Religious Ecstasy

Religious Ecstasy

Based on Papers read at the Symposium on Religious Ecstasy held at Åbo,
Finland, on the 26th–28th of August 1981

Edited by
NILS G. HOLM

Distributed by

Almqvist & Wiksell International
Stockholm/Sweden

ISBN 91-22-00574-9

Printed in Sweden by

Almqvist & Wiksell, Uppsala 1982

Contents

IV

I

Ecstasy Research in the 20th Century- An Introduction

By NILS G. HOLM

1. *Definitions*

Scholars have always been interested in distinctive phenomena in culture and religion. Thus the accounts and achievements of yogis and mystics received attention at an early stage. There is a similar tendency with shamans, different kinds of sorcerers and with the "group-hysterical" phenomena that have appeared from time to time. There is, on the other hand, no major collection of research contributions on all the phenomena belonging to this field. Before I proceed to discuss some of the research produced over this vast area, I shall introduce some of the technical terms and concepts current in this field of study.

Ecstasy is derived from a Greek word, with the original meaning of removing oneself from a given place. By an extended sense of the word, this implies that the ego is no longer in the physical frame. In Latin it can be translated by "alienatio" (Spoerri 1968, 1f.). In research it has come to signify different states of consciousness that are characterised by unusual achievements, peculiar experiences and odd behaviour. In the Encyclopaedia of Religion and Ethics from 1912 we have a fairly short but nonetheless lucid definition as follows: "an abnormal state of consciousness, in which the reaction of the mind to external stimuli is either inhibited or altered in character. In its more restricted sense, as used in mystical theology, it is almost equivalent to 'trance' " (Inge 1912, 157). We have a number of monographs on the subject of ecstatic phenomena both within Christianity and beyond. Older studies include those of Achelis (1902), Beck (s. a.) and

Linderholm (1924); more recent contributions are those of Arbman (1963–1970), Lewis (1971) and Laski (1961).

In addition to ecstasy, other words are used to describe phenomena in the same category. Trance is a term that is employed in almost exactly the same sense as the word ecstasy. Anna-Leena Siikala mostly uses the word trance in her study of shamanism and provides the following definition: "trance is a form of behaviour deviating from what is normal in a wakened state and possessing a specific cultural significance, typical features being modifications of the grasp of reality and the self-concept, with the intensity of change varying from slight alterations to complete loss of consciousness" (Siikala 1978, 39). Siikala points out that, apparently, anthropologists more frequently use the word trance, whereas students of religion employ the word ecstasy (ibid.).

Another concept often associated with ecstasy is mysticism. Attempts have sometimes been made to assign all ecstatic phenomena to mysticism. Thus the Encyclopaedia Britannica defines ecstasy as a term "used in mysticism to describe its primary goal: the experience of an inner vision of God or of one's relation to or union with the divine". It is not customary however to proceed in this manner and the two concepts, as a rule, are only partially allowed to coincide. When we speak of mysticism we imply a much wider field—where aspects of knowledge and intention are prominent—than when we use the word ecstasy. Mystical experiences are perhaps best described as occurrences through which an individual, in an intensive and unusual way, is afforded new knowledge of the innermost essence of the universe. Not infrequently the experience implies some sort of absorption into the great universal whole. In the case of ecstasy however, interest is more concentrated on certain mental changes without any assumptions being made about the constituent qualities of the experience itself (cf. Holm 1979).

Possession is another term which converges on the concept of ecstasy. We have a number of studies dealing with possession, including those of Oesterreich 1921, Bourguignon 1976 and Crapanzano-Garrison 1977. In his introduction to the latter work, Crapanzano provides us with a short but concise definition of possession. It is "any altered state of consciousness indigenously interpreted in terms of the influence of an alien spirit" (Crapanzano 1977,7). We see here that in the case of possession there is a special interpretation of the course of events. There is a god, a spirit or some other supernatural force exerting an influence on the person possessed. This interpretation is thus borrowed from the culture in question and only used by researchers for the purpose of classification. It may thus involve the influence of both good and evil forces.

In recent years another term has come into currency to designate ecstatic phenomena. It is the term "altered states of consciousness". This term has been used in an attempt to cover all states of consciousness except the normal alert state. Ludwig, who classified this state at an early stage, gives the following definition of the concept: "For the purpose of discussion, I shall regard 'altered states of consciousness' [...] as those mental states induced by various physiological, psychological or pharmacological maneuvers or agents, which can be recognized subjectively by the individual himself (or by an objective observer of the individual) as representing a sufficient deviation, in terms of subjective experience of psychological functioning, from certain general norms as determined by the subjective experience and psychological functioning of that individual during alert, waking consciousness" (Ludwig 1968, 69f.). Ludwig's article goes on to provide a comprehensive account of the different ways in which altered states of consciousness occur, together with the characteristics and functions these states assume in different contexts. He classifies these states according to whether the exteroceptive stimulation and activity is higher or lower and whether mental alertness is increased or diminished. It is obvious that the concept of altered states of consciousness is the most comprehensive one hitherto in use and that all ecstatic states can be assumed within it. No value judgements are implied in the concept and it is thus well-suited to a scientific context. The only problem is that the concept is a very broad one and that it does not convey any information about the origin or function of the state. There is thus a continual need for scientific categorisation and clarification of ecstatic states.

After this brief survey we can therefore state that there is a general ecstatic phenomenon, implying alteration of man's mental activity and with attendant consequences for his interpretation of reality and his ego-perception. Within different religions and cultures this phenomenon then acquires different interpretations and meanings. I am here using the terms altered state of consciousness, trance and ecstasy in the same sense. Possession, however, implies the addition of another criterium: the altered state of consciousness must acquire a specific interpretation from the culture or individual concerned. Mysticism is a broad term but it does not focus attention, as do the previously mentioned terms, on the alteration of consciousness. The concept of hypnosis has gained fairly wide scientific currency and clearly converges on the phenomenon I am studying here. It would be carrying things too far to extend our discussion to include research into hypnosis and I therefore refrain from any detailed reference to it. In my final comments however, I provide a link with the results of hypnosis research.

2. *Earlier 20th century research*

After this brief survey of the concept of ecstasy and its related terms, we shall now give further consideration to the literature on the subject. It transpires that the latter may be fairly simply divided into different categories depending on the type of research in question. We have, first of all, a large number of contributions characterised above all by the analysis and meticulous description of some phenomenon or occurrence somewhere in the world, often without any greater aspirations towards a general explanation of the phenomenon in question. Another group of studies aims, however, at a theoretical explanation of ecstatic states. These explanations may of course be very different in character but the theoretical concepts involved may easily be divided into two groups: 1) research which attempts to compare ecstasy with ideas taken from psychiatry or which tries to fit ecstasy into some classification of mental states, 2) research which applies an anthropological or social-psychological point of view. There are of course marginal approaches between the two groups. In what follows, I shall not discuss accounts that are essentially descriptive in character. I shall instead pay closer attention to research that is more interpretative in nature and which attempts to apply a theoretical perspective to the phenomenon.

The purpose of research in the first category of the more theoretical contributions may be regarded as the description of the ecstatic state in as precise terms as possible to provide an opportunity for comparison with other known mental states. There has often been an interest in discovering as many criteria as possible for ecstatic states, which may then be all the more easily compared to other states, particularly those of a pathological nature. Towards the end of the 19th century psychiatry made great progress and also began to display an interest in religious ecstasy. New prospects were provided of understanding a large number of distinctive phenomena within the history of religious enthusiasm. In this context I shall do no more than briefly recall such figures as Janet, Kraepelin, Ribot and, in Sweden, Gadelius, as representatives of psychiatry. There was a tendency to believe that if one found parallels between ecstatic states and proven cases within psychiatry, this in itself was sufficient explanation. The sick states which research tried to "carve out" were often regarded as clear quantities with a specific genesis and a certain characteristic course of events. The pathological state with which connections were most frequently formed was that of hysteria. Students of religion such as Linderholm, Andrae, Voipio and Arbman readily made this connection.

In his study "Die Ekstase" from 1902 Th. Achelis gives us a comprehensive survey of the phenomenon. He uses the psychology and sociology of his day but also shows a familiarity with cultural variations in different parts of the world. He emphasizes, among other things, the use of different narcotic agents to induce ecstasy. He also describes dancing, castration and self-torment of various kinds. He regards people with a weak and, to a certain degree, undeveloped nervous systems as more easily susceptible to every sort of influence from nature and the group and therefore more liable to become involved in ecstatic phenomena. He writes: "Je geringer die Herrschaft des Menschen über sich selbst ist, je weniger er imstande ist, willkürlich seine Aufmerksamkeit zu bestimmen, umsomehr ist er von seiner Umgebung abhängig, je grösser ist seine Suggestibilität, wie der technische Ausdruck lautet" (Achelis 1902, 18). In describing the social importance of ecstasy he claims that many ecstatic movements have been emphatically group phenomena where individual needs have been fused with the group spirit (Achelis 1902, 184).

P. Beck in his study uses an evolutionary approach. He assumes that states of consciousness, just like physical organs, have had different functions and purposes during the course of evolution. Phylogenetically speaking, they are of different ages. He writes: "Nach meine Hypothese ist die Ekstase der Rückfall in einen uralten Bewusstseinzustand, in das Urbewusstsein, das der Differenzierung des modernen Bewusstseins in Ich und Aussenwelt vorangeht. Dieser Zustand ist im allgemeinen verschwunden, wie ein alter Kontinent, der jetzt vom Meer bedeckt wird" (Beck, 50).

In his study of Pentecostalism, E. Linderholm discusses the basis and origin of the Pentecostal movement in the first volume. He calculates that ecstasy is "a deep rooted tendency in man's mental constitution" (Linderholm 1924, 11). The state is produced by various external means of suggestion, both material and nonmaterial in nature. It is characteristic of ecstasy, of which there is both a spontaneous and a voluntary form, that the external senses, particularly those of sight and hearing, cease to function. The awareness of time and space also disappear. The "subconscious spiritual activity" nevertheless continues (14). Linderholm points out that ecstatics from different cultures display certain general similarities, although there are otherwise a host of cultural variations. The similarities or correspondences may be explained by the fact that "in the highest or deepest ecstatic states all notions of the subconscious spiritual life and all memory of the ordinary cognitive universe have been so strongly reduced, that they are no longer able to appear specialised" (21). If, however, the cognitive assertions are more specific in kind, the ecstatic's dependence on a cultural environment becomes evident.

T. Andrae, who in his book "The Psychology of Mysticism" (unfortunately only in Swedish) has given detailed descriptions of the various mystical states in terms of possession or inspiration, also discusses the phenomenon in relation to the theory of hysteria. He finds similarities between the two concepts and writes: "It cannot in my opinion be denied that the penomena of religious possession and inspiration must be regarded as manifestations of hysteria and that consequently most mystics must be called hysterics. We have seen that the clearly defined and highly typical cycle of symptoms that normally accompany possession and inspiration correspond clearly to the stigmata of hysteria" (566f.). But Andrae wishes to point out that the hysterical reaction should not be regarded as particularly more "primitive" than thought or volition. In his studies of sleeping preachers in Finland, particularly the prophetess Maria Åkerblom, A. Voipio has indicated hysteria as an explanation for the distinctive phenomenon involved (Voipio 1923; 1951).

Arbman's great study of ecstasy "Ecstasy and Religious Trance" may also be placed in the category of research that has tried to classify ecstasy in relation to other known mental states. Arbman has given several long definitions of ecstasy and I should like to quote the one which perhaps best clarifies his position: "In all its forms and manifestations ... the ecstasy shows itself unmistakably as a state of mind in which the consciousness of the believer has been involuntarily absorbed in the religious complex which in the state by which it was preceded constituted its sole exclusively dominating content or object, and in such a way that it has in its entirety been drawn under the more or less untrammelled automatic control of the latter ... I have in several passages in the foregoing chosen to designate and describe the ecstasy or the religious trance as a state of *suggestive absorption*" (Arbman 1963, XV).

Arbman's study provides a comprehensive survey of the literature of ecstasy until the middle of the 50's. It also discusses ecstatic phenomena in different religions. An important section is devoted to his treatment of the relation of religious ecstasy to concepts developed within psychiatry. This account is to be found, above all, in the third volume of his work. He adopts a critical attitude to the equating of religious ecstasy with hysteria. He also however opposes Andrae's more sympathetic attitude in this context (Arbman 1970, 238ff.). Whilst he acknowledges that ecstasy can occur in close connection with hysterical states, he strongly emphasizes that the distinctive character of religion is of great significance for religious ecstatics. He writes: "I have, I believe, clearly shown in the foregoing that ecstasy, as a consequence of the states of mind from which it proceeds and of which in the last analysis it only constitutes an abnormal intensification or culmination, cannot, despite its many striking resemblances with the hysteric trance, be regarded as identical with the latter state or in all respects completely similar to it" (Arbman 1970, 45).

I should now like to mention the research that has aimed to provide a classification of different states of consciousness. From the literature written in German we have one scrupulous attempt to accomplish this. W. Gruehn thus speaks of "Überwache" and "Unterwache" states of consciousness. Normal states occupy a small field in a diagram whilst above and below them occur states which can be classified according to their intensity. The "überwache" state is characterised by an intensified alertness although the heightened awareness is often operational within a very limited area. The "Unterwache" states are characterised by varying degrees of sleep. Ecstatic-mystical states, according to the scheme, constitute an "überwache" state (Gruehn 1960, 124 ff.).

K. Thomas works along the same lines in his study of meditation. In this context he introduces the concept of "ausserwache Bewusstseinsstufe" by which he means primarily hypnosis and intoxication of various kinds, particularly by means of narcotic substances. In his chart of states of consciousness he has also introduced a scale according to which these states are evaluated from a religious point of view (Thomas 1973, 10 ff.).

A classificatory approach is also adopted by D. Langen in his study of archaic ecstasy and Asian meditation (1963), and by Th. Spoerri in his book "Beiträge zur Ekstase" (1968). Spoerri distinguishes between primitive ecstasy and cultural ecstasy. Together with C. Albrecht he speaks of a somnambulistic-ecstatic consciousness and of a "versunken-ekstatisches Bewusstsein". In describing different states of consciousness one should, according to Spoerri, pay attention among other things to awareness itself, that is the mechanism of sleep and wakefulness, communication with the environment and the question of integration (1 ff.).

A theoretical innovation that can also be included in this group is W. Sargant's view of religious ecstasy. He starts from Pavlow's research on the effects of overloading the nervous system and discovers that ecstasy may be regarded as a form of collapse of the nervous system (Sargant 1973). From the field of depth-psychology too, wee have a number of studies devoted to ecstatic states. The discussion has largely centred on projection and paranoid forms of self-punishment (cf. Wikström, 203 ff.).

3. *Anthropological and social-psychological research*

Within this area of research there is considerably more interest than in the previous one in understanding ecstasy as a function of cultural and social factors. In several cases we find an emphasis on cultural determinants and other more individual ones. As I have suggested earlier, there is no ques-

tion of a sharp divide *vis à vis* the research contributions I have already
discussed but rather of a shift in emphasis, with attempts at clarification.

I. M. Lewis is an anthropologist who has attempted to consider the
phenomena of trance and possession in a sociological perspective. He
makes a distinction between peripheral cults and what he calls "main
morality possession religions" (Lewis 1971, 34), that is to say religions
where possession constitutes a central part of the dominant culture. He
makes an additional division in the case of the latter between religions that
are concerned with ancestral spirits and those where possession allegedly
resorts to more independent divine powers. To understand the authority
exercised by the key persons within a cult, one must, according to Lewis,
consider the whole spectrum of other more specialised means for the
exertion of political or social control. The relationship between authority
and ecstatic phenomena is expressed by Lewis in the following way: "If
certain exotic religions thus allow ecstasy to rule most aspects of their
adherents' lives, all the evidence indicates that the more strongly-based and
entrenched religious authority becomes, the more hostile it is towards
haphazard inspiration" (34).

Lewis provides a comprehensive survey of the phenomenon of possession in the peripheral cults and discovers that it is almost exclusively
women who are possessed. They are often in a difficult position. They are
subject to male oppression and otherwise without influence with respect to
social and political conditions. By being possessed, the women, as it were,
make a virtue of necessity and can also to a certain extent achieve a kind of
liberation. In the eyes of the ruling groups, possession is regarded as an
expression of evil spirits demanding in turn a ritual or something comparable if the possessed person is to be freed. Lewis writes: ". . . if it is in terms
of the exclusion of women from full participation in social and political
affairs and their final subjection to men that we should seek to understand
their marked prominence in peripheral possession, we must also remember
that these cults which express sexual tensions are yet permitted to exist by
men" (88). Lewis supposes that male tolerance of the cults may reflect a
dim consciousness within the men of the unjust position of women in
society. Peripheral possession is generally directed by subordinates at
superiors, whilst other forms of witchcraft assuming the form of accusations are used between groups of equal status or in relation to subordinates
(Lewis 1971, 120).

In the case of religions where the possession phenomenon has a central
position, however, the carriers are often, acording to Lewis, more highly
regarded people. The phenomenon then functions to maintain the system of
power and control which the dominant groups wish to preserve. It is often

the religious elite that has the technique of ecstasy in its own hands in this case, and in contrast to the situation previously described, it is not used democratically. Instead it is only shamans, sorcereres, priests etc. who can and may practise this art of possession (Lewis 1971, 170ff.).

Erica Bourguignon and her research team have also worked with ecstatic phenomena. They have made special studies of possession in a number of cultures but have also been interested in trance and altered states of consciousness as a general phenomenon. In order to establish the presence of this phenomenon all over the world, they made a survey of 488 societies on the basis of information contained in an ethnological atlas. Results showed 90% of the societies "to have one or more institutionalized, culturally patterned form of altered states of consciousness" (Bourguignon 1973, 11). For Bourguignon, this result has the effect of legitimising research into the phenomena of trance and possession. It is in other words a central phenomenon in various cultures and thus worthy of detailed research.

Bourguignon makes a division between what she calls "possession trance" and "trance", that is between trance interpreted as possession and other forms of trance. Similarly, she calculates that possession can occur without trance. She writes: "We shall say that a belief in possession exists, when the people in question hold that a given person is changed in some way through the presence in him or on him of a spirit, entity or power, other than his own personality, soul, self, or the like. We shall say that possession trance exists in a given society when we find that there is such a belief in possession and that it is used to account for alterations in consciousness, awareness, personality or other aspects of psychological functioning" (Bourguignon 1976, 7–8). Bourguignon thus emphasizes that possession is a special interpretation of a course of events and that it depends on factors within each specific culture.

Bourguignon has made a further division between cultures where "possession trance" occurs either alone or in conjunction with "trance", and those where "trance" occurs quite alone. It then emerges that those cultures in which "possession trance" is found are the most complex ones, having "the largest population and the largest local group, stratification, slavery, sedentary settlement pattern, and a complex hierarchy of jurisdictional levels" (Bourguignon 1973, 20).

In her own interpretation of the theoretical concepts I have presented above, Bourguignon restricts herself to voodoo on Haiti. In her account of this she offers examples of numerous other interpretations made from social, historical or personal standpoints and is far from representing a single narrow view (Bourguignon 1976, 28ff.). The essential part of her analysis of voodoo seems to be that she regards possession as an individual solution in a social situation through models provided by the culture. She summarises as follows: "The people find it possible to play the requisite roles and to have the appropriate experiences, however, not only because cultural learning of this behavior is available but because they have the personality structures, resulting from their particular upbringing and life experiences, that make them apt to engage in such behavior and to find it personally as well as socially rewarding" (Bourguignon 1976, 41).

Bourguignon's collaborators have each become specialised in their own field. I do not therefore discuss their work here, but I should like to emphasize that their theoretical concepts have differed somewhat from those of Bourguignon. Jeannette H. Henney, who has studied the "shakers" on the Island of St Vincent in the West Indies, stresses that the experience of visions found occurs among the shakers has an integrative effect on the individual. She has moreover drawn interesting parallels between "sensory privation" and the method for producing visions practised by the shakers (Henney 1973, 219 ff.; 1974, 3 ff.).

Felicitas D. Goodman, another of Bourguignon's collaborators, has studied a small group of Pentecostalists in Yucután, Mexico, their success, their intensive apocalyptic expectations and the almost total disintegration of the group when the fulfilment of the prophecies did not materialise. Glossolalia behaviour within the group is of central significance in her books and articles. To understand glossolalia Goodman uses a neurophysiological approach, claiming that it is basic cross-cultural structures on a neural level that manifest themselves during speaking with tongues. These are revealed in the special mental state into which the glossolalist is placed. An essential part of Goodman's argument is her examination of how an individual is placed in this state and in what way the awakening from it takes place. The occurrence of glossolalia thus becomes an argument for Goodman to the effect that the state in which the glossolalist finds himself is indeed a special mental state (Goodman 1972; Goodman 1973; Goodman 1974, 267).

I have already discussed Goodman's interpretation of speaking with tongues on an earlier occasion and found that it hardly holds good. The structures which she has found in glossolalia and which she claims are linked with a specific mental state, are so general in most languages that one cannot, on the basis of this alone, support the occurrence of some specific state. This does not of course preclude the appearance of the gift of tongues under unusual mental conditions. It is merely that glossolalia with its attendant structures is not in itself indicative of an altered state of consciousness (cf. Holm 1974; Holm 1976; Holm 1977).

One of the most important studies of possession in recent years is the account published by V. Crapanzano and Vivian Garrison in 1977 under the title "Case Studies in Spirit Possession". I shall not discuss every article in the book, but instead limit myself to reproducing something of the main argument presented by Crapanzano in his introduction. He and the other authors represented in the book combine a modified depth-psychology interpretation of possession with a socialanthropological approach. This means that the authors regard the phenomenon of possession as part of a cultural unity at the same time as they emphasize the individual mental and above all dynamic development in the people they study. There is then, according to these writers, a correspondence between individual needs and the methods provided by society for the enactment and resolution of problems.

When discussing the concept of altered states of possession, Crapanzano joins forces with Ludwig, whose article we have previously discussed. Possession consists of the projection and articulation of emotions and needs, according to the specific model each culture provides to this end. Crapanzano calls this model the idiom. A learning process is necessary, both with regard to the language the possessed person is expected to use and to other extenal procedures, such as the method of entering into a trance, the way of performing expected actions during the trance and sometimes also the way of emerging from a trance. There is then, according to Crapanzano, both a technical and a symbolic side to possession and both must be learned. Many cultures have specific tasks for people who are "called" to function as intermediaries between the spiritual sphere and the human, terrestrial one.

Crapanzano also draws a parallel between the transformation that takes place "within the spirit idiom" and that which occurs on the level of linguistic metaphor. He writes: "Spirit possession may be conceived as a complex series of transformations of (usually negative) metaphorical statements into (occasionally positive, at least ritually neutral) metonomous ones in a dialectic play of identity formation" (Crapanzano 1977, 19). In the phenomenon of possession, needs and demands are transformed into expressions acceptable to the group in question, with the result that purely therapeutic effects are achieved. For Crapanzano it is important to be able to show connections between the procedure and effects of spirit possession and the results achieved by modern psychotherapy. This emerges clearly in a number of articles in the volume, but above all perhaps in Vivian Garrison's contribution, where she describes a 39 year old Puerto Rican woman living in New York. The woman has a nervous attack and goes to visit a "spiritualist" group in order to be cured. She is also the subject of treatment from neurologists and therapists. Garrison shows that there is a

2–Religious Ecstasy

great similarity in the different stages of treatment on the part of both groups (Garrison 1977, 383 ff.).

Together with these social-anthropological studies we have research that has applied the theories of social psychology to ecstatic phenomena. It is regarded as a fact that a given society has ecstatic "modes of intercourse" and the main question asked is by what laws and with what regularity do individuals react. Interest is not therefore focussed on finding individual reasons for the distinctive behaviour. There is instead a desire to fit the behaviour and the whole course of events within a normal psychological process.

This point of view is represented by T. R. Sarbin and V. L. Allen who demonstrate in their theoretical article on role theory that ecstasy can be explained from this perspective. In their study of the intensity of role activity they have introduced a variable called "organismic involvement", which can vary from no involvement at all to an extremely strong personal absorption in the role. On a seven point scale they calculate that ecstasy constitutes the sixth point. It thus approaches one of the limits, represented by "bewitchment", the frequently irrevocable experience of being enchanted or possessed. According to the authors, ecstasy implies "a suspension of voluntary action" (Sarbin-Allen 1968, 489 ff.) and cannot therefore be of any great duration without causing permanent damage to the body. They emphasize that ecstasy is usually enshrined in institutionalised ritual, which effectively regulates its occurrence and control.

Another theoretically inclined article that I would like to mention in this context is R. E. Shor's "Hypnosis and the concept of the generalized reality-orientation". His study is effectively a contribution to the discussion of hypnosis but he also touches fruitfully on ecstatic phenomena and his work has been used, as we shall see, in research into shamanism.

Shor develops the idea that unusual states of consciousness must be understood, using role theory as a point of departure. Normal consciousness has the characteristic feature that the individual, in his interpretation of new stimuli, continually verifies his information against a background of a structured frame of reference that is learned. Shor calls this frame of reference "generalized reality-orientation". In his article he develops 12 postulates emphasizing the importance of this concept for the understanding of altered states of consciousness. According to one of the postulates, this generalized reality-orientation is not maintained without a conscious mental effort on the part of the individual to maintain it. If a person's active ego is not in contact with this generalized reality-orientation, a mental state occurs which Shor denotes by the term trance. He writes: "Any state in which the generalized reality-orientation has faded to relatively nonfunctional awareness may be termed a trance state" (Shor 1969, 241). In trance, therefore, the individual is absorbed in one single special sector of reality and loses control over himself according to how far the generalized reality-orientation has moved into the background. Hypnosis and ecstasy are seen by Shor as the results of similar psychological mechanisms.

In her study of Siberian shamanism Anna-Leena Siikala has used the above social-psychological theories. She first introduces the concept of altered states of consciousness and thus follows Ludwig's suggestion, too. According to Siikala, the mental states of shamans can be accomodated within these concepts and the origin of these states can be explained consistently from theories produced by social psychology and hypnosis research. This implies, she states, that any person with a normal nervous system is capable of becoming a shaman. A pathological disposition is not therefore a prerequisite for the role. Shamanism is a normal institution in Siberian cultures and therefore requires people to carry out its rites. The method for recruiting potential shamans and the way of conducting ritual follows, in principle, the social-psychological mechanisms as other corresponding processes within the society. Siikala therefore regards the state of trance as a gradual absorption into a role and as a variation in the generalized reality orientation, the function of which is dependent on various external influencing factors and of the shaman's experience of his role. The shaman's deep trance is a delicate balance between absorption into the role patterns of the spirit world and deference to the demands and expectations of his audience (Siikala 1978, 28 ff., 340 f.).

4. *An example: Glossolalia in the Pentecostal Movement*

The scholarly view of glossolalia corresponds clearly to the developments in research I have outlined above. At the beginning of the century the gift of tongues was in itself regarded as something ecstatic, and parallel interpretative models were sought, above all, in psychiatry. The gift of tongues was said to appear in individuals of a hysterical disposition and with an otherwise weak mental constitution. Individuals of this type were more liable than stable people to produce so-called automatisms, that is to say behaviour beyond the control of volition. The more influential and animated individuals at a Pentecostal meeting exerted an influence, above all, on people of this type, it was believed.

In later research, the individual mental constitution has not been so strongly emphasized, but a new stress on group-dynamic processes has appeared. In this respect, attention has been entirely removed from abnormal psychology. My own work is based on observation and interview

material from the Pentecostal Movement in Swedish Finland together with
an analysis of tape recordings of meetings. I shall briefly summarise the
main results of my research.

Within the Pentecostal Movement the gift of tongues is connected with
something known as baptism of the spirit. It is seen as a concrete event
through which a person becomes filled with the Holy Spirit in abundant
measure. At this spiritual baptism the individual receives an external sign, a
so-called gift of grace, usually the gift of tongues. The interviews show that
this doctrinal aspect is often attended by experiences on an individual level.
I therefore wonder what mechanisms of a sociological and psychological
nature accompany the emergence of an ecstatic baptism of the spirit in the
individual?

In order to be able to answer this question, I first studied the nature of
glossolalia from a linguistic point of view. I wanted to know what sort of
language was involved and how complicated the gift of tongues was.
Through an analysis of glossolalia on tape, I discovered that no normal
extant language was involved, but rather a pseudo-language with similarities, above all, to the speaker's mother tongue. The linguistic structure of
glossolalia is simple and therefore easy to reproduce on the basis of normal
language acquisition. In all probability, it is barriers of a social nature that
prevent people from using forms of pseudolanguage more frequently. This
suggested to me that it is not the occurrence of glossolalia that is remarkable or that constitutes the ecstatic element in the context, but that other
explanations must be sought for the experiences of an ecstatic type that I
observed and had reported to me.

By the use of symbolic interactionism, above all according Berger-
Luckmann's formulation (Berger-Luckmann 1973) I have shown how the
individual becomes gradually implicated in the symbolic universe of the
Pentecostal Movement. He then becomes conscious of the roles, expectations and positions existing within the social unit constituted by the Pentecostal congregation. Central to this is the doctrine of baptism of the spirit.
Very quickly a newcomer acquires familiarity with the behaviour and
experiences connected with spiritual baptism and an expectation of being
filled by the spirit grows within him. This expectation means in practice a
desire to be able to speak with tongues. But according to tradition and
doctrine the gift of tongues should be inspired by God and not be a false,
humanly inspired glossolalia. It was the process initiated in the individual
mind for the gift of tongues to be interpreted in a certain situation as a gift of
God, or as divinely inspired, that I took to be the interesting question and
the aspect that was connected with ecstasy.

I have also used Hj. Sundén's so-called role-taking theory to explain the process in question. According to this theory, we should take into account mythical roles stored in the religious tradition. These are brought to the fore by familiarity with holy scripture and by an aspiration to share the spiritual experiences of the early Christians. Regarding baptism of the spirit we may state that clear role models are present in the Bible and that a Pentecostalist today can well enter into the situation experienced by the first disciples. Something we might call "the role of spiritual baptism" is now brought to the fore. In a given situation this can so structure the field of perception that an individual gift of tongues is felt to be inspired by God. The assumption of the role brings simultaneously a rich collection of emotional expressions connected with the role within the social community (Holm 1976; Holm 1978; Holm 1978 a).

But role-theory does not entirely explain how it is that misgivings about the gift of tongues are finally dispelled in the individual. I have therefore also indicated various socialpsychological promotion mechanisms present in a cult situation like a Pentecostal Meeting. We find there clear examples of persuasive communication, such as repetition of emotionally charged words, sharp contrasts, ejaculations, song and music, assurances of God's immediate presence and influence, admonitions and exhortations to receive gifts of grace and perhaps most important of all, intercession often accompanied by the laying-on of hands. Such methods of influence ensure that the individual's entire interest is focussed on spiritual baptism and receiving the gift of tongues. This leads to the removal of inhibiting factors within the individual and facilitates the onset of speaking with tongues. If glossolalia occurs this is the external stimulus which initiates role-taking. But the role presupposes a so-called genuine speaking with tongues, inspired by God, and it is not until the individual's conception of reality and ego-perception have combined to suggest the divine inspiration of his glossolalia, that he assumes his role completely. I should like to stress, however, that not all Pentecostalists begin speaking with tongues in a cultic situation in circumstances similar to those described. Many receive their baptism of the spirit when alone, often as they are retiring to bed. If the role of spiritual baptism is developed in them too, however, glossolalia has the same importance in prompting role-taking.

It is, then, the actual experience of being baptised in the spirit with its attendant signs (glossolalia) that I should like to call ecstatic. For most Pentecostalists baptism of the spirit emerges as a unique experience and the descriptions justify our interpreting this event as a form of ecstasy. It is apparent, however, that after the actual experience of spiritual baptism Pentecostalists often use speaking in tongues on their own initiative. Once filled by the spirit and once having received the gift of tongues, they can control the latter at will. Such instances of speaking with tongues are not accompanied by ecstasy, at least not to any greater extent.

In my research, therefore, I regard speaking with tongues as expressions of roles and behavioural patterns instituted and sanctioned by the Pentecostal Movement. It is above all people with a flexible and integrated consciousness who assume the roles and transmit them further. Research has thus moved from a narrow preoccupation with the mental condition of single individuals to an emphasis on the social patterns with which every social unit is endowed. On the individual level, speaking with tongues in all probability acquires a function corresponding to that of meditation in the newer religious movements (Holm 1978; Hutch 1980).

A point that I would like to stress in conclusion is the manner in which ecstatic elements change with the growing institutionalisation within the Pentecostalist Movement. Over the period during which I have been able to study the movement I have noticed that spiritual baptism has increasingly become a routine matter so that it is now experienced increasingly by teenagers often during attendance at a camp and without obvious ecstatic features. Will we one day find that in the Pentecostal movement, too, young people at some form of collective "confirmation act" will be declared to participate in the Spirit and thereby be spiritually baptised without any external signs or gifts of grace becoming apparent? It will, in this case, be a baptism of the spirit without any hard-won ecstatic experience. The Pentecostal Movement will then have taken a large step into the denominational fold.

5. *Conclusion*

A survey of research into ecstatic phenomena reveals that an important kind of development has occurred with regard to theoretical modes of thought. The earlier group of studies that I have discussed is a fairly heterogeneous collection, although they shared a common desire to establish the nature of the ecstatic state as precisely as possible to be able to classify it subsequently with other better known mental states, especially those of a pathological nature. Characteristic particularly of older studies within this group was the tendency to regard mental states as fixed quantities which would serve as explanations for a large number of religious distinctive phenomena. If only the different mental states could be mapped with sufficient accuracy, one would come to a satisfactory understanding of all the curious occurrences that accompanied ecstatic phenomena—or so it was reasoned. Students were partly blind to social-psychological mechanisms, particularly to an understanding of ecstatic phenomena as integrative parts of a working (sub-)culture.

Research of recent years, in contrast to the earlier approach, has emphasized the possibility of understanding distinctive phenomena from the perspective of normal psychology. It is common to speak in terms of an intensification of certain mental mechanisms and processes towards a certain upper limit. In addition, the cognitive content—the system of religious concepts—has received attention as a contributory factor in the process. Without the conceptual world that is specific to every culture, we do not, it is felt, find any ecstatic phenomena. It is also interesting to discover that to the extent that "case studies" have been carried out, an emphasis of intra-psychic, dynamic processes has also occurred.

We may say that the divergence between the two groups is expressed in their view of ecstasy itself, and in particular to what extent the mental state is to be regarded as an explanatory factor. The former group has a more static conception throughout, whilst the attitude of the latter is closer to a process model. The opposition of two such views is apparent in several places. It appears clearly in the case of research into hypnosis. Here we speak explicitly of "state theorists" and "non-state theorists" (Gaunitz 1980, 8). The controversy between the two schools of hypnosis research has gone on for some time and occasionally the data are open to interpretation favouring both tendencies.

Gaunitz has made a contribution with regard to this issue. He has compared, in his research, the state attained by those who practise Transcendental Meditation with the state produced by induction of hypnosis. He proceeded from a claim that the state reached by those who meditated deviated from the normal waking state and also from hypnosis (Gaunitz 1980). The results obtained by Gaunitz suggest that one might, to a great extent, equate religious ecstatic states with hypnosis of varying degrees. There is thus no need to suppose that there is a large number of distinctive mental states, but that there are instead changes along similar lines in hypnosis, ecstasy and possession of various kinds. This opens important theoretical perspectives for ecstasy research in general and invites interesting contributions to the field of religious psychology.

Among the most pressing assignments, the following four appear: 1) continued research into the nature, origin and properties of the mental state itself, particularly in relation to hypnosis, 2) studies of culture-bound models of altered states of consciousness, 3) the significance of ecstatic states for the whole social system of a given culture (sociology of ecstasy) and 4) the use of ecstasy seen from the point of view of the individual (psychology of ecstasy).

An interesting question that presents itself is whether trance can occur without any specific (religious) environment. We have seen that altered states of consciousness appear in religious contexts and that similar states are produced under hypnosis. What role or significance do trance or ecstasy have in our own "secularised" culture, where these phenomena are often pushed into the background?

We know that there exist individual movements and groups that rigorously cultivate the capacity for ecstasy. In this context I am thinking not least of the youth religions with their interest in meditation and religious experience in general. But the latest research into mysticism in the world today also suggests that intensive experiences are present without primary religious interpretation. Many of the experiences exhibit features which have traditionally been regarded as characterising mysticism (Holm 1979). We can therefore state that phenomena of an ecstatic nature have a wide distribution and also occur in (sub-) cultures where they are not given a primary function. The latest observations about human creativity also point in the same direction. Creative people often experience their periods of greatest creativity as being in some way divergent from normal conditions (Ruth 1980). We still do not have any general theory for experiences of the kind suggested. I should nevertheless like to point out in this context that the human neurological structure appears to be such, that different mental states succeed each other in a perpetual cycle. Moveover, man has a basic capacity to condense his needs, desires and relations of various kinds into symbolic form. An interaction between these two phenomena seems to provide both the individual and the culture-bound forms for ecstatic behaviour. The actual cultivation of this interaction seems, however, to be a function of factors within the social environment.

In the articles that follow, ecstasy receives illumination from many sides: there are contributions which treat the phenomenon in a more comprehensive, psychological and sociological fashion and studies that enter deeply into a single phenomenon within one of the religions. We have therefore a survey where different perspectives are able to complement each other.

References

Achelis, T. 1902. *Die Ekstase in ihrer kulturellen Bedeutung*, hrsg. von L. Berg. Berlin.
Albrecht, C. 1951. *Psychologie des mystischen Bewußtseins*. Bremen.
Andrae, T. 1926. *Mystikens psykologi*. Stockholm.
Arbman, E. 1963–70. *Ecstasy or religious trance* 1–3. Uppsala.
Beck, P. [s. a.] *Die Ekstase*. Leipzig.
Berger, P. L.–Luckmann, T. 1973. *The social construction of reality*. London.
Bourguignon, E. 1973. Introduction: a framework for the comparative study of

altered states of consciousness. *Religion, altered states of consciousness, and social change.* Columbus.
— 1976. *Possession.* San Francisco.
Crapanzano, V. 1977. Introduction. *Case studies in spirit possession,* ed. by V. Crapanzano–V. Garrison. New York etc.
Gadelius, B. 1912–13. *Tro och öfvertro i gångna tider.* Stockholm.
Garrison, V. 1977. The "Puerto Rican Syndrome" in psychiatry and *espiritismo. Case studies in spirit possession,* ed. by V. Crapanzano-V. Garrison. New York etc.
Gaunitz, S. C. B. 1980. *Studies on altered states of consciousness and posthypnotically preleased emotions.* Diss. (Acta Universitatis Upsaliensis Abstracts of Uppsala dissertations from the Faculty of social sciences 21.) Uppsala.
Goodman, F. D. 1972. *Speaking in tongues.* Chicago–London.
— 1973. Apostolics of Yucatán: a case study of a religious movement. *Religion, altered states of consciousness, and social change,* ed. by E. Bourguignon. Columbus.
— 1974. Disturbances in the Apostolic church: a trancebased upheaval in Yucatán. *Trance, healing, and hallucination.* New York etc.
Gruehn, W. 1960. *Die Frömmigkeit der Gegenwart.* Konstanz.
Henney, J. H. 1973. The Shakers of St. Vincent: a stable religion. *Altered states of consciousness, and social change,* ed. by E. Bourguignon. Columbus.
— 1974. Spirit-possession belief and trance behavior in two fundamentalist groups in St. Vincent. *Trance, healing, and hallucination.* New York etc.
Holm, N. G. 1974. *Glossolalins kultmönster och ljudstruktur undersökta på ett material insamlat i Svenskfinland.* (Uttryck-kommunikation-religion 2: 2.) Lund.
— 1976. *Tungotal och andedop.* Diss. (Acta Universitatis Upsaliensis, Psychologia Religionum 5.) Uppsala.
— 1977. Ritualistic pattern and sound structure of glossolalia in material collected in the Swedish-speaking parts of Finland. *Temenos* 11.
— 1978. *Pingströrelsen.* (Meddelanden från Stiftelsens för Åbo Akademi forskningsinstitut 31.) Åbo.
— 1978 a. Functions of glossolalia in the Pentecostal movement. *Psychological studies of religious man,* ed. by Thorvald Källstad. (Acta Universitatis Upsaliensis, Psychologia Religionum 7.) Uppsala.
— 1979. *Mystik och intensiva upplevelser.* (Meddelanden från Stiftelsens för Åbo Akademi forskningsinstitut 51.) Åbo.
Hutch, R. A. 1980. The personal ritual of glossolalia. *Journal for the scientific study of religion* 19.
Inge, W. R. 1912. Ecstasy. *Encyclopaedia of religion and ethics.* New York.
Janet, P. 1910. *Les névroses.* Paris.
— 1926. *De l'angoisse à l'extase: une délire religieux, la croyance.* Paris.
— 1928. *De l'angoisse à l'extase: les sentiments fondamentaux.* Paris.
Kraepelin, E. 1915. *Psychiatrie* 4. Leipzig.
Langen, D. 1963. *Archaische Ekstase und asiatische Meditation.* Stuttgart.
Laski, M. 1961. *Ecstasy.* London.
Lewis, I. M. 1971. *Ecstatic religion.* Harmondsworth.
Linderholm, E. 1924. *Pingströrelsen.* Stockholm.
Ludwig, A. M. 1968. Altered states of consciousness. *Trance and possession states,* ed. by R. Prince. Montreal.

Oesterreich, T. K. 1930. *Possession, demoniacal and other among primitive races, in antiquity, the middle ages, and modern times.* London.

Ribot, T. 1924. *Les maladies de la personnalité.* Paris.

Ruth, J.-E. 1980. *Creativity as a cognitive construct; the effects of age, sex and testing practice.* (Unpubl. doct. diss., Univ. of Southern California).

Sarbin, T. R.–Allen, V. L. 1968. Role theory. *The handbook of social psychology* 1, ed. by G. Lindzey–E. Aronson. Menlo Park, Cal. etc.

Sargant, W. W. 1973. *The mind possessed.* London.

Shor, R. E. 1959. Hypnosis and the concept of the generalized reality-orientation. *American journal of psychotherapy* 13.

Siikala, A.-L. 1978. *The rite technique of the Siberian shaman.* Helsinki.

Spoerri, T. 1968. Zum Begriff der Ekstase. *Beiträge zur Ekstase.* Basel–New York.

Thomas, K. 1973. *Meditation in Forschung und Erfahrung in weltweiter Beobachtung und praktischer Anleitung.* (Seelsorge und Psychotherapie 1.) Stuttgart.

Wikström, O. 1980. *Stöd eller börda?* Uppsala.

Voipio, A. 1923. Observations on somnambulic preaching. *Scandinavian scientific review* 2.

— 1951. Sleeping preachers. *Annales Academiae Scientiarum Fennicae* B 75. Helsingfors.

Mystical Experience and the Emergence of Creativity

By ANTOON GEELS

1. Introduction

1.1. *Two current problems within mystic research*

Since the turn of the century, mystic researchers have pointed to the similarities between mystics on the one hand, and artists, poets, mathematicians, musicians, in short, all those who are involved in creative activity. One common denominator, using the terminology of the day, is a state of inspiration, a sort of creative ecstasy, an immediate insight of some form. However, the question of what psychological processes can activate "inspiration" seemed to be unanswerable. According to Evelyn Underhill (1926) it probably arises from the unconscious, where the best and the worst sides of man, "the most savage and most spiritual parts of the character", are located (62 f). Every intuitive person is endowed with a "flexible threshold" to enormous unconscious powers, which can turn him into a genius, a madman or a saint. The mystics themselves, as well as Evelyn Underhill, assume that these creative resources, which the Sufis call "the Constructive Spirit" and the Cabalists "Yesod", lie beyond the world perceived by our senses. The mystic "has a genius for transcendental ... discovery in exactly the same way as his cousins, the born musician and poet, have a genius for musical and poetic discovery. In all three cases, the emergence of these higher powers is mysterious, and not least so to those who experience it" (74 ff). In a later work (1920, 67 ff) Underhill uses other psychological language. Of artists, musicians, philosophers and physicists, she writes that "the twin powers of a steadfast, selective attention and of creative imagination are at work". The creative imagination is expressed in suggestive language, abounding in metaphors and pictures, which makes it possible for others to appreciate to a certain extent the special experiences of the mystic.

A similar view of the relationship between profane and religious creativity is held by James H. Leuba, the author of a classic within the psychology of religion, *The Psychology of Religious Mysticism*, published in 1925. In a chapter on "scientific inspiration or revelation" Leuba states that the word inspiration says something of the suddenness and unexpectedness of the

creative process: "both in the field of imagination and of rational construction, there come, after periods of mental striving or vague brooding, fructi-
fying moments, effortless and unexpected, which give the impression of
inspiration" (243). Mystics, scientists and artists have this process in
common. But while Underhill works mainly with the great geniuses and the
classic mystics, Leuba extends this process to a daily phenomenon, albeit
on a lower level of intensity. "*All* kinds of ideas, and ideas of all degrees of
puerility and importance, appear in our minds under the conditions which
we have found to be those of revelation." These revelations represent for
Leuba "gifts from unknown sources" (244).

In a Swedish context, the concept of inspiration is most often linked with
Tor Andrae, who in his work *Mystikens Psykologi* (the Psychology of
Mysticism) from 1926 wrote "that the religious inspiration in many respects
is so strongly reminiscent of the artistic, that they both can be said to
constitute to a certain extent the same psychic phenomenon ..., that their
initial forms coincide" (581 f). The same view, that is, that there are basic
similarities between mystics and scientists or artists, is found in a more
recent work on mystic experience by Ben-Ami Scharfstein. By presenting
examples from authors, physicists and artists, Scharfstein tries to show,
among other things, that all strive to create unity, be it externally in the
outer world, or internally within man himself (1973, 71–98). However,
Scharfstein shows no greater interest in the psychological process which is
possibly relevant to the discussion in this context.

The first problem I wish to discuss here is whether there exists a common
model for understanding the similarities which many researchers have
hinted at, between religious and profane creativity. This question is inti-
mately linked with another extremely central but little discussed problem
within mystic research: with which psychological concepts should one
describe the special knowledge and experiences which mystics say they
have? What the majority of researchers agree upon is that it appears to be
another type knowledge than discursive thinking. A quick glance at a
couple of common definitions of mysticism is enough to make the problem
clear. The psychologist of religion Walter H. Clark defines mysticism as
"the subjective experience of a person who has what he tells others is a
direct apprehension of some cosmic Power or Force greater than himself
... The experience is *intuitive rather than* sensuous or rational (1969,
263)". In the previously mentioned classic in the psychology of religion by
Leuba, we find that mysticism is "any experience taken by the experiencer
to be a contact (*not through the senses, but 'immediate', 'intuitive'*) or
union of the self with a larger-than-self be it called the World-Spirit, God,
the Absolute, or otherwise" (1972, 1). In an oft quoted classic from the

20's, James B. Pratt (1926, 337) writes that mysticism is "the sense of the presence of a being or reality through *other means than the ordinary perceptive processes or the reason* ... It is ... an immediate and *intuitive* experience." The philosopher of religion, Robert M. Gimello, states that the mystic experience is characterized, among other things, by "*a cessation of normal intellectual operation* (e. g. deduction, discrimination, ratiocination, speculation, etc.) or the substitution for them of some 'higher' or qualitatively different mode of intellect (e. g. intuition)" (1978, 178). To show that the situation has not changed markedly as regards the difficulty of making deeper psychological analyses of the intensive experiences of mystics and other creative persons, I will quote from a newly written work by Robert S. Ellwood Jr. There the mystic experience is defined as "experience in a religious context that is immediately or subsequently interpreted by the experiencer as an encounter with ultimate divine reality in a *direct nonrational way* that engenders a deep sense of unity and of living during the experience on *a level of being other than the ordinary*" (the italics are mine). In an explanatory comment to this definition Ellwood writes that the concept of direct and non-rational means that normal perception is suspended wholly or partially and that the perception of time is disturbed. These symptoms indicate, says Ellwood, that the individual "sees the object of the experience with some nonsensory organ of perception" (1980, 29 ff). What this organ might be he does not suggest.

All the researchers quoted above believe that the experience of the suprahuman cannot occur via "ordinary perceptive processes", via the senses, but only immediately, intuitively. It therefore seems clear that mystic research, if it is to progress, is in need of a model for different (un)conscious perceptual and cognitive processes including insight into how they are activated. It is just such a model that I intend to present here.

This presentation of the problem makes it clear that my starting point is a "general systems approach", an approach perhaps most propagated by Ludwig von Bertalanffy, who defines systems as "complexes of elements standing in interaction". The methodological problem is to formulate problems of a general type. One consequence of "general systems" is "the appearance of structural similarities or isomorphisms in different fields" (von Bertalanffy 1969, 32 f). It is my intention in this article to search tentatively for such isomorphisms within the areas of mysticism and creativity.

The common theoretical base for the areas of mysticism and creativity is, as stated earlier, a model for perceptual and cognitive development. I thus build on the American psychiatrist Silvano Arieti, whose research on schizophrenia and creativity has received a great deal of attention. After this presentation it is natural for a psychologist of religion to ask what are the religious techniques or exercises that can activate such processes. This question is dealt with in the third section of this article. In the fourth section the model's significance for other central problems within mystic research is discussed, for example, the question of whether is is possible to utilize typologies for mystic experience and the relationship between experience and interpretation. In the last section I return to the relationship between mysticism and creativity, and especially to the important question of how the hypothetical constructs can be operationalized and become the object of scientific research.

2. The Intrapsychic Processes

2.1. *Silvano Arieti—a model for perceptual and cognitive development*

It is perhaps unnecessary to mention that Silvano Arieti proceeds from the same "systems approach" that we mentioned earlier. Apart from his highly regarded studies of schizophrenia, he has throughout his research career shown an interest in creativity research and searched for isomorphisms within both areas of study. The results of nearly three decades of research and clinical experience are presented in the great volumes *Interpretation of Schizophrenia* (1974) and *Creativity, the Magic Synthesis* (1976). It is the latter work which provides the foundation for the following presentation.

Arieti also calls his method a "psychostructual approach", which means that with the aid of depth psychology, he searches for structures and the systems on which those structures lie. An important base for his model is the developmental psychologist Heinz Werner, who has the same theoretical viewpoint (see Bertalanffy 1969, 193 ff). Arieti writes that Werner is one of the two authors who have influenced him most (1976 a, 7). The other is Jean Piaget, whose unprecedentedly influential developmental psychology had very much in common with Werner's (Langer and Sugarman, 1978). What both Werner and Piaget lack, according to Arieti, is the integration of the human cognition into a psychodynamic entirety. In Werner's developmental psychology, too little consideration is given to concepts such as the unconscious, motivation and primary process, an unconscious level in the human personality structure where logical and formal relations are not thought to exist. And Piaget describes an increasingly mature adaption to the surrounding reality, but remains on the level of secondary process, that is, logic, reason and knowledge of the external reality. His results are not related to psychopathology or creativity (1976 a, viii, 7 f). These relations in particular are important for this study. When, as we have seen, a number of studies point to the similarities between intensive religious experiences, psychopathological states and creativity, it is then that we need an integrated view of man's cognitive development which also takes psychodynamic factors into consideration. The relationship to psychopathology, however, will only be touched upon in this article.

Before we get further into Arieti's model of human perceptual and cognitive development, I would like to mention a few of his more general viewpoints. According to Werner, development implies an increasing degree of differentiation in a hierarchic structure. Through repetition and learning the child acquires increasing access to a differentiated cognitive structure with which ingoing stimuli are handled and interpreted. As the logical and abstract thinking processes take over, the more primitive cognitive processes are relegated to subconscious and preconscious levels. These more primitive levels nevertheless exist within the human organism as a resource. In certain psychopathological states and even in the creative process, these repressed cognitive processes can be activated. It is characteristic of man's psychological structure, Arieti states, "to use all the levels of activity, whether in succession, in a given sequence, or in simultaneous action" (1976, 51). According to the psychoanalyst Lawrence Kubie (1958) man can be placed upon a scale according to the extent to which pre- or subconscious processes are allowed to influence consciousness. An all too firm foothold in external reality with little access to other processes is a state just as fixated as one characterised by a domination of the pre- and subconscious, as exhibited by schizophrenic patients. Somewhere in the middle of this scale we find the artist, scientist and, we might add, certain mystics.

Arieti divides the distinct cognitive processes of the human psyche into three main categories: the primary process, which dominates in dreams and in certain states of mental illness; the secondary process, that is, a normal waking consciousness which follows the laws of reality-oriented logic; and the tertiary process, a term which Arieti suggests to cover the "magic synthesis" of primary and secondary processes, the springboard of creativity. He admits here his dependence upon Freud, but at the same time notes that the tertiary process does not exist in classic Freudian analysis. Freud was interested in primary process not so much as structures but rather as abnormal phenomena or as bearers of subconscious motivations. Arieti, however, suggests the following for the creative process: "Instead of rejecting the primitive (or whatever is archaic, obsolete, or off the beaten path), the creative mind integrates it with normal logical processes in what seems a 'magic' synthesis from which the new, the unexpected, and the desirable emerge" (1976, 13).

In his discussion of creativity's psychological components, Arieti first looks at the primitive perception, a complex process of whose last phase we become conscious. Experimental research has shown that we first learn to perceive parts, which are eventually welded into units. A three month old child first sees its mother's forehead, eyes and nose, and later the whole mother. Blind people who have regained their sight must first acquaint themselves with the various parts of an object before the parts can build a whole. In certain states of neurological illness the reverse is possible: perception disintegrates, one perceives only fragments of the whole. The phenomenon is called dedifferentiation (1976, 39 ff). The necessary pre-stages of conscious perception, gestalt-free perception, partial perception and perception of obvious parts, are repressed. The reason for this is that we cannot provide them with meaning (1976, 194 f; 1974, 280 ff. See even Schachtel 1959; Goleman 1981).

As opposed to perception, images are purely mental phenomena which are built upon the memories of earlier perceptions. The production of images belongs to the level of the primary process. It is the most primitive form of symbolic functioning. After approximately seven months a child is at the point where it can produce and experience images. From that point on, images are an important part of the inner reality. They occur spontaneously, but appear more easily when the individual is passive, and when external stimuli are reduced. Rest, isolation and meditation aid the production of images (1976, 46).

The most common images are of either the visual or the auditive type. The eidetic images are a special type and are experienced mainly by children. As opposed to other types, eidetic images are most reminiscent of photographic reproductions of earlier perceived objects. But otherwise, images are relatively blurred and defective reproductions of earlier perceptions. Arieti states that this is of considerable importance for the creative process, as the discrepancy between the original perception and its image introduces what is new; it is the seed of creativity. "Imagery thus emerges not only as the first or most primitive process of reproducing or substituting for *the real,* but also as the first or most primitive process of creating *the unreal*" (1976, 49). Its function is to deal with that which is absent in two senses: the absence of, for example, a friend or food; the absence of that which does not exist and must therefore be created. The production of images does not necessarily only indicate wish-fulfilment (classical analysis) but also implies that the individual has not passively adapted to reality.

Thinking in images can even become a goal in itself. At this point it can lead to daydreaming and in more extreme cases to adualism, that is, the inability to differentiate between the inner and outer world. In other cases,

psychedelic drugs like mescaline or LSD-25 are utilized in order to experience primitive or intensive images.

A final note of importance for this section is that images are often
represssed. The result can be frustration. One way of avoiding this is to
externalize the images, through the activation of various psychic levels and
diverse transformatory mechanisms (1976, 44 ff).

The next level is called amorphous cognition, a type of cognition lacking
concepts, that is, lacking forms of expression such as pictures, words,
thoughts or actions. Since this concerns a purely inner process, Arieti has
called this function endocept[1] (from the Greek. endo, within) to differentiate it from concept, a more mature type of communication. Other researchers use concepts like non-verbal, subconscious or preconscious cognition
when referring to the endocept.

The German Würzburg school were among the first to draw attention to
experiences such as surprise, apprehension, doubt, which lie on a preverbal
level. Some individuals have greater access to endoceptual experiences
than others. This brings us back to Kubie, who stated that there are great
differences in individual contacts with pre- and subconscious processes.
Similarly, Arieti also maintains that the endocept is largely repressed in
adult human life. When it appears, the individual is well aware of the
discrepancy between the endocept and verbal explanations. At that point
one may hear the comment "I know what I mean and feel, but I just can't
describe it." The endocept also plays an important role in situations of
intense emotional content, for example, "intense artistic appreciation".
Arieti sees empathy as a form of communication which is built to a large
extent upon a primitive understanding of each others endocept. A typical
example of this is the relationship between mother and child (1976, 56 ff).

What Arieti wishes to emphasize is that a large part of man's cognitive
activity occurs in a non-conceptual, endocept state. The source of this
amorphic activity is twofold: a primitive level, for example, an extended
image or other non-differentiated mental activity; the contents of higher
mental levels which avoid consciousness and return to more primitive
levels. One discovers time and again, says Arieti, that "the psyche functions in two ways, from a low level to a high and from a high level to a low"
(1976, 53 ff).

The endocept tends to be the object of various transformations. This is an
important point for the understanding of inexpressible, intensive exper-

---

[1] Arieti comments: "At the present state of knowledge, we cannot obtain certain proof of the existence of the endocept. It remains the least clear and the least scientifically verifi-able of the ideas presented in this book ... However ... there is some evidence for its existence, both from logical inference and from clinical observation" (1976, 55).

iences. The following possibilities of transformation are mentioned: "1,
into communicable symbols, that is, into various preconceptual and conceptual forms (the symbols are generally words but may also be drawings,
numbers, sounds and so forth); 2, into actions; 3, into more definite
feelings; 4, into images; and 5, into dreams, fantasies, daydreams, reveries,
and so forth. In all these cases they may constitute the springboard to
creativity" (1976, 60).

A higher stage in the creative process is called primitive cognition or
paleological thinking, which belongs to the thinking of the primary process.
This immature thought form occurs in dreams, among other things, and in
certain mental illnesses, above all, schizophrenia. It can arise spontaneously in otherwise healthy individuals who have been overwhelmed by emotions, for example, prejudice, or anger. These primitive thought processes
are the main subjects of Arieti's research (Special note 1974, ch. 16).

While images and endocepts are found in all people, paleological thinking
occurs only minimally for the average person. In its purest form it is studied
in schizophrenic patients (1976, 66 f). Paleological thinking has three characteristics: identification based upon similarity, altered relation between
word and meaning, concretization and perceptualization of the concept.

Identification based upon similarity is built upon a logic which deviates
from common Aristotelian logic. The principle is that one finds at least one
common element for two or more things or people, which is suffcent for
identification. An example is the patient who asserted that she was the
Virgin Mary. When asked why she believed this, she answered: "I am a
virgin. The Virgin Mary was a virgin; I am the Virgin Mary". Since the
predicates of a subject are innumerable it is impossible to predict what type
of identification will take place.

A constructive variation of identification based upon similarity is scientific discoveries. There are innumerable examples of scientists who have
seen similarities between things which were previously viewed as quite
different. After having studied a mathematical problem for 14 days, the
Frenchman Henri Poincaré stepped onto the bus and suddenly, with "immediate wisdom", gained an insight into the similarity between two mathematical Titans which had not been seen before. The discovery led to a
breakthrough in mathematics. Isaac Newton noticed the common quality in
the apple which falls to the ground and the gravitational attraction of the
planets. The result was the law of gravitation. In Arieti's terms, this is a
question of the coupling of the primary process to concepts, that is, the
secondary process. Out of this constructive combination the tertiary process arises, the creative product (1976, 270 ff). This type of thinking is also
the foundation of Freudian symbolism. The common predicate for the

words pen and penis is their long extended form, and for a box and a vagina is that they both can contain something. The same type of thinking is found in children between the ages of $1\frac{1}{2}$ and $3\frac{1}{2}$ years. All adults are called mamma or pappa because they have the element in common of being adults. Finally, Arieti shows that paleological thinking is very common among primitive peoples, although he does not attach any value or evolutionary significance to this (1976, 68 ff).

In an effort to return quickly to what was said at the start of this section, we may notice a fairly recent experimental study by G. Smith and A. Danielsson. The authors showed that the capacity for "symbolic functioning" is a common element in both children and creative adults, that is, they have a greater ability "to perceive several meanings behind a correctly perceived object" (1979, 5). Noncreative people tend to maintain one single interpretation. In order to be creative, regardless of the subject area, the individual must be able to go beyond the conventional interpretations of reality. The symbolic function can serve as a starting place for creativity. The author's operational definition of creativity is "an individual's ability or inclination to transgress the confines of an established (conventional) perceptual context" (1979, 1). This definition can be compared with what Joachim Israel has written about the phenomenon of transgressing. "It is a process through which we actively exceed or transgress the existing boundaries of our knowledge, including our problematized knowledge" (Israel 1980, 56). An example is the chess player, who must be able to exceed known combinations in order to become a chess master. Transgressing is the source of creativity (Israel 1980, 60).

The other characteristic of paleological thinking is that the relationship between a word and its meaning content can change. One can refer to a table, for example, through three different aspects: the table's connotation, its definition; its denotation, the table as a physical entity; and its verbalization, the sound of the word itself. A healthy person in a waking state is most concerned about the table's connotation and denotation. He can also vary his attention between the three aspects. When an individual thinks paleologically, he connotates differently and focuses on the denotation and verbalization at the expense of the connotation. As far as the first change is concerned, words no longer represent classes or groups but rather specific personifications of the same. The word "dog" for example, is not used in relation to all members of a specific species, but rather for "the dog sitting on the corner over there"

The third characteristic is that a concept can be concretized and even perceptualized. In the psychic process which results in a schizophrenic transformation of an individual's personality, concretizing and perceptualizing occur during the fourth and last phase. "Active concretization means that the psyche is still capable of conceiving the abstract but not of sustaining it, because the abstract is too anxiety-provoking or disintegrating. Abstract ideations are thus immediately transformed into concrete representations". In this respect the artist, poet, and the schizophrenic have something in common. All transform abstract concepts into perceptual images or pictures. However, in contrast to the schizophrenic, the artist maintains contact with the abstract plane (Arieti 1976 a, 272; 1974, 218 f).

The perceptualization of concepts is an extention of the concretizing process. There arc many different levels of this phenomenon. A normal perceptualizing process occurs during dreams. An abnormal form of this process is seen, in its fullest expression, in the hallucinatory experiences of the schizophrenic patient. The perceptualization of concepts is the hallucination's most specific characteristic (1974, 266 ff). Paleological thinking tends to build concrete conceptions of what in normal thinking occurs in abstract form. This is common for schizophrenic patients, for whom indefinite feelings become definite, the invisible becomes visible, etc. (1976, 82 f).

Arieti places religious hallucinations among the non-schizophrenic hallucinations, such as those that occur, for example, in a state of panic, or because of organic disturbances in the central nervous system, delirium tremens etc. However, those with religious hallucinations are not to be viewed as sick or schizophrenic. The differences between the two types of hallucinations are the following: 1, religious hallucinations are mainly visual, auditive elements in general being of lesser importance. 2, Contentwise, religious hallucinations often involve older people, parent substitutes, but they are kind parents who guide the person they reveal themselves to. 3, The content is clearly benefical for the individual. 4, They lead to a marked increase in the individual's self-evaluation and a feeling of "his being or becoming a worthwhile and very active person". A more general difference is that "the hallucinatory and delusional experiences of the schizophrenic are generally accompanied by a more or less apparent disintegration of the whole person" (1974, 277).

Before we leave the primary processes, let us remember that these cognitive mechanisms can, according to Arieti, be activated in many ways. One possibility is that they occur spontaneously, like lightning. Among the ways we have previously mentioned are daydreaming, relaxation, intoxication, dreams, meditation and contemplation. This activation is followed by a further reworking on the secondary process level. "It is up to the mental faculties that are part of the secondary process to accept or reject this material" (1976, 84). What occurs there can generally be described as "the formation and use of concepts and their relations" (1976, 87).

One example of how Arieti utilizes his model in relation to the mystic experience is the following. The contact with a divine reality that many religious figures mention is interpreted as an activation of primary processes, which function as supports for the secondary process. The religious revelation is often preceded by doubt or conflicts. An important condition is what Arieti in agreement with James (1904) and Laski (1961) calls "a state of overbelief", in other words, a foundation in a religious tradition. The mechanisms of the primary process can mean the solution to a conflict situation or can be seen as evidence that the deity is on the individual's side. One example of this is Constantine the Great, who according to Eusebius was preparing for battle against his rival Maxentius. On the 27th October 312 AD he had a vision of a flaming cross in the sky coupled with these words: "In this sign thou shalt conquer". Constantine interpreted this vision as a divine exhortation to become a Christian.

Arieti views this vision as an example of concretizing or perceptualization of concepts. The Cross is a symbol of conversion to Christianity and a projection onto the outer world; the message to become a Christian, a step that Constantine as emperor of a heathen tradition dare not take himself, now came from God. The religious hallucination or possibly illusion, is the solution to the situation. The secondary process is now in harmony with the primary process. Constantine's conversion to Christianity, Arieti says, was influenced by the fact that his mother was a Christian. Additionally, it implied a tactical advantage. In Maxentius' army there were many Christians who perhaps refused to fight or at least fought less intensively against the Christian Constantine (1976, 249 ff).

With this instrument we have the opportunity to cast new light upon a decisive experience in the life of the Swedish mystic Hjalmar Ekström (1885–1962). However, a minimum of background information is necessary to understand this interpretation.

After ten years work in his father's shoeshop, the young Ekström was finally able to realize his dream of an active Christianity by studying to become a deacon. His high-flying expectations fell, however, after a couple of years work in the field. He left the deacon service in the spring of 1914, after a deep spiritual crisis. For one and one half years he wandered through Sweden to preach the simple teachings of Jesus, based upon the message of the Sermon on the Mount. Among the motifs predominating in his letters to his wife during this time, is the conviction of God's guidance in everything. "God guides in everything, may we be secure and happy and with courage follow his paths", he wrote in October 1914 (Geels 1980, 125). The necessities of life forced him to return to the deacon service in the fall of 1915, a situation which must have created considerable conflict. The new position did not last long. In the spring of 1916 he requested leave of absence which lasted the rest of his life. He radically severed all ties with the deacon institute and the deacon service and thereby even with its Christian reference system. After all the difficult years he finally took a vacation in Örkelljunga and there had an experience which he several years later described as a mystical death. Despite his reticence concerning his own experiences, he gave the following account of this experience to a good friend as an answer to his pressing questions. "It (that is, the mystical death) is really, at least according to my experience, like a fire which cuts through everything and consumes everything, leaving nothing left for man" (p. 208). The experience's visionary and auditive elements are clearly expressed in a secondary text, written down by a younger friend immediately after Ekström's own account (see 157f, 247, note 18):

... he went wandering in the woods alone. The path led up a hill. Then it was as if the entire world fissured. It was as if God's eternal love and God's eternal wrath had met in one place like a bolt of lightning, "which flamed down and to the sides like a cross, filling all the heavens and the whole earth, consuming everything". At the same time, he heard a voice which said; "Hereafter the path becomes pathless". And he was cast out into nothingness, a resounding, empty nothingness. Heaven was empty and the earth was empty and Hell as well.—In the first moments he hardly knew whether he saw or heard even with his outer senses. He dimly recalled that it was as if the day of judgment had arrived. But he came to his senses again and continued on his way, tremblingly.

This story has much in common with Ekström's description of the Spirit's night of darkness in the published commentary on the Song of Songs. In that spirit's night, everything that is light, both outer and inner, turns to darkness and despair. But ...

... it perceives something in that dark night, it perceives an immense and crushing expanse of space above, out of which there echoes a single word: Nothingness, followed by lightning, as if from the centre and flaming downwards and to the sides like a cross, filling the whole of space, consuming everything.

The visionary element is similar in both renditions. However, the auditive element is lacking, the voice saying that hereafter the path becomes pathless, in the commentary on the Song of Songs. Despite the fact that Ekström does not mention his own experience in a single word of his commentary, we may be relatively sure that it represents a systematic presentation of an experience and development that is his own. The fact that the auditive element is lacking in the commentary can be interpreted as a support for Arieti's opinion that such elements for mystics are subordinate to the visionary contents.

In Arieti's terms, the experience can be understood as follows. The break with the deacon service, where Ekström had spent eight hard years, must have given rise to the question of whether or not he was still led by God. It was, after all, this motif that had come into the foreground during the preceding years. Was God continually with him when he had now so radically withdrawn from the vocation of deacon and expressed such a strong and occassionally aggressive criticism of Christianity in general? The conflict may have taken place at a subconscious level. It found its solution in the vision and audition of the summer of 1916. The vision of the lightning bolt in the form of a cross can be viewed as a perceptualization of Christianity's most central symbol, which is projected upon the outer world. The auditive element served as a reinforcement for the renewed insight that he was still led by God. Even if the path should become pathless, Ekström now knew that there was still a path. However, it became very difficult for him. His health vacillated increasingly, his loneliness was intense, and it took him approximately six years to verbalize the experience in a self-made religious frame of reference. He shared this mystic view of man and existence with a small group of people for whom he served as soul curer and guide on the path of mysticism. The dream of his youth to care for the souls of others was realized, after all, but in a difficult and extremely independent way.

Arieti is aware that some researchers would not consider such experiences as the one mentioned above to correspond to mysticism. According to Stace, the mystic experience is totally devoid of form or content. What Stace is referring to, writes Arieti, is a sort of endoceptual phenomenon which goes beyond time and space, an experience which does not necessarily need to be coupled with a divine dimension of reality (1976, 263).

3. The Mystic's Techniques—The Activation of Other Cognitive Processes

3.1. *Arthur J. Deikman—de-automatization and the cognitive mode*

Deikman's theoretical and experimental studies of meditation and the psychology of mysticism received much attention during the 1970's. Frits Staal evaluates his contributions as "the one promising kind of experimental work I am familiar with" (1975, 119). And Hjalmar Sundén writes that "his approach means an important step forward in the study of the psychology of religious mysticism" (1970, 46). Deikman has, during almost 20 years of studying meditation and mysticism, emphasized the techniques that mystics and meditators have utilized to achieve a cognitive change. He is, however, apparently hesitant when it comes to describing what changes have been

achieved. In articles from the 1960's and 1970's he has also successively
developed and modified his analysis, with the consequence that his conceptual apparatus has become somewhat inconsistent. What Deikman lacks,
above all, is a total view of perceptual and cognitive development in the
light of which perceptual changes in his subjects can be analysed. These
faults can be compensated by Arieti's integrated model. I would like to
point out however, that the proposed coupling of Arieti and Deikman is
merely a tentative suggestion. I hope to be able to point out a course along
which mystic research should work more than it has done in the past. We
shall see that this theoretical foundation can even be fruitful for the interpretation and understanding of certain religious phenomena.

Deikman has presented two experimental studies on meditation (1963;
1966 a). In both cases the subjects were asked to concentrate on a blue vase
for a period of 15 to 30 minutes without allowing either internal or external
stimuli to distract them. The technique was called contemplative meditation
or perceptual concentration. Already after the first short series of experiments, the subjects reported considerable changes in perception. The analysis of the taped interviews gave the following thought provoking results
(1966 b, 331; 1976, 72).

(a) an increased vividness and richness of the percept- "more vivid", "luminous";
(b) animation in the vase, which seemed to move with a life of its own; (c) a marked
decrease in self-object distinction, occurring in those subjects who continued long-
est in the experiments: "... I really began to feel, you know, almost as though the
vase and I were perhaps merging, or that vase and I were ... It was as though
everything was sort of merging ..."; (d) syncretic thought and a fusing and
alteration of normal perceptual modes: "I began to feel this light going back and
forth", "When the vase changed shape I felt this in my body ..."

How is one to explain these perceptual changes? In order to understand
Deikman's reasoning here, we must first study his theoretical starting
points. Some of the important concepts in this theoretical analysis are
automatization and de-automatization. Automatization implies in short that
man, through the socialization process and through learning, has access to a
large number of stereotypical interpretation patterns, which are utilized in
an automatized way to understand and interpret stimuli. When one looks
out of a window and sees a park there is no need to think first about what
one sees, but rather the interpretation occurs spontaneously. However, a
blind person who had once again received his sight would not automatically
find meaning and structure in the flow of stimuli. The nervous system must
first be codified with these interpretation patterns.

Now Deikman contends, with the support of other researchers, that these
stereotypical models can either partially or completely cease to function if

one manipulates, so to speak, with attention. The result is an "un-undoing of the automatizations of apparatuses—both means and goal structures —directed toward the environment" (quoted by M. Gill and M. Brenman in Deikman 1966 b, 329). Gill and Brenman attempt to understand deautomatization as an "advance or retreat in the level of organization" (ibid.).

We have thus reached the next landmark in this discussion. If we are to judge whether deautomatization is a step forwards or backwards (regression)[2] in man's perceptual and cognitive development, we must first answer a few questions pertaining to developmental psychology. Deikman refers here to Heinz Werner, whose orthogenetical principle underpins our ensuing discussion. This principle implies that "whenever development occurs it proceeds from a state of relative globality and lack of differentiation to a state of increasing differentiation, articulation and hierarchic integration" (Werner 1957, 126). This means that man's development leads to continual differentiation, while earlier developmental stages are integrated into a hierarchic structure. With the aid of such a principle we can speak of an "advance or retreat in the level of organization".

Now Deikman shows that the previously mentioned perceptual changes coincide on all points with Werner's characteristics of the child's and "primitive" man's thinking, a developmental stage which precedes analytical, abstract, intellectual thinking. Is it then a question of regression? Deikman seems unwilling to use this term. The reason is that deautomatization occurs in "an adult mind, and the experience gains its richness from adult memories and functions now subject to a different mode of consciousness" (1966 b, 331). Instead, he is most inclined to speak of changed states of consciousness, which are analogous to the experiences of the classical mystics. The results indicate, however, that meditation as a psychological technique "is a central element in the production of the trained mystic experience" (1963, 216). The majority of the subjects reported experiences that belong to the "sensate" category, that is, that they are based on common affects, sensations or conceptions (more on this below). But there were even indications of experiences of the transcendental type, beyond the "sensate" category. From a psychological perspective, however, the concept of transcendence seems to be problematical, a difficulty I shall return to later on.

In the article on deautomatization and the mystic experience (1966 b), Deikman writes that the effect of deautomatization is amplified by the activities that mystics have always engaged in, namely various forms of

---

[2] The concept of regression has lately become the object of criticism (see below p. 46).

privation, such as poverty, chastity, isolation, silence, and meditation. We are simply dealing with various techniques that the mystic utilizes to direct attention away from the world and instead become totally directed towards an experience of God's nearness. A further similarity between Deikman's subjects and mystics is that both learn not to react to distracting stimuli. Both groups develop psychological barriers, which EEG studies with Zen monks confirm (see for example Kasamatsu and Hirai 1963; Hirai 1978). There are, in other words, a great number of techniques which can elicit deautomatization. For the mystic these are, above all, privation and meditation. Deikman draws the following conclusions (1966, 337 f):

A mystic experience is the production of an unusual state of consciousness. This state is brought about by a deautomatization of hierarchically ordered structures that ordinarily conserve attentional energy for maximum efficiency in achieving the basic goal of the individual: biological survival as an organism and psychological survival as a personality. Perceptual selection and cognitive patterns are in the service of these goals. Under special conditions of dysfunction, such as in acute psychosis or in LSD states, or under special goal conditions such as exist in religious mystics, the pragmatic systems of automatic selection are set aside or break down, in favor of alternate modes of consciousness whose stimulus processing may be less efficient from a biological point of view but whose very inefficiency may permit the experience of aspects of the real world formerly excluded or ignored. The extent to which such a shift takes place is a function of the motivation of the individual, his particular neurophysiological state, and the environmental conditions encouraging such a change.

In his last two articles (1971, 1976) Deikman places emphasis upon the previously discussed shifting between different states of consciousness. Meditation aids the shift from an active to a receptive cognitive mode. This model of a "bimodal consciousness" has been mentioned is earlier articles, but is now developed to a considerably higher degree. It integrates both psychological and biological variables, which are coordinated in two positions: "action mode" and "receptive mode".

The active mode is directed towards dealing with the environment. Seen physiologically this implies an activation of the musculature and an increase in muscle tone, while the EEG registers beta waves. Seen psychologically, one finds focal attention and dominance for the logic-objective thinking process. Perception of objects is steered to a greater degree by a priori concepts than by the experience of the senses. Perception of form dominates perception of color. The perceptual qualities of this "action mode" have developed so that man can influence the world with success.

Opposed to this active cognitive mode is the receptive mode, an organisational state which instead of dealing with the environment has the function of being receptive to it. The functions of the senses are more active than the muscular system. Now the para-sympathetic nervous system dominates. EEG readings tend toward the alpha and theta wave levels. Muscle tone is low. Attention is more diffuse and subject-object distinction becomes unclear, likewise the experience of ones own ego. Thought processes proceed along paralogical paths.

In order to illustrate these cognitive modes, Deikman gives two examples. A taxi driver who has been given the task of getting to the airport on time is totally preoccupied by this goal. He weaves through the traffic, sees things mainly as obstacles and is unconcerned with the colours of other cars. The blue sky or the beauty of the passing buildings he simply does not see. During this time his entire attention is concentrated on the streets and sideroads. He tries to remember alternative routes to the airport. His posture indicates tension and his EEG would without a doubt show quick beta waves.

In contrast with this taxi driver, the psychological and physiological processes of a monk are quite different. In the experiential world of the monk, the distinction between himself and the environment seems more dim. His muscles are relaxed and his EEG would probably register alpha or theta waves. In contrast to the taxi driver, he is not concerned with the future but is totally consumed by what he experiences at the moment.

The characteristics of both of these modes build a coherent system in the sense that a change in one of the system's components effects all the others. The choice of cognitive mode depends upon the individual's motivations. The completely dominating mode is the "action mode". This follows because, among other things, it is needed for survival, it is confirmed during childhood at the expense of the more basic receptive mode, and because, in a larger socio-cultural perspective, it is emphasized by western effectivity thinking. It is difficult for many to return to the receptive mode.

3.2. *The relation Arieti-Deikman*

A summary of Deikman's research results gives us the following picture. Experimental meditation leads to a shift from the active to the receptive cognitive mode, a shift that can result in a deautomatization of normal perceptual and cognitive functions. A possible result of this process can be a disturbance in the individual's perception of reality. "The sense of reality normally bestowed on objects is now 'transferred' to abstract psychical entities" (Deikman 1966a, 111). Deikman calls this phenomenon "reality transfer". To my way of thinking, this is most reminiscent of what Arieti calls the perceptualization of concepts. Another possibility, according to Deikman, is that the perception is broken down in the direction of a more primitive visual experience. Arieti calls this dedifferentiation (above p. 32), a concept which Deikman seems to use in approximately the same way (1963, 335; 1966a, 110f). Dedifferentiation, writes Deikman, can also lead to an experience of unity, when "the self is no longer experienced as a separate object and customary perceptual and cognitive distinctions are no longer applicable" (1966b, 330). Through perceptual concentration, the individual can become aware of certain intrapsychic processes which are normally withheld from consciousness. Deikman refers here to Heinz Werner, according to whom development implies, among other things, a structuring of the perceptual and cognitive world, a selective process, which occurs at the expense of certain stimuli. It is possible that the individual in these experimental conditions experiences intrapsychic, amorphic processes. Another logical possibility, Deikman continues, is that the individual perceives a characteristic of the phenomenological world (1966b, 334f). These experiences are strongly reminiscent of Arieti's description of endoceptual experiences. By these comparative examples I hope to show that Deikman's results can very well be viewed in the light of Arieti's psychology. A few circumstances facilitating a coupling of these two researchers is that both begin from a "general systems approach" and that both build to a large extent on the developmental psychology of Heinz Werner.

Deikman's concept of deautomatization and Arieti's cognitive model can be seen to complement one another. Deikman has studied the techniques which lead up to a psychological process, but he is unsure of how to describe this process. Arieti continues where Deikman stopped: deautomatization can lead to a situation where more primitive cognitive mechanisms, repressed by the environment's demands for secondary processes, can be reactivated.

Such an activation naturally need not only occur through renunciation and meditation. There are a considerable number of other techniques which mystics utilize within different traditions. Many of these classical exercizes entail that the individual is either placed in a situation of sensory deprivation, a state where a minimum of stimuli can be received, or a situation of sensory overload, where, for example, sight or hearing senses receive a given stimuli over a long period of time. The research on this phenomenon from the 1950's can, according to Arieti, be summarized in the following way. When a person is first put into a situation of sensory isolation, she experiences in the beginning a hunger for stimulation, then "indulgence in reveries occurs, finally the reveries assume a perceptual quality and become hallucinations, predominantly or exclusively of the visual type". Similar phenomena have been reported earlier by people who have through certain circumstances been placed in a situation of understimulation, for example, lone seaman or polar explorers. According to a theory of L. J. West,

effective sensory input ordinarily serves to inhibit the emergence into consciousness of previously recorded precepts. If effective sensory input is impaired, recorded perceptual traces are released and emerge. According to West, effective sensory input can be impaired in three ways: (1) absolute decrease or depatterning; (2) input overload, or 'jamming the circuits'; (3) decreased psychological contact with the environment through the exercise of mental mechanisms (dissociation).

West believes that if, at the same time as the input is decreased, there is sufficient internal arousal of the brain (through the reticular formation of the brain stem) to permit vivid awareness, the released perceptions may be dynamically organized and reexperienced as fantasies, dreams, or hallucinations (quoted in Arieti 1974, 272f).

This theory is of importance for the understanding of diverse phenomena within the psychology of religion. One example is the repetitive prayer, which exists in different places throughout the religious world, above all, in Islamic mysticism or Sufism. Through a persistent repetition of God's name, combined with specific body movements and a special breathing technique, the Sufis place themselves in a situation of "input overload". It is interesting to note that sensory under- and overstimulation, at least at one level, appear to be two sides of the same coin, as overstimulation occurs at the expense of other stimuli. These phenomena are also related to ecstatic dance, to overstimulation of the sense of hearing through rhythmic music, and to cries of hallelujah at charismatic meetings, to give only a few examples. There is here a great area for research in the psychology of religion.

If we return to the comparison between Arieti and Deikman, we can state that traces of Deikman's so vital distinction between active and receptive cognitive modes are also found in Arieti. In connection with the neo-Freudian Ernest Schachtel's division into autocentric and allocentric perception, that is, perception with a low degree of objectification and a predominance of feelings of lust and discomfort, and a perception which actively directs itself towards the object (Schachtel 1959, chp III), Arieti remarks that this deals with important attitudes, but is not sufficient for creativity (1976, 28).

Schachtel's distinction has a number of intersecting points with the active and receptive modes (van der Lans 1980, 79ff). If I interpret Arieti correctly, the receptive mode and allocentric perception can be creativity promotive cognitive attitudes. On images on the level of the primary process, for example, Arieti writes: "Images occur spontaneously, but they are made to occur more easily if the person *refrains from action and if external stimuli are reduced or eliminated. Rest, solitude, and meditation facilitate their occurrence*" (1976, 46. My italics). Among the nine "simple attitudes" and the circumstances which promote creativity in the individual, he lists first aloneness, thereafter inactivity, and daydreaming as the third point. In other words, three conditions which are not valued in western success-oriented society. Through aloneness the individual is less susceptible to the influence of society and its clichés, a sort of partial sensory deprivation, which facilitates the manifestation of the primary process. When it comes to the choice of cognitive mode, the authors seem to be in agreement.

It appears that Deikman has also seen something of Arieti's tertiary process. The shift to the receptive mode can, according to him, give rise to creative intuition. The first phase in this process is characterized by an intensive struggle with the problem (action mode). When one is conscious of having arrived at a dead end, a stage of self-surrender (receptive mode) ensues, during which the answer can come like a flash—the creative synthesis. During the last phase, one shifts back to the active mode in order to integrate the new formulation with previous knowledge and in order to share it with others (Arieti 1976, 83 f; 1971, 83. Compare also Wallas's (1926) four studies of the creative process). It is however clear, as we have already suggested, that the value of Deikman's deautomatization concept and the cognitive modes lie on a different level to that of Arieti. The relationship between Deikman's and Arieti's concepts then is that they complement and partially overlap one another.

3.3. *The concept of regression*

One central question which we previously mentioned (p. 41) is whether an activation of more primitive cognitive processes implies a regression to an earlier stage of development. One of the leading figures in this field for a number of years was the neo-Freudian, Ernst Kris. In his work on the psychology of creativity (1950, 1952) Kris suggested that creativity should be understood as "regression in the service of the ego". The creative individual has access, so to speak, to primitive cognitive processes without losing contact with reality. The difference between creative and schizophrenic regression is that the former implies a temporary regression while the latter implies a more permanent one.

In latter years, the concept of regression has been the point of critical debate (Kragh and Smith 1970; Rothenberg 1979, 1981; Suler 1980). Kragh and Smith point out that the concept of regression could easily become misleading because of its clinical connotation. The authors feel that instead of talking of regression one should talk of reconstruction, a concept which implies that subconscious or preconscious material "is exploited within the frame of an individual's present perceptual-cognitive activity'' (Smith 1981, 4). In connection with Rothenberg (1981) Smith comments that the activated cognitive processes do not apparently represent ''a primitivization of mental functioning although they utilize certain aspects of primary process characteristics beneficial to creativity'' (1981, 6). I believe that this is an important point, which harmonizes with the integrated hierarchical model previously presented, based upon Heinz Werner's developmental psychology. With a starting point in Rothenberg and Smith, I shall therefore speak of reconstruction (more on this concept follows on p. ●). A reflection comes to mind, however, concerning intensive religious experiences. It would seem reasonable to assume that secondary processes are more or less connected to primary processes. The predominance of the former or the latter might be a function of the intensity of the experience. During intensive experiences the secondary thought process is inhibited completely, during less intensive experiences only partially.

4. Two Problems Often Discussed within Mystic Research

4.1. *Types of mystic experiences*

Many pioneers within mystic research have worked with typologies in order to differentiate between mystic experiences. One of the first was presented by William James. His division into cultivated and sporadic mysticism (1904, 393 ff) still seems to be of use. Deikman utilizes a similar division which I shall come to shortly. One advantage of these typologies is that they are free from apologetic elements, which cannot be said of many other classifications in mystic research in the 20th century. One exception is James B. Pratt, who in his classic study on the psychology of religion from the 1920's differentiates between mild and extreme experiential types. The former is found in completely normal people, while the latter is usually ''so striking in its intensity and in its effects that it attracts notice and is regularly regarded as a sign either of supernatural visitation or of a pathological condition ... And in these more intense cases of mysticism the simple 'sense of a Beyond' develops into the ecstasy and the vision'' (1926, 339).

What is interesting in Pratt's distinction is that, like James, he was aware that there are differences in mystic experiences with regard to intensity, which implies that such experiences in their less intensive forms are more common than is generally assumed. There is a tendency in older mystic research to consider the mystic experience as unique, unattainable for the average person, remote from his day to day life.[3] Marghanita Laski has a completely different view. In the very title of her book *Ecstasy, a Study of some Secular and Religious Experiences,* she expresses the view that this type of experience is not unique to the world of religion. She has the support of the well-known humanistic psychologist Abraham Maslow, who has lowered, so to speak, the religious prophet's and ecstatic's "core-religious" or transcendental experiences to the level of everyday psychology. "It is very likely, indeed almost certain, that these older reports, phrased in terms of supernatural revelation, were, in fact, perfectly natural, human peak-experiences of the kind that can easily be examined today" (1973, 20). One consequence of Maslow's view is that in a western secularized society of the 1980's we utilize a different language than that used in an older society, where religion played a more important part as a pattern for interpretation of diverse experiences. We are once again dealing with socio-cultural factors, which always play a central role. It is quite apparent that in the pluralistic society of today, with its strong influence from meditation movements of the East, for example, it is much easier to talk of religious and mystic experiences. Indeed, mystic experiences appear so common today that the American sociologist of religion, Andrew Greeley, asks in an article from 1975, "Is America a Nation of Mystics?" His survey study showed that four out of ten Americans had had, or believed that they had had, mystical experiences. The American Gallup study of religion showed similar results in their index from 1977–78 (quoted in Ellwood 1980, 1f; Hay 1978; Hay and Morris 1979).

Arthur Deikman has in his studies of mysticism presented a distinction which, with certain additions and restatements, can be of practical value. He differentiates between "untrained-sensate, trained-sensate, trained transcendent" types (1966b, 324f). In the first category, which is largely commensurate to the previously mentioned sporadic type, are included people who normally do not engage in prayer, meditation or other exercises. This category also includes the majority of intensive experiences elicited by drugs. James gives many examples of experiences elicited by laughing-gas, chloroform and ether. After the second World War, especially during the 1960's, many studies were done on the importance of psychedelic drugs for mystic experience (Geels 1980a). These experiences, however, need not always belong to the spontaneous category. The question of with what intent and in what kind of environment drug usage occurred, in

---

[3] A similar tendency has been found within the field of creativity research, where the great geniuses are often emphasized. The modern view seems to be, however, that the creative process is similar both with regard to various subject areas and to various degrees of intensity.

other words, the set and setting, is of decisive importance. There is a great difference, especially in set and setting, between, for example, the North American Indians' peyote rites and the hippie culture's uncontrolled self-experimentation with LSD-25, mescaline or psylocibin during the 60's.

It can be difficult to differentiate between the categories "untrained-sensate" and "trained-sensate" if one only studies the texts. The difference is that the latter consciously and with the aid of given exercises strive towards a directly experienced relationship with God. The socio-cultural difference is of decisive importance. The trained mystic often functions in a special environment, for example, the monastery life, and has a system of concepts at his disposal with which he can interpret his experiences.

The great mystics as well as their commentators, writes Deikman, "divide the effects and stages through which mystics progress into a lesser experience of strong emotion and ideation (sensate) and a higher, ultimate experience that goes beyond affect or ideation" (1966b, 325). The latter experiential type belongs to the "trained-transcendent" group, a state where multiplicity steps back for a sort of experience of unity. Such experiences are often the result of considerable ·practice. An important difference, Deikman states, is if the experience is founded upon normal affects, sensations and concepts, or if it is reported to extend beyond them (1966b, 327).

I believe that one experiential type is missing among Deikman's distinctions, namely the "untrained-transcendent" category. Transcendental experiences in Deikman's sense can also occur sporadically or spontaneously. Often it is this type of experience that Zaehner (1967) calls panenhenical, unity in existence. Instead of the categories "sensate" and "transcendent", I suggest, therefore, a differentiation between structured and unstructured experiences. By structured is meant a clearly discernible content, for example, the face of Christ, a figure and so on. The experience is unstructured when the individual refers to more abstract categories such as emptiness, nothingness, peace, light and so on. These two types are to be viewed in relationship to the two qualitites of cultivated and spontaneous. We then gain the following axial system.

$$\text{structured} \underset{\text{spontaneous}}{\overset{\text{trained}}{\rule{4cm}{0.4pt}}} \text{unstructured}$$

There is one disadvantage with the concept pair sensate-transcendent. Since the human organism always strives to provide stimuli with meaning, and since the mystic experience always contains some form of stimuli, the concepts are poorly chosen. The question becomes rather, what sort of stimuli are we dealing with? From this point of view, the concept pair structured-unstructured is more appropriate. At this point, I should also like to add that I am sceptical of the concept transcendence in Deikman's sense. An experience must always have some sort of content, otherwise it is not possible to communicate it. On the other hand, the content can be of a completely different type to that which is experienced in everyday life. What is lacking is a language with which to communicate it. Another side of the transcendent is that the individual's experiential platform is not the ego that he is used to identifying by, but rather a "deeper" dimension of personality. That which one "goes beyond" (transcends) is one's own identity. After the experience, the ego concept is extended. It is in this sense I feel that one should understand humanistic psychology's talk of self-realization and expansion of consciousness.

4.2. *Mystic experience and interpretation—a perceptgenetic view*

It is mainly the philosophers of religion who have shown an interest in the relationship between mystic experience and interpretation. Since the beginning of the 1960's there has been a clear distinction between a mystic experience and, in the words of W. T. Stace, "the conceptual interpretations which may be put upon it" (Stace 1960, 31f). According to Stace, this distinction is comparable to the relationship between a perception and its interpretation. The former relationship is, however, very difficult to get at. By interpretation Stace means "anything which the conceptual intellect adds to the experience for the purpose of understanding it" (1960, 37). Stace's concept of interpretation belongs, in other words, to the reconstruction phase and to a phase which can occur after the first description of an experience. I will return to his perspective on the experience- interpretation problem. In any case, we are dealing with the conscious reworking of an experience on the basis of a given tradition.

Stace inspired researchers in various places to examine this problem (see, for example, Smart 1962, 1966; Hof 1967). One of the latest and most indepth examples of analysis of this problem from the perspective of the philosophy of religion was made by the Englishman, Peter G. Moore. In an article from 1973, Moore points out that mystic research has underestimated this problem. His contribution consisted of a recommendation for three "possible junctures at which interpretation could relate to experience" (Moore 1973). Five years later the distinctions were increased to four, which indicated that Moore himself had also underestimated the problem. The first type is called "retrospective interpretation", that is, interpretations influenced by tradition arising after the experience. Moore did not however, discuss what importance the time interval had for ex post facto descriptions. From a psychological perspective, however, this is a not uninteresting detail. The majority of descriptions of mystic experiences are given long after, perhaps years after, the experience itself. The intention of the description is also important to note. When dealing with old texts, even various Church censorship bodies can have played a part. In any case, one must take the knowledge of memory psychology into consideration with regard to retrospective interpretations.

The second type Moore calls "reflexive interpretation", spontaneous interpretations formulated during the experience or immediately thereafter. When the mystic's own beliefs, his expectations and intentions influence the experience, Moore speaks of "incorporated interpretation". This third type is divided into two subgroups: "reflected interpretation", ideas and images that are reflected, so to speak, in the experience in the form of visions and such; "assimilated interpretation", the experiential type which builds a phenomenological analogy to a belief or doctrine. And the last type in Moore's categorization consists of experiences which are supposed to be uninfluenced by the mystic's earlier belief, expectations or intentions. He speaks in such cases of "raw experience" (1978, 198 f).

Let me add immediately that the latter category is a theoretical abstract. From the psychological point of view, the mystic's original experience is very difficult if not impossible to get at. Further, it is unthinkable that the individual is totally uninfluenced by earlier life developments. Researchers always work with interpreted experience, most often verbalized in various forms. However, it is possible to speak of "raw interpretation". But this category coincides, as far as I can see, with that of "reflexive interpretation".

The most important contribution of the above mentioned philosophers of religion is that they have been aware of the various levels of interpretation concerning mystic experience. One must agree with Peter G. Moore, however, that it is the psychologist's task to clarify the relationship between experience and interpretation (1973, 178). Moore emphasizes the importance of the individual's cognitive structure before the experience. No more comments of a psychological nature are to be found. It is therefore apparent that a psychological conceptual apparatus is needed to carry this discussion a step further. With the aid of percept-genetic theory, I feel that a new perspective is unfolded.

Before we consider this new perspective I would like to direct attention to an almost trivial point, which is a consequence of both the previously presented cognitive model and of analyses by philosophers of religion. The text which the psychologist of religion studies must be seen as a conscious and developed final product of a process which has a number of sub- and preconscious pre-stages. The well-known semanticist Alfred Korzybski differentiated as early as the 1950's between a number of "silent, unspeakable levels" which preceed the verbal fixation of an experience (1951, 172). An occurrence, for example, the dropping of a matchbox, first leads to a retinal image and thereafter reactions like "feelings" or value judgements. These phases in the perceptual process are still to be found on a preverbal level. The last phase in this greatly simplified model is the various forms of manipulation with the aid of the language system (1951, 172ff). When dealing with these systems, Korzybski differentiates between primitive and Aristotelian language structures, the latter comprising the Indo-european languages. The former are characterized by a lack of abstraction and "identification based upon similarity", an expression we recognize from Arieti (Korzybski 1951, 178).

What is interesting about Korzybski's article is that he points to the importance of the language structure for our perceptions. Without going further into this, I would like to direct attention toward a point of great importance for the problem of how an unspeakable experience is interpreted and in turn influences new experiences. I have pointed out in a previous work that a mystic must at some point have had his first mystic experience and thereby a possible problem of how to describe with words the "indescribable" (Geels 1980, 27f). It is this that the former American psychologist Richard Alpert, now Ram Dass, calls a "labeling conflict" (1977, xif). With what frame of reference is one to interpret an intensive experience? Ram Dass chose a religious interpretation, accepted the consequences of this and left his job as an academic teacher. Such a conflict, however, need not occur. The problem is minimal if the mystic belongs to a tradition where experiences of this type are a possibility and indeed something worth striving for. In that case, there are probably what social psychologists call significant others in the mystic's environment, who can, with the aid of tradition, explain the experiences, thereby making them easy to integrate into the personality and with one's concept of reality. The problem arises when the mystic does not have access to a mystic tradition. In such cases a time lapse will probably be found between the original experience and its verbalization. This is not an unusual phenomenon in the context of intensive religious experiences. One of Shri Aurobindos biographers mentions for example, that this well-known Indian mystic of the 1900's had no language with which to interpret his decisive religious experiences. The explanations came much later (see Goleman 1975, 207). It is then possible that the mystic, after reflecting upon the experience and having gathered more information from other mystics, subsequently adds new formulations and explanations. These new "cognitive schemes" (Neisser 1978) in turn influence a renewed experience. We will see below that perceptgenetic theoreticians support such a view.

This aspect of the experience-interpretation problem is also confirmed by Korzbyski's research, according to which "all languages have a structure of some kind, and every language reflects in its own structure the world as assumed by those who evolved the language. Reciprocally, we read mostly unconsciously into the world the structure of the language we use" (1951, 177). A clarification of this mutual relationship between language and experience is that we expect the lapse of time between the experience and its interpretation to become shorter when the mystic possesses a cognitive scheme with which to describe the experience. According to Korzybski, a linguistic fixation always implies a risk: we tend to identify the verbalization with the preceding preverbal levels. However, "statements are verbal, they are never the silent 'it' " (ibid, 173).

If one assumes that the mystic experience is some sort of perception, which is a common assumption, then the perceptgenetic argument should be of the greatest importance for the experience-interpretation problem. Viewed in this way, an intensive religious experience should follow the same psychological process as all other perceptions. The big difference is clearly the degree of intensity. It is important to keep this in mind when comparing mystic experiences and the perceptual process.

The perceptgenetic research at the University of Lund[4] is linked to pre-World War II continental psychology, including the developmental psychology of Heinz Werner, so important for our model. In connection with Werner, perceptgenetics (PG) builds upon the assumption that perception's microgenesis, that is, its development during a very short period of time, is related to the individual's ontogenesis, that is, her personal and personality development (Westerlundh 1976, 313; Smith and Westerlundh 1980, 95 ff). With the aid of various techniques, one attempts to plot the different subconscious—or more correctly preconscious—pre-stages of conscious perception. Empirical research indicates that these pre-stages run from deeply rooted archaic function levels to relatively wellstructured and reality adapted levels. The development from the subjective, preliminary phases (so-called P phases) to the concluding C phase ("concluding") is described as a *construction in the direction of the object*. It is during this phase that the individual, in the context of her own life development, gives meaning to stimuli. When the individual, then, can on a conscious level grasp the

---

[4] The development of percept-genetics arises out of experiments in perception. For a review see Kragh & Smith 1970; Smith & Westerlundh 1980. The concept apparatus of percept-genetics has shown itself to be fruitful in other areas, for example creativity research.

constructed contents, she is influenced partially by her current cognitive structure and partially by her defense mechanisms. The latter is called *reconstruction,* a concept we have met earlier (p. 46). On the relationship between construction and reconstruction, Smith and Westerlundh write (1980, 113):

... during our lives, we will consciously experience more and more (reconstruction). This successive experiencing is incorporated in the life-historical meaning system and is thus activated in later acts of construction. In terms of the historical personality, the act of construction implies an activation of the individual's earlier reconstruction.

Perceptgenetics assumes that perception, during this construction from phase P to C, can go through many "descriptive transformations". The first is *cumulation,* the retention of previously gained insights; the second is *elimination,* an exclusion of material via an automatizing process; the last is *emergence,* the development of new insights (Westerlundh 1976, 313; Smith and Westerlundh 1980, 111). Transferred to the area of mysticism, cumulation is commensurate with what Moore calls "incorporated interpretation". Cumulation implies namely, that there is a certain continuity between the individual's "life history", where faith and expectations are a part, and experience. Such a continuity is probable when the mystic's intensive perception is structured, for example, in the form of the face of Christ or perhaps a voice that speaks to the individual. Visions and auditions, in other words, should reinforce rather than demolish a religious frame of reference.

If we return again to Moore's categories, we can, from a psychological perspective, combine the reflexive interpretation and the "raw experience". As far as his third category, "incorporated interpretation" is concerned, it can possibly explain the cumulation effect, but not the emergence phenomenon. The first category, the retrospective interpretation, is too broad to be of use, for Moore does not seem to have considered the time lapse between the original experience and later additions, repressions, and other changes. (Regarding regulatory aspects and the psychology of memory see earlier work (Geels 1980)).

Over and above the previously mentioned points concerning the latter problem, I would like to direct attention to a similar phenomenon within psychoanalysis—the interpretation of dreams. In his classical work on dreams (1900) Freud assumes that dream contents are successively reinterpreted. Through this reworking, dreams gain a better logical construction and inner context. Since the later versions are steered by the secondary process, Freud calls this reworking *secondary revisions.*

I believe that this concept is of interest for the experience-interpretation problem. Grønbaek (1935) has from the direction of the psychology of religion, shown what principles are active in post-descriptions. The four tendencies that he found, including the order and intellectualization tendencies, are all of the secondary process type. What is not clear in Grønbaek's results, however, is the tendency to add to previously made interpretations or the tendency to practice censorship, so to speak, of one's own interpretations. This can be motivated in both cases by the mystic's need to integrate the experience into the religious frame of reference (inner motive) or by the environment's demands for orthodoxy (external motive).

One example of a secondary revision is the following quotation by Martin Buber (1961, 43):

... from my own unforgettable experience I know well that there is a state in which the bounds of the personal nature of life seem to have fallen away from us and we experience an undivided unity. But I do not know—what the soul willingly imagines and indeed is bound to imagine (mine too once did it)—that in this I had attained to a union with the primal being or the Godhead. *That is an exaggeration no longer permitted to the responsible understanding.* Responsibly—that is, as a man holding his ground before reality—I can elicit from those experiences only that in them I reached an undifferentiable unity of myself without form or content. /- - -/ This unity is nothing but the unity of this soul of mine, whose 'ground' I have reached ... (italics mine)

Buber refers here to an experience of undifferentiated unity, which he at one time interpreted as a unity with God. However, based upon what he terms "responsible understanding", that is, loyality to his own Jewish tradition with its strong emphasis upon a transcendental God, he calls this previous interpretation an exaggeration. Instead, he chooses to interpret this experience as an experience of unity with his own soul, without God being involved. In other words, it is a clear example of secondary revision.

5. The Mystic Experience and Creativity

The concept of emergence is very interesting for the psychology of religion. In creative people, emergence is combined as a "revolutionary" principle with the conservative influence of accumulation (Smith 1981). I believe that it is reasonable to assume that the possibility for new insights increases when the mystic's intensive perception is unstructured, for example, an experience of unity in nature, an intense experience of light, peace etc. Seen psychologically, such stimuli should be a good starting point for the primary process in Arieti's sense. Experiences of an endoceptual nature or paleological thinking or a transition from the former to the latter should be factors that greatly facilitate a rich picture language, metaphors, paradoxes and possibly new linguistic constellations. Its not surprising, then, that the two great linguistic reference systems, the profane and the religious, merge into one another.

With the concept of emergence we have also provided a link between perceptgenetics and our model of perceptual and cognitive development. For perceptgenetics does not describe *how* emergence's new insights come to the individual, only *that* they arise. According to the model based upon Arieti and Werner, we are dealing with the activation of processes that can lead to creativity. In addition to the (un)structured nature of the experiences, even defense mechanisms and socio-cultural factors play an important role. In dealing with historical mystics however, it is difficult to get at the former variable, which makes a psychological study even more difficult.

It is apparent that the unstructured intensive experience is of the greatest importance for the activation of cognitive processes that aid creativity. Emergence leads to new insights, new contents. It is a well-known fact that many of the classics of world literature are the contributions of religious mystics. Juan de la Cruz's *Cantico* is judged to be "avec deux ou trois sonnets de Gongora, ce que la poésie espagnole a jamais produit de plus étrange et de plus sublime" (quoted in Sundén 1970, 35). Among the mystics less bound by tradition we find both Plotinos and William Blake. Examples are many. One can say in any case that intensive religious experiences have motivated mystics to write and often led to literary masterpieces.

Intensive religious experiences can be seen, in other words, as a motivational factor. We must remember, however, that the verbal expression of this represents only one of a number of reaction patterns (see p. 36). The methodological problem for researchers is to find criteria for the creative process, a very important problem which I shall come to shortly. The combination of primary and secondary processes discussed above is to a large extent a hypothetical construct. It should perhaps be said here that Arieti is not the only one to present a dichotomy of the creative process. Other researchers who have had similar ideas include D. Rapaport, A. Maslow and U. Neisser (see Ruth 1980, 25). Even A. Koestler's (1964) distinction between associative and dissociative thinking indicates similarities with this dichotomy.

Marianne Jeffmar is one of those who has taken research a step further. Instead of using a dichotomous model, she works with a trichotomous model which serves her purpose of explaining the similarities between intelligence and creativity. She differentiates between three cognitive processes: a primary imaginative process and two secondary processes, the ductive (inductive, deductive) and the annotating process. The imaginary (I) process is described as intuitive, global and sensitive. The ductive (D) process is analyzing and abstractive, and the annotative (A) process is observant and ordered. The I process is the least dependent and the A process is the most dependent upon the environment (Jeffmar 1978; 1978 a, 16 f). The combination of the I and D processes can lead to creativity, while the combination of D and A processes gives rise to intelligence. It is worth mentioning, however, that the I process in comparison with Arieti's primary processes, is a more limited category. It is mainly of a cognitive type, while Arieti's primary processes are of both a cognitive and affective nature.

In a later work, Jeffmar (1980) suggests in connection with Ornstein et al, that the I and D–A processes have their physiological counterparts in the specialization of the two brain hemispheres, a coupling which acquired new topicality when Roger W. Sperry was awarded the Nobel prize in medicine in 1981 for precisely similar research. The left hemisphere's logical-analytical thinking is commensurate with the secondary processes, while the right hemisphere's spatial and holistic specialization is commensurate with the pre-and subconscious primary processes.

Jeffmar has also contributed with suggestions concerning the previously mentioned problem of finding criteria for when the the creative process has been active, in other words, to operationalize these processes. A subprocess to the I process is *syncretism,* "a tendency to build up new combinations and/or conglomerations of disparate concepts or elements in an emotional way. Syncretism can also be described as a tendency to keep separate phenomenon and fact, feeling and perception. The term syncretism is borrowed from Werner (1948) who used it to describe 'primitive' cognitive functioning." A subprocess to the D process is *flexibility,* that is, "a tendency to interpret phenomena and/or facts intellectually in different and/or new ways." *Exactness,* finally, is an expression of the annotative process (1978 a, 17 f). I believe that these subprocesses are applicable to mystic research. A good reason for supplementing with Jeffmar is that, like Arieti and Deikman, she starts from a "systems approach" and, as we have seen, also builds upon parts of Heinz Werner's theories.

It is not difficult to find examples of syncretism in the mystic texts. Out of consideration to space, I will limit myself to a few. On a general level, the mystic's rich flora of pictures, metaphors and symbolic language can be viewed as an expression of verbal syncretism. The use of pictures and metaphors clearly coincides with the most important characteristic of the mystic experience—its indescribability. The pressing need to somehow

describe the indescribable can lead to metaphors, among other things.
According to Arieti, they offer the opportunity to express "the similar in
the dissimilar".[5] Even Aristotle understood the importance of the metaphor: "The greatest thing by far is to be a master of metaphor; it is the one
thing that cannot be learnt from others; and it is also a sign of genius, since
a good metaphor implies an intuitive perception of the similarity in the
dissimilar" (Poetics, 1459 A. Quoted in Arieti 1976, 136).

Another example of syncretism is the tendency for many mystics to
assume relatively freely the ideas and wordings of other authors. The
combination of what in themselves are old words and phrases leaves us
with something new, a unique combination of ideas. We can call this
ideational syncretism. We should not however forget the socio-cultural
environment, for example, the possibility to express oneself freely, without
external demands for orthodoxy. Thus Hjalmar Ekström in twentieth century Sweden can use a very old image which it would not have been
possible to interpret in that way in the Catholic Europe of the 1300's. The
image contains two components, iron and fire, which illustrates man's
relationship to God during *unio mystica,* the mystical unity. As iron's
characteristic qualities disappear when it is glowing red, so also does man's
nature disappear when consummed in the divine fire. But, Ekström writes
in November 1929, "the more often the iron is in the fire, the more it is
consummed by the fire, until nothing is left, and the iron has gone to
another existence" (Geels 1980, 209). Ekström refers here to the dissolution of the personal identity in the mystic experience, a unity with God in
the sense of a coalescence, a wording which would not have been allowed
in another time and place.

New linguistic constellations, such as Simone Weil exemplifies, can be
seen as an example of flexibility. The phenomenon is well-known and is
similar to the linguistic mobility that many mystics bear witness to. Here
we have reached the subprocess of flexibility. It can go together with the
unstructured nature of the experience and the mystic's independent attitude
in relation to tradition. An example of this is once again Hjalmar Ekström,
who in certain collections of letters utilizes a language with a strong
infinitudinal coloring and in others describes the mystic experience with
concepts taken from the personality category. One example of each will
illustrate this phenomenon (see Geels 1980, 193–213). On his experience of
God Ekström writes:

---

[5] Compare Hans Hof's analysis of *analogia
attributionis* with Meister Eckhart (Hof
1952).

it's as if you are *sucked up and drown* in Him in heaven and become one with Him, as if nothing else exists except Him, no other will except His. This unity cannot be described with words, it is full of the wonders of heaven and earth . . .
/–––/
Yes, *everything drowns in God's transparent stillness* and in It becomes as one: everything is transparently transformed, everything becomes as crystal, until one for a moment or a while falls back into one self . . . And so the Heart's space opens again, more widely than before, radiating with great light, and so bubbling with life that the body staggers and shakes (consumed as the flame consumes the wax—'life blooms with a swaying crown') (Italics Mine).

This description with its clear feeling of infinity can be compared to the next quotation which is characterized by fertility, pregnancy, and birth symbolism:

And with this seed of life he fertilized everything that believes in Him, so that His heavenly body and spirit was born in it (to be born out of it in its time). During the time that the new life grows within man, man is taken ever closer to the death of the old, for the new and the old life can never be united—the one must do away with the other.

The concepts born-in and born-out are probably new linguistic constellations, possibly influenced by Master Eckhart. Other examples of creative reactions of the flexibility type are where old terms or doctrines receive new meaning. In this category we may also include the innumerable commentaries and personal explanations of religious texts that one often meets. In certain religions, for example, Hinduism, it has become a tradition that the great leaders of the various religious branches should comment on the texts that are common for all the religious branches. For Christianity I will give a couple of examples. Jan van Ruusbroec builds his most important work "The Spiritual Marriage" on the Bible verse "Behold, the bridegroom cometh; go ye out to meet him" (Matt. 25:6), a Bible verse that he then comments on for 150 pages! It is clear that with this commentary he strayed far from the exegesis of his time. Another example is commentary, common with in Christian mysticism, on the Song of Songs. Hjalmar Ekström's personal commentary, published in 1937, is one of the latest examples of such creativity.

6. Conclusion

The aim of this article was to provide a partially new method for mystic research, largely by utilizing modern research from the psychology of creativity. Much has happened during the last decade in the area of creativity. This research, in turn, has been strongly influenced by the new direction within the development of psychoanalytic theory during the 1960's and 70's. Central concepts such as the primary and secondary process and regression have become the objects of revision and empirical testing (see for ex. Suler 1980). These aspects are of great importance, I feel, for creativity as well as for mystic experience. Much, however, remains to be done. It is my intention to test, with the aid of the hypothetical-deductive method (Naess 1980), a number of the consequences of the previously presented theoretical view. It is therefore important to work with individuals that are still alive. Since many studies (for ex. Greeley 1975, Hay 1979) seem to indicate that intensive religious experiences are relatively common in the western world, there should be ample opportunity for carrying this out.

References

Arieti, S. 1974. *Interpretation of schizophrenia*. New York.
— 1976. *Creativity, the magic synthesis*. New York.
— 1976a. *The Intrapsychic self, feeling and cognition in health and mental illness*. New York.
Bertalanffy, L. von, 1969. *General systems theory, foundations, development, applications*. New York.
Buber, M. 1961. *Between man and man*. London.
Clark, W. H. 1969. *The psychology of religion*. Toronto.
Dass, R. 1977. Foreword. D. Goleman, *The varieties of the meditative experience*. New York.
Deikman, A. J. 1963. Experimental meditation. *Journal of nervous and mental disease* 136, 329–343.
— 1966a. Implications of experimentally induced contemplative meditation. *Journal of nervous and mental disease* 142, 101–116.
— 1966b. Deautomatization and the mystic experience. *Psychiatry* 29, 324–338.
— 1971. Bimodal consciousness. *Archives of general psychiatry* 25, 481–489.
— 1976. Bimodal consciousness and the mystic experience. *Symposium on consciousness,* ed. by P. Lee et al. 67–88. New York.
Ellwood, R. S., Jr. 1980. *Mysticism and religion*. Englewood Cliffs.
Freud, S. 1962. *Drömtydning*. Stockholm.
Geels, A. 1980. *Mystikern Hjalmar Ekström (1885–1962)*. Lund.
— 1980a. William James och drogforskningen. O. Pettersson,–H. Åkerberg, *William James då och nu* 129–151. Lund.
Gimello, R. M. 1978. Mysticism and meditation. *Mysticism and philosophical analysis,* ed. by S. T. Katz, 170–199. London.
Goleman, D. 1975. The Buddha on meditation and states of consciousness. *Transpersonal Psychologies,* ed. by C. T. Tart, 203–230. London.
— 1981. Forgetfulness of things past. *Psychology today,* October 17–20.
Grønbæk, V. 1935. *Om Beskrivelsen af Religiøse Oplevelser*. København.
Hay, D. 1979. Religious experience amongst a group of post-graduate students—a qualitative study. *Journal for the scientific study of religion* 18.

Hay, D.–Morisy, A. 1978. Reports of ecstatic, paranormal, or religious experience in Great-Britain and the United States—a comparison of trends. *Journal for the scientific study of religion* 17.

Hirai, T. 1978. *Zen and the mind.* New York.

Hof, H. 1967. Att säga det outsägliga. *Myt och symbol,* red. av F. W. Dillistone, 143–215. Stockholm.

— 1952. Scintilla Animae. Lund-Bonn.

Israel, J. 1980. *Språkets dialektik och dialektikens språk.* Arlöv.

James, W. 1904. *The varieties of religious experience.* London.

— 1956. *Den religiösa erfarenheten i dess skilda former.* Stockholm.

Jeffmar, M. 1978. *Ways of cognitive action.* Lund.

— 1978a. *Intelligent eller kreativ?* Lund.

— 1980. Den kreativa processen—pedagogiska implikationer. *Nordisk Psykologi,* Vol. 32, 3, 266–275.

Kasamatsu, A.–Hirai, T. 1972. An electroencepahlographic study on Zen meditation (Zazen). *Altered states of consciousness,* ed. by C. T. Tart, 501–514. New York.

Korzybski, A. 1951. The role of language in the perceptual processes. *Perception, an approach to personality,* ed. by R. R. Blake and G. V. Ramsey, 170–205. New York.

Kragh, U.–Smith, G. 1970. *Percept-genetic analysis.* Lund.

Kragh, U.–Smith, G. J. W. 1974. Forming new patterns of experience, a classical problem viewed within a percept-genetic model. *Psychological research bulletin* 14, 6.

Kris, E. 1950. On preconscious mental processes. *Psychoanalytic quarterly* 19, 542. (Reprinted in Kris 1952).

— 1952. *Psychoanalytic explorations in art.* New York.

Kubie, L. S. 1958. *Neurotic distortion of the creative process.* Lawrence.

Langer, J.–Sugarman, S. 1978. Die Entwicklungstheorien von Heinz Werner und Jean Piaget. G. Steiner, *Die Psychologie des 20. Jahrhunderts,* 8, Piaget und die Folgen, 568–583. Zürich.

Lans, J van der. 1980. *Religieuze ervaring en meditatie.* Deventer.

Laski, M. 1961. *Ecstasy, a study of some secular and religious experiences.* London.

Leuba, J. H. 1972. *The psychology of religious mysticism.* London.

Maslow, A. H. 1973. *Religions, values, and peak-experiences.* New York.

Moore, P. G. 1973. Recent studies of mysticism, a critical survey. *Journal of religion and religions* 3, 146–156.

— 1978. Mystical experience, mystical doctrine, mystical technique. *Mysticism and philosophical analysis,* ed. by S. T. Katz, 101–131. London.

Næss, A. 1980. *Vitenskapsfilosofi.* Oslo.

Neisser, U. 1978. *Kognition och verklighet, den kognitiva psykologins principer och konsekvenser.* Stockholm.

Pratt, J. B. 1926. *The religious consciousness, a psychological study.* New York.

Rothenberg, A. 1979. *The emerging goddess.* Chicago.

— 1981. A protest for creative theory. *Contemporary psychology—in press.*

Ruth, J.-E. 1980. *Creativity as a cognitive construct; the effects of age, sex and testing practice.* (Unpubl. doct. diss., Univ. of Southern California).

Schachtel, E. 1959. *Metamorphosis.* New York.

Scharfstein, B.-A. 1973. *Mystical experience*. Oxford.

Smart, N. 1962. Mystical experience. *Sophia* 1, 1, 19–26.

— 1966. Interpretation and mystical experience. *Religious studies* 1, 75–85.

Smith, G. J. W. 1981. Creation and reconstruction. *Psychoanalysis and contemporary thought*—in press.

Smith, G. J. W.–Danielsson, A. 1979. The influence of anxiety on the urge for aesthetic creation. *Psychological Research Bulletin*, 19, 3/4.

Smith, G. J. W.–Westerlundh, B. 1980. Perceptgenesis, a process perspective on perception-personality. *Review of Personality and Social Psychology*, ed. by L. Wheeler, 94–124. Beverly Hills.

Staal, F. 1975. *Exploring mysticism*. London.

Stace, W. T. 1960. *Mysticism and philosophy*. London.

Suler, J. R. 1980. Primary process thinking and creativity. *Psychological bulletin* 88, 1, 144–165.

Sundén, H. 1970. Meditation and perception. *Mysticism*. ed. by S. S. Hartman and C.-M. Edsman, 34–46. (Scripta Instituti Donneriani Aboensis 5.) Stockholm.

Söderblom, N. 1975. *Till mystikens belysning, Uppenbarelsereligion; Tre livsformer, Två skrifter med förnyad aktualitet*. Lund.

Underhill, E. 1926. *Mysticism*. London.

— 1960. *The essentials of mysticism and other essays*. New York.

Wallas, G. 1926. *The Art of thought*. New York.

Werner, H. 1957. The concept of development from a comparative and organismic point of view. *The Concept of Development*, ed. by D. B. Harris, 125–148. Minneapolis.

— 1948. *Comparative psychology of mental development*. New York.

Westerlundh, B. 1976. Perceptgenes. *Psykologisk uppslagsbok*, utg. av J. Johannesson, 313–314. Stockholm.

Zaehner, R. C. 1967. *Mysticism sacred and profane*. London.

Some Psycho-physiological Aspects of Ecstasy in Recent Research

By NORA AHLBERG

1

In this article it is my intention to present some psycho-physiological perspectives of recent date concerned with the phenomenon of ecstasy. As almost none of this research has as yet been assimilated by comparative religion and as it would not be possible for me to make a substantial contribution to the field in this connection, I will concentrate on illustrating some of the background for renewed speculation on the relationship between psyche and soma.

Traditional Western science has usually operated with a distinction between external and internal processes. Thus the nervous system of vertebrates has been thought of in terms of a central and an autonomous part. The latter is involved in such inner processes as digestion, heart rate or hormone balance. Because it is thought to be independent of our will power it is called autonomical.

Perhaps owing to this idea of the independence of our internal processes from our intentional consciousness, reports from other cultures such as those concerning the extraordinary achievements of holy men (e.g. their capacity to lie buried for days, or survive unclothed at very low temperatures) have tended to be ignored as fantastic rumours (which, to some extent, is certainly true) and myths. In a similar way the varieties of religious ecstatic states have often been countered with a shrug by psychiatrists. The recently renewed interest in consciousness within general psychology, together with what may be called marginal psychology and the drug revolt of youth culture have, however, provoked new speculation concerning human potential, speculation which in due time might also benefit comparative religion. This is particularly true with regard to research into so-called Altered States of Consciousness (which include ecstatic religious phenomena) (Ludwig 1968; Holm 1979, 13–62), although there is reason to warn against growing dilettantism in this field (Ahlberg 1980).

There are some known characteristics of this type of experience that are commonly used as criteria, such as ineffability, accompanying analgesia, loss of ego-identity (that is the experience of wholeness or oneness) in addition to the basic ecstatic wellbeing to which there are a few exceptions, sometimes called the dark night of the soul. As I shall try to show, it is with respect to these characteristics that recent research is able to contribute by offering some psycho-physiological perspectives.

Some of the explanatory models which have gained renewed topicality in recent literature are actually rather old. Ernst Arbman deals with many of them in his comprehensive book *Ecstasy or Religious Trance* (1968). I would particularly like to emphasize his excellent treatment of hypnotical phenomena in relationship to, for example, the practice of yoga (Arbman 1968, I, 260–90) and his treatment of hysteria (Arbman 1968, II, chap. IX) which demonstrates his thorough knowledge of the field of psychiatry. At the present time, however, his book might in some respects seem rather old—fashioned, based as it on the solid psychiatric theory of his time. Since then, anti psychiatry has done away with many previous attitudes towards mental illness and related religious phenomena. It is, however, only to be regretted that the book has not gained the reputation it so undeniably deserves within the field of the psychology of religion.

2

Arbman's (1968) interest in hallucinogenic drugs seems less marked, and perhaps rightly so, as the classic debate on authentic versus non-authentic or false mysticism, crystallized by Aldous Huxley (1954) and R. C. Zaehner (1957; 1972), has become unduly emphasized through the interest of the "flower-power generation" in drug-induced Altered States of Consciousness and their claims of mysticism (Ahlberg 1981, 232–43).

I shall not consider this question here but merely point out that the discovery of endogenic opiates in the human brain has given this debate a rather new direction. In the light of recent research it seems that not only the non-authentic but also the authentic mystical experiences might be connected with drugs; thus much of the former debate has become superfluous. In any case, from the perspective of comparative religion the primary concern is with cultural tradition and interpretation, although the hallucinogenic drugs have opened up possibilities for a more experimental design as a complementary development in this area.

It was in 1973 at the John Hopkins School of Medicine in Baltimore that a team of researchers led by Dr. S. H. Snyder discovered that the human brain contained special opiate receptors (Pert & Snyder 1973), and soon afterwards another team succeeded in isolating a system of endorphines and one of encephalines located in parts of the brain thought to be connected mainly with emotions. It could now be asked whether these substances might be a key to the understanding of the typical euphoric and analgetic effects of spontaneous, non-drug induced Altered States of Consciousness.

Opiates are commonly held to be dangerous narcotics with mindaltering effects and it has now been shown that all of us are literally speaking addicted to ourselves. Expectations of having found the ideal analgetic substance were thus thwarted as it was discovered that these natural opiates have the same side effects as our ordinary opiate-derivative, the analgetic morphine.

Why do we have them? It is not yet known, but what is known is that like morphines they regulate the experience of pain. Thus we do know that patients with chronically severe pains exhibit a lower level of endorphines, that the concentration in all of us varies around the clock, and that these substances may also be involved in the explanation of the effect of acupuncture. An supply of morphias inhibits the production of endogenous opiates by invading the above-mentioned opiate receptors in our brain (so that no need for further internal production is triggered). This could be an explanation for the symptoms of abstinence connected with extended misuse of these types of drugs until the internal production through the feedback system again starts functioning. Furthermore, acupuncture has been used with some success in the treatment of drug addicts perhaps by stimulating the production of endogenous opiates. Besides, researchers now believe that the endogenous opiates may be active in connection with the so-called placeboeffect (that is, the effect of sugar-pills) which has previously been entirely attributed to psychic mechanisms (Mardsen 1979; Snyder 1977).

What does all this indicate? Human beings probably have a separate internal autonomic control system for pain which is activated in extraordinary circumstances as for example extreme stress (which could explain the often reported feeling of peace in the face of death). It is fascinating to speculate about a possible human capability for deciding the level of pain for oneself, for instance by means of yogic exercises. Could this be what so many a holy man has been reported to have done while enduring extreme heat, cold or other torture? We here face a correlate in the natural sciences to what common sense has known for a long time, that is the knowledge of cure by faith or the belief that with faith it is possible to move mountains at least in the inner landscape.

Moreover, it is also known that these natural opiates cooperate with a transmitter substance in the nervous system of our brain called serotonine which in its chemical structure resembles LSD. LSD has been regarded as a key towards understanding Altered States of Consciousness in the laboratory, with special reference to the experience of ego-loss (Harkness 1973, 161–64; Axelrod 1974). It has also been found that auditory hallucinations, which are so pronounced in schizophrenia but also found in religious experiences, correspond to an increased level of endogenous opiates and can be neutralized with the opiate antagonist naloxone (Mardsen 1979; Snyder 1977).

3

Among our many new potential methods for better understanding ecstatic phenomena by means of experimental methods, biofeedback has been the most sensational one. I have speculated on human ability to control the production of endogenous opiates. And it is above all the research in biofeedback that has forced many scientists to reconsider their view of the autonomic nervous system as a system completely independent of human will and control.

Typically, it was a rat experiment that was necessary to shake the convictions of many a sceptical researcher. This was first and foremost the achievement of Neal Miller and Leo DiCara at the Rockefeller University, their results indicating that a certain amount of learning by operant conditioning within the autonomic system could take place apparently without the involvement of will-controlled skeletal muscles (Miller 1969; DiCara 1970).

Despite a total paralysis due to curare the experimental rats showed themselves able to change the blood-flow in one ear as opposed to the other, being rewarded by electrical stimulation of the so-called pleasure centre of their brains. Unfortunately later attempts at replication of this brilliant series of experiments have not succeeded, a fact which has no satisfactory explanation. Later however, this type of experiment was continued and extended at Harvard by measuring different physiological processes such as blood-pressure or heart rate in students who had been instructed in biofeedback (Shapiro, Tursky & Schwarts 1970).

Biofeedback rests on the simple idea of letting a measuring apparatus register internal physiological changes which people normally, or because of some disease, do not seem sensitive enough to recognize. The intention is to examine the relationship between the physiological outcome on the measuring apparatus and consciousness in order to improve conscious control (Blanchard & Epstein 1978; Sagberg 1977). Fig 1. Although the majority of these studies, in addition to their theoretical implications, have been adapted to therapeutic purposes (biofeedback training has been used

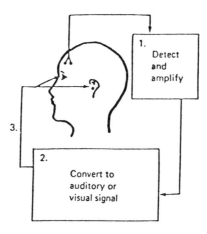

Fig. 1. 1, Detection and amplification of *bio*electric potentials; 2, Convert bioelectric signals to easy-to-process information; 3. *Feed* this information *back* to the patient; 4, With immediate feedback, patient learns voluntary control response. (Blanchard 1978, 3.)

in the treatment of different psychosomatic illnesses such as hypertension) they have also initiated a more or less sensational so-called "alpha-cult" (Ahlberg 1980).

This alpha cult is connected with biofeedback research into the possibilities of voluntarily influencing brain activity as measured through EEG (that is, measuring electrical brainwaves). There has been some speculation that different EEG patterns would correlate with different forms of experience, thus alpha with ecstatic or meditative consciousness. Some counterculturally oriented persons have through biofeedback believed themselves to have found a short cut to nirvana or "nerve-ana". Although this "electronic yoga" practice has gained the largest number of adherents among the public searching for happiness it is probably the most complex form of biofeedback utilization concerning which there is much debate among researchers (Blanchard 1978, 128–29).

These "nerveanic" expectations are again connected with the equally recent experimental research in meditation, a theme which would need a separate article and thus cannot be dealt with here. It must suffice to state that a majority of these experiments concern recordings of physiological changes due to meditation (Lægevidenskabelig og psykologisk forskning 1978). Like the related research in biofeedback these experiments shake our conviction that the autonomy of inner processes excludes all possibilities of influencing the system, and thus to a certain extent demystify those strange phenomena reported by the study of religion.

Most studies point in the direction of a gradual lowering of metabolism as a significant characteristic of the practice of meditation. It is Transcendental Meditation in particular that has been the object of research but some studies even try to explain the course of events during so-called coffin funerals which are reported to have taken place among oriental yogies (Anand et. al. 1961). One could probably state that whereas the method of biofeedback strengthens the internal signals so that they may be recognized, the practice of meditation often to the contrary lessens external distractions so that normally unconscious or autonomic internal processes can be brought into consciousness and thus controlled.

4

Most of the increasing interest in Altered States of Concsiousness could probably be integrated into the research and the more or less wild speculations produced in connection with study of the cerebral hemispheres. The human brain in fact actually consists of two bilaterally symmetrical brains. And one may naturally therefore ask whether man, accordingly, is equipped with two forms of consciousness and is thus a sort of Dr. Jekyll and Mr. Hyde.

It has been maintained that the father of experimental psychology Gustav Fechner (1801–87) was already concerned with this problem in that he speculated about the possibility of splitting our consciousness by cutting the corpus callossum or brain bridge, which constitutes the only connection between the two hemispheres (Blakemore 1977, 155). But it was not until the 1960s that a daring surgeon in California decided to cut the corpus callossum in patients afflicted by grave epilepsy which threatened to spread from one to the other hemisphere.

Strangely enough the results of this drastic operation turned out to have only minor negative effects in the everyday life of these patients and on the positive side the operation meant relief for their epileptical seizures. After closer examination, however, bizarre symptoms indicating that the hemispheres functioned independently of each other were discovered. Roger Sperry (who was later awarded the Nobel Prize for his discoveries in 1981) reported that the incision had left these patients with two separate spheres of consciousness (Sperry 1964; 1968). What was experienced by the left hemisphere seemed totally outside the consciousness of the right hemisphere. Later studies with normal experimental subjects (with an intact corpus callossum) or mental patients under electrical shock treatment in the Soviet Union also point in the same direction (Filbey & Gazzaniga 1969; Deglin 1976).

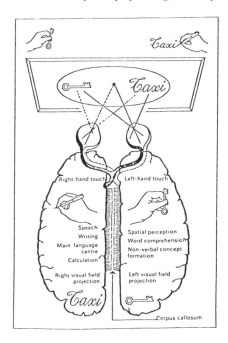

LEFT HAND, RIGHT HAND

Drawings below illustrate the different capacities of the brain's two hemispheres. They were done by a patient whose left hemisphere had been separated from his right. He was asked to copy the cross and cube (centre) first with his left hand, then with his right hand. Although the patient was actually right-handed, he did a far better job with his left hand (controlled by the brain's right hemisphere, which excels at space perception) than with his right hand (governed by the spatially inept left hemisphere).

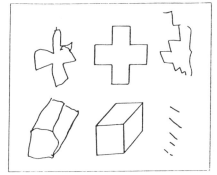

Fig. 2. Reprinted from the Unesco Courier Jan. 1976.

But the left consciousness is not totally identical with the right one. The most important difference is the fact that it is the left hemisphere which controls speech. Because the hemispheres control the opposite side of the body the right hand is for example controlled by the left hemisphere and vice versa. If a so called split-brain patient with his eyes shut receives an object in his left hand he will be unable to identify even the most common object verbally. But given the task of pointing out the object in question from among other objects lying in front of him he will be able to do this with his left hand. His right hand/left brain, however, seems to be totally unconscious of what happens to the other side (Gazzaniga 1967; Deglin 1976). Fig. 2.

The right hemisphere is associated with non-verbal visio-spatial skills (such as visual images or music) in contrast the the verbal, left side. This point is also supported by findings in connection with damage to the respective hemispheres (Bogen 1964–72; Deglin 1976, 13–14). The discovery of hemispheric specialization has since resulted in a growing movement of protest aiming at the liberation of the right hemisphere in what is felt to be our verbal-logically and technologic-scientifically dominated western society, where—according to these enthusiasts—there exists a sort of dictatorship by the left hemisphere.

Perhaps the best known exponent of such ideas is the American psychologist Robert Ornstein (1969; 1972; 1973) whose writings may, from the point of view of comparative religion, often seem unduly simplified. Like others of the same opinion he connects the specialization of the hemispheres with a fundamental dualism between reason and emotion or consciousness and unconsciousness. He reports, for example, an experiment where the right non-verbal or unconscious hemisphere, in the middle of an otherwise boring laboratory experiment, is confronted with a photograph of a nude woman. Verbally, the subject in question denies that he has seen anything special which, due to the design of the experiment, is the case with his verbal, left hemisphere. But at the same time he blushes and giggles "without reason", as Ornstein (1972, 60) comments, with his conscious ego.

Unconsciousness would thus be a question of the degree of communication between the hemispheres through the brain bridge. Analogically to this, creativity would be a capacity to translate unconscious experiences in the right hemisphere to left hemispheric verbal categories or an integration by means of the corpus callossum. With creativity is also associated religious ecstatic or meditative states, while schizophrenia is explained as a sort of disintegration of the inter-hemispheric coordination in this simplified organically oriented thinking (Fisher 1975; Deglin 1976; 14–16, 31–32).

But anthropological circles have also, somewhat unexpectedly, shown interest in this question, an interest which can be traced back to an article by Robert Hertz (one of Durkheims pupils) "La Prééminence de la main droite: étude sur la polarité religieuse" from 1909, where he states that the explanation of the almost universal dominance of the right hand over the left is, in the last resort, to be found in the human organism, that is, we are right handed because we are left-brained (some of the approximately 5 % of left-handed persons constitute exceptions).

At the same time he emphasizes the cultural constructions based on this fact, and traces the dichotomy back to the primitive concept of cosmos as divided into two spheres; a masculine one, which is strong, good and holy and a feminine one, which is weak, evil and profane. This cosmic division is said to be reflected in primitive man's own microcosmos so that the positive side is identified with the naturally more developed right hand (which is dominated by the left brain).

The article is reprinted in the book Left and Right edited by Rodney Needham (1973) and serves as a point of departure for a number of interesting articles concerning right-left symbolism in different cultures.

They deal with such concepts as yin-yang in China, right and left in Greek philosophy or against the background of Arabic evidence, but in particular there are examples from African cultures. Probably the most notable of these is Evans Pritchards "Nuer Spear Symbolism" (1973), where he interpretes the spear as an extension of the dominating right hand in Nuer culture, and gives the credit due to Hertz's pioneering work. At the present time, one can only state that there is a tendency towards idealizing the right hemisphere and attributing to it introvertive capacities and experiences connected with so-called human peak experiences such as, for instance, creativity or ecstasy (Maslow 1959).

With considerable foresight, Heinz concluded his article as follows:

> If the constraints of a mystical ideal have for centuries been able to make man into a unilateral being, physiologically mutilated, a liberated and enlightened society will strive to develop the energies dormant in our right cerebral hemisphere, and to assure by appropriate training a more harmonious development of the organism (Hertz 1973, 22).

And forty-four years later Ornstein (1972, 66) writes that it is precisely the complementarity of the two hemispheres which is his central interest as it finds expression simultaneously on many levels. One side, according to him, is analytical, the other holistic, one linear and rational, the other arational and intuitive.

The idea of a split in our consciousness or its complementarity is not unknown as such either to psychologists/psychiatrists or to students of comparative religion interested in Altered States of Consciousness. What is more interesting is that this duality seems to a certain extent to have an anatomic-physiological as well as a psychological and cultural dimension, and that the first mentioned fact increases our possibilities of research in ecstatic phenomena with methods borrowed from the natural sciences.

5

In the future, discoveries in such traditionally remote fields as psycho-physiology, will probably to a greater extent complement the data of comparative religion and contribute to a growing understanding of the internal processes which are so important to religion. Not least, some of the traditionally more inaccessible phenomena of the psychology of religion such as religious ecstasy, may be introduced to the laboratory under strictly controlled conditions. This again will contribute to the prestige of the psychology of religion, which has been somewhat neglected within comparative religion since the beginning of this century.

I should like to conclude with the following hypotheses:

— that the ecstatic consciousness is, if not produced by, at least dependent on so called natural opiates in the human brain
— that this explains its analgetic effects
— that the basis for the unifying mechanisms of mystical ecstatic experience is a transfer of mastery from the left to the right hemisphere. Some EEG recordings seem to imply that this is the case at least as far as dreams, hallucinations or meditation are concerned (Goldstein & Stoltzfus, 1972 a, 1972 b, 1973)
— that the ineffability of Altered States of Consciousness is related to the inability of the right hemisphere to express itself verbally as shown in connection with Sperry's splitbrain patients.

References

Ahlberg, N. 1980. Biofeedback som marginalpsykologiskt fenomen (unpubl. manus.).
— 1981. Vastakulttuuri todellisuutta haastattelemassa. *Äidinkielen Opettajain Vuosikirja*.
Anand, B. et al. 1961. Studies on Shri Ramananda during his stay in an airtight box. *Indian journal of medical research* 49, 82–89.
Arbman, E. 1968. *Ecstasy or religious trance* 1–3. Uppsala.
Axelrod, J. 1974. Neurotransmitters. *Scientific American* June 58–71.
Blakemore, C. 1977. *Mechanics of the mind*. Cambridge.
Blanchard, E.–Epstein, L. 1978. *A biofeedback primer*. Massachusetts.
Bogen, J. 1964. The other side of the brain 1. *Bulletin of the Los Angeles neurological society* 34, 73–105.
— 1969. The other side of the brain 2–3. *Bulletin of the Los Angeles neurological society* 34, 135–62 & 191–220.
— 1972. The other side of the brain 4. *Bulletin of the Los Angeles neurological society* 37, 49–61.
Deglin, V. 1976. Our split brain 1–4. *The Unesco Courier* Jan, 4–16 & 31–32.
DiCara, L. 1970. Learning in the autonomic nervous system. *Scientific American* Jan, 30–39.
Filbey, R.–Gazzaniga, M. 1969. Splitting the normal brain with reaction time. *Psychonomic science* 17, 335–36.
Fischer, R. 1975. Cartography of inner space. *Hallucinations. Behavior, Experience & Theory*, ed. by I. Stegel–L. West. New York. 213–20.
Gazzaniga, M. 1967. The split brain in man. *Scientific American*. Aug 217, 24–29.
Goldstein, L.–Stoltzfus, N. 1972 a. Drug-induced changes of interhemispheric EEG amplitude relationships in man. *5th international congress of pharmacology*. July. Abstracts 505. San Francisco.
— 1972 b. Changes in interhemispheric amplitude relationships in the EEG during sleep. *Physiology and behavior* 8, 811–16.

— 1973. Psychoactive drug-induced changes of interhemispheric EEG amplitude relationships. *Agents and actions 3,* 124–32.

Harkness, G. 1973. *Mysticism.* London.

Hertz, R. 1909. La prééminence de la main droite; étude sur la polarité religieuse. *Revue philosophique* 68, 553–80.

Holm, N. G. 1979. *Mystik och intensiva upplevelser.* Åbo. (Publications of the Research institute of the Åbo Akademi Foundation 51.)

Huxley, A. 1954. *The doors of perception.* New York.

Lægevidenskabelig og psykologisk forskning på yoga & meditation. 1978. København.

Ludwig, A. 1968. Altered states of consciousness. *Trance and possession states* ed. by I. Prince. Montreal.

Mardsen, C. 1979. The emotion of pain and its chemistry. Symposium on Brain and Mind. *CIBA Foundation* (new series) 69, 304–14.

Maslow, A. 1959. *Religious values and peak experiences.* New York.

Miller, N. 1969. Learning of visceral and glandular responses. *Science* 163, 434–45.

Ornstein, R. 1969. *On the experience of time.* Harmondsworth.

— 1972. *The psychology of consciousness.* San Fransisco.

— 1973. *The nature of human consciousness.* San Fransisco.

Pert, C.–Snyder, S. 1973. Opiate Receptor: demonstration in nervous tissue. *Science* 197, 1011–14.

Pritchard, E. 1973. Nuer spear symbolism. *Right and left,* ed. by R. Needham. Chicago.

Sagberg, F. 1977. Biofeedback—psykologisk adferdsterapi. *Impuls* 31, 28–37.

Shapiro, D.–Tursky, B.–Schwartz, G. 1970. Differentation of heart rate and systolic blood pressure in man by operant conditioning. *Psychosomatic medicine* 32, 417–23.

Snyder, S. 1977. Opiate receptors and internal opiates. *Scientific American* March, 44–56.

Sperry, R. 1964. The great cerebral commissure. *Scientific American* Jan, 142–52.

— 1968. Mental unity following surgical disconnection of the cerebral hemispheres. *The Harvey lecture series* 62, 293–323.

Zaehner, R. 1957. *Mysticism sacred and profane.* Oxford.

— 1972. *Drugs, mysticism and make-believe.* London.

Ecstasy from a Physiological Point of View

By KAJ BJÖRKQVIST

Religious ecstasy can be studied from as many points of view as there are disciplines in the scientific study of religion. It can be studied, for example, from a sociological, phenomenological, historical or a psychological point of view. But there is also a physiological aspect to the experience of ecstasy; and a physiological study of ecstasy might bring to light new facts that would add to our general knowledge of the phenomenon and perhaps lead to a better understanding of it from other points of view, too. The very close relationship between psychology and physiology can hardly be questioned. The biological study of man is one of today's most rapidly advancing sciences. There is no reason for not utilizing these methodologies of research and the knowledge already gained when studying ecstasy and other similar religious phenomena. It is not my opinion that ecstasy should be solely or even principally studied in a physiological context; the shortcomings of such a reductionistic viewpoint should be obvious, and have been pointed out, for example, by Staal (1975, ch. 8). To the comments of Staal, I would like to add that sociological factors, like the social role of the person experiencing ecstasy, and cognitive factors, like the interpretation of the experience, are two variables that undoubtedly will have a great effect when the experience of ecstasy is shaped in the human consciousness. But physiological data, meaningfully integrated with other bodies of data, will no doubt broaden our understanding of the phenomenon of ecstasy.

In everyday language, the word "ecstasy" denotes an intense, euphoric experience. For obvious reasons, it is rarely used in a scientific context; it is a concept that is extremely hard to define. Ecstasy-seeking religious movements have always existed, and they seem today to be as numerous as ever. There is perhaps no reason yet to abandon the concept entirely. I will not attempt to define the term ecstasy here, but I will say that I consider ecstasy, mysticism and trance to be partly overlapping concepts. In mystical experience, there is always an element of ecstasy, although the presence of this element is not, in itself, enough to justify calling an experience mystical. In trance, there is often, but not necessarily, an element of ecstasy. In the literature, trance has nonetheless often been used almost synonymously with ecstasy. Furthermore, an experience can be ecstatic without being either mystical or trance-like. An experience can also be ecstatic without having any religious connotation whatsoever. Since the borderline is so hard to draw, I will in this discourse consider not only clear cases of ecstasy, but also phenomena that are closely related to it.

Something should also be said about the body-mind-issue, the relation between *psyche* and *soma*—an age-old problem in philosophy. There are almost as many theories about their relationship as there are philosophers. The materialists stress soma at the total cost of psyche; the idealists do the opposite. Of dualism, there are many different versions, for instance parallellism, which proposes that the two coexist without directly affecting each other. Without discussing any of these further, I will simply state that I here regard body and mind as *two sides of the same coin;* the same phenomenon seen either from the point of internal subjective experience, or from the point of external objective observation. When a change occurs in soma, a simultaneous change also occurs in psyche, and vice versa. There cannot be a change in one without a simultaneous change in the other. In the act of thinking, neural activity takes place in the brain. Although we do not know what a person is thinking by studying his brain waves, we do know that different types of thinking result in different types of brain waves (alpha and beta waves, etc.).

The claim that there cannot be a change in psyche without a simultaneous change in soma is of course hard to prove, since our instruments are not, and perhaps never will be, sufficiently sensitive to register all the subtle changes in the human nervous system. But in my opinion it is the most plausible viewpoint, judging from the present scientific data. Whether one wants to call this dualism or materialism is a matter of taste. But this soma-psyche relationship is the basic assumption which I will use as the starting point for this discussion.

Since mental states and physiological correlates always accompany each other, it is obvious that the human mind can be affected by external means, for instance by drugs. But the opposite is also true; mental changes affect the body, as they do in the case of psychosomatic diseases.

Aldous Huxley was the first one to suggest that mystical experiences are directly related to physiological changes (Huxley, 1969; first published in 1954). He based his hypothesis mainly on his own experiments with mescalin. Huxley believed that adrenochrome, which is a product of a decomposition of adrenalin and has a chemical composition resembling that of mescalin, might be the cause of so called "spontaneous" mystical experiences, since this substance, he thought, might occur spontaneously in the human body in sufficient amounts (Huxley, *ibid.,* 12). He also suggested that mystical experiences could be achieved by means other than exogenous or endogenous hallucinogenics. The breathing exercises of yogis, for example, might increase the amount of CO_2 in their lungs and blood, and hence also in the brain (Huxley, *ibid.*, 113). When the ascetics of medieval times used to beat themselves repeatedly, histamine was released into the blood, which according to Huxley (*ibid.*, 120) might have caused an intoxication reminiscent of that achieved with hallucinogenic drugs. He explained the prevalence of mystical experiences in medieval times in a similar fashion: it could have been the result of severe lack of vitamins (Huxley, *ibid.*, 117–119).

In his proposals as to how the different ecstasy techniques work physiologically, Huxley was probably often wrong (a point to which I shall return). Modern research data have refuted many of his hypotheses, or at least rendered them unlikely. All this does not make Huxley less important; he started a new paradigm in the psychology of religion. We certainly have to agree with Huxley that physiological variables must be taken into account when we ponder the question of why religious practitioners all over the world have used such similar ecstasy techniques. They have altered their physical constitution by fasting or adhering to vegetarianism; they have changed their hormonal balance by living in celibacy; sometimes they have bombarded their nervous system with drugs. At times the physiological implications are more subtle and not so easily apprehended, as in the case of meditation, prayer and the use of music. The music might be slow and "soothing" such as one may hear in a Christian mass or in a Tibetan temple, or it can be fast and rhythmic, often combined with drumming and dancing, as in voodoo. Meditation, prayer and music are undoubtedly psychological rather than physiological, but studies of brain waves have made it clear that they also have physiological implications.

Drugs have been used in all parts of the world as an ecstasy technique (Furst, 1972). How the hallucinogenics work, however, is not quite clear. Most researchers agree that they seem to interfere with the transmitter substances in the nervous system. The adrenochrome hypothesis, suggested by Huxley (1969; see also above), appears unlikely to be true—there does not seem to be enough adrenochrome in the human body to account for any radical effects. Instead it has been thought that LSD might interfere with the action of serotonin. In some situations LSD has been shown to act like serotonin, and in others to be a powerful antagonist to it; thus LSD might either facilitate or block the neurohumoral action of serotonin in the brain (Barron *et al.*, 1971). But it is far from proved that the effects of LSD can be explained this way. It may be that LSD creates an imbalance among several different neurohumors. The question is still not settled.

Even less is known about how fasting and vegeterianism work. There has been surprisingly little study of the physiological effects of reducing food intake and adhering to special diets, and even less of the psychological effects. EEG recordings obtained from the participants in a fasting march from Jyväskylä to Helsinki in Finland three years ago showed more alpha activity after the march than before (Björkqvist, S.-E., 1980). This is a quite natural result of the participants being tired, and of course a combined result of both marching and fasting; in what proportions is impossible to say.

That celibacy can also be considered as a "physiological" ecstasy technique has been almost overlooked by the psychologists of religion. It has not, to my knowledge, been discussed at length in the literature. The psychodynamic implications of sublimating the libido (in Freudian terms) have been discussed, but the physiological implications have been neglected. Still it is a fact that the vast majority of all widely-known mystics have been living in celibacy. In medieval times, when monasteries were common in Europe, mysticism flourished. When the number of monasteries decreased, mysticism also declined. Celibacy was of course only one factor of many, but nevertheless probably an important one. In Hinduism, celibacy or *brahmacārya* has always been a highly emphasized technique. How it works can at the present only be guessed at. But it is evident that celibacy must have a profound influence on hormonal balance in the body.

Some authors (e. g., Ornstein, 1972) have suggested that, neurologically, religious experiences are a function of the right cerebral hemisphere. From the work of Sperry and Gazzaniga (Gazzaniga, 1971), among others, we know that the two brain hemispheres have, in part, very different functions. The left hemisphere is connected with the right side of the body, the right hemisphere with the left side. In most people, the left hemisphere is dominant—a good example being righthandedness. During childhood, the two brain halves develop partly different functions. For instance, the area of cortex dealing with hearing is in the left hemisphere connected with speech; the corresponding area in the right hemisphere is connected with the musical ear and the comprehension of music. Speech, logical thinking and mathematics are governed largely by the left hemisphere (Luria, 1978). The right hemisphere seems to be the more intuitive, artistic half of the brain. However, to claim that religious experience is governed by the right hemisphere would be to jump to conclusions.

Ecstasy is often described as an extremely joyful experience; this pleasure must necessarily also have a physiological basis. It is of course too early to say anything for certain, but the discovery of pleasure centres in the brain (e.g., Olds, 1971) might offer an explanation. These pleasure centres are situated at different locations in the midline region of the brain, but mostly in the hypothalamus. If an electrode is inserted into the brain of an animal at a spot where a pleasure centre is situated, and through a special arrangement such as by stepping on a pedal the animal is able to give itself electric stimulation in that specific spot, something remarkable occurs; the pleasure is so intense that the animal will forget everything. It will no longer care about food or drink, and it will often simply stimulate itself until it dies.

These same pleasure centres also exist in the human brain. Could it be that in the future we will find humans with electrodes inserted into their brain, giving themselves electric stimulation every now and then? A new, more horrible addiction, worse than heroin? Let us hope this will not be the case. But it is not far-fetched to suggest that when a person experiences euphoric ecstasy, it might, in some way or other, be connected with a cerebral pleasure center.

The best known studies of ecstatic experiences utilizing physiological measurements have been the electro-encephalographic (EEG) investigations of meditation. A number of studies (e.g., Anand et al., 1961; Wenger & Bagchi, 1961; Kasamatsu & Hirai, 1963, 1969; Wallace, 1973; Banquet, 1973) have shown that the most typical finding during meditation is a general slowing down of the brain waves. Slow alpha waves with increased amplitudes, sometimes even still slower theta waves (which usually appear only during light sleep) are frequent during meditation, regardless of the type—yoga, zen, or TM. In one study, faster beta waves were more frequent (Das & Gastaut, 1955) but in this study the subjects used a special technique, Krya yoga, which involves strong concentration on the point between the eyebrows with the eyes crossed. Strong concentration is always correlated with beta waves in the EEG. And even in this study, the yogis in question had abundant alpha activity after finishing meditation. Another observation (Banquet, 1973) is that the deeper the meditation, the more synchronized this activity seems to be, so that the same type of activity takes place simultaneously all over the cortex. The neurons seem to fire off in the same rhythm, regardless of where they are located.

Alpha waves are usually associated with a relaxed and positive mood. Other physiological measurements have corroborated this. During meditation, skin resistance is higher, which is a sign of released tensions. The amount of lactate in the blood decreases, which is also a sign of reduced tension (Wallace, 1973). Heart rate and breathing slow down. Taken as a whole, the entire metabolism slows down, with the person remaining in a state of peaceful rest.

The question can be raised: How is it possible that by practising meditation a person can learn to increase, at will, the amount of alpha activity in his brain? Although alpha activity also appears in untrained subjects when they are relaxed and have their eyes closed, it has been shown (Wallace, 1973; Kasamatsu & Hirai, 1963, 1969) that the better subjects are trained in meditation, the more frequent and slower is their alpha activity; theta activity, which is still slower than alpha, generally appears only among trained meditators.

Functionally, man has two nervous systems: one through which he can voluntarily control certain muscles of the body, and another called the visceral or autonomic nervous system (ANS). Through the ANS are governed the activity of the heart, the stomach and other internal functions. It has been thought that we are unable to control these voluntarily to even the slightest degree, but this has lately been shown to be false. Miller (1971) was the first to demonstrate that learning in the ANS can take place at least to some degree. For instance, through a feedback mechanism, subjects, whether they are animals or humans, can to a *slight* degree learn to slow down or speed up their heart beat. This phenomenon has been called biofeedback. Biofeedback can also be applied to the activity of the brain. It has been shown that people can learn to increase their alpha activity (e.g., Kamiya, 1969) or even their theta activity (Green, 1975) at will. In this learning process the person sits with electrodes attached to his head, through which brain wave activity is registered. Whenever alpha activity appears in the EEG, a special sound automatically registers through a loudspeaker; and when the alpha disappears, quite another sound is aired. In that way, the subject can acquire a "sense" for how alpha activity feels, and is slowly able to increase it at will. This can also have a therapeutic effect, reminiscent of that of meditation (Green, 1975).

The experiments with brain wave feedback give a hint of how meditation works. In a way, meditation can be seen as a kind of biofeedback without the alpha activity monitored out through speakers; instead, the meditator listens to subtle inner signals. To help in this process he can use one of several meditation techniques which differ slightly depending on the religious tradition or group he belongs to.

In India, breathing exercises have been used as an ecstasy technique. But also in zen, the counting of inhalations or exhalations has been used as a meditation technique (Kapleau, 1970, 32). As mentioned earlier, Huxley thought that breathing exercises could cause religious experiences by increasing the amount of CO_2 in the brain. This is highly unlikely—breathing CO_2 is a very unpleasant experience, which anyone knows who has been in a room with extremely bad air.

There is another possible explanation, which I have suggested in an earlier work (Björkqvist, K., 1976). Breathing is an exceptional function in that it is controlled both by the ANS and the somatic or voluntary nervous system. Some breathing occurs automatically all the time, and we cannot at will stop breathing altogether. The ANS sees to that. But we can voluntarily change the rhythm as well as the depth of our breathing. Moreover, breathing is closely related to a number of functions governed solely by the ANS, such as heart beat, perspiration, and various mechanisms related to emotions. As a consequence, breath control or simply being attentive to one's breathing would probably be the easiest biofeedback technique to learn, since it does not involve any direct or difficult learning in the ANS.

If meditation increases alpha activity, then listening to slow, soothing religious music, like Christian hymns or Tibetan temple music, can be expected to have a somewhat similar effect: a slowing down of the brain waves. But how can we then explain that the complete opposite—fast, rhythmic music combined with drumming and dancing—has been a popular ecstasy technique in many cultures?

Pavlov (1928), in his conditioning experiments with dogs, had already observed something which he called the ultraparadoxical phase. Both when the dogs were totally overstimulated and when in certain stages of drowsiness, there occurred a distortion of the effects of the conditioning stimuli. The positive stimuli lost their effect, and the negative became positive. Sargant (1951, 1957) suggested that something similar could be the case in man when sudden political or religious conversion occurred. He interpreted this phenomenon, which he called "transmarginal inhibition", brought on by these transmarginal stimuli (=stimuli exceeding the limit), as some kind of collapse in the reactiveness after intense mental tension or excitement.

This has direct relevance in the study, for instance, of the physiological effect of voodoo dancing. Oswald (1959) found to his surprise that when he repeatedly gave strong electric shocks to his subjects, they fell asleep! He also found (Oswald, *ibid.*) that the signs of sleep in the EEG could repeatedly come and go in rhythm with regular stimuli at intervals of only a few seconds. When people were dancing to the rhythm of a popular dance band, they could actually fall asleep for a few seconds while still moving. In another experiment (Oswald, 1960), he taped the eyelids of his subjects so that they were unable to close their eyes. He then gave them electric shocks and bright visual stimulation to the rhythm of a blues band. All his subjects fell asleep.

Voodoo dancing, and similar practises, can easily be understood in terms of the inhibition caused by transmarginal stimulation. All the time they are dancing, dancers are on the border between sleep and wakefulness, at times actually sleeping while dancing. It is easy to understand that visions can be seen in such a state. Sundén (1967) has interpreted the experiences of zen monks in similar terms to Sargant and Oswald.

The spiritual practice of prayer, on the other hand, seems to have a lot in common with meditation. Neither prayer nor meditation are in themselves necessarily ecstatic experiences; but they are practices during which ecstasy frequently occurs. It is therefore reasonable to consider them as ecstasy techniques. The effect of prayer on the body has not been studied very much with physiological methods. When Mallory (1977) used EEG in her investigation of monks and nuns at prayer, she found no increase in alpha activity during prayer compared with the activity recorded in a control situation. She did find, however, that extraverted subjects had more abundant alpha activity than others, and that the abundance of alpha correlated positively with contemplation and negatively with neuroticism. Synchronization of alpha activity was another interesting point; it was reduced when subjects had difficulties in contemplating. Contemplation was thus associated with both alpha abundance and alpha synchronization. Mallory, summing up her results, says that subjects who were good at contemplation tended to have the same degree of alpha abundance as experienced yoga or zen practitioners. The only possible difference was that the alpha activity of her subjects remained the same in the control situation, sitting with closed eyes, but not praying, as in the experimental situation, sitting with closed eyes, contemplating. Having abundant alpha activity seemed to be the natural state for these subjects when relaxed (Mallory, 1977).

In a study in progress, I have been measuring EEG, GSR (skin conductance and skin potential), heart beat and eye movements (EOG) of ten persons while they pray. All belong to a sect calling themselves "rukoilevaiset" (The Prayers), whose members live in South West Finland. The members of this sect pray regularly and often.

The subjects were first told to sit still with their eyes closed, and simply to tune themselves in on being close to God, but not actually to pray. This was called the contemplation condition. They were then told to pray as they normally did, either with words or silently, whichever they preferred.

Some typical results are seen in figures 1–6. Two records are shown for three subjects.

During the contemplation condition, alpha activity was common among most subjects. A typical case is shown in fig. 1. One subject (fig. 3) even had very slow theta activity.

During the prayer condition, the alpha was immediately blocked and replaced by faster beta activity. This is typical when a person is involved in some active, concentrated activity. Either they said their prayers aloud (fig.

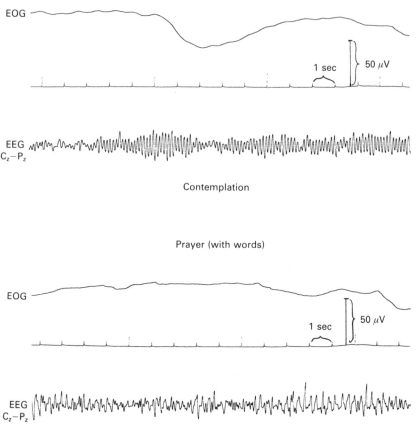

Figs. 1–2. EEG and EOG recordings of a middle-aged man during contemplation and prayer. Note the symmetrical alpha during the contemplation condition. During prayer, the alpha is blocked by faster, irregular beta activity. Beta always appears during concentrated mental activity.

2) or repeated them only mentally and silently (fig. 4), the result was the same: beta activity was generated.

One of the subjects asked if she could be allowed to speak in tongues. Though this is not a usual practise in this particular sect, she had acquired the habit. I was of course delighted. So she spoke in two "languages". While switching to something she described as an "African" language, she immediately started doing large, irregular rolling movements with her eyes (fig. 5). When she switched to the other language, the eye-rolling immediately stopped (fig. 6).

In this study, prayer and contemplation certainly mean something different from that in Mallory's investigation. Her subjects were Catholic monks and nuns, who used totally different techniques to my subjects, who were

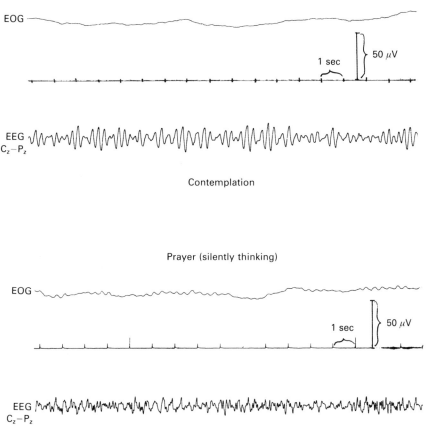

Figs. 3–4. EEG and EOG recordings of a middle-aged man during contemplation and prayer. In the contemplation condition, very slow theta activity appears. In the prayer condition, the theta is blocked by fast beta waves due to the concentration, although the subject is sitting silently with his eyes closed. There are almost no eye movements in either condition.

saying their prayers in a traditional, Lutheran manner. Nevertheless, the results are compatible, and seem to indicate that Christian prayer in a contemplative state generates abundant alpha, in certain cases even theta activity. Active praying, on the other hand, blocks the alpha and replaces it with beta activity. It might be added that the electrodermal measurements indicated that praying relieved psychological tension.

I have previously mentioned or described several ecstasy techniques, all of which have one thing in common: all affect the body in one way or another. I have also suggested possible mechanisms by which they might work. In fact, they are so many and varied, that it might seem confusing. But is only one explanation right, and are all the others wrong? Can it be, for example, that religious ecstasy is attained only by some mechanism

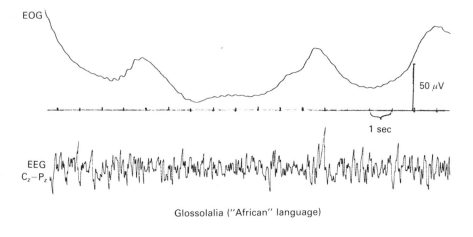

Glossolalia ("African" language)

Glossolalia (unknown language)

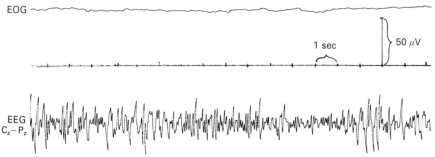

Figs 5–6. EEG and EOG recordings of a middle-aged woman while speaking in tongues; two different languages. Fast beta activity is dominant in the EEG. The spike-like waves occurred when she aspirated phonemes loudly, and seem to originate from verbal motor cortex. Note the rolling eye movements during the speaking of the "African" language.

triggering off changes in the balance of the transmitter substances? Or is it reached only via a change in the hormonal balance, or only by a slowing down of the brain waves, or is a pleasure centre activated?

I am not proposing that one of these possible explanations is correct, and that all the others are wrong. Future knowledge will probably refute some suggestions (if not all of them) and corroborate others. My suggestion is that an ecstatic experience can be reached by many different means, which might affect the body in slightly or quite different ways.

Whatever the physiological basis of the experience—and as I said, it might vary in different cases—we must not neglect the cognitive side. An experience is something that happens in our consciousness. We interpret in a certain way, depending on how we have been "programmed" by our social background and past experiences. Schachter & Singer (1962) with their widely accepted two-factor theory of emotion, proved that at least in the case of physiological arousal, the cognitive interpretation is of utmost importance. An aroused person might interpret his experience as anger, fright or euphoria, depending on what he expects. They showed this by injecting their subjects with adrenalin and telling them that they had re-cieved a new drug called "suproxin". Because the researchers gave differ-ent information to different subjects about how the drug would work, the subjects tended to behave differently in the expected direction compatible with the information they had received—although all subjects showed signs of physiological arousal.

The possibility cannot be excluded that by a feedback loop the cognitive interpretation might in turn have affected physiological functions. But Schachter and Singer's experiment clearly demonstrated the power of expectations.

When a person is using an ecstasy technique, he usually does so within a tradition. When he reaches an experience, a traditional interpretation of it already exists. The Hindu mystic experiences unity with Brahma, while the Catholic mystic sees visions of Jesus and Mary. It is true, however, that within the Christian tradition, too, the experience of *unio mystica* resem-bles the Hindu *samādhi*. But the power of cognitive expectations can clearly be seen when we study the literature of the mystics.

In some cases, a person might obtain an ecstatic experience "by mis-take". Maybe the person unintentionally triggers one of the, probably many, physiological mechanisms through which such an experience can be reached. In such cases, it is not rare to find that the person later, by reading, looks for an interpretation and maybe finds it within a tradition. The well-known Swedish "mystic of Vällingby" was perhaps such a case (Dahlén, 1976).

Much is still unknown about the physiological basis of the experience of ecstasy. We still deal mostly in vague guesses and suggestions. However, because knowledge of the central nervous system is continuously increas-ing, it is likely that in the future we can base our speculations on firmer ground. The science of psychophysiology is developing rapidly; this devel-opment will of necessity also be reflected in the psychology of religion.

References

Anand, B.-Chhina, G. 1961. Investigations on yogis claiming to stop their hearts. *Indian journal of medical research* 49, 90–94.

Banquet, J. 1973. Spectral analysis of the EEG in meditation. *Electroencephalography and clinical neurophysiology* 35, 143–151.

Barron, F., Jarvik, M.-Bunnell, S. 1971. The hallucinogenic drugs. *Altered states of awareness*, ed. by T. Teyler. San Francisco.

Björkqvist, K. 1976. *Vetenskapliga undersökningar av yoga och meditation*. Unpublished graduate thesis, Åbo Akademi. Åbo.

Björkqvist, S-E. 1980. Unpublished research. Åbo.

Dahlén, R. 1976. *Visionär i tjugonde århundradet*. Stockholm.

Furst, P. 1972. *Flesh of the gods*. London.

Gazzaniga, M. 1971. The split brain in man. *Altered states of awareness*, ed. by T. Teyler. San Francisco.

Green, E. 1975. *Biofeedback and beyond*. Topeka.

Huxley, A. 1969. *The doors of perception and Heaven and hell*. Aylesbury.

Kamiya, J. 1969. Operant control of the EEG alpha rhythm and some of its reported effects on consciousness. *Altered states of consciousness*, ed. by C. Tart. New York.

Kapleau, P. 1970. *The three pillars of zen*. Boston.

Kasamatsu, A.-Hirai, T. 1963. Science of zazen. *Psychologia* 6, 86–91.

— 1969. An electroencephalographic study on the Zen meditation (Zazen). *Altered states of consciousness*, ed. by C. Tart. New York.

Luria, A. 1978. *The working brain*. Aylesbury.

Mallory, M. 1977. *Christian mysticism: Transcending techniques*. Assen-Amsterdam.

Miller, N. 1971. Learning of visceral and glandular responses. *Biofeedback and selfcontrol*, ed. by T. Barber et al. Chicago-New York.

Olds, J. 1971. Pleasure centers in the brain. *Contemporary psychology*, ed. by R. Atkinson, San Francisco.

Ornstein, R. 1971. *The psychology of consciousness*. San Francisco.

Oswald, I. 1959. Experimental studies of rhythm, anxiety and cerebral vigilance. *British medical journal* 105, 269–293.

— 1960. Falling asleep open-eyed during intense rhythmic stimulation. *British medical journal* 1, 1450–1455.

Pavlov, I. 1928. *Lectures on conditioned reflexes*. New York.

Sargant, W. 1951. The mechanism of conversion. *British medical journal* 2, 311–316.

— 1957. *Battle for the mind*. London.

Schachter, S.-Singer, J. 1962. Cognitive, social and physiological determinants of emotional state. *Psychological review* 69, 379–399.

Staal, F. 1975. *Exploring mysticism*. London.

Sundén, H. 1967. *Zen*. Halmstad.

Wallace, R. 1973. *The physiological effects of transcendental meditation*. Los Angeles.

Wenger, M.-Bagchi, B. 1961. Studies of autonomic functions in practitioners of yoga in India. *Behavioral science* 6, 312–323.

Possession as a Clinical Phenomenon
A Critique of the Medical Model

By OWE WIKSTRÖM

In this article I will limit myself to the individual's specific experience of his personality being possessed, either partially or completely, momentarily or for an extended period of time, by evil spirits.[1] The individual is so disturbed by this experience that he cannot experience himself as freed, despite exorcism within his sect or the efforts of exorcizing experts.

My intention is to deal with the experiences of the group of individuals who, sincerely convinced that they are possessed by demons or evil spirits, have sought psychiatric or clinical psychological aid or who have received such aid through the efforts of relatives.

One way of defining this type of personality transformation in modern psychiatric terminology is "cacodemonomania" (Shendel, 1980).

I should first like briefly to present four cases. These can be said to represent the most common possessional states found in clinical praxis (Whitwell 1980). In conjunction with these four cases I will discuss a few more fundamental aspects of the explanations often provided in medical-psychiatric literature. I wish to supplement narrow medical perspective with one from the psychology of religion. At the very outset I wish to maintain that the structure of possession can above all be understood as an *interaction* between a cognitive, linguistic level, and an emotional, affective level. Only if one unites these two levels can one attain a deeper understanding of the individual's possession experience.

When dealing with the *dynamics* of possession, that is, the importance of the experience for the individual's total psychic economy, one must differentiate between the "normal" and the "pathological". The possessional experience which temporally is initiated, experienced and concluded within a cultic ritual frame, within a specific religious context, is a well-known phenomenon in the phenomenology of religion. This experience, however,

---

[1] Bibliographies in these themes: Anthropological and Cross-cultural Themes 1977. Spirit possession and spirit mediumship. An annotated bibliography, 1978. Overviews: Bourguignon, 1976. Case Studies in Spirit Possession 1977. An important report with detailed bibliography is Spanos-Gottlieb who discusses the "demythologizing" of psychological language from Possession through Mesmerism to Hysteria, 1979.

must be kept *separate* from the anxiety-filled and temporally enduring possession experience. The latter, however, can be initiated by the former and remain as a pathological/neurotic symptom if *before* the cultic possession experience there were neurotic/psychotic determinants in the individual's personality. Naturally, there are also compound forms of these "normal" and "pathological" types (Buzzuto 1975, Ward-Beaubrun 1981). Our article will deal particularly with the latter phenomenon.

Where the psychology of religion borders on clincial psychology and psychiatry, the concept of the "psychopathology of religion" has been coined. It is mainly in Germany that attempts have been made to delimit mentally anomalous states where religion has an important part in the genesis or manifestation of respective symptoms (Weitbrecht 1948). We can, in other words, differentiate between religious function in pathogenesis and in pathoplastics. It has long been known that psychotic patients often express their misconceptions in religious temrs. Jung has systematized this and drawn extensive conclusions for comparative religion, perhaps all too extensive. Depressed individuals of an endogenous nature often express notions of sin in religious terms. Others develop paranoid tendencies which, clothed in religious garb, are interpreted as if they were persecuted by demons or spirits or were sinning against the Holy Spirit.

To gather material for a more careful study of these phenomena one can work strictly with statistics and attempt to correlate different variables such as sex, age, denomination, etc. This is an important part of research but these studies must be supplemented by more individual-oriented case studies. *Günter Hole,* professor in Ulm, has published the largest study known to us of the relgous conceptions of the mentally disturbed. He uses there a strictly statistical method. But in his concluding discussion he contends that one can actually go "further" by "verstehende und einfühlende Kontakt; also der Einzelfallerhellung" (1977, 216). In the context of clinical psychology, as in psychiatric work, the case study is an important part of the scientific material. Within the psychology of religion it should therefore be necessary to concentrate on individual cases although methodological stringency is then harder to maintain.[2]

The following case studies are based upon notes written after interviews with the respective individual. Tape recordings were not allowed. The interviews are supplemented by letters and files. They are published by consent and after being read by the individuals involved. Some have been

[2] The necessity of case-studies in the psychology of religion is stressed by Beit-Hallahmi 1980. Rizotto 1976, shows the importance of case-studies, especially when dealing with possessional states.

changed to avoid identification. Publication in other than scientific periodicals is not desired.

Case studies

Case A. A 29 year old male, married with two children, social group 3. Never religiously active before, either during childhood or as an adult. Politically active in leftist groups. No prior history of psychiatric treatment. One and one half years prior to his relatives seeking aid, his activity level successively increased. Besides his regular employment, he began intensive business activity. He became increasingly restless and anxious. Among other things, he purchased wholesale a large quantity of Bibles. These he could not sell. The purchase was completely unexpected and he could not explain it himself. Stress increased both at work and at home. He purchased more religious literature, storing the books in his cellar for future use. God had chosen him for something great. He slept less and less. He telephoned the USA and purchased two Bolivian boats, and, again by telephone, he rented exhibition halls in Buenos Aires. Bank transactions followed in rapid succession. At this point the family and friends began to have their doubts.

A few neighbours who were active in a small Pentecostal group told the man's wife that her husband was obviously possessed by some sort of spirit. A travelling preacher visited the family, laid hands upon him and prayed for him, attempting to drive out the spirits he could discern in his eyes. The day after the preacher's attempted exorcism, the tempo had further increased. But now the thought arose that he was persecuted by demons who wanted to thwart his great project. The demons controlled not only his wife but even the preacher and the neighbours who spoke of his seeking aid. The demons were at times even in his own body. During these periods his relatives experienced him as completely changed. He ridiculed everything that was religious, spat at his wife's prayers and urinated on a Bible and the religious books he had earlier collected. During those periods when his mind was not filled with demonic behavior, he was tired, nervous and restless; he was intensely afraid of Hell and demons. A few days before his arrival at the psychiatric clinic he slept only three hours a night.

Obviously, this man felt himself to be possessed by the Devil. We shall return shortly and discuss the medical explanation and its plausibility, but above all its limitations.

Case B. A male, 19 years of age, admitted two years ago to a psychiatric ward for "border-line psychosis?". Since junior high school he has only worked temporarily. Childhood is described as closed and lonely. Very active, non-conformist parents. At the age of 16, he had an intensive attack of anxiety and anguish. During the same period, he became a member of a Free Church, having experienced "salvation" during a tent meeting. During one period, he was active in the musical activity of his church. But his anxiety was overwhelming. A decisive phase in his development was the reading of Nicko Cruz's description of his path from drug abuse to Christian faith. Cruz describes this process as his liberation from a drug demon. Then "he understood that he was possessed". The anxiety continued, but it was coupled to a religious world. The idea of his being possessed increased. For one year now he has been convinced that his anxiety and depression are the result of being possessed by the Devil. He writes,

"One day it burned in my soul and a veil was placed before my eyes. It still remains. I experienced a lot of strange things. One guy said to me, you are a demon. That hurt me deep in my soul, it seared like a fire.

From the beginning, my sexual feelings were almost animal-like. The same thing I went through was experienced by another person called Nicko Jonson. In the book he wrote, it said that he was possessed by the Devil. For over two years I've been here in the psychiatric ward and I don't feel a bit better. I am so anxious and restless that life is unbearable. Inside me an eternal fire burns that never ceases. I believe that I prayed too little, so that an evil spirit and seven other demons have once again possessed my soul, as it says in Matt. 12. Please, help me ... My head is so heavy and I am a so-called devil."

B, too, has often been the object of prayer, exorcism and Bible reading with the laying-on of hands, but has not felt that it has helped in the slightest.

Case C. C. is an unmarried, childless, 33 year old female. From childhood she has been a member of a Free Church. She herself sought aid at a psychiatric clinic after contact with the parish priest, convinced that she was possessed by demons. The following is an extremely simplified summary of 43 hours of psychotherapy.

Despite a high academic degree and a good position, C always wanted to be a pastor. In particular, the charismatic movement's persuasive and enthusiastic leaders appealed to her. Those "filled with the Holy Spirit and fire" have always enjoyed her boundless admiration. However, since she could in no way meet these "spiritual criteria", but rather regarded herself as withdrawn, inhibited and shy, she has increasingly bemoaned her inability to become a pastor. In spite of this, she experienced a call from God and began her theological education. But her own evil nature and her inability to be filled with the Holy Spirit, which she sees other receiving, has concerned her increasingly. Eventually she developed an (obsessive) compulsion to observe the spirituality of others and her own lack of it. Despite the fact that she felt herself to be called by God, she could still lie, act falsely etc. Why? Subsequently she understood that her evil was Satan's cunning; she must be possessed.

All impulsive tendencies, which she classified as wrong, were not at all neutral in her eyes but rather interpreted as consequences of a diabolical eruption from her own evil heart. To get away from this and be instead completely filled with the Spirit, she had tried nearly everything, the Salvation Army's altar of repentance, the spirit-filled meetings of Pentecostalism, the convent life, fasting and exorcism in Norway. Finally she sought psychotherapeutic help.

Case D. D is a 42 year old female, married for 16 years, with 3 children. Up until five years before our meeting she had never been religiously active. After a series of meetings she had become »saved» and received the Baptism of the Holy Spirit, subsequently becoming active in her congregation. In the same congregation some four years before our interview, a visiting preacher had made a great impression upon her. He had preached, among other things, on judgement and about the Devil who went round like a roaring lion. The evil of our time, (we lived according to the preacher in the last days), was regarded as the Devil's direct deception of mankind. The Devil made particular use of sexuality and infidelity as a means of snaring man in his net.

This is documented in D's carefully written diary. Six months after the preacher had left, she began to experience evil, devilish impulses within. Gradually she developed the insight that devils were in her body. They whispered to her that she didn't really love her husband at all. They made sexual allusions and, above all, she could now and again hear blasphemous words. This was experienced as something completely foreign to her and caused considerable suffering. At first she struggled against these impulses. Sleepless and desperate, having taken tranquilizers, she finally sought the aid of her pastor to whom she revealed her thoughts. After Bible reading, prayer, speaking in tongues and singing in the Spirit, he had in the context of a small group driven out the devils in Jesus's name. She had immediately felt freed, received once again her feelings for her husband and her God and could function for three years, the entire time convinced that exorcism worked. After three years, however, she abandoned her marriage and her religious role and then interpreted the exorcism as a "naive repression".

Discussion

How is one to interpret these individual's possession from the perspective of comparative religion? How are we to understand conditions, structure and function of the experience for the individual himself? In the following discussion I hope to augment the psychiatric medically-oriented model.

In older psychiatric terminology, the Devil was found as an accompanying factor at least in the plastic form of the illness. Krafft-Ebbing in his day could speak of Demonomania or Demonomelancholia, but psychiatric terminology has become successively demythologized (Spanos-Gottlieb 1979) and the constituent elements of paranoia, for example, are no longer part of the diagnosis. These are replaced by the structural changes that arise in the personality in what we now call psychosis, such factors as daily variations, reality constancy, perceptual changes etc. Interpretations of the intensive experiences as the result of spirits or radiation or cosmic forces are not, in other words, a part of diagnostic work. What does this mean for the individual himself and for the psychological attempt to understand his experience?

In *case A,* with its hectic pace and hyperactive behavior, the psychiatrist will soon find the classic symptoms of the manic phase of a manic-depressive psychosis.

When the individual experiences his mood as increasingly intensive and undertakes increasingly fantastic projects, and when the need for rest drops to a minimum, then the clinician recognises the manic phase.

For the medical doctor, the case is neither interesting or comprehensible from the individual's description of being possessed by devils, but rather through the differential diagnostic process which observes the pathogenesis of abnormal emotion.

However, from the perspective of comparative religion, it is precisely this content, the cognitive content in the paranoid conception that is of decisive interest. At first, the paranoia is projected onto the world around him, but it is later introjected on A himself. He then not only experiences himself as a devil, but also behaves like one. Our question, in other words, must be: how is it that the paranoid experience is clothed in specifically religious garb? Naturally, the medical classification of A as a manic psychotic is adequate from one perspective, for we thereby gain an insight into how, behind certain possessional states, there can lie bio-chemically conditioned, extremely intense emotional states coupled with a paranoid tendency. It is, in other words, important to remember that to increase understanding of the *structure* of possession, we must relate the individual's (bio-chemically conditioned) intensive feeling experience to the surrounding subculture's way of defining these intensive feelings. *Religious language* provides one way of dealing verbally with the unstructured and terrifying aspects of a developing psychosis. The talk of spirits by friends and neighbours served here as triggers and only reinforced A's self-understanding: "possessed".

The strictly medical model is, in other words, narrow and inadequate and must be supplemented by this interactional perspective.

Case B is described as typically schizophrenic. The autism and vague hallucinations contribute more than a little to this diagnosis. He was given classic anti-psychotic medicine consisting of fentiazine derivatives, but in spite of this he experienced no change for the better. No one has seriously discussed the psycho-dynamic function of the demonic experiences in a therapeutic context, but rather B has been judged as impervious to psycho-therapeutic treatment. Even here it is one of the figures in religio-mythical language representing evil and anxiety, the Devil, who verbalizes the intense anxiety felt by B.

Through Nicko Jonson's uplifting account of his entrapment in the agony of narcotics, the Devil's power, B received a *model* which he adopted as his own. The anxiety has, in other words, become bearable and received a name in that it is ascribed to the Devil. For B there exists no alternative to the theological interpretation of suffering. The biological or psycho-dynamic explanations of anxiety are only seen as the Devil's tricks to snare even the therapist in his power.

Here, too, we can say that we have an increased understanding of B if we relate the *emotional* disturbance to the way in which he uses religious *language:* an interaction.

When it comes to the *dynamic* function of possession, we find in both A and B's case that it is similar and must be considered pathological. There exist, in other words, strong overdetermining factors of a psychotic nature to which the talk of supernatural evil powers in the surrounding group can be coupled thus becoming reinforced. In this way exorcism cannot help since it is based to a large extent upon strong suggestions and a well-integrated ego in the psychoanalytic sense. The latter was not present in either A or B and we may therefore speak of "psychotic possession experiences", where the majority of treatment must be medical, even though psychotherapeutic support should naturally utilize the dynamic function of religious language.

Case C represents the form of possession most commonly described in the classic literature of the psychology of religion. Here the psychoanalytic model has mainly been utilized. C's experience may be said to have its origins in the repression of certain elements from consciousness and precipitated anxiety. This anxiety, however, is never described neutrally but is instead covered or encapsulated with the aid of religious language. In the older literature it was often aggressive or sexual impulses that were forced to submerge through the strict discipline of the monastery. This resulted in the feared or desired impulse being manifested outside the individual consciousness and thereby beyond one's own responsibility. It was converted into hysterical symptoms or a gush of obscene or blasphemous words uttered by a demon in the body.

In the case of C however, it is doubt and the desire to avoid having to become a pastor which result in her unconscious development of *cleptomania*. This she forces herself to keep secret. In both major and minor situations she *must* imperatively steal things. Being the pious woman she is, she experiences this as something terrible.

In the depth-psychological sense, we interpret this as a classic defense manoeuvre. With the aid of this she remains unconscious of her doubt and anxiety over becoming a pastor. Repressed impulses break out in refined form; if she were found out she could avoid becoming a pastor. Even here we can say that an interaction exists between the religious terminology of evil or demons, and the anxiety and apprehension that C feels inside. In the symptom "possession idea", which develops into a compulsive obsession, an *alloying* occurs between anxiety and religious language. C thus remains unresponsible for her actions. C is a plaything in the power of the demons.

We have the opportunity to analyse *case D* more carefully from a psychodynamic point of view, since D later underwent psychotherapy. We thereby can state the following: during the strongly suggestive meeting that D attended, she obtained a religious model for interpretation of evil impulses. Marital infidelity and sexual acts, in particular, were described there as the results of the intervention of spirits.

At the same time, D lived in a marriage full of conflict. The impulse to criticize or desert her husband was therefore repressed from consciousness with the aid of religious words. When she saw that her husband did not share her convictions and he began to criminalize, the tendency to question their relationship increased, although this was driven down into D's unconscious. Instead, a converted form of apprehension broke forth. Encapsulated in religious language, she did not need to confess her "sinful impulses". Instead, it was the Devil who was playing his games. Thus she herself was not responsible for her blasphemous thoughts.

The exorcist who was summoned supported her defense against the developing impulses. Through the use of strongly suggestive exorcist treatment, evil was held in check for a period of months. However, in the long run the religiously moulded defense mechanisms of isolation, repression of affect and above all, the projection onto an externally perceived devil, could not hold their own against the approaching conflict. Later, doubt over her marriage broke out instead, no longer encapsulated in religious language, but now expressed »neutrally» as discontent, meaninglessness and apprehension. It is, however, interesting from our point of view to note that exorcism, the command to obsessive demonic thoughts to desist, actually worked. It could not hold its own, however, with the conflict lying behind, for the defences broke when the anxiety over marriage and married life finally became insurmountable.

In both *case C* and *case D,* possession has a similar dynamic function. It serves the neurotic defense. Strong emotions are repressed from consciousness, but later return in an altered form. The religious terminology for evil appeals to the emotive level and at the same time provides cognitive frameworks for denial and repression. Thus the possession experience, here too, is a result of an interaction between cognitive linguistic processes and emotive, affective processes. Neither is it a possession which is initiated, experienced and abandoned during a specific ritual situation. We have hear an anxiety which is partially bound to the possession idea, and at the same time accessible either to occasional support therapy using its own terminology, or to insight therapy treatment.

Theories of Possession

I. *The neurophysiological theory*

The neurophysiological theory has been paid special attention by *Sargant* (1969, 1974). He builds his entire theory of the psychology of religion on a few of the fundamental aspects of the Pavlovian theory of conditioning.

When the stress became too great for the test dogs one could observe a psychic breakdown. A reduction of the dog's resistance was obtained through exhaustion, starvation, drugs, and forced wakefulness. Sargant was interested in the brain inhibition which occurs under extreme stress, and of which one can discern two stages. One stage is where previously learned responses are erased and the other, which is more important for the psychology of possession, results in the greatly increased subseptibility of the individual to suggestion and conditioning. These breakdowns, which can be explained purely by brain physiology, also apply to humans. One can, according to Sargant, even regard Wesley's violent and lengthy testimonies on the tortures of Hell as so inducive of stress that individuals quite simply collapsed.

The same processes have later been alleged to occur during the desired and anticipated possessional states in Loa and in the Voodoo cults. The combination of ceaseless drumming, intensive hyper-ventilation, noise, dancing and song, result in over-stimulation. This prepares the way for erasure of previously learned patterns and for the conditioning of new ones. Neher has criticized this theory, emphasizing instead the epileptoid tendency which is latent in every human. He has attempted to demonstrate that rhythmic stimulation in the form of dance, movement and rhythm lies in close proximity to the brain's alpha waves and can very well release a multiplicity of subjective experiences such as fright, disgust, anger and total exhaustion. Finally, spasms can occur which approximate epileptoid states of consciousness. The 7–9 hertz which the drum rhythms on Haiti are said to maintain, lie directly under the brain's alpha waves; 8–13 hertz.

These theories only concentrate on the biological conditions for the external *form* of possession. What these theories, on the other hand, *do not* discuss is the specific *content* that the experience has for the individual and the collective. One decisive factor both for the initiation of these experiences and for the understanding of them must be the language which gives meaning to the experience.

It must be more plausible to view the ritual drama in its entirety, that is rather as a process between the perhaps physiologically explicable conditions for this type of consciousness, *and* the mythical linguistic world with the aid of which this consciousness is interpreted or even initiated. Consequently, the physiological can not automatically be a *condition for* possession, it can even be understood as a *result of* other group-psychological processes.

With regard to our previously described clinical cases, not one of them can be understood in these narrow neurological terms.

II. *The psychoanalytic theory*

The psychoanalytic explanation in its earliest stages stated that possession was actually nothing more than hysteria.[3] Both Charcot and Janet had, at an early date, attempted successfully to heal patients in this way. Freud, on the other hand, worked at trying to understand Haizmann, an artist from the 1800's. Haizmann had made a pact with the Devil in order to get out of a state of deep depression. The melancholia had arisen because he had lost his father. Freud viewed both God and the Devil as derivatives of the child's ambivalent attitude towards its father. If God is the good, loveable, warm father, then the Devil is the strict, feared, aggressive father. In Haizmann's case, Freud assumed that the Devil was a substitute for his own father and that the state of possession was a struggle against his own

---

[3] Most papers dealing with possessional states in the medical literature use a psychodynamical theoretical framework. McAlpine-Hunter 1954, Diecköfer 1971, Schatzmann 1973, Bron 1975, Ehrenwald 1975, Taylor 1978, Diecköfer 1979, Ward 1980, Griffith 1980.

feminine, passive wishes, including a desire to bear a child for his father. Freud's ideas here have been criticized. Above all, critics claim that Freud's interpretation of Haizmann lacks the support of the sources. The Devil can instead symbolize *both* mother and father. Archaic pregenital procreation fantasies may exist in their own right and arise independent of passive homosexual wishes. Later, mainly from the direction of neoanalysis, it has been maintained that possession experience must be interpreted according to objectrelations theory. It is possible to understand the internalized object as an introjection or fantasized incorporation of either one or both parents. These introjected objects are experienced as either good or evil depending upon which feelings the child projects into them. What can then arise is a persecution of the self from the introjected bad or evil object. This leads to a persecutory-paranoid anxiety. It is here that possession can function as an *interpretation* of this inner anxiety. Otherwise, the general psychoanalytic view is that thought, feelings, fantasies and impulses are repressed from the conscious by the super-ego. Aggressive and sexual components inparticular lie as a loaded potential in the depths of the individual. This inner impulse material can, in distorted form, come to the surface and invade the personality in the form of self-hatred. The evil that one feels, however, can alternatively be repressed from consciousness by being projected outwardly onto a culturally sanctioned scape-goat, in our culture a devil, thereby shifting the fear and apprehension to an externally perceived figure. However, it can also be introjected and thus both belongs to personality itself and is at the same time experienced as an alien, a devil. The Devil's impulses are then beyond the individual's control; anxiety decreases.

If the neurological model is seen as a typically monogenetic theory and all too concentrated on biological conditions, we may say that the psychoanalytic explanation speaks far too narrowly of the psychodynamic determinants. The problem is *why* is it just one "person", the Devil, who is created to function as the recipient of projections of evil? Consequently, we must say that this theory too is far too narrow, although our cases C and D can largely be understood with the aid of this theory.

III. *The hypnosis theory*

The hypno-theoretical explanation was especially common at the turn of the century and in the developing psychotherapy. Possession was related to hysterical phenomena which, as had been known for a long time could be cured through hypnosis.

But even the hypnosis research of the 1970's, especially that involving dissociative states, has proved very useful for attaining a deeper under-

standing the psychological genesis and structure of religious possession.[4] It
was observed quite early that central elements within the mind could be
dissociated from the flow of the rest of consciousness. Previously it stated
that different qualities of experience were guided to different association
centres within the consciousness. There they could live a shadow existence
of their own, separate from normal waking consciousness. Janet related this
to the perceptions of devils.

For a long period of time, this area of hypnosis research has lain dor-
mant, and it is only in recent years that the question of so-called "multiple
personalities" has been reconsidered. It has been discovered that in hypnotic states, where we know that the degree of suggestibility is greater, but
also that the barriers for what is repressed or "dissociated from consciousness" are weaker, that so-called alter-personalities can appear. A new
personality can spontaneously take command. The individual's language,
diction, sentence rhythm, dialect, voice level, etc., can then change. An
apparently completely new personality speaks through the lips of the
person hypnotised. These are well documented experiments.

Instead of assuming the existence of personalities flying around the room
in accordance with reincarnation theories, it is now assumed that the
interviewer with his question: Who are you?, provides the subject with a
suggestion. This is above all the case with deep regressions, where people
have been enabled to imagine themselves living, for example, in the 14th
century. At the same moment as the interviewer says it is the 14th century,
the subject unconsciously compiles all he knows about the period and in
this way creates a new personality. Thus, during hypnosis, a subtle role-
playing emerges between the subject and the interviewer, so that very
diffuse questions such as: "Who are you?, Where are you? How are you
dressed?", can create clear perceptions and change the subject's behaviour. Whether the hypnotic state is a "state or non-state" phenomenon or
whether it should be described as a sophisticated role-play is difficult to
clarify. It is, however, tempting tentatively to understand many possession
experiences, even in a neurotic sense, as the results of suggestive states.
We can say that an intensive religious revivalist meeting with its multiplicity of suggestive stimuli perpares the individual suggestively for a message
on possession.

The classical *exorcismus probartivus* is not the least of the phenomena
which it is possible to clarify theoretically with the hypno-theoretical
framework. When an individual filled with conflict and anxiety becomes the

[4] Ravenschroft 1965, Ludwig 1972, Allisson
1974, Kampmann 1976, Larmore 1977, Berwick 1977, Hilgard 1978 and Hildén 1981.

object of intensive "treatment" from an exorcist who desires contact with alien personalities with the individual's own inner world, it is possible that everything that is incomprehensible and anxiety-filled, is welded together by the exorcist's suggestions into an especially diabolical individual.

In D's case, it appears that the preacher's talk of devils functioned like a post-hypnotic suggestion, that when the impulses to leave her husband arose, they were "captured" immediately by the religious language and were thus kept from consciousness: it was the effect of the devil. That the exorcism worked can be seen as strong support for D's neurotic defense against affect: isolation and repression.

Even doctors have, in certain situations, felt obliged to work with priests who have performed exorcism, when the problem was judged to be inaccessible to insight-oriented treatment (Cappannari 1975). So we see that even hypno-theoreticians have begun to approach a theory which actively attempts to combine emotive and cognitive elements.

IV. *Interaction between language and emotion*

Bourguignon, inparticular, has worked with Haiti's Voodoo cults (1976). She has found that the essence of the obscenities and blasphemies flowing from the mouth of the possessed, must be understood as divided or dissociated elements of the personality itself. The culture provides the *forms,* that is the possibility of dramatically providing shape and figure and even the *words,* verbal representatives for evil. If there are concepts current in a culture according to which people during certain rites become the helpless victims of interventions by spirits, then these concepts fit into collectively sanctioned hysteroid attacks. The culture thus provides both form (possession by spirits) and words (blasphemies, obscenities) for them. In this way, a repressed experience constituent interacts with a cultural world concept of mythical character (Ward 1980, Leon 1975).

"In a sense these attacks manifested by one who consciously knows that they will be followed by exorcism, simultaneously demonstrate a breakthrough of the repressed feelings, and constitute an appeal for the help of the community in dealing with the overwhelming force of the individual's own contradictions and anxieties which they produce" (Bourguignon 1976, 78). This hysterical reaction can then be treated by the exorcist who supplies a culturally sanctioned form of psychotherapy. In general, the word possessed is probably a powerful and appealing metaphor implying that a person feels "beside himself". He is then no longer responsible. Possession can here unconsciously symbolize a form of magic escape.

One can say that the mythological expressions of a culture for what lies beyond the individual's control, serve to symbolize certain psychological dispositions, and the relationship that is obtained between these elements may be symbolic of certain psychological processes. In this way, the conflict is removed from the intra-particularistic level to the cultural-universalistic level and is restructured as possession by a spirit.

It is, therefore, far too simplistic to call spirits or devils purely the results of projections in a psychoanalytic sense or of paranoid tendencies. Even the ethnologist *Crapanzano* maintains the double perspective: "Thus there can be projections only where there have been introjections. If the spirit qua exterior existents serve as means for the articulation of what the westerner would regard as within him as outside him, then strictly speaking there can be no projection of what was within outside, for there was no within to begin with" (1977, 12). Language and emotions *interact*.[5]

Summary

It must be seen as necessary to supplement the narrow medical model for interpreting states of possession.[6] The clinically interested psychologist of religion, inparticular, needs consider aspects of the phenomenology of religion and clinical psychology in order to gain a broader understanding of this phenomenon. Otherwise, there is a risk of falling into the trap that James warned us about. He called it medical materialism. With reductivist zeal one regards multi-dimensional experiences such as mysticism, conversion or prayer as the result of primarily biological drives. James strongly criticized those who for example felt that saint Theresa's spiritual marriages were "nothing but" hysterical reactions.

There is, in other words, a danger within more clinically oriented psychology of religion that one unconsciously adopts a medical model and falls into the "monistic-method" fallacy or that one "totalizes ones own perspective".

To declare that possession experiences are "nothing but" psychosis, mania, epilepsy or schizophrenia, are examples of this type of over-simplification. The same can be said of the assertion that possession is "nothing

---

[5] A few have tried to maintain a unity between ethnographical facts and psychiatric theories, Parson 1974. Particulary Yap 1960, tried to compare what we have called the arbitrary, process initiated possessional state with hysterical, pathological phenomena. Cf Kiev 1961. Hes 1975 but even more Figge 1973 and Leon 1975 implicit use a "interactionalistic" perspective stressing the dynam-

ic relation between emotions and cognitions. Cf. Wikström 1980.
[6] The scientific exploration of this field is also ethically desirable as is shown in the "Case Klingenberg", where the German student Anne-Lise Michel, suffering from epilepsy died after long-term exorcist "treatment". Goodman 1980. Cf Roth 1970.

but " an obsessive neurotic symptom. I maintain, rather, that one must attempt to produce a multi-factoral model for explanation. In our cases we have tried to understand "clinical cacodemonomania" as a process. It is possible to describe it as a *dynamic relationship* between the *verbal* representatives for evil or the Evil One in the world of mythological language, and the intrapsychic, anxiety-filled *emotive* state, regardless of whether this inner state is considered to be the result of neurosis, psychosis, or the consequence of intensive suggestion.

References

Allisson, R. B. 1974. A new treatment approach for multiple personalities. *American journal of clinical hypnosis* 17, 15–32.

Anthropological and crosscultural themes in mental health. 1977. An annotated bibliography. Ed. by E. Favazza. London.

Beit-Hallahmi, B. 1980. Psychology of religion. *Archiv für Religionspsychologie* 11, 228–237.

Berwick, P. R. 1977. Hypnosis, exorcism, and healing: a case report. *American journal of clinical hypnosis* 20, 146–149.

Bourguignon, E. 1976. *Possession.* San Francisco.

Bron, B. 1975. Zum Phänomen der Besessenheit. *Confinia psychiatrica* 18, 16–29.

Buzzuto, J. C. 1975. Cinematic neurosis following "The exorcist". *Journal of nervous and mental disease* 161, 43–48.

Cappannari, S. C. et al. 1975. Voodoo in the general hospital. *Journal of American medical association* 232, 938–940.

Case studies in spirit possession. 1977. Ed. by V. Crapanzano–V. Garrison. New York etc.

Diecköfer, K. 1971. Zum Problem der Besessenheit. *Confinia psychiatrica* 14, 203–225.

— 1979. Katamnestische Betrachtungen zum Fall einer Obsession. *Confinia psychiatrica* 22, 219–225.

Ehrenwald, J. 1960. *Psychotherapy: myth and method.* London.

Figge, H. H. 1973. Zur Entwicklung und Stabilisierung von Sekundärpersönlichkeiten im Rahmen von Besessenheitskulten. *Confinia psychiatrica* 16, 28–37.

Goodman, F. D. 1980. *The exorcism of Anneliese Michel.* New York.

Griffith, E. 1980. Possession, prayer and testimony. *Psychiatry* 43, 120–128.

Hes, J. P. 1975. Shamanism and psychotherapy. *Psychotherapy psychosomatica* 25, 251–253.

Hildén, L. 1981. Secondary personality as an adjunct to hypnoanalysis. *Svensk tidskrift för hypnos* 8, 114–117.

Hilgard, E. R. 1978. State of consciousness in hypnosis. *Hypnosis at its bicentennial,* ed. by H. Frankel et al. New York–London.

Hole, G. 1977. *Der Glaube bei Depressiven.* Stuttgart.

Kampmann, R. 1976. Hypnotically induced multiple personalities. *Svensk tidskrift för hypnos* 2, 10–25.

Kiev, A. 1972. *Transcultural psychiatry.* London.

Larmore, K. 1977. Multiple personality. *British journal of psychiatry* 131, 35–40.

Leon, C. A. 1975. El Duende and other incubi. *Archives of general psychiatry* 32, 155–162.

Ludwig, A. M. 1972. The objective study of a multiple personality. *Archives of general psychiatry* 26, 298–310.

McAlpine, A.–Hunter, M. 1954. Observations on the psychoanalytical theory of psychosis. *British journal of medical psychology* 27, 175–191.

Parson, A. 1974. Expressive symbolism in witchcraft and delusion. *Culture and personality,* ed. by R. A. le Vries. Chicago.

Ravenscroft, K. 1965. Voodoo possession. *International journal of clinical and experimental hypnosis* 157–182.

Rizutto, A. M. 1976. Freud, god and the devil and the theory of object representation. *International review of psychoanalysis* 31, 165–172.

Roth, G. 1970. Epilepsia est morbus non possessio. *Confinia psychiatrica* 13, 67–72.

Schatzmann, M. 1970. *Soul murder.* London.

Shendel, E. 1980. Cacodemonomania and exorcism in children. *Journal of clinical psychology* 41:4, 119–123.

Spanos, N. P.–Gottlieb, J. 1979. Demonic possession, Mesmerism and hysteria: a social psychological perspective on their historical interrelation. *Journal of abnormal psychology* 88, 527–546.

Spirit possession and spirit mediumship in Africa and Afro-America. 1978. An annotated bibliography, ed. by B. Zantzky. New York.

Taylor, G. 1980. Demoniacal possession and psychoanalytical theory. *British journal of medical psychology* 53, 287–295.

Ward, C.–Beaubrun, M. H. 1981. Spirit possession and neuroticism in a West Indian pentecostal community. *British journal of clinical psychology* 20, 295–296.

Ward, F. et al. 1980. The psychodynamics of demon possession. *Journal for the scientific study of religion* 19, 201–207.

Weitbrecht, H. 1948. *Beiträge zur Religionspsychopathologie.* Heidelberg.

Whitwell, F. 1980. Possession in psychiatric patients in Britain. *British journal of medical psychology* 53, 287–295.

Wikström, O. 1980. A case of possession. *Archiv für Religionspsychologie* 14, 212–226.

Yap, P. M. 1960. "The possession syndrome: a comparison of Hong Kong and French findings". *Journal of mental science* 106, 114–147.

II

The Siberian Shaman's Technique of Ecstasy

By ANNA-LEENA SIIKALA

The Siberian shaman's function as mediator between the normal and the supranormal world is based on systems of beliefs according to which difficulties threatening the even peace of life are caused by representatives of the spirit world, and can be forestalled and eliminated with the help of benevolent spirits. There are several methods used in the areas in which shamanism appears that are thought to influence the working of supranormal beings. The essential feature in the functioning of the shaman is the creation of direct and reciprocal states of communication directed at the spirit world. The shaman is thus first and foremost a supplier of information and a "negotiator", whose task is to find out the measures required to resolve a crisis that has already arisen or to prevent crises in the future. Although the tasks of the shaman vary somewhat in different communities, they do have one thing in common in that direct communication with the spirit world is always considered necessary in carrying out the shaman's duties. A shamanic rite is not made shamanistic merely by the nature of the task to be carried out, i.e. the aim of the rite, but by the way in which the goal is sought. The shamanic rite is an attempt to solve the problems of the normal world through ecstatic contact with the supranormal.

Shamanism and the altered states of consciousness

The Siberian shaman's technique of ecstasy, regarded sometimes as symptomatic of a pathological state and sometimes as "cold-blooded" playacting, is one link in a series of extensive phenomena highly varied in form. The anthropological literature uses the words *trance, ecstasy* and *possession* as general terms for given states. The last of these, sometimes wrongly used as a synonym for the first two, arises from culturally-bound concepts. It is based on native theory according to which a supranormal being may enter a person's body and take command. As terms, 'trance' and 'ecstasy' do not differ greatly from each other except that the former is favoured primarily by anthropologists, the latter by students of comparative religion. They both refer to forms of behaviour deviating from what is normal in the wakeful state and possessing a specific cultural significance, typical features being an altered grasp of reality and the self-concept, with the intensity of change ranging from slight modifications to a complete loss of consciousness. Recent research has adopted the general term, altered states of consciousness, ASC's, to express this sphere.

In order to be able to understand or interpret correctly the incomplete reports of ecstasy and possession based on the momentary impressions of eyewitnesses appearing in ethnographic literature, the reader must be familiar with the features characteristic of altered states of consciousness. The matter cannot be approached completely objectively. The scale describing the outward behaviour of the ecstatic, and similarly his feeling or observations, is very broad. The same external stimulation may also, in the case of various individuals, lead to ASC's differing from one another. As I shall attempt to show later, the factors leading to personal ASC experiences lie at many levels and are always weighted according to the demands of the situation and the motivations and hopes of each individual (van der Walde 1968, 56).The subjective content of experience is influenced by what is culture dependent, e.g. belief, frames of reference the ecstatic has learnt to associate with ASC's, i.e. during his trance the shaman meets his spirit-helper, a Christian possibly Christ or the Virgin Mary. Differences in the nervous systems of individuals also affect their responses to various stimuli and thus shape the nature and degree of the alteration of consciousness. The phenomena classified as altered states of consciousness do, however, have certain common features with the help of which their close relationship can be shown. Arnold Ludwig has tried to define these natural properties, whilst emphasizing that some are more, some less typical of different individual cases. He mentions alteration in thinking, disturbed time sense, loss of conscious control, change in emotional expression, body image changes, perceptual distortions, hallucinations and pseudo-hallucinations, change in meaning or significance, sense of the ineffable, hypersuggestibility (Ludwig 1968, 77–83).

Examining shamanic phenomena in the light of Ludwig's list of features, we see that most of the properties he mentions well describe the state reached by the shaman during his ritual activity. Changes in the field of observation and body image, attenuated grasp of reality and self-control, which may lead to identification with authority in the case of the shaman with supranormal powers, are all identifying features of shamanic ecstasy. It also appears that some of the basic elements of the shamanic tradition can be explained on the basis of typical marks of identification of altered states of consciousness. A sense of depersonalization and transcendence may in itself act as an impetus to cosmic journey fantasies. Without doubt, such feelings are at the very heart of the tradition containing the schism between mind and body. Thus, by placing the shamanic technique of ecstasy beside parallel modes of behaviour, possibly of different cultural background, we discover the guide lines for analysing its basic psychophysical properties.

The ways in which people have pursued trance or an altered state of consciousness, or found themselves in such a state, are generally speaking highly varied, ranging from mechanical stimuli of the nervous system to chains of effect caused by such mental factors as states of mind and motivations. We may, however, mention four regions of the human organism the disturbance of whose balance, in one way or another, leads to altered consciousness. These are a) the normal inflow of sensory stimuli, b) the normal outflow of motor impulses, c) the normal 'emotional tone', or d) the normal flow and organization of processes of recognition.[1]

Arnold Ludwig has presented an extensive list of the methods used in the pursuit of an altered state of consciousness. He divides these methods into five groups, according to the nature of the technique, and points out that different methods may overlap.[2]

1. Reduction of exteroceptive stimulation and/or motor activity:
   — result of absolute reduction of sensory input, changes in pattern of sensory data, or constant exposure to repetitive, monotonous stimuli.
   — includes hypnotic trance; ASC's from prolonged social isolation, e.g. mystics, aescetics.
   — (lethargy of initiation period).
2. Increase of exteroceptive stimulation and/or motor activity and/or emotion:
   — excitatory mental states resulting mainly from sensory overloading or bombardment, which may or may not be accompanied by strenuous physical activity or exertion. Profound emotional arousal and mental fatigue may be major contributing factors.
   — dance and musical trance in response to rhythmic drumming; hyperkinetic trance states associated with emotional mental contagion, often in a group or mob setting; religious conversion and healing trance experiences during

---

[1] Ludwig 1968, 30; see also Fischer 1969 and 1970. The part played by emotion as a factor leading to ecstatic behaviour has attracted the attention, above all, of students of mysticism and deep religious experiences. Orlo Strunk links the arousal of emotion with the process of perception and finds himself on the track of one fundamental fact in saying that the closer perceived aspects (concerning religion) come to self-concept, the greater is the attendant emotional experience. Strunk 1962, 67. See also Sundén 1959, 49 ff.

[2] Ludwig 1968, 71–75. Quoted here is Sheila S. Walker's summary, which concentrates in particular on a broad presentation of the parts that concern institutionalized and religious connections Walker 1972, 12.

meatings of a revivalist type; mental aberrations associated with certain rites of passage; spirit possession states; shamanistic, divinatory, prophetic and ecstatic trances.

3. Increased alertness or mental involvment:
— results from focused or selective hyperalertness and from peripheral hyperalertness for prolonged periods.
— fervent praying; total involvment in listening to dynamic speaker; trance resulting from watching a revolving object.

4. Decreased alertness or relaxation of critical faculties:
— passive state of mind with minimum of active, goal-directed thinking.

5. Presence of somatopsychological factors:
— results from alterations in body chemistry, or neurophysiology, which are deliberate or due to a situation over which the individual has no control.
— drowsiness; dehydration; hypoglycemia from fasting; (hyperventilation); hormone disturbance; sleep deprivation.

It is interesting to note that the ASC technique appearing in religious connections cover all five of Ludwig's classes. For example, the pursuit of trance through meditation comes under classes 1 and 4, the mass frenzies brought on by charismatic preachers under class 3. Ludwig places shamanism in the group 'Increase of exteroceptive stimulation and /or motor activity and/ or emotion', but it is clear that the use of hallucinogens he places in class 5 also serves to characterise the shamanic technique of ecstasy (Cf. Harner 1973). It appears from some of the reports of shamanizing that the séance is preceded by a period of concentration, a type of meditation (Jochelson 1926, 205), which is in marked opposition to the strongly motoric behaviour of the séance itself. A study should be made of the types of combinations appearing among forms of shamanism representing different cultures. The most common Siberian hallucinogen, for example — amanita — is not used everywhere (Siikala 1979). In some areas it is among the normal, revered tools of the shaman, in others it marks out the user as belonging to a class of poorer or less skilled shamans. From the reports of séances we can also observe clear regional differences in the motor behaviour of the shaman. Thus Ludwig is right to suggest that the means of ecstasy he classifies may possibly overlap. The technique of ecstasy, especially in its ritual connections, seems to constitute a cumulative process in which factors aiming at the same result but operating at various levels of man's psychophysical mechanism act as mutual reinforcements. These component processes may also come in succession. Sheila S. Walker notes that the initial stages of possession trance may be due to one factor, later stages to a different one (Walker 1972, 12–13). Thus the shamanic séance, like many other enactions of cult, begins as a current given momentum by rhythmic music, dance and song. We may then think of a gradual alteration of consciousness induced by sensory stimulation as opening the way to mechanisms at a psychological level.

Changes in states of consciousness are moulded by many factors: external stimuli, personal expectations and motives, social, cultural and situational demands, even properties connected with the inherited psychophysical make-up of the aspirant. In the most highly patterned connections, even the combination of so many variables leads to individual differences. On the other hand, when studying a phenomenon such as shamanism, where the method of inducing trance is marked by the occurrence of certain common features and whose culturally-bound meaning and social function are, broadly speaking, uniform, we may assume that despite individual variation the basic mechanism of the technique of ecstasy may be delineated. What, then, is the ideal process of the shamanic trance technique? What factors exert particular pressure on the behaviour of the shaman? On the basis of Ludwig's classification we may already conclude that some of these factors have a 'mechanical' influence at the neurophysiological level, whilst others are among more complicated brain functions, i.e. are formed from processes of a psychic nature.

In setting out to discover a basic psychic mechanism for the shaman's technique drawing on a knowledge of Western hypnosis, I wish to emphasize immediately that it is impossible to make an exact equation between these phenomena. Differences in cultural environment, cognitive system and functional context, alone, push them in different directions. Also of great importance is the fact that the Western hypnotic trance does not involve any of the neurophysiological changes discernible by EEG that are most clearly characteristic of shamanic ecstasy.[3] Thus although the shaman's technique of ecstasy does display many factors influencing at a neurophysiological level which do not appear in Western hypnosis—the use of hallucinogens will suffice as one such factor—I consider that the basic psychic process by which the shamanic trance is channelled into a specific form and content is the same as the process of influence in hypnosis.[4]

The induction phase of hypnotic trance has been analysed best by those researchers who have stressed the nature of the phenomenon as goal-oriented striving or social interaction. Mention should be made in this sense, above all, of two theorists with complementary views each illuminating our understanding of the shaman's technique of ecstasy: Ronald E. Shor

[3] See Raymond Prince's list of features indicating neurophysiological changes, Prince 1968, 121.
[4] New studies concerning the active-alert induction of a hypnotic-like ASC support this assumption, see Bányai 1980, Bányai-Hilgard 1976, Bányai–Mészáros–Greguss 1980.

and Theodore Sarbin. Both set out to develop the theories of Robert W. White which stress the importance of motivation as a basic element of hypnotic behaviour and which are crystallized in the following definition: "hypnotic behaviour is meaningful, goal-oriented striving, its most general goal being to behave like a hypnotized person as this is continuously defined by the operator and understood by the subject" (White 1941, 483).

Ronald E. Shor's article "Hypnosis and the concept of the generalized reality-orientation" is significant in the sense that it tries to show how an alteration in consciousness occurs as a result of this goal-orientend striving. He starts from the theory that a normal state of consciousness is characterized by the mobilization of a structured frame of reference behind the attention which supports, interprets and gives meaning to all experience. This frame of reference he calls the usual generalized reality-orientation (Shor 1959, 585). Generalized reality-orientation develops slowly during life and remains a superstructure of consciousness only by means of active mental striving, which in fact is not usually conscious. According to Shor hypnosis is a complex of two fundamental processes. The first is the construction of a special, temporary orientation to a small range of preoccupations and the second is the relative fading of the generalized reality-orientation into non-functional unawareness (Shor 1959). This basic process of the altering of awareness, or actually the two fundamental processes, illustrates the psychich mechanism by which the shaman attains a state of trance. To the shaman preparing for a séance his generalized reality-orientation remains without significance. He directs all his energy towards active performance, by means of which he recalls the other reality to which only he has access, the shamanic world. His special temporary orientation is directed at shamanic knowledge.

Shor himself points out that this basic mechanism of hypnotic trance was in fact described earlier, only with the emphasis on slightly different aspects: "While the concept of new, special orientation is defined from the standpoint of cognition, it is identical with what White has called goal-oriented striving from the standpoint of motivation or what Sarbin has called role-taking from the standpoint of social psychology" (Shor 1959, 598).

The supranormal shamanic world is personified in separate supernatural beings which, being capable of communication, are social beings. Correspondingly the shamanic séance as a forum for communication between this world and the next is a social occasion at which the shaman, as medium, holds reciprocal relationships with both sides. If we assume that the basic psychic mechanism of the shaman's technique of ecstasy is the same as that in Western hypnotic practices or, on an even wider scale, in all trance behavior,[5] Theodore Sarbin's socialpsychological formulation "hypnosis is one form of a more general kind of social psychological behavior known as role-taking" (Sarbin 1950, 255) then provides the analytically most fertile point of departure for studying this mechanism. This view does not contradict the explanation starting from a personality psychology basis, according to which controlled trance phenomena can be explained as regression in the service of the ego.[6] The reason why, in examining shamanism, the social-psychological aspect takes precedence over the personality-psychological is simply that the former provides a better terminological and conceptual frame of reference for the sounding of the social dimensions of an institutionalized phenomenon.[7]

The conditions for controlled ecstatic behaviour

Although social reasons, such as the striving for prestige or material advantage in the case of poor young men, may lead a man to become a shaman (cf. Bogoras 1904–1909, 424), the bulk of the shamans' own personal reports give "the shaman's disease" as the basic stimulus. The story of the wife of Shaman Kyzlasov is typical: "That was how he became a shaman, after the sickness, after the torture. He had been ill for seven years. While he was ailing, he had dreams: he was beaten up several times, sometimes he was taken to strange places" (Diószegi 1960, 58). The symptoms are both mental and physical; there are frequent mentions of pains in the head and the limbs, states of torment, with visions and voices, fits reminiscent of manifestations of hysteria, and so on. The patient turns to shamanizing in order to be healed, and this means is often mentioned as being the last and the only way of attaining equilibrium. Whatever the nature of the psycho-physical disturbances that the symptoms of shaman's so-called sickness refer to, it is clear from the reports that equilibrium can be attained and maintained precisely by shamanizing. Often the shaman's account mentions that neglect of shamanizing causes a return of the sickness. If the shaman's initiatory sickness is equated with hysteria, as is done by many scholars,

---

[5] Cf. the view put forward by van der Walde, based on cross-cultural comparisons, according to which the basic mechanism of hypnotic trance is the same as that in all goal-oriented trance behaviour van der Walde 1968.

[6] On the theory of hypnosis as controlled regression, se Merton M. Gill and Margaret Brenman 1959.

[7] Hjalmar Sundén and Lauri Honko have mapped out the potential of role theory spe-

cifically as an explanation of the psychological prerequisities for the encounter between man and the supranormal (Sundén 1959 and Honko 1972). In his article "Role-taking of the Shaman" (1969) Honko has also discussed the shaman's art of social role-changing. In my earlier publication *"The Rite Technique of the Siberian Shaman"* (1978) I have deliberated these principal ideas and paid special attention to the concept of role-taking. See also Peters–Price–Williams 1980.

the novice stage must be regarded as a therapeutic period during which the initiate, generally under the guidance of an older shaman, learns to order and control his ego-functions by means of ready models within the belief tradition so that a real fit of hysteria during the initiatory stage *becomes* a fit in the control of the ego. No universally accepted conclusions as to the nature of the shaman's initiatory 'sickness' have been made, however, and it is difficult or even impossible to draw any from the wide range of symptoms mentioned in the reports. It is more or less agreed that one feature of the shaman novice is some sort of nervous sensitivity or reactional susceptibility. When we remember, for example, that the future shaman of a clan may be selected for training even as a child, that seeking to become a shaman may be influenced by social reasons and, above all, that even a person with a normal nervous constitution may be means of a suitable technique reach an altered state of consciousness,[8] it is obvious that it is impossible to name any specific nervous disorder qualifying a person as a shaman. The basic qualification for becoming a shaman is control of the technique of ecstasy and the formal study of this technique. People with a certain nervous susceptibility are, however, best suited for this, and people easily roused to hysteria have the best potential. Thus it is often exceptional individuals who seek to become or are sought out as shamans. The long initiatory stage is then preparation for the control of ecstatic behaviour. The shaman must execute faultlessly traditionally-patterned ritual functions before the critical eyes of an audience.

Study centres round ways of using mechanical means of stimulating the nervous system — rhythmical music, singing, dancing and drugs — as best suits each individual, and practice in the psychic mechanism of the technique of ecstasy. The psychic side of the shaman's technique of ecstasy may be regarded as a phenomenon related to Western hypnotic behaviour, in which an altered state of consciousness is attained as a suggestive consequence of dynamic experience. As a result of the shaman's position as a vehicle of communication between this and the other world, this experience takes place by means of role-taking directed at representatives of the spirit world. The assumption of the role of the other is a covert cognitive process which denotes the ability to place oneself symbolically in the place of another.[9] Living the spirit roles, manifesting them to the point of identification does, however, mean that these roles have been learnt.

---

[8] See i.e. Andrew Neher (*A physiological explanation of unusual behavior in ceremonies involving drums,* 1962) and V. J. Walter and W. G. Walter (*The central effects of rhythmic sensory stimulation,* 1949).

[9] On role-taking and the role-concepts of symbolic interactionism, see Mead 1934, Sarbin 1950 and 1954, Turner 1956, Allen-Sarbin 1964, Cooley 1972.

Sarbin and Allen, for example, who observed that role-taking and role-performance concern man's entire psychophysical being, stressed the need for previous experience in a role-taking situation (Sarbin-Allen 1969, 522–523). During his initiation period the novice constructs his supranormal counter-roles in accordance with the models provided by tradition, i.e. he acquires his spirit-helpers. The way in which the young shaman selects elements of the belief tradition in shaping his supranormal helpers is illustrated in the shaman's songs and the visions requiring a deeper assimilation of the tradition. For example, the songs of the Chukchi shaman, based on tradition but moulded into individual shapes, came into being precisely during the novice stage. The content of the songs is to a great extent the shaping of supranormal roles: they describe the regions inhabited by the spirits, the essence of the spirits and their characteristic features, the tasks they are able to carry out, and so on (Siikala 1980, 88–92). The ways of manifesting the spirit roles are also traditional. Shirokogoroff, for example, describes typical modes of behaviour of the Manchu shaman from which the shaman's assistant and those present can recognise the spirit in question (Shirokogoroff 1935, 337). The ecstatic experiences of the initiation period, which shamans have, when interviewed, been able to describe feature by feature, are repeated in the songs sung during séances. There are frequent references for example to the motif of 'the dissecting of the shaman by spirits', i.e. the culmination of the process of becoming a shaman, the 'birth' of the shaman. It is interesting, as appears from the initiatory visions of the Samoyed shaman, that these experiences are completely traditional not only in content but also in form (Siikala 1978, 193–197). In other words the structure of the visions is in the main similar, and the motifs are repeated in the songs sung while shamanizing.

The induction of trance

In public ritual proceedings the technique of ecstasy transferring the shaman to an altered state of consciousness appears as a cumulative process in which elements acting at the physical and mental levels reinforce one another. In addition to a mechanical stimulus (rhythmic music in the case of Siberian shamans), the following suggestive factors affect the change in consciousness: a) the motivation of the shaman, which may be social (there is an acute need for the séance) and recognised or may lie in the realm of unrecognised personal hopes and wishes, b) study by the shaman of matters representing the supranormal, c) the actively expressed concentration of the attention, hopes and wishes of the audience on the shaman and d) a strong emotional pressure that is the sum of all these elements. It is characteristic of the course of the séance that these factors influence the séance in different ways at different stages, and the degree of change in the shaman's consciousness likewise varies. I shall here attempt to outline the basic features of the shamanic technique of trance and to distinguish the factors shaping the shaman's ecstatic behaviour.

The preparation for the séance is the stage at which ties with the ordinary waking state, the normal world, are broken. The séance may be preceded by a period of fasting or contemplation. Whether the period of concentration is long or short, it includes the assembly of requisites and the donning of the shaman's dress, these representing the concrete transition to the faculty of shaman. The dress, on which are depicted the shaman's supranormal assistants or other objects necessary for moving about in the spirit world, in itself helps to focus the shaman's thoughts. All measures taken during the preparatory stage—the tuning of the drum, the removal of any icons, which were already relatively common by the end of the 19th century, the extinguishing of the fire, the making of idols, the excitement and hushed expectation of those present—generate favourable emotional charges in those present and above all help the shaman to concentrate on his coming task as shaman and on the supranormal helpers required in the task.

The induction proper of trance, the stage at which the shaman attains an altered state of consciousness, is, according to shamanic theory, the period of assembling the spirit-helpers. Practices are surprisingly similar throughout Northern and Central Asia. The chief principle may be described as follows: *connected with the rhythmical, sensory stimulus slowly gaining momentum and directly influencing the central nervous system is the gradual actualisation of the supranormal counter-roles and a slowly intensified assumption of supranormal roles in conjunction with the sensory stimulus*. It has been experimentally proved that rhythmical stimulus alone is sufficient to bring about changes in the electrical activity of the brains of people with normal nerves and, according to the reports of the test subjects, it also produces unusual observations (Neher 1962). The shaman's drumming technique is by and large uniform over the whole area: a slow, soft initial phase is followed by an increase in tempo and volume. The effect of the rhythmical stimulus is in some areas fortified by various intoxicants, such as amanita, and in latter times in particular strong tobacco and alcohol. The use of hallucinogens and other such intoxicants is not, however, a vital element of trance technique in any part of Siberia. The mechanical stimuli mentioned thus form a necessary basis for the shaman's trance behaviour. Shamanic practice does, however, differ from other means of attaining ecstasy with its emphasis on the ritual role-taking technique aimed at the supranormal counter-roles, the "spirit-helpers". The shaman's generalized reality orientation is cut off by means of suitable ritual requisites, the extinguishing of the lights and the noise of intensified drumming. Its place is taken by special orientation, a world created by the shamanic tradition, fantasies of supranormal beings and their dwelling places. The shaman actualises one spirit role after another according to a set pattern. Very often (e.g. in the shaman's songs of the Khants (Karjalainen 1918, 558–591), the Nentsy (Lehtisalo 1947, 493–496), and the Chukchi (Findeisen 1956, 141–156)) the shaman, in calling on his spirits, almost as it were brings them concretely near him. The objects described in the song are firstly the figure of the spirit and its dwelling in the other world, then the spirit's journey to the shaman stage by stage, reaching its climax with the arrival at the séance. The course of the account of the journey described in an invocatory song such as this coincides with the curve representing the rise in ecstatic frenzy on the part of the shaman, i.e. during the songs the shaman reaches an altered state of consciousness. The invocation of the spirit-helpers during the induction of the trance may be manifested more simply. The imitation of the sounds of the spirit-helpers, constituting the first act of the most common séance, is one of the most established elements of the séance. More precisely, this is the imitation of the sound of spirits imagined to be in animal form, and this acts almost without exception in the function of a call. Corresponding growling, whistling and other sounds are also encountered later in the séance, but then it is a question of manifesting the spirit roles present. Simple shouts of invocation or request to the spirits for help fall in between the songs, dividing them up into shorter entities. Note that the nature and scope of the invocatory songs seems to correlate with the modes of manifesting the spirit roles. Instead of a long description of the spirit world there may simply be a statement of the reason for the séance and request for help (cf. Orochi séances, Lopatin 1946–1949, 365–368). In such cases improvisation plays a relatively large part in contrast, for example, to the long poetic song episodes of the Nentsy (Lehtisalo 1947).

The audience plays a relatively small part at the trance induction stage. It chiefly concentrates on supporting the shaman through invocations or urgings addressed to the spirits. Many observers mention a growing expectation, which is a feature characteristic of the opening stages of the séance. The part played by the audience is probably greater at this stage as an emotional factor. The shaman feels the weight of expectation as he concentrates on his performance.

Variations in the presentation of spirits

Meetings with the spirit-helpers, either in this world or the other, constitute the ecstatic climaxes of the séance. As the shaman manifests his supranormal counter-roles his consciousness has already clearly altered. This degree of alteration is not, however, the same in different séances, nor does it remain constant within the course of one séance. The depth of the shaman's trance varies in the different stages of the séance, and he may from time to time rest in order to seek ecstasy again. In addition to individual differences arising from ecstatic ability the depth of the trance also seems to be regulated by traditionally bound factors. Comparison of the descriptions of séances shows that the supranormal counter-roles are manifested by means of a few alternative techniques. These are: a) the shaman identifies completely with the spirit role, he is regarded as having changed quite concretely into a spirit (role-identification); b) manifesting both his own role as a shaman and that of the spirit, the shaman creates a dialogue situation in which the spirit is regarded as acting and speaking from outside the physical being of the shaman (dual role); c) the shaman creates an image of the role performances of his spirit-helpers purely verbally, in which case only the shaman is regarded as "seeing" or "hearing" the spirits during the séance (description of counter-role).

Complete role-identification, which is common in Central and Eastern Siberia (among e.g. the Yukagir (Jochelson 1926, 196–199), Evenks (Anisimov 1963, 100–105), Yakuts (Hudjakov 1969, 311–355), Manchu (Shirokogoroff 1935, 308–309, 313–314), Nanay (Lopatin 1960, 169–172) and Orochi (Lopatin 1946–1949, 365–368) signifies possession. One or more spirit-helpers is thought to enter the body of the shaman and to speak and act through him. Jochelson's description of the changing of a Yukagir shaman into a spirit is highly characteristic: "The shaman half-opens the door and inhales his spirits in deep and noisy breaths. Then he turns to the interior of the house, holds his hands like claws, rolls his eyes upwards, so that only the whites are seen, sticks out his tongue, curling it under the chin and, without uttering a word, walks to the centre of the house and sits down on the ground. Having sat down, he straightens his hands and pulls his tongue in with his eyes still turned upwards and a blown up belly he sits there and already one of the spirits speaks through him" (Jochelson 1926, 201). Features that recur are a) the arrival of the spirit at the door, b) the inhaling of the spirits and c) the expression of the spirit's nature in words, mimicry and movement: a Manchu shaman, transformed into a wolf, claws the ground like a wolf (Shirokogoroff 1935, 337) and an Orochi shaman transformed into a bird leaps across the tent shouting, "I fly, I fly" (Lopatin 1946–1949). As regards the role relations of the séance, the shaman's complete identification with one of his supranormal counter-roles means that the position of the shaman as a *mediator* between the two worlds remains, as it were, unfilled. Role-identification is regularly followed by the someone present at the séance, usually the assistant, taking over as mediator. A dialogue then ensues between the mediator, which may sometimes be the entire audience present at the séance, and the spirit, in which the reasons for the crisis leading to the séance and the chances of eliminating them are discussed. The shaman's identification with a spirit role is often momentary, it comes at different stages in the séance and is susceptible to disturbances. In the course of one séance the shaman may identify with several spirits.

It is worth noting that the area in which role-indentification occurs largely coincides with the areas in which the spirit of the ancestral shaman plays a major role as the initiator of the novice shaman. In these areas, the spirit of the ancestral shaman may also remain as the shaman's chief spirit. In this case the spirit of the ancestral shaman enters the shaman at the séance and speaks through him. This points to the possibility that identification with the spirit role, i.e. the possession-type séance, is linked precisely with the development of family-bound and ultimately clan shamanism. In parts of Central and East Siberia the typical explanation for illness is that a disease spirit has entered the patient's body. During a séance the Yukagir shaman identifies with the roles of both his chief spirit and the disease spirit alternately (Jochelson 1926, 201–205). Both forms of possession are basically similar — the spirit is inhaled with noisy gasps, it speaks through the mouth of the shaman, who manifests it with his whole being. The spirit is deactualized by being blown out. Only the characteristic features of the spirits are manifested in different ways. Since shamanic séances are for the most part precisely healing events, it is scarcely a coincidence that basically parallel spirit and demon possessions appear in the same regions. Thus the explanation for illness "the demon has penetrated the patient" would in turn add to the popularity of the possession-type technique of shamanizing. On the other hand, the possession-type of séance is not the only form of séance found in these areas and the shaman's journey-type also appears. Among the Evenks, for example, there were further séances in which the shaman met the spirits in this world, i.e. in the tent, and also travelled to the upper and lower worlds in their company (Anisimov 1968, 207 ff). As a result the shaman might well manifest the roles of the spirit-helpers in different ways during the course of one séance: identifying with the spirit role or in some other way manifesting its presence, and describing its behaviour in words only.

The shaman might also manifest spirit roles without identifying with them completely, and create an illusion of communication between several spirit figures appearing simultaneously. In the background is the idea of the meeting of shaman and spirit in such a way that the spirit or spirits remain all the time outside the shaman's body. This dual role of the shaman does not require any active contribution from an assistant or from the audience to carry the séance through; the shaman creates the whole performance before them. As regards the manifestation of spirit roles, the ventriloquism produced, for example, by the Chukchi shaman is brilliantly skilful and the séance takes on the form of a great show in which the shaman brings in one spirit after another (Findeisen 1956, 159–167). 'Dual role' is in this case an inadequate expression, for the shaman sometimes tries to create the illusion of the simultaneous presence of several spirits. As well as in Northeast Asia, the shaman's dual role is a typical means of manifesting supranormal counter-roles in the western parts of Siberia, although the technique of manifestation is more reminiscent of the possession-type than the ventriloquism-type: by his sounds and movements the shaman indicates that a spirit is present. The shaman's songs also contain imitations of the sounds of animals, i.e. zoomorphic spirits. Displays of this type are sometimes difficult to distinguish from those of the possession type.   According to Munkácsi, for example, the possession tradition might be found among the Khants, whereas Karjalainen, on the basis of his own subsequent experiences, puts this claim open to doubt (Karjalainen 1918, 593). The typical dual role situation of the west is found in the shamanizing séance of the Minusa Tatars (Lankenau 1872, 281–283). It is the specific duty of the assistant to sprinkle water for the spirtis to drink so that they do not come too close to the shaman. Even so the shaman, by imitating the sounds, for example, of a zoomorphic spirit, indicates that it is present, and creates the direct illusion of a conversation between the shaman and the spirit.

Describing the supranormal counter-roles in songs is a common element of the invocation of the spirits. In many cases the course of the entire séance is expressed through song. The shaman meets the spirits in either this or the other world, describing his meeting and his conversations in the songs. It is sometimes difficult to draw a line with the former mode of behaviour, and the presentation of the spirit roles purely by description is also more common in the northern and western parts of Siberia than in the central and eastern regions. Particularly the rich song tradition of the Samoyeds, with its visionary themes, is suitable for carrying out séances of this type (Lehtisalo 1924, 152–155). It is natural that at séances in which the shaman's soul is thought to depart for the supranormal world these experiences are described in the songsections. In this case the outward journey, for example, may be described in song, the arrival there is marked by loss of consciousness, and the return journey again in song. The séance basis typical of the northern regions, performed by means of visionary songs, is always the jorney of the shaman's soul. The special nature of this type of séance is revealed when contrasted with the ways of manifesting the shaman's journey employed by e.g. the Evenks and the Nanays. If it was an important and difficult undertaking they might become great shows the setting for which—the objects laid out, the shamanizing site, etc.—was prepared beforehand. The shaman manifested the stages of his journey and the counter-roles he met on the way both through frenzied movement and singing, and also through mimicry. The number of people attending big séances such as this, typical of clan shamanism, was sometimes so great that similar events would have been impossible among the small hunting communities of the north.

Role-taking and control of the degree of altered consciousness

The ways of manifesting supranormal counter-roles in the shamanic séance thus vary from total involvement by the shaman in living out the role to a mere outlining of the counter-role. We noticed that role-identification, the playing of a dual role or verbal description of a counter-role are, on the one hand, typical behaviour models bound to tradition, but that on the other hand the intensity with which the shaman lives a counter-role varies even in the course of a single séance. The latter point means that the depth of the trance varies according to the course of the séance. The variations in intensity are understandable when we remember that 1) the role relationship of the séance is in fact made up of a triad, for in addition to the shaman and the supranormal role figures he creates there must always be a third party at the séance: the audience, and that 2) the séance always has a goal, something the shaman bears in mind during his actions. As a result, the shaman always has two sorts of other-roles, radically differing in nature, in operation at the séance. For the séance to be duly conducted he must direct his role-taking at the representative or representatives of either group according to need, i.e. during the séance the target groups for the shaman's role-taking change. Then it must be noted that in directing his role-taking at one other-group, the illusory spirit roles, the shaman to a greater or lesser extent keeps an eye on the reactions of the second other-group, the representatives of the community present. Since the supranormal counter-roles act primarily as the objects of reincarnation and identification for the shaman, this other group might be called the *identification* group. Correspondingly the "clients" taking part in the séance, neighbours or relations who guide the shaman's behaviour by their wishes and reactions, are called the *audience* group. The role adopted by the shaman with regard to the supranormal is therefore dictated by the extent to which he follows the reactions of the audience group or factors connected with the traditional execution of the séance. Alternative forms of role-taking may thus be examined from the standpoint of role-taking or its reflexiveness.[10] The latter refers to the shaman's self-consciousness—his awareness of how he appears in the eyes of others—and is characteristic precisely of role-taking directed at the audience. Role-taking directed at the audience does not include identification, either; its starting point is selective consideration of the hopes of the audience and the correct execution of the rite. In the light of the above criteria the chief types of 'shaman—supranormal' relations would appear to be as follows:

'Shaman—supranormal' relation

	A. Dual role	B. Role-identification	C. Verbal construction of role
Reflexiveness of role-taking:	Reflexive	Reflexive and non-reflexive	Non-reflexive
Role-taking standpoint:	The audience	The spirit role (and the audience)	The shaman (his previous vision experiences)
Depth of trance:	Light trance	Depth of trance varies—comes in waves	Trance deep, most often ends in loss of consciousness

The shaman's role-taking with regard to the supranormal, not merely a cognitive process at the séance, but finding an outlet through this process in active operation, the manifestation of roles, thus varies in intensity, influencing the degree of change in the shaman's consciousness. In this respect type A is in a different position to types B and C. Keeping an eye on the reactions of the audience requires a stronger link with waking reality (A) than complete identification with the spirit role (B). In the latter case, the responsibility for directing the rite is in fact transferred to the assistant, whose job is also to help the shaman, where necessary, return from too deep a trance. Séances in which the construction of supranormal roles takes place at a verbal level (C), i.e. in the shaman's songs, permit in turn the

---

[10] See Ralph H. Turner's article "Role-taking, role-standpoint, and reference-group behavior", 1956.

greatest concentration on supranormal reality. To use Shor's concepts (see p. 108), the direction of the shaman's generalized reality orientation is replaced by complete special temporary orientation. Séances of this type very often end in complete loss of consciousness; all in all, the curve showing the shaman's ecstatic frenzy is simpler — often consisting of a rise, climax and fall — than in séances in which the shaman must be constantly aware of the audience's reactions, or where identification and audience groups change repeatedly as the objects of the shaman's role-taking. In this case, the curve showing the shaman's ecstasy is wave-like, with several climaxes. Although the part played by the audience as a suggestive factor can under no circumstances be denied — on the contrary, it does exert some sort of basic pressure on the shaman's quest for ecstasy and also provides active support for the shaman during the séance — it is nevertheless clear from the accounts of séances that when the roletaking is directed at the audience the degree of the shaman's altered consciousness falls just as it rises when role-taking is directed at the supranormal world.

The relationship between the shaman and the audience attending the séance, which influences ecstatic activity, is determined according to the position of the shaman and shamanism in the community. It is interesting to note that among the Chukchi Type A (dual role) manifestation of the supranormal based on ventriloquist skill was held in greater esteem than type C (verbal construction of role), typical of small group shamanism in northern Siberia and connected with the shaman's journey. The former type of séance, in which the shaman was able to observe the audience's reactions throughout the performance, is in fact more suited to the independent professional shaman seeking the favour of the audience than is the latter form. The Chukchi's manner of bringing in the spirit roles, which demanded great skill, and the great show-like shaman events of the southern regions have been mistakenly regarded as indications of the degeneration of shamanism merely because there was seldom a loss-of-consciousness stage. In the case of rite performances involving a wealth of requisites and many episodes, it is rather a question of more developed forms of tradition, reflecting the importance and scope of the shaman in the community rather than a degeneration in the shaman's ecstatic ability.

References

Allen, V. L.–Sarbin, T. 1964. Role enactment, audience feedback, and attitude change. *Sociometry* 27.

Anisimov, A. F. 1963. The shaman's tent of the Evenks and the origin of the shamanistic rite. *Studies in Siberian shamanism,* ed. by H. N. Michael. (Arctic Institute of North America. Translations from Russian sources 4.) Toronto.

— 1958. *Religija evenkov*. Moskva–Leningrad.

Bányai, E. I. 1980. *A new way to induce a hypnotic-like altered state of consciousness: active-alert induction*. Problems of the regulation of activity (4th meeting of psychologists from the Danubian countries). Budapest.

Bányai, E. I.–Hilgard, E. R. 1976. A comparison of active-alert hypnotic induction with traditional relaxation induction. *Journal of abnormal psychology* 85. Stanford, Cal.

Bányai, E. I., Mészáros, I.–Greguss, A. C. 1980. Alteration of activity level: the essence of hypnosis or a byproduct of the type of induction? *28th International congress of physiological Sciences*. Budapest.

Bogoras, W. 1904–1909. The Chukchee. *The Jesup North Pacific Expedition*, ed. by F. Boas. (Memoir of the American Museum of Natural History 7.) Leiden, New York.

Cooley, C. H. 1972. Looking-glass self. *Symbolic interaction, a reader in social psychology*, ed. by J. G. Manis and B. N. Melzer. Boston.

Diószegi, V. 1960. *Tracing shamans in Siberia*. Oosterhout.

Findeisen, H. 1956. W. G. Bogoras' Schilderung zweier schamanischer Séancen der Küsten-Tschuktschen (Nordost-Sibirien). *Abhandlungen und Aufsätze aus dem Institut für Menschen- und Menschheitskunde* 38. Augsburg.

Fischer, R. 1969. The perception-hallucination continuum (a re-examination). *Diseases of the nervous system* 30.

— 1970. Prediction and measurement of perceptual-behavioral change in drug-induced hallucinations. *Origin and mechanism of hallucinations*, ed. by W. Keup. New York.

Gill, M. M.–Brenman, M. 1959. *Hypnosis and related states: psychoanalytic studies in regression*. New York.

Harner, M. J. 1973. *Hallucinogens and shamanism*. London, Oxford and New York.

Honko, L. 1969. Role-taking of the shaman. *Temenos* 4.

— 1972. Rooliteorian soveltamisesta uskontotieteessä. L. Honko, *Uskontotieteen näkökulmia*. Helsinki.

Hudjakov, I. A. 1969. *Kratkoe opisanie Verhojanskogo okruga*. Pod red. V. G. Bazanova. Leningrad.

Jochelson, W. 1926. The Yukaghir and the Yukaghirized Tungus. *The Jesup North Pacific Expedition*, ed. by F. Boas. (Memoir of the American Museum of Natural History 9.) New York.

Karjalainen, K. F. 1918. *Jugralaisten uskonto*. Porvoo.

Lankenau, H. v. 1872. Die Schamanen und das Schamanenwesen. *Globus* 22.

Lehtisalo, T. 1924. Entwurf einer Mythologie der Jurak-samojeden. *Mémoires de la Société Finno-ougrienne* 53. Helsinki.

— 1947. Juraksamojedische Volksdichtung. *Mémoires de la Société Finno-ougrienne* 90. Helsinki.

Lopatin, I. A. 1946–1949. A shamanistic performance for a sick boy. *Anthropos* 41–44.

— 1960. *The cult of the dead among the natives of the Amur Basin*. (Central Asiatic Studies 6.) 's-Gravenhage.

Ludwig, A. M. 1968. Altered states of consciousness. *Trance and possession states*, ed. R. Prince. Montreal.

Mead, G. H. 1934. *Mind, self and society*. Chicago.

Neher, A. 1962. A physiological explanation of unusual behavior in ceremonies involving drums. *Human biology* 34.

Peters, L. G.–Price–Williams, D. 1980. Towards an experiential analysis of shamanism. *American ethnologist* 7.

Prince, R. 1968. Can the EEG be used in the study of possession states? *Trance and possession states,* ed. R. Prince. Montreal.

Sarbin, T. 1950. Contributions to role-taking theory: 1. Hypnotic behavior. *Psychological review* 57.

— 1954. Role theory. *Handbook of social psychology,* ed. G. Lindzey and E. Aronson 1. Cambridge, Mass.

Shirokogoroff, S. M. 1935. *Psychomental complex of the Tungus.* London.

Shor, R. E. 1959. Hypnosis and the concept of the generalized reality-orientation. *American journal of psychotherapy* 13.

Siikala, A.-L. 1978. *The rite technique of the Siberian shaman.* (FF Communications 220.) Helsinki.

— 1979. Kärpässienen rituaalinen käyttö pohjoisessa Euraasiassa. *Alkoholipolitiikka* 44.

— 1980. Two types of shamanizing and categories of shamanistic songs. A Chukchi case. *Genre, structure and reproduction in oral literature,* eds. L. Honko and V. Voigt. Budapest.

Strunk, O. 1962. *Religion. A psychological interpretation.* New York, Nashville.

Sundén, H. 1959. *Religionen och rollerna. Ett psykologiskt studium av fromheten.* Stockholm.

Turner, R. H. 1956. Role-taking, role standpoint, and reference-group behavior. *American journal of sociology* 61.

van der Walde, P. H. 1968. Trance states and ego psychology. *Trance and possession states,* ed. R. Prince. Montreal.

Walker, S. S. 1972. *Ceremonial spirit possession in Africa and Afro-America.* Leiden.

Walter, V. J.–Walter, W. G. 1949. The central effects of rhythmic sensory stimulation. *Electroencephalography and clinical neurophysiology* 1.

White, R. M. 1941. A preface to the theory of hypnotism. *Journal of abnormal and social psychology* 36.

The *Noajdie* and his Ecstasy—A Contribution to the Discussion

By LOUISE BÄCKMAN

It is obvious that the trance state of the *noajdie* (the Saami shaman) and his supposed abilities to discover hidden and unknown things have fascinated the neighbours of the Saamis ever since the first contacts were established. The view of the Saamis as *the* wizards (trollkarlar) has been dominant in the history of the Saamis from time immemorial right up to the present day, a history that has been written for example by the Scandinavians. From the Viking sagas (Strömbäck 1935, 184, for example), we know that a *noajdie* had an aura of sorcery, and that the "Finns", meaning the Saamis[1] were in general looked upon as skilled in the arts of magic. In the historical sources, as well as in the archives, there are also documents from the time of the colonization of the Saami area, in which amazement at, and dread of, Saami sorcery is profoundly expressed by the intruders.

During the course of history, there developed tales varying in content about the strange culture of the Saamis, and it is evident that their concepts of belief were very difficult to understand and thus repulsive (Campbell 1954 and Tillhagen 1969 for example).[2] In these tales, the *noajdie* appears as a very frightening man, and he himself willingly adds fuel to this fear, as he feels the power he possesses to terrify individuals.

From their own traditional beliefs (Lid 1950), the Scandinavians (cited here as an example) saw the behaviour of the *noajdie* merely as general "trolldom" (sorcery), in which different elements were included, such as *hamnskifte* (changing of shape), sending of *gand* (magic projectiles), singing of *galdrar* (magic spells), and predicting the future etc., all elements famil-

---

[1] There has been discussion as to whether "Finne" in the Saga literature really describes an ethnic grouping or whether it serves to denote the "mountain-inhabitants" and "finders" (finnare) in general, i.e. a people of undefined genesis who found their livelihood in the mountain-regions, an area which was looked upon as a very inhospitable place by the people living in the plains (Koht 1923, 161 and Kválen 1925, 44). According to Collinder "Finne" in historical accounts means "Saami" (Collinder 1953). "Finne" in the Norwegian language today means "Saami".

[2] See also Bäckman 1978 where another theme of "ethnocentric legends" is discussed.

iar to the Scandinavians, which is partly proved by the vocabulary in the sources. But sorcery, at least the "black kind", was a negative factor in the community (the early medieval Church condemned it very strongly), and the Scandinavians externalized their own beliefs on to the Saamis and accused them of being masters of the magic arts.

Concerning the Saamis themselves, the *noajdie* was regarded as *the* soothsayer and diviner, but above all he was associated with what was looked upon as *passe*, (*bissie* in Southern Saamian), the sphere of the spirits and the gods, the *sacred* one might say. He was the true mediator between man and the supernatural powers on which man was dependent. Like his colleague in Siberia, the *noajdie* was the talented one, who learned and taught the mythological traditions and functioned as the "mytho-poet", that is he renewed the religious traditions by means of his poetic talents. He was an ordinary member of his group, but when needed, he acted on behalf of his groupmembers. By means of his knowledge and by the technique he had acquired—thanks to a long apprenticeship—he was able to fall into a trance and of his own volition direct his "free-soul" wherever it was necessary—to the *passeworld*, or elsewhere. He was a *guovdi ilmmi vázzi*, a wanderer in two worlds,[3] and thus he lived up to the expectations of the members of his own community and fulfilled the religious tradition.

In Saami popular tradition, the memory of the *noajdie* and his extraordinary skill is still alive, but he has lost his religious function and become a diviner or a wizard, or a juggler, almost in accordance with the view of the Scandinavians. There are numerous tales of his fantastic abilities as a wizard, told by the Saamis as well by their neighbours. The tales vary, however, depending on the cultural milieu where they develop; in non-Saami popular belief, the *free-soul* or *alter ego* of the *noajdie* is often said to materialize in front of the onlooker and is then able to perform real deeds while the noajdie himself is lying in a trance far away. Arbman has given a true instance of such an event (Arbman 1955, 49–52): a judge and his driver were caught in a snow-drift with their sledge, but they were helped by an old »spålapp» (Saami-wiseman) who turned up and thereafter immediately disappeared without saying a word. On reaching their destination, the two men, to their astonishment, met the old Lapp again. The explanation was that the old man concerned had entered into a trance and sent away his "free-soul/alter ego" to find out the reason for the delay of the judge and his companion.

Another motif in the tales of "spålappar" in Nordic tradition is that the

---

[3] From Professor Israel Ruong.

noajdie is able to demonstrate his spiritual visit to a far distant place by means of an object which is wellknown to his client. Or, furthermore, his "visit" is certified later on by a trustworthy person who had seen his materialized "alter ego" at the place concerned. Let us return to Arbman again: a Norwegian soldier on a mission in Denmark was anxious to know of his wife's safe delivery of a child. "With the help of the bottle" an old Lapp "sitting by the tiled-stove" was induced to find out what had happened to the soldier's wife and the expected child. The Lapp sat down as if lost in thought. His head soon dropped down and after a while he seemed to be "stone-dead". He woke up, however, after an hour, saying that everything was in order at home. As proof of his "visit" to the soldier's home in Norway, he took out two silver-spoons that belonged to the soldier's family (Arbman 1955, 54–55).

The following is a variant of the motif: A Lapp, Lördal by name, offered to prove his "magic art" to the Archbishop of Uppsala who was visiting his home in Lappland. Lördal burnt some herbaceous plants, inhaled the smoke and seemed to "pass away". After an hour he woke up and told the Archbishop that his wife was working in the kitchen, and he gave a detailed and exact description of the room. As evidence of his "visit" to Uppsala, he said that he had hidden the wife's wedding-ring in the coal-box. The Archbishop's wife confirmed his "visit" in a letter later on and the ring was found in the coal-box, as the man had said (Arbman 1955, 52–54).

In Saami folk tradition one can seldom, if ever, find such motifs as those mentioned above. There are a great many tales of the *noajdie* and his ability to perform fantastic acts, such as knowing about conditions in other places, but it is never said that his "alter ego" could turn up in distant places far away from his body in a trance. It is also seldom or never said that he had to prove his "visit" with an object of some kind; one saw and heard the result of his "journey" and took it for granted. Instead, it is stated that a *noajdie* has "capabilities" beyond the intellect of ordinary human beings and that this is due to help from supernatural "powers". These "powers" are incomprehensible but real; they are the "givers of knowledge and skills", and once they have chosen their man, he has to obey.

As an example of Saami tradition regarding a *noajdie's* powerful skill and its results, we will cite a tale from Swedish Southern Lapland. It was related at the beginning of the 20th century by an old Saami who had memorized an episode from his childhood. We will repeat only the substance of his account here and leave aside the details: Madter-Trorie, a respected *noajdie,* was once able to drive home a herd of reindeer-cows and calves from a distance by manipulating his drum while singing a *jojk*. Unfortunately, the narrator, who was then just a little boy, was unable to understand the words of the song. After some initial preparations at the site of his *kota* (hut), we are told, the old Madter-Trorie beat his drum and performed his *jojk*. Very soon, to the boy's astonishment, the cows and calves come running to the hut, behaving as if they were haunted by some monstrous thing. The boy and Madter-Trorie were then able to milk the cows and remove the sticks which had been bound over the tongues of the calves, in order to stop them from sucking the cows.

The *noajdie* of former days, my informant told me, had "powers" that we know nothing of today, because they took their secrets with them. Madter-Trorie had, according to him, asked his "powers" or "spirits" for help, but he did not know the nature of these "powers/spirits"; they belonged, however, to "the other world". To my question about »a *noajdie* sending out his alter ego or free-soul, which could be visible to the onlookers» my man answered that he had never heard of that kind of skill. A *dead noajdie* could show himself to a living person, he knew for sure, but not a *noajdie* in a trance; he used his "helpers from the other world". In my opinion, my informant's statement is characteristic of all the tales of *noajdies* among the Saamis. (My informant was Jonas Israelsson 1887–1974.)

Saami shamanism coincides with that of the North-Eurasian type, though there are variations of expression, for instance in the behaviour of the shaman in the séance. The fundamental elements are, however, in agreement, such as the invocation of the helping spirits at the beginning of the séance, the shaman's ritual movements, the rhythmical sound caused by the drum or, as amongst the Saamis, by other clatter »instruments» as well, the shaman's state of trance, and the cooperation of the audience. We are familiar enough with the external happenings at a *noajdie's* séance where ecstasy is of importance, but we know nothing of what was really happening in the trance. According to the religious tradition the *noajdie* was led to the world of the spirits or gods—to the *passe* world—by his supernatural helping-spirits and, above all, to the realm of the dead according to our early sources. His personal experience of the trance is, however, concealed; the informants did not reveal these kinds of secrets to the chroniclers. However, there is an attempt to describe a *noajdie's* experience in a so called "soul-journey" in our older sources. A writer from the 17th century, Lundius by name and Saami by origin, narrates: When a *noajdie* was returning from the 'nether world', the 'spirit of divination' (spådoms-anda) led the 'man's spirit' (lappens anda) in great haste through mountains and across valleys so that stones and sand whirled about like rain and hail ... (Lundius 1905, 7). This is the only record of an "inner experience" we can find in our older sources, and later popular tradition contains just as

few accounts of this matter. An old Saami has, however, given us a hint of a
"soul-journey", in this case a journey to the realm of the dead, and we will
use the story as an illustration of a *noajdie*'s speculation on this question.
Lars Pirak, a Saami artist and author, has recalled a *subtsasav,* a story, that
he heard as a boy. The story is related to a descendant of a *noajdie* and it
describes a journey to the realm of the dead. When a person dies, it says,
his "soul" will dive into a hole behind the *boassjoe*—in former days this
meant the *holy* area of a *kota*—and fly away like a bird through a long
corridor in the inner parts of the earth. It will be necessary to take food, for
the journey will last a long time. During the voyage the "soul" will be
surrounded by deep darkness and a terrible noise. At the end of the corridor
he will see a luminous point like a star to which he will come closer and
closer, and, when he reaches it he will be enclosed in a hot and colourful
illumination, and the heat will be almost unbearable. He will see his own
body lying on the earth in the distance, for now he will be flying through
space at a tremendous speed over mountains and over vast, green areas. All
the time he will be surrounded by colours like those of the rainbow, and in
his hair there will be sparkling stars. After his flight through space he will
reach a long beach with sand, and the surrounding area will be covered with
green grass and yellow flowers in abundance. Then he will know that he has
arrived in the realm of the dead—he has reached the home of his ancestors
(Lars Pirak 1932—. His story will be published in full.)

There is a common pattern in the conception of sorcery held by the
peoples of Northern Scandinavia: they all believed that there were persons
who were able to influence their surroundings by supernatural knowledge:
"to use trolldom" (with all its connotations) in the Scandinavian language,
but "to get into contact with the helping spirits of the *passe* world" in the
Saami language, by my own interpretation. There was also a common belief
in the conception of the soul: one's soul could leave one's body and be
materialized in an animal and then function as one's alter ego and guardian
spirit. In the Scandinavian tradition a person who was skilled in *hamnskifte*
(change of shape) was able to influence another person in his "soul-animal-
shape" (Ström 1967, 206), but in my opinion we do not find this conception
among the Saamis, where a *noajdie*'s knowledge and skill depended on his
helping-spirit from the *passe* world. Maybe we can say that the difference
was on the cultic level.

The history of the Saamis has been written by people other than the
Saamis themselves, and their customs, both religious and secular, have
mostly been described from a foreign point of view in our older sources.
Thus the trance-state of a *noajdie* was sometimes believed to be *hamnskifte*
in accordance with the tradition of, for instance, *fylgja* as a human-

(woman-)shaped being.[4] The chroniclers are, so to speak, limited by their own frames of reference and the "legends" that were created about the Saamis were formed from their own point of view.

References

Arbman, E. 1955. Shamanen, extatisk andebesvärjare och visionär. *Primitiv religion och magi,* ed. by Å. Hultkrantz. Stockholm.

Bäckman, L. 1978. The dead as helpers? Conceptions of death amongst the Saamit (Lapps). *Temenos* 14. Helsinki.

Campbell, Å. 1954. Om lapparna i svensk folktradition och etnocentrism. Utkast till ett forskningsprogram. *Scandinavica et Fenno-Ugrica. Studier tillägnade Björn Collinder den 22 juli 1954.* Stockholm.

Collinder, B. 1953. *Lapparna.* Stockholm.

Koht, H. 1923. Var "finnane" alltid finnar? *Maal og Minne.* Kristiania.

Kvålen, E. 1925. Kva meinast det med finnar i gamalnorsk litteratur? *Maal og Minne.* Oslo.

Lid, N. 1950. Trolldom. *Nordiske Studiar.* Oslo.

Lundius, N. 1905. Nicolai Lundii Lappi descriptio Lapponiae. *Svenska Landsmål 17, 5.* Uppsala.

Ström, F. 1967. *Nordisk hedendom.* Lund.

Strömbäck, D. 1935. *Sejd.* Lund.

Tillhagen, C.-H. 1969. Finnen und Lappen als zauberkundige in der skandinavischen Volksüberlieferung. *Kontakte und Grenzen. Festschrift für Gerhard Heilfurth zum 60. Geburtstag.* Hrsg von seinen Mitarbeitern. Göttingen.

---

[4] The Scandinavians believed that a man's *inner ego, his soul,* named *hugr,* could free itself from the human body, for instance in dreams, and be materialized in an animal. This transformation was called *hamnskifte* (change of shape) and this "soul-animal" was named *fylgja.* Among Saami traditional beliefs we find the same thing: a man's soul freed itself from its human covering and manifested itself in an animal, a bird above all. These "soul-animals" functioned as an alter ego and a guardian spirit in both cases. The Scandinavians believed, however, that *fylgja* sometimes turned into a woman-shaped being, but, in my opinion, this idea was foreign to the Saamis. Furthermore, in his "soul-animal-shape" a person could do evil or good to another person, according to the Scandinavians, while a *noajdie* had to obtain help from the "other world», where his helping-spirits lived.

The Professional Ecstatic in His Social and Ritual Position

By BIRGITTE SONNE

The title of this paper will need some elucidation below. Its aim is to delimit the social status of the professional ecstatic, by means of a series of mostly sociological criteria. These, then, are tested on historical material, the sources of the traditional cultures of the Eskimos.

Definitions

The professional ecstatic is according to my definition: a religious specialist, who has become recognized as a person able to carry out an ecstatic ritual, corresponding with the local cultural expectations in force. The ecstatic ritual per se comprises a number of persons, i.e. it is a collective ritual. It consists of a regular sequence of acts entailing the entry of the recognized specialist, the professional ecstatic, into one of the dissociated psychic states under the common denomination of ecstasy (I shall not go into the physio-psychology of these states and their attending perceptions). A possible effect of the collective ecstatic ritual is that the other participants also enter into a state of ecstasy, but by definition only the professional himself is required to do so. Thus the definition does not cover ecstatic rituals intended to induce all participants, by turns or simultaneously, to enter a state of ecstasy. Obversely, the definition requires that in the culture or subculture referred to, the ecstasy is ascribed a religious content irrespective of the forms of this content. Thus it is irrelevant whether the culture or subculture in question interprets the ecstasy as possession by a super-natural being, or gives it any other religious content.[1]

Part of the criteria that may be employed as a measure of the professional ecstatic's social status, is covered by the determining designation, social

---

[1] E. Bourguignon (1973) analyzes data in Murdock's Ethnographic Atlas to arrive *inter alia* at this result: on statistical probability, the degree of complexity in a society will determine the type of interpretation that society will prefer, whether possession and/or other types of phenomena. Murdock's data have been criticized, so Bourguignon's result may be questioned. Yet, Siikala's more detailed analysis of written sources for Siberian shamans also points to the fact that the preferred type of interpretation varies with social factors (1978, conclusions). If the preferred interpretation is thus a dependent variable, its influence on the professional ecstatic's status cannot be independent.

and cultic position. The explanation of these two terms will follow in reversed order.

By the ritual position of the professional ecstatic I denote his ritual place in the entire ritual pattern of his society. Or put more distinctly: what ecstatic ritual duties does he have, and how large a part in the whole range of collective rituals within his society will his duties comprise? The latter question is rarely raised in specialist literature, but the answer may give an indication of the status of the professional ecstatic, as I shall demonstrate towards the end of this paper.

The social position of a professional ecstatic can profitably be regarded as a position in society that he has come to obtain. Previous to his recognition as an ecstatic specialist he has one social position, and after being recognized presumably another. The social position thus acquired can be measured by many possible criteria, but I shall concentrate on the following: the economic conditions of recognition; its inherent possibilities, partly for control of social morals, partly for influence on political and juridical decisions, in the society in question.

The delimitations of social position by these criteria depend, in certain types of society, on the social radius employed as a yardstick. The traditional Eskimo societies were relatively small autonomous entities, with a simple division of labour, a relatively loose social structure and with a varying but never very complicated political organization. (The complexity of political organization is measured by the existence or non-existence of juridical institutions on a local or higher level, and of a leadership structure with institutionalized rights in an inherited or non-inheritable succession.) In these and in corresponding societies the social position of the professional ecstatic can be simply gauged with reference to society in its entirety, because the entire autonomous society is his field of action. In larger and considerably more complex societies, on the other hand, his field of activity does not comprise society to its full extent, that is, society as a political entity. This is only the case if through his ecstatic ritual practice he has the possibility of exerting influence upon decisions taken at the highest level of juridical and political authority. But if he does not have these possibilities of influence, his active field is restricted to a subgroup within his complex society. Here his social position can be measured on two different social radii: one including the subgroup, and another embracing the entire society. In contemporary large modern states, the professional ecstatic acts for the lower or intermediate social strata; while in the smaller autonomous kingdoms or chieftaincies of the past, he could rise to influence in high places, if recognition allowed this possibility. Indeed, he *could* do so,—for these autonomous and relatively complex societies are coming to be a thing of the

9–Religious Ecstasy

past. International market economy and political hegemony reach deep into decision-making processes in most societies to-day. And so the question arises of social change in relation to ecstatic religion. Analysis and delimitation of a professional ecstatic's social position is simpler in relatively stable societies, than in societies undergoing continuous and dramatic changes. Sometimes the ecstatic's potential for influence will increase, sometimes decrease, and at times new cults will arise around fresh ecstatic specialists; all this because the social and economic bases for his recognition change. But I shall not enter into the methodological problems arising when social change complicates the analysis of the professonal ecstatic's social position. My subject is his social and ritual position among the Eskimos in their traditional, and thus relatively stable, societal cultures. Here the criteria are social order and the ritual patterns of the various societies in their entirety. As professional ecstatics among the Eskimos may be defined as shamans, I shall henceforth call them so.

A note on Eskimo culture

The Eskimos have their habitat around the polar circle from Siberia to Greenland, from the North-Easternmost point of Asia, on the islands of the Bering Strait and the Bering Sea, along the coastal line of the North American continent, from the coast of Alaska turning South towards the Pacific, and in the arc up to the Hamilton Inlet on the Eastern coast of Labrador (Newfoundland) and across to Greenland and on to its South-Eastern coast.

Hunting and fishing formed the basis of subsistence for all Eskimos. Most groups[2] would hunt both sea animals from the coast, and land animals in the interior. A few groups, the inland Eskimos, only hunted and fished in the interior, whilst a single group, the Polar Eskimos in North Greenland, only exploited the resources of the sea.—The annual cycle of all Eskimos fell into two, sometimes more, periods: a sedentary, and a more or less nomadic period. During the sedentary period several families would live together in societies proper, which during the second period would dissolve into smaller family groups. In districts with permanent habitation, as for example among the Pacific Eskimos, single families would go on longer trips during this period; while most other Eskimos, the semi-sedentary, would spend their whole nomadic period moving from place to place. The duration of the sedentary period, in relation to the more or less nomadic one, would vary considerably from one Eskimo group to another. These

---

[2] "Group" designates each sector of Eskimos who spoke a common dialect and hunted within a delimited territory.

relative variations depended on the quantity and character of local resources, and the extent to which they were exploited. Thus the sedentary period was longer among the coastal Eskimos, hunting large marine animals in spring and early summer (e.g. Baffinlanders and Iglulik), than among those hunting seal at breathing holes in settled communities on sea ice in winter only, and which dispersed into families to hunt along the shores and in the inland in spring and summer (Netsilik and Copper).—The same ecological variations seem to have been the decisive factor behind the rich variations in types of society characterizing the Eskimo territories as a whole. The Polar Eskimos would live in small, labile and preponderantly nomadic societies, and were informally led by mature, experienced hunters. In contrast, the Pacific Eskimos were divided into very large, relatively stable, and preponderantly sedentary societies; they carried on collective hunts for big marine animals, and went to war under the leadership of single persons, who had taken over their leadership status from a father, uncle or elder brother.—Between these two extremes, all other Eskimo societies represented every conceivable intermediate form. It is thus in fairly different societies that the social positions of Eskimo shamans must be measured.

The economic background of Eskimo shamans

Apart from a single possible exception, any Eskimo male or female could train himself to be a shaman. In addition, an Eskimo shaman was paid for his individual performances. But even if these payments might be a welcome incidental surplus for shamans of low economic status, no shaman could make a living on these alone. In other words, the shamans were only part-time specialists among the Eskimos. In everyday life the male shamans had the same occupations as other men in the division of labour, and the female ones the same as other women. Individual shamans would lead a normal family life like all other persons—sons, daughters, fathers or mothers.

But since most Eskimos were men, I shall here cite them in the masculine gender. It should be stressed, though, that male shamans would not necessarily have any greater shaman gifts or powers than female ones.

The possible exception may be the shamans on Kodiak in the Pacific. According to a unique and unverifiable source (Black 1977), the Kodiak shamans were born as boys, educated like women, and remained unmarried. They were destined for the task of shaman from their birth, and therefore evidently prevented from exploiting the outlets for prestige which were open to ordinary men and women. These unmarried shamans had a special status, and they were presumably members of well-to-do families, where their position was that of servingmaid. All other Eskimo shamans, like any man or woman, could exploit the given possibilities for obtaining prestige, dependent on the individual's family situation and his or her exertions as a hunter or in the household.—I shall currently denote the shaman's varying positions on this scale of prestige as his Economic Status.

To summarise: no Eskimo shaman could live from his shaman activities. He was paid for each performance, but although this profit would be a welcome surplus for shamans of low economic status, it could never afford him a living. So the shaman was a part-time specialist, and the primary basis of his economy rested on his economic status.

Siikala's Siberian shaman typology

The economic conditions of Eskimo shamans correspond to those prevailing for shamans among Chukchee and Koryaks in North-Eastern Siberia. Anna-Leena Siikala (1978) has established a typology for the Siberian shamans and places Chukchee and Koryak shamans within the type she calls The Professional Shaman. Her meaning differs slightly from my sense of the word professional by denoting that the shaman receives payment for each of his shamanistic performances. Siikala further characterizes this type of Professional as follows: the shaman is not bound to any definite group of people; on the contrary, he can shamanize for anybody. He does not obtain his recognition through a separate ritual of initiation, and he has no ritual duties in the collective economic rituals of his society.

As stated, the Eskimo shamans apparently tally with this type, because they were paid for their separate performances. Furthermore they could shamanize for anybody. But here the similarities end (apart from the shamans of a unique eskimo group, the Taremiuts at Point Barrow, who fulfill all of the criteria for Siikala's Professional Shaman). For all other Eskimo shamans the following points obtain: they did have ritual tasks in the economic rituals of their society, and most of them had to pass a special ritual of initiation to obtain recognition as a shaman. In this point they resemble the shamans in Siikala's additional three types: the Small Group shaman; the Clan shaman; and the Professional Regional shaman. But as the Eskimo shamans, as noted, could shamanize for anybody, they do not tally with any of these three shaman types. For they were bound to shamanize respectively for the small group or the clan whose members they were, and within the limited geographical area in which they had obtained their recognition enabling them to shamanize.

In short: the Eskimo shamans cannot be placed within Siikala's Siberian typology.

One certain exception is provided by the above shamans at Point Barrow

(Spencer 1959, 303 f); while a single fact about a group of Inland Eskimos in North Alaska, Nunamiut, points to their having maintained small-group shamans at some time in the past (ibid., 314). This serves to emphasize that Siikala's typology, which is fully applicable to Siberian shamans, cannot be simply transferred to Eskimo ones. And yet, of Siikala's typological criteria, the economic one and the one about the shaman's duties in collective rituals can be profitably applied for delimiting the personal, social status of Eskimo shamans. The economic criterium I treated above; but the question of shamans' ritual duties must be treated in depth, when I have elucidated their possibilities of political and juridical influence.

The shaman's possibilities of influence

The question of the shaman's possibilities of influence on social morality and on decisions concerning the collective, requires an extended and more differentiated answer.

In his 'Ecstatic Religion' (1971) with its cross-cultural analyses of ecstatic cults, Ioan Lewis places the professional ecstatic's possible influence in three fields: control of social morality; influence on decisions of courts on a local or higher level; and influence on the succession of political leaders.

Lewis preferably selects his instances from East Africa, but one example is taken from Eskimo shamans. This analysis leads to far-reaching conclusions and must definitely be characterised as a daring venture, since Lewis obtains his whole knowledge of Eskimos from only one book (Rasmussen 1929) and two papers (Balikci 1963 and Murphy 1964). As this literature concerns only one Bering Strait and two Central (Canadian) Eskimo groups (Iglulingmiut, Nestilingmiut and St. Lawrence Islanders), Lewis has been hard put to discover the wide relative differences in Eskimo societal conditions that I mentioned above. But in addition Lewis selects his information from the two books so as to correspond with his theoretical considerations. Lewis's extensive theory about ecstatic cults is built on a typology, whose differentiating criterium is the relation of the cult to the collective morality of the society in question. Of the three types that Lewis establishes in this way, I shall deal with only one, the Central Cult type, because Lewis uses the Eskimo shaman rituals as one instance of this type.[3]

The Central Cult is characterized by its intimate connection with the collective morality of society, because its ecstatic specialist exerts a decisive control on this morality in his cult practises. In the societal envelopment of the central cult, crisis situations are interpreted as the negative

---

[3] My treatment involves some criticism of Lewis' Central cult type. For criticisms of his second type, the Peripheral Cylt, see Bour- guignon 1973; Douglas 1975; Sibisi 1975; Swantz 1976.

reactions of forefathers or nature spirits to social conflicts and infringements of morality, and the culprits are pointed out by the professional
ecstatic through the cult rituals.

Lewis further states that in societies with a certain degree of political
organization, the central-cultic specialist shares his moral control with the
political leaders and judges; while in societies without a political organization proper, he has complete control within his own hands.

I. *The Eskimo shaman's control of social morality.* Among the latter
societies the Eskimo ones are numbered, notes Lewis. They have no
juridical institutions, and as their informal leaders have no juridical authority, the shaman must exercise a considerable control of social morality.
Furthermore, the shaman can here function simultaneously as informal
leader, which is an impossible combination in societies with some degree of
political organization.

II. *The Eskimos' means of social control.* In his description of the
Eskimos, Lewis is exclusively concerned with the shaman's possible control of social morality, the only possibility left that Lewis can see, because
he finds no juridical institutions among the Eskimos. And there were none.
But other means of social control existed, of which a couple are described
in the literature from which Lewis takes his information.

The strongest social control was executed by public opinion, which is
extremely effective in groups of the manageable size that characterized
Eskimo society. Besides, the Eskimos had even more institutions functioning as the long arm of opinion, viz.: the song contest; the joking partnership; the song–and song-dance festivals.—In the song contest and the
joking partnership (Hoebel 1967; Lantis 1946 with references; Kleivan
1971) two persons would alternately deride each other to the delight of the
public. Resounding acclamation arose if the derision fully corresponded to
public opinion; but enthusiasm waned if insults were below or above a
justified level. The song–and the song-dance–festivals served the accepted
and appreciated self-praise of single individuals. They depicted their own
and/or their near forefathers' outstanding experiences and deeds in songs
that left no listener in doubt as to the moral value of these weighty events
(Sonne 1978). All these institutions exercising control and even an exemplary effect on morality, was outside the domains of the shaman.

"Juridical" decisions

The song contest channeled some part of dyadic conflicts, because the rules
of this institution prevented conflicting parties from coming to blows.[4] On

---

[4] Underlined by Kleivan 1971 for the Western Greenlanders in particular.

the other hand, the Eskimos did not demand that two persons who had fallen into serious disagreement laid their conflict open to public 'judgement' in a song contest. Their difference was a private affair, which did not necessarily involve other parties than the conflicting persons, and possibly their close relatives. Dyadic conflicts did not become public affairs, unless one person developed into a habitual criminal and so posed a threat to economic cooperation within the society. In that case, a more or less formal deliberation was held about the criminal's possible extermination, exile, isolation or reproof.[5] During the deliberation people would listen most to the honoured, mature and aged men, and to their *primus inter pares,* the informal leader, who as a rule had the decisive word. But his 'judgement' had to correspond with the consensus he could infer from pronouncements of the honoured, mature men. No more in such deliberations was the shaman's professional assistance required. He would take part as an ordinary person, on a par with other men, whose weight of opinion depended on their economic status.[6]

The ways in which the Eskimo shaman executed his main social control nevertheless causes Lewis certain problems. Contrary to other societies with central cults which serve as examples for Lewis, the Eskimos did not interpret a crisis situation as the result of some transgression of social morality. The most frequent cause was seen in infringements of taboos, i.e. the breaking of rules in force for relations with surrounding nature. Thus any direct control of morals could hardly be the effect of shaman rituals in crisis situations, a fact which Lewis does admit. But he continues: as most infringements of taboo can cause a common crisis situation, such transgressions must be synonymous with infringements of morality; and, as the Eskimo shaman controls the execution of taboo rules, he would by this leverage execute an important indirect control on social morals.

I should like to make the following comment on Lewis:

It is questionable whether the Eskimo shaman exerted any wider control on social morality because of his control of taboo rules, which was his acknowledged area of authority. Taboo rules were numerous, and where they were most numerous, infringements of taboo were inevitable. The Eskimos did not react with strong negative sanctions against grown-ups, who might from time to time break a taboo. Only the extremely few persons

---

[5] In some groups of small societies, the culprit's close kin made the decision and did away with their relative themselves (Steenhoven 1962).

[6] Bilby 1923 offers a single case from the Eastern Baffinlanders where the shamans, probably irrespective of economic status, had a greater influence on such "juridical" procedures than was the case among the other Eskimos.

who time and again seriously broke taboos, leading to a serious common crisis situation, had to be reprimanded with a reminder.[7]

In his argument Lewis chiefly stresses one collective ritual led by the shaman, which I might dub 'the public confession'. It was a widespread ritual in the larger part of the Eskimo world, for neutralizing a common serious situation of crisis. All grown-up members of society took part and in turn confessed all the breaks of taboo, of which they had recently been guilty. The shaman who presided at the public confession had the task of pointing out the special break of taboo which, according to his special knowledge, must be the cause of common misery. As a rule, this break of taboo was the last one disclosed in a long series of confidences; and when the shaman declared himself satisfied, relief would spread among the participants. As the very disclosure would neutralize the ominous effects of the many breaks of taboo, a public confession removed all imaginable causes of the critical situation. The ritual did not serve to point out a guilty person for chastisement. The participant who had confessed the infringement of taboo which, according to opinion and the shaman's assessment, was the proper cause of the crisis, neither incurred any odium or was made the object of other negative social sanctions.

The prevalent mood when the ritual was ended was relief. And it is my view that the public confession served primarily as a therapeutic ritual for reducing the anxiety, which a serious situation of crisis would produce among all members of society. Or stated theoretically: the shaman exerted a minimal indirect control on morals in his function as the guardian of taboo rules.

Status as shaman and leader

The Eskimo shaman could attain leader status, says Lewis. To be sure, this was a theoretical possibility in most Eskimo societies; but a shaman never became a leader due to his shaman powers in isolation. A leader's qualities were not identical with a shaman's powers. A leader was always a reliable person, an outstanding provider, an experienced adviser in hunting affairs, and besides, he was generous with the surplus resulting from his excellent providing capacity. In societies where hunting demanded organized cooperation under a single man's leadership, he should also have organisatorial gifts. If a shaman, apart from his recognized shaman powers, possessed

---

[7] This statement is based on my extensive reading in Eskimo literature. It is sustained by van den Steenhoven's conclusion on the topic (1962), based on a detailed analysis of written sources and personal field notes from Caribou and Netsilik Eskimos. The latter group had one of the most comprehensive and restrictive taboo networks in all the Eskimo territories.

these qualities, he could attain a leader's status. His advice as a shaman, in common situations of crisis, combined with his authority as a leader, would endow him with particularly great authority.

As stated, the combination of leader and shaman status in the same person was a theoretical possibility in the majority of Eskimo societies. In practice it was another matter. I shall return shortly to this point. But before that, one question must be answered: suppose the Eskimo shaman was not one of the honoured, mature men, nor their informal leader with high economic status; would he then have any appreciable part in social control? The reply is, yes.

The shaman as witch-finder

Premature deaths, illnesses, and common situations of crisis, which could not be explained by breaches of taboo, were interpreted as the effects of witchcraft. According to Lewis, the accusations of witchcraft would always be raised against a shaman from outgroup societies.—My comment here is that this was often the case, although it was far from being an invariable rule. Such accusations might be directed against both ordinary people and shamans, in other societies and in one's own. Possible witchcraft accusations were always a favourite subject of conversation behind closed doors; but the shaman could raise such accusations in public during a séance. Only he then had to be certain of support; for if he accused a person enjoying widespread confidence and/or respect, the shaman could fall foul of public opinion, with the effect that suspicion would turn against his own person. In his function of witch-hunter, the shaman in other words exercized a certain control but, at the same time, he was in this capacity himself under social control.

Because of his special powers, which he could use to the harm or to the advantage of others, the Eskimo shaman, like his colleagues all over the world, fell an easy prey to suspicion and accusations of witchcraft. Thus there arose the ambivalent attitude toward the shaman which was conspicuous in all Eskimo territories. The attitude contained a mixture of respect and fear, which might be combined with confidence, if the shaman had high economic status, and at the same time was reliable and sociable in behaviour. In the contrary case, that is: when his economic status was low; if his diagnoses often went against the consensus; and if his prognostications, too, often failed, he was classed with habitual criminals, the treatment of whom has been described above. Yet it was always a risky affair to attack a shaman, because his spiritual means of defence were numerous and efficient. Murders of unpopular shamans did nonetheless occur at intervals.

This ambivalent attitude to the shaman was, as noted, pronounced in all

Eskimo societies. In itself, recognition of the shaman gave him no clearly
delimited and riskfree social position. The shaman's tasks constituted no
office. They gave him limited economic advantages, and a limited influence
on social control. Only by virtue of high economic status together with
sociable qualities could the Eskimo shaman support his prestige, which was
measured by the extent of his shaman powers. If he lacked these qualities,
the fear that his shamân prestige engendered could break out in a joint
decision leading to his isolation, exile or even extermination.

With this risk in mind the question then arises: what advantages would
the shaman's duties confer among the Eskimos? In my opinion, the answer
is to be found in the special prestige that shaman powers would confer, in
spite of the accompanying drawbacks. They increased the shaman's personal security in all dyadic conflicts in which he and any other individuals
might become entangled.[8] As formerly mentioned these dyadic conflicts,
which would include the claim of blood revenge, were private affairs which
the parties involved had to tackle themselves. In such conflicts, too, the
low-status shaman was better situated with his spiritual means of defence[9]
than were ordinary persons of any status. The shaman's powers would thus
afford increased personal security but, as has been emphasized, only up to
a certain point.

Geographical differences in the economic status of shamans

From the above conclusion it would also follow that all Eskimos who
underwent a shaman education rose from a low-status situation; that they
remained low status persons within the division of labour by sex; but
through their recognition as shamans they would obtain increased personal
security in their low-status situation.—This conclusion, however, can only
be made to hold good with any certainty for shamans in three Eskimo
groups in Alaska: Nuniwagamiut, on the Island of Nunivak in the Bering
Sea (South Alaska) (Lantis 1946); the whale hunting Eskimos at Point
Barrow in North Alaska (Spencer 1959); and their neighbours to the South,
Nunamiut, who were inland Eskimos with caribou hunting as their chief
source of provision (ibid.).

Sources for other Eskimos in Alaska (and Siberia) do not yield sufficient
information about the recruitment and economic status of shamans. The
sources for Canada and Greenland, on the other hand, are more complete
on these points, and in these two areas shamans with a high economic

---

[8] My evaluation is based on sources (and
stories) from most Eskimo groups, e.g. Sandgreen 1967, I–II; Qúpersimân 1972; references to Western Greenland in Sonne, n.p.;

Balikci 1970; Spencer 1959; Lantis 1946; Nelson 1899; and Ray 1966.
[9] The Eastern Greenlanders' synonym for
spirit helpers (Sandgreen 1967 I–II).

status were frequent. Similarly, in Canada and Greenland informal leaders who were at the same time shamans were not infrequent. But this combination was only a theoretical possibility in the three above-mentioned Alaskan groups, where in practice the shamans had a low economic status.

In the following I shall take three groups to represent respectively South Alaska: Nuniwagamiut; the whale hunting cultures of North Alaska: Taremiut at Point Barrow; and the Northernmost inland Eskimos of the same region: Nunamiut. This restriction is made for reasons of economy, and each mention implies my reservations as to their representativity for the three entire regions.

For reasons which will shape my final conclusion, the shaman's task was definitely more attractive in Canada and Greenland than it was in Alaska. This is seen not only in the different economic statuses of shamans in the West and in the East, but also by the way in which the shamans were recruited. In Alaska a person rarely became a shaman of his own free will. He was most often "called" through illness or acute psychotic seizures, a "call" which as a rule was unavoidable if the called person wanted to survive. In Canada and Greenland the "call" to be a shaman was a far rarer occurrence, and if it did occur the person struck could in some instances (Lynge 1955, 1967) himself decide whether he or she would follow the "call" or not. Most frequently a person would commence a shaman education on his own resolve, unless his parents had already taken this decision while he was still in the womb. In that case the parents executed certain rituals at his birth, which in later life were to make him attractive to the spirits: that is, the spirits would be attracted by his person and offer their service as his future helping spirits.

But why, then, was the shaman's task more attractive in Canada and Greenland than in Alaska? Why was shaman-and-leader status a more frequent combination in East than in West? As far as my analysis is concerned, the answer lies in two factors: 1. The ritual position of the shaman, and 2. The degree of complexity in the leadership structure of society.

As regards 1, a table with corresponding graph shows the following facts: In Canada, Greenland, and among Nunamiut in North Alaska, these ritual tasks made up a far larger share in the aggregate ritual pattern, than among the whale-hunting Eskimos of North Alaska or among South Alaskan Eskimos. But the degree of complexity in leadership structure within the societies in question shows a slightly different distribution. To this latter point I shall return when I have commented upon the typology in the graph of collective rituals, and the tasks that the shaman executed within these.

The collective rituals of the Eskimos I have divided into four types. Type

Table 1. *Collective rituals and shaman participation among Eskimos*

Shaman participating + −

| | Calender rituals | Situation rituals | | Show-off séances |
		Expectable	Crisis	
Siberia	Many +/−	?	+	?
N. Alaska		Few −	+	
Whaling	Few +/−			Period?
(Pt. Barrow)	Few −			Dec.–Jan.
Nunamiut, caribou	1 +			Dec.–Jan.
S. Alaska	Many +/−	Many −	+	Trad. rit. + other?
Pacific coast	Few? ?	Many −	+	Period?
Canada		O/Few −	+	Winter season
S. E. Baffinland	1 +			
N. Labrador	1 +			
Iglulik	1? (+)			
Rest of Canada	0− −			
Greenland	0− −	O/Few −	+	Winter season

A are the Calendar Rituals, which were fixed by regularly recurring natural events in the annual cycle. Types B and C are jointly called Situation Rituals, since their occasion is an event that occurs in the life of the individual or of society, and so is without any fixed "date" within the annual cycle. Rituals of type B were celebrated for Expected Situations or events. Whether these befell single persons or the entire society, they would of course have to concern society as a whole to call forth the collective ritual. They might fall both in the life cycle of individuals (chief rites of passage) and in connection with seasonally fixed occupations under the latter sub-heading. Expected situation rituals as a rule immediately followed the event in question, although at times and in certain groups the event might be celebrated in two other ways: 1. Both immediately and later in a calendar ceremony, where it formed only a link in a long sequence of rituals. 2. Not immediately but only later within a calendar ceremony. The rules that governed those three groupings of celebrations, would vary from society to society.

Rituals of the C-type could be called Unexpected Situation rituals, since the event that produced them was a non-expected occurrence, and it may best be characterized as a situation of crisis.

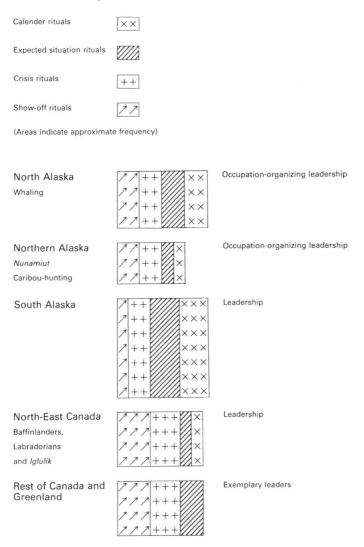

Fig. 1. Graph of collective ritual types by frequency and territories.

The final type D is the Show-Off Ritual, a free shaman séance with no religious end in any direct sense. Their aims were twofold: firstly, the shamans gave clear proofs of their powers in order to further their own shaman prestige, and for their entourage to realize their powers and performance. Secondly, the show-off séances served as entertainment and enacted information about the ways of the world—odd and complicated yet understandable. In this way the function of these séances came to be a sort of object lesson, and a corroboration of the lore contained in the commonly held store of tales.

From the graph it will be seen that in Alaska, shamans' show-off rituals were limited to two months of the year, the dark winter months (Spencer, 1959).—It may be added about of these rituals on Nunivak, that they took place most frequently in connection with the ritualized trading festivals celebrated by two or more villages. They would host them in turn, so that over a couple of years the festivals as a rule became fixed annual events (Lantis 1946).—In Canada and Greenland these rituals, as shown in the graph, were not limited to the same extent as in Alaska to a brief span of time. They were spread throughout the whole winter season, and usually they took place on the shaman's own initiative, or in connection with visits from other settlements.

The shaman's ecstatic tasks in other rituals were distributed as follows across the entire Eskimo territory: the rituals of crisis were his speciality, but it was extremely rare for his expertise to be called for in the collective rituals for expected situations. And in the event that his society had a single or several calendar festivals, the shaman had ritual obligations in at least one calendar festival. (Point Barrow presents a single certain exception op. cit.). In North Alaska (and Siberia) the shaman's tasks were limited to a few minor ecstatic leavens in several calendar festivals, each in itself often considerable in extent. He had corresponding brief functions in the calendar festivals of South Alaska and of North-Eastern Canada, but in Canada he would also function as obligatory leader of ceremonies; and in South Alaska he could be requested to undertake that ceremonial task. In North Alaska the *umialik* or leader would always carry out such tasks.

Digression on calendar rituals

The exclusive occurrence of calendar ceremonies among most Western (=Alaskan+Siberian) Eskimos and North East Canadian Eskimos (Labrador, Baffinlanders and Iglulik) seems to depend on two social factors: 1. the longer duration of the sedentary period as compared to the nomadizing one, and 2. leaders who would organize and direct the common hunt on a contractual basis (see below p. 144). Thus the Baffinlanders, the Labrador, and to some extent the Iglulik Eskimos, formed settled winter-to-spring communities of much longer duration than those of other Canadian Eskimos (Caribou, Netsilik, Copper). The first mentioned groups had an annual ceremony (not entirely certain for the Iglulik (Boas 1888, 669)), whereas the latter three did not.

The longer sedentary period cannot, however, account for the calendar ceremony among Nunamiut in North Alaska (Spencer 1959). They cohabited in sedentary communities for only a couple of months twice in the annual cycle, to nomadize all the rest of the year. In contrast to the other Inland Eskimos in North Alaska and Canada, who celebrated no calendar rituals, the Nunamiut's common caribou hunt was directed by a contractual leader, the *umialik*. This leader both arranged the annual ceremony and paid the hired shamans for their services in the cult (ibid.). This contractual type of leadership may thus explain the calendar ceremony among the Nunamiut.

A third, and perhaps primary, factor underlying calendar rituals could be the sheer size of communities. Baffinland censuses from the 1880's to the 1920's give the number of temporary Eskimo settlers around European whaling stations at 150 to 250 persons during the whaling season (Milleward 1930). For the same 50 years of intensive European whaling, we have descriptions of the Sedna cult celebrated at these stations. Whether the smaller Eskimo settlements actually celebrated the cult too, we are not directly told; but they formed a maximum of 50 persons (ibid.). The number of persons at settlements in pre-European days, with native whaling, is of course unknown. Archeology may provide a clue.

Sources then leave us with two documented factors: the longer sedentary period; and contractual leaders organizing hunt and celebrations.

The ritual positions of shamans

The graph (p. 141) shows the five patterns of ritual types in their proportional distribution. It indicates a distinct preponderance in Alaska of two types which called for the cooperation of the shaman's ecstatic abilities, to a limited extent only or not at all, viz. the calendar festivals and the expected-situation rituals.—In Canada and Greenland and among the Nunamiut, two other types were dominant, the shaman's rituals of crisis and of show-off.

The whale-hunting cultures of North Alaska are the ones most fully described in this area. They are on an intermediate level both as regards number and distribution of the four ritual types. (Sources are few however for the smaller coastal cultures, so no patterning can be given for their rituals.)

To sum up: the shamans' ritual position, i.e. their relative parts in ritual patterns within the five areas, are not identical. Their parts were large in Canada, Greenland, and among the Nunamiut; less in the whale-hunting cultures of North Alaska; and negligible in South Alaska.[10]

We could then make the following assumption: the shaman's ritual position, high or low, will coincide with his high or low economic status. If

---

[10] Marsh (1954) makes the same observation, although his interpretation in a setting of evolutionary theory would need further criticism, beyond the limits of this paper.

so, the formula would run as follows: a proportionally large part in the ritual patterns should correspond to high economic status; and obversely, a small part in rituals would conform to a low status in economy. But this relationship is contradicted by the conditions among the Nunamiut: here the shaman's ritual participation was extensive, but his economic status was poor. Thus ritual position can not be the sole factor determining the shaman's economic status. But when we introduce a second factor, the degree of complexity in leadership structure, the jigsaw forms a neater picture.

Leadership

I select this factor from one of Lewis's conclusions above, viz: in societies with a well-developed organisation, shaman tasks and leadership are separate functions which cannot be united in the same person. But in societies without political organisation, this combination is possible.

Eskimo leadership may be roughly divided into four categories, taking the leader's authority and his responsibilities as criteria. In some societies, an organized cooperation under a single person's leadership was necessary for carrying out the chief occupations, as also for making war expeditions, which could be lucrative too). We find two categories of leadership in these societies: one is inheritable (Pacific Eskimos), the other is non-inheritable. In addition, this latter is no properly elected leadership, since a man would offer himself as economic leader and be accepted as such, without any elective process (North Alaskan whale-hunting cultures, and Nunamiut, with their organized collective hunting of whales and caribou).—In the remaining Eskimo societies, hunting as a rule was carried out on a more individual basis. But when at intervals coordination was necessary in collective hunts, the latter were led by a person who did not have the same authority and responsibility as the occupation-organizing leaders. These latter would contract with the single participants in a hunt, and their bond obliged the leader to take upon himself rather considerable economic obligations towards the participants. A similar bonding with built-in obligations is unknown in other Eskimo societies. The possible leader of a collective hunt and the other participants took part on identical economic conditions.[11] Each participant, including the leader, had his share in the catch which he himself killed or had taken part in killing, in conformity with the rules in force concerning shares of catch.

---

[11] In Western Greenland a collective hunt e.g. of caribou, was led by some acknowledged specialist, irrespective of his total economic status, which might be low. From the expedition's start till its end he was a leader, but neither before not after (Professor Robert Petersen, field notes, and personal communication).

The leader in South Alaska (Bering Sea area) and in North Eastern Canada constitute the third type, with less formal obligations than the above two types. In S. Alaska he took the initiative in the ritualized trading festivals, and in N. E. Canada he watched the sharing of meat, which followed fairly complicated rules.

At this point we can return to the shaman's status in relation to two factors: his ritual position, and the complexity of leadership structure.

The highest complexity was found among the Pacific Eskimos with their inheritable and occupation-organizing leadership. And, if the isolated source for Kodiak in the Pacific is reliable, the combination of leader and shaman status in the same person was not even a theoretical possibility there (the Kodiak shaman, an unmarried transvestite and thus placed in the female line, as a matter of course could not inherit leadership status from a possible near male relative).

One step farther down in complexity, we find the leaders in the whale-hunting cultures, and among the Nunamiut the leader organizing occupations and war. In those two cultures, the combination of leader and shaman status in the same person was theoretically possible, but in practice it was rarely or never realized. The shamans had a low economic status, in contrast to the high status of respected mature men. And in spite of the fact that the shaman among the Nunamiut had a high ritual position, this was obviously without importance within their relatively complex structure of leadership.

But when we compare Nunivak (South Alaska) and Northeast Canada, where the shaman's social position was respectively low and high, this difference cannot be explained by differences in the leadership structures, which can be placed at the same level on the last but one step in the complexity scale. On the other hand, differences in the shaman's ritual positions correlate neatly with differences in their economic status.

Finally, at the bottom of the scale, we find the exemplary leader. He was the leader type in the rest of Canada and in Greenland, where the shaman's economic status was often high, and his part in the ritual pattern equally considerable.

In other words: the task of shaman was more attractive in Canada and Greenland, because the shaman had a central place in the ritual pattern. Within this pattern it was mainly during the shaman's séances that the collective asserted their common religious ideas. In Alaska his task was less attractive; either because the shaman had only a small part in the ritual pattern; or because a relatively well-developed leadership had obviously tended to prevent the professional ecstatic from obtaining leadership status.

Conclusion

The Eskimo data appear to confirm Lewis's first hypothesis: the more complicated the political organisation of a society, the greater the probability of the statuses of leader and of shaman never being united in the same person. But Lewis's view of the Eskimo shaman's potentiality for social control, via his supervision of the rules of taboo, has to be revised. The shaman exerted a certain control in his function as a witch-finder who was himself the object of social control. His further influence depended on a high economic status, and on positive traits of character, which might endow him with leadership status. But the more complex the type of leadership, the smaller were his obvious possibilities of obtaining this leader's status. With the type of leader becoming increasingly simple, this possibility would grow: always dependent on the centrality of the shaman's position within the ritual pattern.

This represents the limit of my hypotheses, which can also be tested against the social and ritual positions of professional ecstatics in various societies. In ethnographical literature, sociological criteria have often been employed in delimiting his status; whereas his part in ritual has not been the subject of similar interest and proper research in depth. That ritual position may provide an indication of the ecstatic's status has been demonstrated as the preliminary result of this analysis.

The next step in analysis must be as follows: taking the ritual position as an analytical tool, the social conditions that influence the socioreligious content and extent of ritual patterns can be clarified (as far as sources will allow). This analysis, however, must await another occasion.

References

Literature on Eskimos is categorised by regions:

(General)   all regions.
(S.)   Siberia and St. Lawrence Island.
(Pac.)   Pacific: Southern coast of Alaska and the Aleuts.
(S.A.)   South Alaska: Bering Sea region.
(N.A.)   North Alaska and Bering Strait Islands.
(C.Can.)   Central and North West Canada.
(N.E.Can.)   North Eastern Canada.
(N.G.)   Northern Greenland.
(W.G.)   Western Grenland.
(E.G.)   Eastern Greenland.

The Alaskan Eskimos. 1952. Ed. by H. Ostermann. (Report of the 5th Thule expedition 10,3.) Copenhagen. (N.A. + S.A.).

Balikci, A. 1963. Shamanistic behaviour among the Netsilik Eskimos. *South West-ern journal of anthropology* 19.
— 1970. *The Netsilik Eskimo.* New York. (C. Can.).
— 1973. The Netsilik Eskimos: adaptive processes. *Man the hunter,* ed. by R. B. Lee and I. de Vore, Chicago. (C. Can.)
Bilby, J. W. 1923. *Among unknown Eskimo.* London. (N. E. Can.).
Birket-Smith, K. 1924. Meddelelser om Grønland 66. *The ethnography of the Egedesminde district.* Copenhagen (W. G.).
— 1929. *The Caribou Eskimos.* (Report of the 5th Thule expedition 5.) Copenhagen. (C. Can.).
— 1953. *The Chugach Eskimo.* (Nationalmuseets skrifter. Etnografisk række 6.) Copenhagen. (Pac.).
Black, L. I. (ed.) 1977. The Konyak (The inhabitants of the Island of Kodiak) by Iosaf (Bolotov) (1794–1799) and by Gideon (1804–1807). *Arctic anthropology* 14, 2. (Pac.).
Boas, F. 1888. The Central Eskimo. *Sixth annual report of the Bureau of ethnology.* Washington. (N.E.Can.).
— 1901–1907. The Eskimo of Baffin Land and Hudson Bay 1–2. *Bulletin of the American museum of natural history* 15. (N.E.Can.)
Bogoras, W. 1913. *The Eskimo of Siberia.* (The Jesup North Pacific expedition 8, 3.) New York. (S.).
Bourguignon, E. 1973. *Religion, altered states of consciousness, and social change.* Ohio.
Curtis, E. 1930. *The North American Indian* 20. New York/London. (S.A. + N.A.).
Dalager, L. 1915. *Grønlandske Relationer ... 1752.* (Det grønlandske Selskabs Skrifter 2.) København. (W.G.).
Damas, D. 1968. The Eskimo. *Science, history and Hudson Bay,* ed. by R. Beals 1. Ottawa. (C.Can. + N.E.Can.).
— 1973. The diversity of Eskimo societies. *Man the hunter,* ed. by R. B. Lee and I. de Vore. Chicago. (N.E.Can. + C.Can.).
Douglas, M. 1975. *Naturlige symboler.* København.
Egede, H. 1925. *Omstændelig og udførlig Relation ... og Grønlands nye Perlustra-tion og Naturel Historie.*(Meddelelser om Grønland 54.) København. (W.G.).
— 1971. (Same, ed. Finn Gad). København.
— 1939. *Continuation of Relationerne ... 1734–1740.* (Meddelelser om Grønland 120.) København.
— 1971. (Same, ed. Finn Gad). København. (W.G.).
Fejes, C. 1966. *Peoples of the Noatak.* New York. (N.A.).
Giddinge, J. L. 1961. Kobuk River People. Univ. of Alaska. *Studies of Northern Peoples* 1. College. (N.A.).
Glahn, H. C. 1771. Anmærkninger over ... Crantzes Historie om Grønland. (W.G.).
— 1921. *Dagbøger for Aarene 1763–64, 1766–67, og 1767–68,* ed. by H. Ostermann. (Det grønlandske Selskabs skrifter 4.) København. (W.G.).
Gubser, N. J. 1965. *The Nunamiut Eskimos: Hunters of Caribou.* New Haven/London. (N.A.).
Hawkes, E. W. 1913. The "Inviting-In" feast of the Alaskan Eskimo. Canada, Department of Mines, Geological Survey, Memoir 45: 3, *Anthropological Series,* Ottawa. (S.A.).

— 1914. The dance festivals of the Alaskan Eskimos. Univ. of Pennsylvania, *The Univ. Mus. Anthropological Publ*, 6, 2. Philadelphia. (S.A. + N.A.).

— 1916. The Labrador Eskimo. Canada Geological Survey, Memoir 91: 14. *Anthropological Series*. Ottawa. (N.E.Can.).

Himmelheber, H. 1951. *Der Gefrorene Pfad*. Eisenach. (Kassel). (S.A.).

— 1953. *Eskimokünstler*. Eisenach. (Kassel). (S.A.).

— 1980. *Ethnographische Notizen von den Nunivak-Eskimo*. (Abhandlungen und Berichte des Staatlichen Museums für Völkerkunde. Forschungsstelle Dresden 38.) Berlin. (S.A.).

Hoebel, E. A. 1967. Song duels among the Eskimo. *Law and Warfare*, ed. by P. Bohannan, New York. (General).

Holm, G. 1888. *Ethnologisk Skizze af Angmagssalikerne*. (Meddelelser om Grønland 10.) København.

— 1911. *Ethnological Sketch of the Angmagssalik Eskimo*. (Meddelelser om Grønland 39,1.) Copenhagen. (E.G.).

Holm, G.–Petersen J. 1921. Angmagssalik distrikt. *Grønland i Tohundredeåret for Hans Egedes Landing*. (Meddelelser om Grønland 61, 2.) Copenhagen. (E.G.).

Hrdlička, A. 1944. *The Anthropology of Kodiak Island*. Philadelphia. (Pac.).

Hughes, C. C. 1958. An Eskimo deviant from the "Eskimo" type of social organization. *American anthropologist* 60. (S.A. + S.).

— 1959. Translation of I. K. Voblov's Eskimo ceremonies. *Anthropological Papers of the University of Alaska* 7, 2. College. (S.).

Ingstad, H. 1954. *Nunamiut*. London. (N.A.).

Jacobsen, J. A. 1977. *Alaskan Voyage 1881–1883*. Chicago. (S.A. + N.A.).

Jenness, D. 1922. *The life of the Copper Eskimos*. (Report of the Canadian arctic expedition 1913–18 12.) Ottawa. (C. Can.).

— 1928. *The people of the twilight*. New York. (C.Can.).

Jochelson, W. 1933. *History, ethnology and anthropology of the Aleut*. Washington. (Pac.).

Keithan, E. L. 1976. *Alaskan igloo tales*. Anchorage. (N.A.).

Kleivan, I. 1971. Song duels in West Greenland. *Folk* 13. (W.G.).

Lantis, M. 1946. The social culture of the Nunivak Eskimo. *Transactions of the American philosophical society*. N.S. 35,3 Lancaster. (S.A.).

— 1947. *Alaskan Eskimo ceremonialism*. (Monographs of the American ethnological society 11.) Seattle/London. (S.A.).

— 1960. *Eskimo childhood and interpersonal relationships*. (The American ethnological society, Monograph 33.) Seattle/London. (S.A.).

Lewis, I. M. 1971. *Ecstatic religion*. Middlesex.

Lynge, H. 1955. *Inegpait eller fornemme mennesker ... Upernavik Norddistrikts Ældre Historie*. (Meddelelser om Grønland 90, 2.) (W.G.).

— 1967. *Inugpat. Upernaviup ergâta oqalugtuagssartai*. Godthåb. (W.G.).

Marsh, G. H. 1954. A comparative survey of Eskimo-Aleut-religion. *Anthropological papers*. Alaska University. (General).

Mathiassen, T. 1928. *Material culture of the Iglulik Eskimos*. (Report of the 5th Thule Expedition 6,1.) Copenhagen. (N.E.Can.).

Michael, H. N. (ed.). 1967. Lieutenant Zagoskin's Travels in Russian America, 1842–44. Arctic Institute of North America. *Anthropology of the North: translations from Russian sources* 7. Toronto. (S.A.).

Milleward, A. E. 1930. *Southern Baffinland*. Department of the Interior North West Territories and Yukon Branch. Ottawa. (N.E.Can.).

Moore, R.D. 1923. Social life of the Eskimo of St. Lawrence Island. *American anthropologist*, N.S. 25. Menasha. (S.).

Murdock, G. P. 1967. *Ethnographic atlas*. (U.S.A.).

Murphy, J. M. 1964. Psychotherapeutic aspects of shamanism on St. Lawrence Island, Alaska. *Magic faith and healing*, ed. by A. Kiev. London/New York. (S.).

Nelson, E. W. 1899. *The Eskimo about the Bering Strait*. (18th Annual Report of the Bureau of American ethnology 1.) Washington. (S.A. + N.A.).

Qúpersimân, G. 1972. *taimane gûtimik nalussûgama*. Godthåb. (E.G.).

Rainey, F. Q. 1947. *The whale hunters of Tigara*. (Anthropological papers of the American museum of natural history. 41, 2.) New York. (N.A.).

Rasmussen, K. 1905. *Nye Mennesker*. København. (N.G.).

— 1908. *The people of the polar north*. London. (N.G.).

— 1921. *Myter og Sagn fra Grønland 1*. Kjøbenhavn. (E.G.).

— 1929. *Intellectual culture of the Iglulik Eskimos*. (Report of the 5th Thule expedition 7, 1.) Copenhagen. (N.E.Can.).

— 1930. *Observations on the intellectual culture of the Caribou Eskimos*. (Report of the 5th Thule expedition 7.) Copenhagen. (C.Can.).

— 1931. *The Netsilik Eskimos*. (Report of the 5th Thule expedition 9.) Copenhagen. (C.Can.)

— 1932. *Intellectual culture of the Copper Eskimos*. (Report of the 5th Thule Expedition 9.) Copenhagen. (C.Can.).

— 1938. *Knud Rasmussen's posthumous notes on the life and doings of the east Greenlanders in olden times*. Ed. by H. Ostermann. (Meddelelser om Grønland 109, 1.) Copenhagen. (E.G.).

Ray, D. J. (ed.) 1966. The Eskimo of St. Michael and vicinity as related by H. M. V. Edmonds. *Anthropological papers of the University of Alaska* 12, 2. College. (S.A.).

Rink, H. 1974. *Tales and traditions of the Eskimo*. Copenhagen. (W.G.).

Rooth, A. B. 1971. *The Alaska expedition 1966*. (Acta Universitatis Lundensis. Sect. 1, 14.) Lund. (N.A.).

— 1960. *Isímardik*. (Det grønlandske selskabs skrifter 20.) København. (E.G.).

— 1963. *Sagn og saga fra Angmagssalik*. København. (E.G.).

— 1970. *Kimilik*. København. (E.G.).

Sandgreen, O. 1967. *isse issimik kigutdlo kigúmik* 1–2. Godthåb. (E.G.).

Sibisi, 1975. Spirit possession in Zulu cosmology. *Religion and social change in southern Africa* ed. by M. G. Whisson and Martin West.

Siikala, A. L. 1978. *The rite technique of the Siberian shaman*. (FF Communications 220.) Helsinki.

Sonne, B, 1978. Ritual bonds between the living and the dead in Yukon Eskimo society. *Temenos* 14. (General).

— *Blodhævnens ideologi og virkelighed i Vest- og Østgrønland*. (W.G./E.G.) Forthcoming in *Etudes/Inuit/Studies*.

Spencer, R. F. 1959. *The North Alaskan Eskimo*. (Bureau of American ethnology. Bulletin 171.) Washington. (N.A.).

Steenhoven, G. van den 1962. *Leadership and law among the Eskimo of the Keewatin District. Northwest Territories*. (C.Can.).

Steensby, H. P. 1910. *Contributions to the ethnology and anthropology of the Polar Eskimos*. (Meddelelser om Grønland 34.) Copenhagen. (N.G.).

Swantz, M.-L. 1976. Dynamics of the spirit possession phenomenon in Eastern

Tanzania. *Dynamics and institution,* ed. by H. Biezais. (Scripta Instituti Donneriani Aboensis 9.) Uppsala.

Søby, R. M. 1969/70. The Eskimo animal cult. *Folk* 11–12. (General).

— 1977/78. The kinship terminology in Thule. *Folk* 19–20. (N.G.).

Saabye, H. E. 1816. *Brudstykker af en Dagbog holden i Grønland.* Odense. (W.G.).

Thalbitzer, W. 1941. *Social customs and mutual aid. The Ammassalik Eskimo 2.* (Meddelelser om Grønland 40, 4.) Copenhagen. (E.G.).

Thornton, H. R. 1931. *Among the Eskimos of Wales, Alaska 1890–93.* London. (N.A.).

Turner, L. M. 1894. Ethnology of the Ungava District. *11th annual report of the Bureau of ethnology.* Washington. (N.E.Can.).

Weyer, E. M. 1932. *The Eskimos.* Hamden. (General).

Spirit-possession in Theory and Practice— Séances with Tibetan Spirit-mediums in Nepal

By PER-ARNE BERGLIE

This paper is a short study of the séances and trance-performances of three Tibetan spirit-mediums (*dpa' bo*) from a refugee-community in Nepal.

For each *dpa' bo* a summary of personal thoughts and beliefs concerning possession is provided, followed by an example of how a séance was structured. In a concluding section the inner experiences of the mediums during the séance will be related and a few comments given.

For further details on this type of spirit-mediumship and for relevant background-material, the reader is referred to some previous studies by the present author (Berglie 1976, 1978, 1980). The field-work on which this study is based was carried out in a Tibetan refugee-village in Nepal during 1970 and 1971.

dBang phyug

He was a man about forty years old. He was married and had one son. He was suffering from tuberculosis, but worked as a porter or doing various odd jobs. He was born in Eastern Tibet.

Before he let himself be possessed at a séance, he had to send away his *rnam shes,* "consciousness". This had to be effected immediately before possession took place, as the moment when the body was "empty", i.e. without *rnam shes* and before it was possessed by a god, was considered extremely dangerous. Evil spirits and demons of various kinds were always thought to be trying to disturb the séances. In this case a demon could very well seize the opportunity to enter the spirit-medium's "empty" body, pose as a god and thereby create great dangers for the spirit-medium as well as for those seeking help. It was considered equally dangerous if the *dpa' bo* let his *rnam shes* remain in his body after he had let the god in. Then he would be "half god, half man" and what he said and did could not be trusted.

dBang phyug sent his *rnam shes* to the mirrors placed on the altar through the "channel", *rtsa,* opening at the top of the skull. These mirrors

are considered to be the most important parts of a *dpa' bo*'s equipment, as
the gods are thought to reside in them during the séance. His *rnam shes* is
then taken care of by *Padma 'byung gnas* (Padmasambhava).

Essential to an understanding of how possession is thought to take place
is the belief in the existence of "channels" in the human body. This is not
the place for a study of the very important role played by this belief in
Indian medicinal and religious speculation. Suffice it to say that it occurs in
most of the Buddhist Tantras and their commentaries (see, e.g., Dasgupta
1958: 153–158; Eliade 1969: 236–241; Govinda 1959: 103, 155, 170, 173;
Snellgrove 1957: 88, 90; 1959: 25, 27, 35 ff.; Stablein 1976: 57 ff.; Tucci
1961: 108–133; 1970: 72–79; Wayman 1973: 151 f., 192 f.; 1977: 65, 205 f.).
According to this religious physiology the human body, or perhaps rather
the "subtle" body the Tantric practician may develop, has a very great
number of "channels" or "veins" (nāḍī, *rtsa*) of which there are three chief
ones. They are Avadhūti (*dbu ma rtsa*), Rasanā (*ro ma rtsa*), and Lalanā
(*rkyang ma rtsa*). The three are united at the base of the genitals from
where they run upwards in the body. The central one, *dbu ma rtsa*, runs
straight up to the top of the head, while *ro ma rtsa* runs to the right and
rkyang ma rtsa to the left up to the nostrils. It may be noted that *ro ma rtsa*
is associated with the blood, while *dbu ma rtsa* is associated with air and
rkyang ma rtsa with water (Stablein 1976: 57 ff.). *dBang phyug's* view of
these things differed, however, from this literary tradition in a number of
ways. Thus, according to him, the three "channels" unite in a point in the
middle of the chest with *dbu ma rtsa* having its opening at the top of the
head, *ro ma rtsa* in the tip of the fourth finger of the left hand, and *rkyang
ma rtsa* in that of the right hand. Furthermore, according to him both *dbu
ma rtsa* and *ro ma rtsa* are white, while *rkyang ma rtsa* is red.

It is through these "channels" that possessing gods enter the body of the
dpa' bo. Each "channel" has at its opening a door (*rtsa sgo*), which can be
opened to let the possessing god in. These doors were often mentioned at
the séances with *dBang phyug*, soon after possession had taken place,
together with the names of certain deities. These deities were not necessarily the same at every séance. The pantheon of the *dpa' bo* is divided into
three classes: *lha, btsan,* and *klu,* and the three "channels" are assigned to
members of these classes. *dBu ma rtsa* was always guarded by a *lha,*
rkyang ma rtsa by a *btsan* or, less often, by a *klu* and *ro ma rtsa,* finally, by
a *klu* more often than by a *btsan*. The deities mentioned in this connection
functioned as guardians of the *rtsa*-doors with an obligation to make it
impossible for demons to enter. During the séances they were called *rtsa
lam sang mkhan*, "cleaners of the *rtsa*-road", which perhaps indicates that
these deities had other functions as well.

Furthermore there were other gods present to guard these "channels".

Theirs was, moreover, the main responsibility that nothing happened to *dBang phyug* during possession. They were *gnyan chen Thang lha mi dkar rta dkar*, here carrying the title *rtsa bdag*, "Master of the *rtsa*" and *Ma sangs rkyang khra mchor bo*, with the title *rtsa rogs*, "Helper of the *rtsa*(- master)". These gods *dBang phyug* had inherited from elder spirit-mediums in his family. They are, therefore, common to all *dpa' bo*s belonging to his lineage.

During the séances, a further number of supernatural beings were mentioned in connection with the "channels" and their protection. They were called *rtsa ba'i bla ma*s, "root-lamas", a term otherwise used to designate a pupil's personal gurus. It is not clear to what degree the semantic ambivalence of the word *rtsa* has influenced the connection between these figures and the "channels" in the body of the spirit-medium. Nevertheless it is quite clear, that to *dBang phyug* they were powerful protective beings to be invoked just before he let himself be possessed. It is, however, difficult to see any primary connection between these figures, among whom we find the Dalai lama, Karmapa, Padmasambhava, Vajrapāṇi, Hayagrīva, Amitābha and many more, and spirit-medium activities. Perhaps we have here important figures in Tibetan religion, who due to their importance have been connected, in a protective function, to a crucial situation in the ritual of the *dpa' bo*s. But not only is the initial phase of possession considered dangerous, it is also necessary for the *dpa' bo* to be protected by gods during the whole of the séance. Thus a number of supernatural beings arrive at the séances and place themselves by certain parts of the body of the *dpa' bo*, from where they guard and control proceedings. These gods were usually mentioned soon after *dBang phyug* had put on his *rigs lnga*, headdress, but before possession had taken place. The five parts of the body thus serving as abodes were: the top of the skull, the right and the left shoulder, the back (i.e. the part between the shoulder-blades), and the chest (i.e. the heart). Only during one séance was one god mentioned, the latter obviously thought of as guarding the whole of *dBang phyug*'s body. These gods were not the same at every séance. Apart from gods more properly belonging to the pantheon of the *dpa' bo*s, we find such prominent figures as Hayagrīva guarding the back, and *Ye shes mtsho rgyal*, the female consort of Padmasambhava, guarding the chest of *dBang phyug*.

As can be seen from the above, a séance involves rather a large number of gods. In addition to the hundreds of gods attending the séance in the mirrors on the altar, several gods both high-ranking and more obscure play important roles in the ritual.

As an example of what might take place during a typical séance with *dBang phyug*, I will now give extracts from my notes taken at a séance for a

woman and her grown-up married daughter. The mother thought she had
been bitten by a dog infected with rabies, while her daughter had pains in
what she thought was her liver. In addition to this, the mother also suffered
from headaches. "(6.05 p. m.) *dBang phyug* has already started to arrange
the special séance-altar when I arrive at the house of the sick people. He
builds it up in front of the house-altar, which is placed on his right side.
During this work he chats with the people present. He has laid out a *g.yung
drung* (svastika) of rice on the shelf on which he now arranges his altar. He
fills two small bowls with *spags* (i.e. *rtsam pa,* roast-flour, mixed with
water or tea) and one with rice, forming the contents to conical *gtor mas.*
The bowl with the *gtor ma* of rice is placed to the left. In the bowl in the
middle, he then places a round metal mirror and, behind it, a stick to which
three small *tsagle*-pictures are attached. These pictures represent, according to *dBang phyug, Sa skya gong ma, Guru drag po,* and *mGon po phyag
drug.* In the bowl to the left, he then places a stick with pictures of *U rgyan
rin po che* (Padmasambhava) and Karmapa. In the bowl to the right he puts
a stick with the picture of *dPal ldan lha mo* attached. Over these small
paintings he then puts a white *kha btags* and pieces of red cloth. In front of
these bowls he then places three smaller ones, the right one filled with tea,
the middle one with water to which he adds some milk-powder, and the left
one with water. A bundle of white feathers is placed to the far left of the
altar and two white conch-shells on either side of the middle bowl. Over the
small bowl with tea, a spoon is laid and, finally, a small oil-lamp and some
incense-sticks are placed on the altar. Thus the altar has been built up in his
customary way. (6.21 p. m.) He starts his introductory prayers, which soon
lead on to the invocations proper. A great number of gods belonging to
different classes are mentioned by name and asked to come to the place.
(6.43 p. m.) The invocations are now concluded, the gods having arrived
and installed themselves. *dBang phyug* chats with the people present in a
relaxed and joking way. He then puts on a special séance-shirt and hangs a
thin metal mirror around his neck and ties a piece of red cloth around his
head. (6.53 p. m.) He lifts his headdress with both hands and holds it up in
front of him, singing the names of the five *mkha' 'gro ma*s (ḍākiṇīs), who
during the séance are associated with the five lobes of the *rigs lnga.* (6.56
p. m.) He fastens his headdress to his head with two strings and then starts
to sing, accompanying himself with his small drum and his flat bell, *gshang.*
The drumming is steadily becoming more intense and violent and he jumps
several times on the bench where he is sitting cross-legged. Suddenly he
jumps out onto the floor, crying "phaṭ" three times and starting to dance.
After a short time he jumps back up on the bench, where he kneels turning
to the altar. He now sings about the gods in the mirror and about the cave at

Mount Targo (on this cave and its importance to the *dpa' bo*s, see Berglie 1980). After some time, a *kha btags* is put over *dBang phyug*'s headdress, as a greeting to the possessing god, in spite of the fact that no one in the room has heard the god introduce himself. The task he has to carry out is then presented to the god by the man appointed as intermediary. The god makes a few comments on this and the intermediary answers. Then the god starts to make rather harsh and sarcastic comments on a séance which *Nyi ma don grub*, another *dpa' bo*, held a few days ago for his sick brother (see below). *Nyi ma don grub*, who is present, listens to the god with a troubled look on his face. The god says that the young man has not been cured. (7.22 p. m.) *dBang phyug* is now going to perform *rtsis*, which is the *dpa' bo*s' designation of the method of drum divination they commonly used. He puts his drum in front of himself on the bench and places seven grains of rice on the drumskin. When he then asks the gods to carry out the divination, the grains move with sudden jumps on the drumskin. After that he carries out another divination, where he asks the gods to make the grains rotate on the drumskin. The grains accordingly started to rotate clock-wise rather fast. These divinations were made for the prognosis of *Nyi ma don grub*'s brother's illness and the result was auspicious: he was going to get well. (7.25 p. m.) The god talks about the divination and about the nature of the illness. The intermediary tries to say something but is rebuffed by the god. The god, however, soon resumes the singing and asks the elder to sit down in front of him. She does so. The god is now rather irritated for some reason or other. He calms down and starts to drum. Then he takes his horn, *rkang gling* and strikes the woman three times over her right shoulder crying "phaṭ". (8.00 p. m.) The god now explains the course of the illness and complains about being asked to cure at this early stage. During his singing, the god also expresses great displeasure at the behaviour of the intermediary, who is subsequently replaced by another man. *dBang phyug* alternates between song and talk, when he now mentions several of the supernatural animals which can possess the *dpa' bo* to effect the actual removal of the illness from the patient. (8.19 p. m.) The curing animal now takes possession of *dBang phyug*. Some believe it is *Zangs spyang dmar po*, "Red Copper-Wolf" (this proves to be wrong, see below). The woman has bared her back and a piece of red cloth is put over her shoulder. *dBang phyug* moves his horn over her back, arms, and head. Then he blows his horn once. Then he sucks several times through the horn with its opening placed at various points of the woman's back and neck. He then spits into a small bowl of water. Nothing, however, is visible in the water when it is inspected by the people present. The bowl is now filled with fresh water. Then he again sucks through his horn, moving it around her shoulder. He again spits in the bowl, but still nothing is to be seen. *dBang phyug* then moves his drum over the shoulder and neck of the woman. He drums violently. Then he proceeds to suck from her head, at the same time moving his drum, which he holds in his right hand, over the woman's back. When he now spits into the water, some black colour is seen. He then drinks several bowls of water handed to him by the intermediary. The animal has now left *dBang phyug*'s body and the god has resumed control. He talks about what has happened and what has been sucked out. He asks the onlookers if it is a lump or if it has fallen apart in the water and, if that is the case, if all parts are there. The god asks everyone present to look closely and carefully. The intermediary then tells the god what is to be seen in the bowl. The god also asks us to inspect the horn and the hands and mouth of "the red one" (*dmar po,* i.e. *dBang phyug*), to see whether any cheating has taken place. No one, of course, does this. Then he tells us that it was a bird, *mtho nam mkha'i Khyung chen + dernga,* who sucked out and thus cured the illness. (8.37 p. m.) The god now continues talking and singing about various illnesses and their symptoms. He is then going to treat the younger woman, who now sits in front of him. He says that he cannot do much for her but that he will try just to ease her mind. If there is anything to be sucked out, he will take care of it. He also asks about her symptoms; has she lost her appetite, does her back ache, has she pains in the liver? The intermediary afirms all of this. The god then enumerates a number of illnesses which correspond to the symptoms and says, as far as can be understood (see below), that he is going to send for *Zangs spyang dmar po.* He then hits her three times over the back with his horn and cries "phaṭ". The woman now bares the upper part of her body and the piece of red cloth is put on her back. *dBang phyug* starts a fast and violent drumming and tinkling and the supposed wolf arrives sniffing and howling. He then pats her lightly on her back with the drum. Thereupon he sucks twice through the drum, one edge of the drum in his mouth and the opposite edge against the piece of red cloth. When he spits into the small bowl of water, a faint red colour can be seen dissolving. He then places the drum against the woman's chest, at the same time pressing his horn against her back. The red cloth is now put between her breasts. *dBang phyug* then suddenly and very quickly grabs the cloth and thrusts it into his mouth. He takes it out and holds it up; a black lump in the wrinkled cloth is the removed illness. The lump is about 5–6 mm long and 2 mm thick. After the lump has been shown to everyone, *dBang phyug* sucks through his horn from a point between the woman's breasts. At the same time he is patting her on the back with his drum. He then spits out what looks like saliva mixed with blood on the drumskin. Then the animal leaves him and the god returns. He immediately starts with an explanation of what has been done. During the singing he tears a piece of yellow cloth into ribbons, one of which he gives to the elder woman and one to the younger. He says they should wear these ribbons as a protection and as a blessing. (9.00 p. m.) The task has now been carried out and the gods are ready to leave. *dBang phyug* mentions them one by one and they all receive a drop of tea, thrown by one of the onlookers from the small bowl on the altar. (9.15 p. m.) The gods have now all been formally taken leave of and the concluding part of the séance, the so-called *rigs lnga*-game, the playing with the headdress (*ri rtsed*), starts. It soon becomes rather violent, *dBang phyug* shaking his head and body while singing to a very rapid and loud drumming. (9.35 p. m.) He now unties one of the two strings with which the headdress is held onto his head and continues the agitated movements. He sings that he is going to ask the leaving gods to tear feathers from their mounts, the *thang dkar*-birds, as they fly away. Soon small white feathers are falling in the room and the onlookers are eager to catch them before they reach the ground, as they are considered to be auspicious. Again *dBang phyug* pulls at one of the wings of his headdress, as if to show how well it is kept on his head by the *mkha' 'gro ma* (the *rigs lnga* is believed to be guarded and kept on the head on the *dpa' bo*s by one or two of these female deities.). The "play" continues while feathers swirl in the room. Then *dBang phyug* makes a short stop, while he moves his head as if following the flight of the birds. (10.06 p. m.) *dBang phyug* shakes violently, the drumming now has an intense and pulsating rhythm. (10.19 p. m.) With his left hand he now picks up a piece of grey cloth. The headdress is sliding slowly backwards on his head as the "play" nears its end. Finally, it slides off his head and stays around his neck with the wings spreading over his shoulders. He puts the grey cloth over his face and drums violently. (10.24 p. m.) The drum and the *gshang* fall out of his hands, the séance is over. For a short while *dBang phyug* sits shrunken on the bench but soon recovers and starts to collect his equipment. As he is folding his headdress two men from the audience step forward and ask to be blessed with it. They kneel in front of him and *dBang phyug* puts his folded headdress on their heads and says a prayer. Most of the onlookers have now left the house and those of us who remain are offered some food. There is now a relaxed conversation on what has happened that evening and *dBang phyug* is informed about the proceedings."

Sri gcod

He was about thirty-two years old, married and with one child. He was born in North-Eastern Tibet. He worked mainly as a porter.

Sri gcod was very reluctant to tell anything about how he conceived the possession. There are a few hints that his ideas differed from those of *dBang phyug* but nothing can be said with certainty. As in the case of *dBang phyug, Sri gcod* must send away his *rnam shes* before the possessing god enters. It is then taken care of by a certain deity, the identity of whom *Sri gcod* did not wish to reveal. He maintained, however, that it was not the whole god, so to speak, who entered his body but just the god's *rnam shes.*

The three "channels" through which possession took place according to *dBang phyug* were never mentioned at the séances of *Sri gcod* as far as could be heard. Instead the *rtsa*s were spoken of as being tripartite and the three parts as guarded by three gods: a *lha*, a *btsan,* and a *klu.*

Nor did *Sri gcod* want to speak about his *rtsa bdag* but others claimed that it was the god *A bse rgyal ba + dung dmar,* who carried out this function for *Sri gcod.* This, they said, could be understood from the fact that *Sri gcod* emitted a loud piping sound during the dance just after having become possessed. The term *rtsa ba'i bla ma* was also heard at *Sri gcod*'s séances but whom he meant specifically is not known.

At one séance, in addition, a list of deities attending and guarding the five parts of his body, as mentioned in the case of *dBang phyug,* could be heard. Of these gods, *mkha' 'gro Ye shes mtsho rgyal,* who protected his back, is perhaps the most well-known.

As an example of how his séances were structured, extracts from notes made at one of them are given here.

"When I arrive, the altar has already been built up. It consists of three flat wooden bowls, on which *gtor ma*s have been constructed. The left one is made of rice, the two others of *spags.* In front of these bowls, two smaller bowls have been placed, one filled with water and the other with milk. Between them is an oil-lamp. At the front is a bowl with tea over which a spoon has been laid. In each of the *gtor ma*s is a stick to which *tsagle*-pictures are attached. *Padma 'byung gnas* to the left, *Guru drag po* in the centre, and *mGon po ber nag* to the right. A *kha btags* is stretched over the three small paintings. In the centre bowl there are two metal mirrors of circular shape, a smaller one in front of a larger one. On the altar there are also burning incense-sticks and, on the floor, a larger bowl with burning incense. *Sri gcod* is sitting on a cushion on the floor with the altar on his left side. The séance, which is held on my account, takes place in the temple room of the small *Karma bka' brgyud pa* monastery in the village. The onlookers, mostly novices, are sitting behind *Sri gcod.* (7.50 p.m.) He whirls his drum for a few seconds, then starts to sing the invocations. During the singing he slowly rocks the upper part of his body. All the gods arrive in due order to the mirrors on the altar. When the invocations are finished he attaches a piece of red cloth to his head and starts to sing again. His voice is now louder and harsher and the rocking more violent. After a few minutes *Sri gcod* stops singing, having almost yelled the last words. Suddenly he laughs derisively; the god has taken possession of him. He puts on his headdress and sings for a short while. Then he jumps up to a standing position and executes a slow dance, standing on one leg at a time. He dances up to me, then to the lama, who is sitting on my left. The lama sprinkles him with a few drops of water with his peacock's feather. Then *Sri gcod* dances up to the temple altar, making a sort of circumambulation in the room. After that he again moves up to the lama and kneels there. The man appointed as intermediary now puts my questions to the god, *Chos skyong + chag med.* The questions concern my relatives in Sweden. The intermediary is also blessed by the lama. During the questioning the inter-mediary puts a *kha btags* over *Sri gcod*'s headdress. The god then starts to sing, explaining that he never before has been consulted by a foreigner and that it will be hard to give any answers. Then he starts to talk about Sweden, but unfortunately it is difficult to hear the details. Then he moves back and sits down in front of his altar. The god now says that a drum divination has to be performed in order to find the answers to my questions. This he performs in the following way. He holds his drum, with one of the drumskins upwards, in his right hand and lets a few grains of rice fall down on the skin from his left hand. From the configurations of the grains on the drumskin he receives the answers. This is repeated until all questions have been answered. The answers are all positive and reassuring. During the procedure he keeps his eyes closed, opening them only occasionally and showing the whites of the eyes. When he now starts to sing, he mentions things of more general interest, explaining the various parts of the séance. Among other things he says that the dance chases away the demons and he also gives some details about the first four *dpa' bo*s in Tibet, living in the time of *Padma 'byung gnas.* Then the gods prepare to leave the place. *Sri gcod* mentions them all by name and the intermediary sprinkles a few drops of tea for everyone. Then the *mkha' 'gro ma,* who has kept his headdress on his head during the séance, is asked to loosen her grip and the headdress begins to slip backwards slowly. (9.20 p. m.) The headdress falls off and he rather abruptly stops drumming. He hiccups once and slumps but remains sitting. He seems very tired but soon begins to gather his equipment. He asks the lama if he has done a good performance. On receiving an affirma-tive answer he finishes dismounting the altar.''

Nyi ma don grub

He was twenty-six years old and unmarried. He was born in Northern Tibet. He worked as a carpet-weaver in the handicraft centre in the village.

He was a friendly informant but, as he was not yet fully established as a spirit-medium, he had not completed his training. This must be remembered, as there are a number of inconsistencies in the material emanating from him, in spite of his continuous additions and corrections during interviews and informal conversations. He was clearly a very creative personality in a formative period of his life when I met him. The period of calling was not yet over and his behaviour accordingly was frequently rather eccentric.

Like *dBang phyug* and *Sri gcod, Nyi ma don grub* maintained that he had to send away his *rnam shes* before the god entered his body. He sent it to the altar, where it was taken care of by *mkha' 'gro Ye shes mtsho rgyal* during the duration of the possession. But, as he was not yet a fully trained *dpa' bo,* he sometimes carried out special séances under the supervision of his teacher *Sri gcod.* Then his *rnam shes* was taken care of by his teacher.

Concerning what happened when he became possessed, he gave apparently contradictory versions on different occasions. At one time he said that first a member of the *lha*-class arrives through *dbu ma rtsa* and stays in the head, then two members of the *btsan*-class arrived through *ro ma rtsa* and *rkyang ma rtsa* and stay in his chest and the lower part of his body, respectively. After these two another two gods arrive directly at his shoulders and stay there. Finally the two female deities in charge of his headdress arrive. One of them stretches the string which is tied around his head and the other sees to it that the knot does not become untied.

On another occasion, however, he said that the members of the *lha*-class always use the *rtsa* opening in his left hand, while members of both the *btsan*- and *klu*-class use the *rtsa* to the right. After entering, the members of the *lha*-class move upwards to the upper part of his body and the head, the members of the *btsan*-class stay in the middle part, while the members of the *klu*-class move downwards to his legs.

On a third occasion he said that members of the *lha*- and *klu*-class never enter the body of a spirit-medium, they only send their "light", *'od gzer,* into it. Only members of the *btsan*-class can possess a *dpa' bo,* he maintained.

From the tape-recordings of séances with *Nyi ma don grub,* it could be established that the *lha*-class was linked to *dbu ma rtsa,* the *btsan*-class to *ro ma rtsa,* and the *klu*-class to *rkyang ma rtsa.* Furthermore, several lists of deities associated with the five parts of the body of the *dpa' bo* could be enumerated with the help of these tape-recordings. Among these gods perhaps *Pha dam pa sangs rgyas,* a well-known historical figure, may be mentioned.

Below follows an extract from notes taken at one of the séances with *Nyi ma don grub* that I attended. It was held on account of his sick younger brother. This was the séance for which he later would receive such heavy criticism from the god during one of *dBang phyug*'s séances (see above).

"(5.40 p. m.) I arrive at the house as *Nyi ma don grub* is constructing his altar. As he has not much equipment of his own, he has borrowed most of the items from *dBang phyug* and he builds the altar in roughly the same way as he does. As for the *tsagle*-paintings, however, he has put two on a stick in the left *gtor ma* depicting, according to him, *Phyag na rdo rje* (Vajrapāṇi) and *Sa skya gong ma*; two on a stick in the bowl in the centre representing Karmapa and *lHa btsan* and two on a stick in the right bowl, depicting *mkha' 'gro Ye shes mtsho rgyal* and *shar lho Me ri mkha' 'gro.* (6.08 p. m.) The introductory prayers begin. Soon, however, he begins to sing accompanying himself with drum and *gshang.* As the singing goes on, the drumming becomes louder and his face grows paler and tighter. His eyes are closed. (6.35 p. m.) He stops singing and puts down his instruments. He takes a piece of red cloth and ties it around his head. Then he drums and tinkles violently for a short while. He puts down his *gshang* and takes up his headdress with his left hand and holds it up in front of him, while increasing the drumming. (6.42 p. m.) He puts the drum down and holds his headdress in both hands, while he sings. Then he binds it to his head, groaning and snorting. After this he starts the violent drumming again and jumps out on the floor. He dances in front of the altar and then kneels facing it. Then he jumps back up on the bench. From there the god, who is *Ma sangs rkyang khra mchor bo,* now asks why he is wearing the headdress and why he has been asked to come on this inauspicious day. He orders the questions to be put without delay and without lies. In the meantime, the intermediary appointed for the evening has lighted incense-sticks and put them on the altar. He now takes a *kha btags* and holds it in the smoke from the sticks before he puts it over *Nyi ma don grub*'s headdress. He then, with great politeness, asks the god to help the sick youth. *Nyi ma don grub* begins singing to a rather slow drum-rhythm. He first tells us about the gods, whom he can see in the mirrors. He then proceeds to describe the cave of Mount Targo in which there are the three copper-ladders that play such a significant role in one of the versions of the initiation procedure of spirit-mediums (cf. Berglie 1980: 40). The god then says that he has now borrowed a body that is like a hollow tree and that it does not belong to one of the best *dpa' bo*s but neither to one of the worst. As he sings, he rises to a kneeling position. Then he takes a few grains of rice and says he is going to perform *rtsis,* i.e. drum divination. He also describes the three members of the *lha*-class, who will supervise the procedure. (7.00 p. m.) He puts the drum on a small table in front of him and places the rice on the drumskin. He asks the onlookers to watch closely. When he then starts to sing and tinkle with the *gshang,* the grains start to move towards the altar. The intermediary tells the god what is happening. *Nyi ma don grub* then flips the grains away from the drum-skin with his index-finger, takes up the drum and starts drumming. In rapid succession he then performs two further divinations, now using only one grain at a time. The first time the grain moves noticeably towards the altar, but the second time there are different opinions among those present as to how and if the grain moved. The intermediary has a hasty discussion with one of the onlookers, and it is agreed that he is to tell the god that the grain rotated clockwise, the auspicious direction. When this has been done, *Nyi ma don grub* takes his instruments and starts the music and the song. He now sings about the young man's illness, explaining that it has been caused by eating meat of different kinds and by drinking "bad" *chang,* rice-beer. The intermediary then asks the god to do what has to be done. The god accordingly asks the patient to sit down in front of him. (7.12 p. m.) The god says he is going to expel a demon, *'dre,* from the body of the patient. The onlookers arrange themselves so that there is a free passage from the patient to the door. Then *Nyi ma don grub* presses the patient's body in the chest and in the back with his drum and bell. (7.20 p. m.) The god again mentions the causes of the man's illness: he has eaten meat, drunk *chang* from unclean cups etc. Then he feels the patient's pulse at a point on the forearm. He starts to sing again, saying that the illness is going to be sucked out but, as the borrowed body (i.e. *Nyi ma don grub*) has not yet learned this, it is going only to be an experiment. The intermediary takes a piece of red cloth, while the god summons *Zangs spyang dmar po.* Soon *Nyi ma don grub* starts a violent drumming and begins to growl and howl. The red cloth is placed on the naked back of the patient. *Nyi ma don grub* now wears a very fierce expression on his face as he growls menacingly. Suddenly he grabs the red cloth with a swift movement of his right hand and then puts it into his mouth. He chews and swallows and then puts the cloth back. Then he sucks through his drum, having placed it on its edge against the cloth. He spits out into a small bowl of water. The content of the bowl is then inspected by the intermediary and several onlookers and there follows a discussion on what is to be seen. To me it looks like small greyish particles dissolving in the water. The god is told the result of the discussion and starts to sing, pausing only to swallow the content of the bowl. (7.46 p. m.) The patient dresses when the god asks for a red-hot iron. He is told that there is not such a thing in the house, and so he takes a ribbon of red cloth and ties a knot in it while he whistles. He soaks the ribbon with oil and sets it on fire. He then puts the burning ribbon into his mouth three times, every time spitting on the patient's back. After a short song he repeats the procedure another three times, now spitting over different parts of the patient's body. Then the god, singing and talking alternatively, gives him good advice. He then takes another ribbon and holds it up in front of the altar, before giving it to the patient to keep and wear around his neck as a blessing. (7.55 p. m.) The cure has now been effected and the patient withdraws into a corner of the room, while *Nyi ma don grub* proceeds to the concluding part of the séance. He shakes his head vehemently as he sings. The intermediary refills the oil-lamp on the altar and also lights some incense-sticks. The *kha btags,* which was put over the *rigs lnga* at the beginning of the possession, now slides off but is put back by the intermediary. The gods are now leaving the place. The intermediary, however, cannot keep up with *Nyi ma don grub*'s pace and therefore fails to give some of the gods their drops of tea as a farewell offering. For this he receives scornful remarks from the god. (8.10 p. m.) The concluding part of the séance is now well under way, with *Nyi ma don grub* making violent movements of the head and upper part of his body. The singing is now and then interrupted by snorting. He leans to the right and to the left so that the wings of his headdress cover his face. The headdress is now slowly sliding backwards. (8.29 p. m.) The headdress falls off his head and stays around his neck. He snorts loudly. He is slumping backwards in a sitting position, while his head falls forward against his chest. The séance is over.''

Concluding remarks

In the notes on séances given above, only the external procedures have been recorded. What, on the other hand, the spirit-mediums themselves experienced, they found hard to describe. When they sang the invocations, which mostly consisted of names of gods interspersed with urgings and pleadings for them to come to the place, they could see the gods arrive, some of them riding on birds, others on horses. They also saw them dismounting, putting away their saddles, weapons etc. and arranging themselves according to rank. This ability to see the gods in the mirrors is not, however, restricted to spirit-mediums, I was told. Lamas and *sngags pa*s are also supposed to have it. When all the gods summoned have arrived, possession took place by the god most suited to carry out the task of the evening. *dBang phyug* said that he then saw all the colours of the rainbow in the mirrors and that all became very bright when the gods arrived. When then the god was to take possession of him, his body felt enlarged and as if filled with air. *Sri gcod* said that when his *rnam shes* was going to leave his body, he saw a glowing fire of many colours. This fire grew bigger and bigger and finally entered his body, as it were. After that, everything became black and he remembered nothing further. At the end of the possession all this happened in the reversed order. *Nyi ma don grub* was able to give a somewhat more detailed relation. Every time he sang the invocations, he said that he saw three stars in the mirror: one white, one red, and one blue. They corresponded to the three classes of gods: the *lha-*, the *btsan-*, and the *klu*-class respectively. During the introductory part of the séance his experiences of his surroundings were altered. The people in the room seemed to become smaller and smaller, while their voices became thinner and squeakier. Their eyes became brighter and glittered and shone. The mirrors on the altar, on the other hand, grew larger and larger and finally filled his entire field of vision.

The actual change of the ritual status of the spirit-medium is marked by the putting on of the headdress. From now on, until it falls off at the end of the séance, it is the god who speaks and acts through the medium, who afterwards claims that he has no recollection whatsoever of what then passes. The onset of the possession is also marked by motoric agitation, sometimes of a violent nature, as often in the case of *Nyi ma don grub,* followed by a dance on the floor or on the sitting-bench. *dBang phyug* said that there were different dances, e.g. the dance of the *mkha' 'gro ma,* of the elephant etc., but could not give any details. After dancing the god usually sits down, introduces himself and asks, often in very rude and offensive language, why he has been called. From then on the séance moves on as outlined above.

A necessary condition for the activity of a spirit-medium is, of course, the conviction that their possession is genuine. Theoretically, when a *dpa' bo* has passed the period of calling and has been tested and has received the necessary training, this genuineness is proved (cf. Berglie 1976: 88–93). Of an established *dpa' bo* no further proofs are therefore required in addition to the satisfactory solution of the problems put to him at the séances. If, after all, someone has doubts about a *dpa' bo,* he can call a lama, a *sngags pa,* or another *dpa' bo* and let him look into the mirrors to make sure that it is gods who have arrived and not demons in disguise. No such check, I was told however, had ever been made in the village. In spite of this, it is hard to avoid the impression that the spirit-mediums felt a continuous need to prove the reality of the possession. As mentioned above, rather spectacular features were often added to the séances, although not necessarily required. I am referring to the throwing of glowing charcoal and the playing with fire in the séances of *Nyi ma don grub* and to the falling of *thang dkar*-feathers in the séances of *dBang phyug*. All religious rites and ceremonies do of course exhibit varying degrees of theatricality and the séances of the *dpa' bo*s, largely "one-man-shows", are no exception. Although features such as those mentioned perhaps more properly belong to this dimension, they can also be ascribed to a medium's aspiration to show the audience the powers of the gods and impress on it the reality of their presence. This must not be regarded as overshadowing the main aspect of every séance, which is that of a serious and purposeful ceremony in which the principal actor, the possessing god, is treated with trust and humility.

In another study I have tried to show that beliefs in possessional states are to be found at many levels and in many contexts in Tibetan religion (cf. Berglie in press). They involve consciousness-transference of one kind or another and are, as in the case of the *dpa' bo*s, expressed in Indian Buddhist terms. To these spirit-mediums and to their clients and audience therefore, possession is neither anything mysterious or inexplicable nor anything demanding analysis and speculation. Their séances were, normally, well-ordered procedures where nothing unexpected was likely to happen if the *dpa' bo* knew his procedure.

References

Berglie, P.-A. 1976. Preliminary remarks on some Tibetan "spirit-mediums" in Nepal. *Kailash, a journal of Himalayan studies* 4, 1, 85–108.

— 1978. On the question of Tibetan shamanism. *Tibetan Studies,* ed. by M. Brauen and P. Kvaerne, 39–51. Zürich.

— 1980. Mount Targo and Lake Dangra: a contribution to the religious geography of Tibet. *Tibetan Studies in Honour of Hugh Richardson,* ed. by M. Aris and Aung San Suu Kyi, 39–44. Warminster.

— in press When the corpses rise: some Tibetan Ro langs stories. *Indologica Taurinensia* 9. Torino.

Dasgupta, S. B. 1958. *An introduction to Tantric Buddhism.* Calcutta.

Eliade, M. 1969. *Yoga: immortality and freedom.* (Bollingen Series 56.) New York.

Govinda, A. 1959. *Foundations of Tibetan mysticism.* London.

Snellgrove, D. L. 1957. *Buddhist Himalaya.* Oxford.

— 1959. *The Hevajra Tantra* 1. (London Oriental Series 6.) London.

Stablein, W. 1976. Tantric medicine and ritual blessings. *The Tibet Journal* 1, 3/4, 55–69.

Tucci, G. 1961. *The theory and practice of the Maṇḍala.* London.
— 1970. Die Religionen Tibets. *Die Religionen Tibets und der Mongolei* 1–291. (Die Religionen der Menschheit, ed. by C. M. Schröder. 20.) Stuttgart.
Wayman, A. 1973. *The Buddhist Tantras: light on Indo-Tibetan mysticism.* New York.
— 1977. *Yoga of the Guhyasamājatantra.* Delhi.

The Taʿziya Ecstasy as Political Expression

By JAN HJÄRPE

The cover of a number of the Iranian Islamic Republic Party Weekly Bulletin,[1] from August 1981, consists of a picture, a drawing representing a large building, demolished evidently by a bomb planted there by some enemy. Among the debris we can see pools of blood. Outlined against the dark sky above we read the words:

> bi-ʾayyi dhanbin ḳutilat ("for what sin she was slain")

Beneath the legend appears dimly a coffin carried by many hands. On the coffin is a carpet with the inscription

> yā maẓlūm Karbalāʾ ("Oh Thou wronged one of Kerbela")

The picture, with its inscriptions, provides a highly concentrated illustration of how Islamic concepts and Shīʿī-Islamic historiography serve as patterns of interpretation in the political field in revolutionary Iran.

The picture of the demolished house symbolizes the activities of the militant opposition against the theocratic regime of Iran, especially the assassination of leading personalities by means of planted bombs. The inscriptions and the coffin hint at the regime's view of this opposition. They relate the events to the frames of reference, the "cognitive universes" (to use Peter Berger's terminology) of Shīʿī Islam, and thus provide the legitimation,[2] or part thereof, of the measures taken against the opposition. In other words, we find here religion as a pattern of interpretation, and thus also of behaviour; religion as a source of attitudes and feelings leading to political standpoints and acts.

The first legend is a quotation from the Quran, from the description of the Day of Resurrection and Doom, in Sura 81:

And when the female child that had been buried alive shall be asked (8) for what sin she was slain (9).

Traditionally this verse is seen as alluding to the pre-Islam Arab custom of the disposal of newborn children for whom they could not provide by

---

[1] IRPWB 1: 44, Aug. 28, 1981, cover.
[2] For this use of the term "legitimation", see Berger, 29.

burying them alive.[3] The quotation of these words constitutes an interpretation of the sabotage and the attempts on the lives of the leaders. The victims are innocent as newborn children, and the assassinations as criminal as the killing of those infants; a crime against God and his Law.

The coffin, carried by a host of hands, implying a crowd of mourners, is interpreted via the inscription and symbolizes an identity or similarity between those killed among the leading IRP members, and the victims of Kerbela and even some sort of identification with Imām Ḥusayn himself.

The crucial event in the history (and the historiography) of Shīʿī Islam is the battle of Kerbela in Iraq (680 A D) where the third Shīʿī Imām, Muḥammad's grandchild al-Ḥusayn, fell attempting a revolt against the Umayyad Caliph Yazīd.[4] In the Shīʿī historiography there is a multitude of traditions about Kerbela and all the persons involved, traditions about all they said, all they did, and everything that happened. Much of the material is obviously legendary, but even this, in all its detail, indicates the central role of Kerbela in the Shīʿī part of the Muslim world.[5]

The tragedy of Kerbela has left its mark on the spirituality of Shīʿīsm and its view of religion and politics. Shīʿīsm is the religion of sorrow, of martyrdom, of sentimentality, but also of opposition and insurrection. To put it in another way: Opposition and insurrection, self-sacrifice and hatred of enemies can find legitimation, i.e. patterns of interpretation, in the Shīʿī traditions of the martyrdom of Ḥusayn and his followers at Kerbela. The drama constitutes a set of roles, with which one can identify oneself and one's friends and enemies; because the drama of Kerbela is alive, living history, always present in the minds primarily by means of the liturgical repetition, the annual commemoration of Kerbela in the ʿĀshūrāʾ celebration.[6]

Taʿziya, "consolation", has become the Shí technical term for the liturgical mourning and commemoration of the martyred Imāms, particularly the ritual lamentation for the death of Ḥusayn, celebrated formerly often in the form of passion plays in which the heart is the drama of Kerbela, but in which in addition the whole of human history is viewed *sub specie Kerbelae*. Nowadays the celebration is first and foremost in the form of processions (in our Western mass media called "demonstrations"), engag-

---

[3] Cf Andrae, KHÅ 1924, 220, and Paret ad loc. This interpretation of the verse is not the only possible one, cf Blachère I, 37f, but it is the one which would most readily come to the mind of the Muslim reader.
[4] For a comprehensive account of the insurrection and its consequences, see Veccia Vaglieri, 608 ff.

[5] For its role in contemporary Shīʿī historiography, cf Ende, 153 ff and 160 ff.
[6] For the use of the term "role" here, and for the importance of the liturgical repetition in role-creation, cf Sundén 1966,, 51 ff, and passim, but especially 214 ff.

ing huge masses of people in emotion-evoking behaviour, also including processions to the cemetery.

For the contents of the classical Shī'ī passion plays and their performance, and for the theological interpretation of the sacrifice of Ḥusayn and the other martyrs, we refer the reader to the available literature on the subject.[7]

The Ta'ziya of Ḥusayn falls in the month of Muḥarram, with its culmination on the 10th day (rūz-i ḳatl, "the day of the murder"), the 'Āshārā' festival, and is followed up by the mourning ceremony on the 40th day (rūzi arba'īn) from the 'Āshūrā' (20th day of Ṣafar).

It is important to note the immense impact of the Ta'ziya on the emotions of the participant masses, emotions aroused by several means. We have here the suggestive sentimentality of the speeches held by the Mullās, dwelling on the tribulations and sufferings of Ḥusayn and his family and followers, on the cruelty and baseness of his enemies, and on the courage of the 72 noble-hearted martyrs of Kerbela. In the processions, the emotions are aroused by the rhythmical repetition of formulae expressing mourning for the martyrs and hatred of their murderers. Many of the participants are dressed in shrouds, many wear chains, ropes and scourges, and the lamentations are accompanied by self-flagellation of the naked backs. People beat their breasts, some have put earth on their heads. Women weep, bewailing the pains of Ḥusayn and the 72.[8]

With regard to the exaltation of the masses, the sentimental raptures of the participants, we may speak of the Ta'ziya-ecstasy, ecstasy at least in the sense of self-induced excitement, but also ecstasy as abnormal states of consciousness,[9] provoked by the flagellation, the repetition of the formulae etc, but not ecstasy in the sense of total loss of reaction to external stimuli.[10]

The feverish exaltation of the participants sometimes proves dangerous for others. The hatred of the murderers of the Imāms and the martyrs is channelled against non-Shī'īs, foreigners etc, identified in the excitement with the enemies of *ahl al-bayt,* the family of the Prophet. But the reaction can also occur in such a way that the positive component predominates: a fervent desire to help the oppressed, the wronged.[11]

The theological speculation and systematization around the tribulations of the Imāms constitute an important part of the Shī'ī interpretation of

---

[7] See Monchi-Zadeh, passim, and for a short orientation Strothmann, 590f.

[8] A very sympathetic account by an eye-witness from the year of the Revolution, from the 'Āshūrā' in 1978, is given by Hunt, 87f.

[9] Cf. Inge, 157.

[10] Cf. Sundén 1974, 50f.

[11] Cf. Hunt, 88f.

existence. Some of this became relevant to political action during the Revolution (and afterwards). In a widely circulated pamphlet about martyrdom, Āyatullāh Murtaḍā Muṭahharī (himself killed during the Revolution and thus considered a martyr)[12] explains the roles of the martyrs. He relates several of the traditions about the early martyrs, and the rules regarding their burial—their bodies shall not be washed and dressed in shrouds as in the case with the ordinary dead, but they are to be buried in their own blood-stained clothing.[13] From the tales of the early martyrs he concludes that martyrdom is necessary to save Islam from corruption. The blood of the martyrs gives life to the whole *Umma,* and thus they live forever in the people.[14] From the rules for burial he concludes that the martyrs are pure, the ablution is performed in their own blood.

The martyrs are like candles which are burnt out,[15] giving their light to all believers. This theme frequently recurs in the "iconography" of the Revolution.[16] In several respects the martyrs are above other human beings. Their "logic" surpasses the capacity of the ordinary man's comprehension,[17] they have the power of intercession on Doomsday, etc. Martyrdom is a role to assume, a pattern to follow. Muṭahharī quotes a prayer which is read on the nights of Ramaḍān:

Oh God! let us be killed in your way, in the company of your friend (Imam) and attain martyrdom.[18]

We can find allusions to this identification in the interpretation of the war with Iraq. Let me quote a passage in a message from Khumaynī:

A number of leading army officers were here with me two days ago, and they urged me to prohibit further visits here of the 'peace mission', for they would not quit fighting. They told me 'we entered the battlefields like Imam Hussein and we welcome a martyrdom like that of Hussein'.[19] (Quoted from the English version printed in IRPWB)

The role ascribed to martyrdom is also stressed very strongly in the constitution of the Islamic Republic.[20]

Let us now consider the dates of some important events in Iran, not according to our Gregorian calendar but in the Islamic Hidjra calendar. We find that the first part of the month of Muḥarram is of significance, particularly the days around the ʿAshūrāʾ, the commemoration of the tragedy of Kerbela on the 10th day of the month.

---

[12] He was shot on May 1st, 1979. Cf the eulogies in IRPWB 1: 28, May 8, 1981, 7–16.
[13] Mutahery, 12.
[14] Mutahery, 28 f.
[15] Mutahery, 11.

[16] The picture (Fig. 2) is reprinted frequently, e.g. in ash-Shahīd.
[17] Mutahery, 26 f.
[18] Mutahery, 22.
[19] IRPWB 1: 38, July 27, 1981, 30.
[20] Kānūn-i asāsī, 5.

الشهيد مهدي رزاقي   مشاعل على الطريق

Fig. 1. Caption and inscription: "Caravan of Martyrs", "Lights on the road". (From ash-Shahīd 16/8 1399, 11/7 1979, 42.)

The uprising in 1963 (end of May, beginning of June) coincided with this period. This occasion was also the definitive break-through of Āyatullāh Khumaynī[21] as a popular and well-known religious leader. He was arrested on June 4th. On June 5th (in the Iranian calender: 15th of Khordad) occurred the great uprising against the Shah. In the Hidjra calendar it was the third day of the 'Āshūrā'. In the revolutionaries' own historiography this was the beginning of the end for the Shah. Khumaynī in a speech on the celebration of the anniversary of the uprising in 1981, makes the following statement (here quoted from the "English" version in IRPWB):

With its 'no' for an answer to the Yezidians, on the day of Ashura, Islam cast them away from the scene of all history and sent them to the grave, and so too our people sent the Pahlavid and the Pahlavians to the grave by their uprising /on the 5th of June 1963/ ...[22]

In Shī'ī historiography the tragedy of Kerbela (in 680) is considered the beginning of the process which led to the fall of the Umayyads (in 750).[23]

In 1978 the 'Āshūrā' coincided with the climax of the demonstrations against the Shah (10th and 11th December). The ritual cry "Death to

---

[21] Cf also Nyberg, 40.
[22] IRPWB 1:33, June 12, 1981, 23.

[23] For contemporary Shī'ī historiography and its tendencies, cf. Ende, 113–169.

Yazīd" became the political slogan "Death to the Shah". The 'Āshūrā' processions assumed the role and function of demonstrations.[24]

In 1979 the days around the 10th of Muḥarram (the turn of the month November–December) were marked by huge demonstrations outside the then occupied[25] US Embassy in Tehran. We could see pictures from the demonstrations on TV showing that many of the participants were dressed in shrouds, the symbolic expression of willingness to accept martyrdom.[26]

In 1980, the 'Āshūrā' celebration provided an interpretation of the war with Iraq—or rather, in the view of the regime in Tehran, the war imposed by the "atheist" Saddām Ḥusayn. To fight in the war is considered "a Ḥusaynic act".[27] The concept of martyrdom, and the interiorization of this concept by the liturgical repetition, undoubtedly played a considerable role in creating the morale of the Iranians in their resistance against the Iraqi attack. Enthusiasm for martyrdom entails courage, self-sacrifice, perseverance, and also includes the frenetic hatred of those who are identified as "Yazīdians". In combat, the Taʿziya ecstasy becomes a reality.[27a]

We find these interpretative patterns all the time: Āyatullāh Khumaynī is called "heir of Ḥusayn", "the Ḥusayn of our time" etc, both in prose and in popular poetry,[28] and the murderers of President Radjāʾī are "worse than Ibn Muldjam"[29] (who killed ʿAlī b. Abī Ṭālib). It is of special interest here to study the reactions to the blowing-up of the IRP Headquarters on June 28th (1981), where Beheshtī, among others, was killed. This event is obviously alluded to in the picture first mentioned.

News of the number of victims spread immediately: 72 people killed, and it was underlined that the June 28th martyrs were of the same number as the martyrs of Kerbela.[30] Even when it became apparent that the number of victims was greater, the figure was retained. An editorial in the evening paper *Kayhan* after the deaths of Radjāʾī and Bāhonar mentions the event of June 28th with the words "as a result of which more than 72 aides of Imam Khomeini ... were martyred".[31]

Living history; the interpretation of the "now" is made by the comparison with the "then". I quote here from the description of the funeral of

---

[24] Cf. Hjärpe, 8.
[25] The Embassy was occupied on November 4th, i.e. immediately after the ʿĪd al-aḍhā that year. The Occupation coincided in time with the "Stoning of Satan" in the Ḥadjdj rituals.
[26] Cf also Nyberg, 147.
[27] See e.g. Mahjubah 1: 1, April 1981, 17.
[27a] For a description of the enthusiasm in battle, cf. e.g. Time, March 22, 1982, 32 f.

[28] See e.g. ash-Shahīd, 13th of Ṣafar 1400, 40 f.
[29] IRPWB 1: 45, Sept. 4, 1981, 22.
[30] Cf. IRPWB 1: 43, Aug. 21, 1981, 24, and IRPWB 1: 37, July 10, 1981, 6.
[31] Kayhan, Shahrivar 11, 1360/Sept. 2, 1981, 2.

Indian newspaper praises young martyr

TEHRAN -- The weekly Islamic English-language newspaper 'Radiance', published in New Delhi, recently devoted a 2½ column feature to the memory of a young martyr. Excerpts follow:

"A few days ago, the radio and television of the Islamic Republic of Iran had announced that a thirteen year old boy had after fastening several bombs around his waist, jumped before an Iraqi tank. Consequently the enemy tank was blown up with many Iraqi soldiers.

"The name of that young martyr was Muhammed Hussein Fahinidah. Some Guards of the Islamic Revolution paid a visit to the family members of the young martyr in Qom. The information obtained through this interview is given in brief.

"Father: Muhammed Hussein was a very active boy. He had many virtues. We never saw him do any thing wrong act. He always tried to tread God's path during his studies and also in all other activities.

"Mother: My son's martyrdom is a glorious matter for me. Every one tells me how merciful is Almighty God upon me by gifting such a child to me. I am not at all regretful about my son's sacrifice in his path.

"Brother : Even while schooling he had devoted himself to the Islamic Revolution. Once when we heard on radio that a thirteen year old boy was killed by throwing himself beneath a tank, he became angry with his parents.

"At that time we did not know that he was our own brother. We thought, alas we should have died in his place. Twelve days thereafter the Revolutionary Guards informed us about his martyrdom. They were praising his courage.

"Aunt: We are very pleased that Hussein was martyred in this path. We would not have hesitated to offer even a greater sacrifice. Hussein was a very handsome boy. He loved his mother father and family members very much. He was regular in his namaz and was always obeying God's order in every respect. He never hurt anybody. He was always helpful to all."

"Inna Lillahe Wa Inna Rajeoon".

Fig. 2. (From Tehran Times, Ordibehesht 22nd 1360, May 12th 1981, 2.)

Radjā'ī and Bāhonar in IRP's Weekly Bulletin, reproducing the account by the Pars' correspondent (the report was in English):

Pars correspondent in front of the Majlis reported at 8:30 a.m. on 31st August, 1981 that crowds entered the area while a tape of President Rajai'e was being played for the people. While the people were crying and heading towards Behesht-e Zahra Cementery they shouted: "We are not like the inhabitants of Kufa, to desert Hussein—even if the Ummat dies, the Imam will never be abandoned" ... At 8:45, crowds filled the streets around the Majlis and chanted "Today is the day of mourning, today, Rajaie and Bahonar are with the martyrs." The people also shouted: "Death to Banisadr" and "Death to the U.S." and "The Party of Allah may die but it never submits to compromise" ... The crowds of mourners set out at 10: 50, while they were beating their chests and crying "Hussein, Hussein", to carry the pure bodies of President Mohammad Ali Rajaie and Prime Minister Mohammad Javad Bahonar to Behesht-e Zahra Cemetery near Tehran.[32]

We know that the cemetery in question served as a centre for the opposition to the Shah. Those killed before and during the Revolution were considered martyrs, and the ritual mourning, especially on the 40th day after death, became political demonstrations, with more victims. Many have observed both the periodicity (every 40th day) of these manifestations and their highly emotional character.[33] This continued after the Revolution. In connexion with the celebration of the 40th day of the June 28th victims, a speech was held, among others, by the 15 year–old son of Ḥasan Āyat—who was murdered a few days earlier. Kayhan reports:

According to the report after the speech of Dr Ayat's son, the crowd of worshippers burst out chanting: "Ayat! Ayat! We swear by your chaste blood that your way is continued'." "The measures of the prosecutor's office perpetuate the revolution, our martyr's blood is awaiting answer." "The armed hypocrite! it is the last moment for you!" "Hezbullah, Hezbullah fights atheism, Hezbullah, Hezbullah will never abandon the scene".[34] (Ḥizb Allāh, "God's party").

In all the papers and magazines issued by the present regime in Tehran, the martyr-motif is stressed. Stories constantly appear about those who have sacrificed their lives for the sake of God (i.e. the Islamic Republic).[35] It is very interesting to note that this concept of religio-political martyrdom also operates in the interpretation of events outside the Muslim world. Official Iran declares its support for the IRA in Northern Ireland and its great sympathy for the "martyrs", the hungerstrikers. A delegation of Iranian Mullās was even sent to Ulster to convey the Islamic Republic's support and sympathy to the IRA. They also visited Bobby Sands' mother, presenting her with a portrait of Imām Khumaynī, all of which was reported and commented upon in the Iranian press.[36] The Shī'ī theologians visiting Ireland recorded with astonishment the lack of enthusiasm among the Catholic priests for the suicidal hunger-strikes.

Even in a hopeless situation where flight or surrender would be possible and more profitable, the martyrdom, the voluntary self-sacrifice, is regard-

---

[32] IRPWB 1: 45, Sept. 4, 1981, 24 and 27. Also in Kayhan, Shahrivar 10, 1360/Sept. 1, 1981, 1.

[33] Cf Nyberg, 144 f, 126.

[34] Kayhan, Mordad 17, 1360/Aug. 8, 1981, 1 and 4.

[35] Cf Fig. 2, quoted from Tehran Times, Ordibehesht 22, 1360/May 12, 1981, 2.

[36] Cf. e.g. Kayhan, Mordad 21, 1360/Aug. 12, 1981, 3, and Kayhan Shahrivar 1, 1360/Aug. 23, 1981, 6, and Mordad 30/Aug. 23, 6.

ed as something positive. Several of the "martyrs" during the Revolution and in the war with Iraq fall into the category of death in suicidal actions against the enemy. Such acts are also frequent in the *attacks on* the IRP regime in Iran. But also those killed unprepared, in ambush or by bombs, are regarded as martyrs.

The highly emotional evaluation of martyrdom sometimes finds expression in remarkable ways. Let me here quote, in its entirety, a eulogy to Āyatullāh Beheshtī after his death in the June 28th outrage. The following prose poem was published in the Ṣawt al-Umma:

> Oh Beheshtī!
> Oh blood of God, shed on the miḥrāb of djihād!
> Oh blood belonging to God, poured out at the threshold of submission to God and the obedience, which painted the fruits of Islam's tree with its deep-red colour, this colour which will continue to tell our future generations the tale of heroism and of the combat of expiatory sacrifice (*al-fidā'*), and emit the radiations of power and the charges of resistance in the hearts which beat in faith and determination.
> Criminal hands were extended, moved by dark black hearts, and guided by a headquarter of infidels; they were extended from the darkness (or: from the oppressors), in order to pick a generous and pure flower; and so a ripe noble fruit was broken off, and to extinguish a sun among the suns of guidance and truth, and to blunt a sword among the sharp swords of Islam, and to break a javelin among its victorious javelins, and to obliterate a soul among the original and firm souls, and to silence a tongue among the tongues of faith which did not haggle and did not dispute.
> The troops of error saw in you the power which threatened their weakness, the originality which vanquished their hypocrisy, and the words of truth and honesty which chase away their vanities and idle talk, and the clarity which tears to pieces the veil of scepticism.
> They found in you the tongue of Abū Dharr, the firmness of Maytham, the sublimity of Hagar and the faith of 'Ammār, and they imagined that by killing you they would be able to recover their languishing breath and bring back the /faculty of/ motion to their trembling collapsing body, and the power to their weakened heart.
> And it eluded them that the blood of Ḥusayn which appeared from the earth of Karbalā' was the sun which illuminated the paths of the mudjāhids, and that his martyrdom was the resounding cry which awoke the "enveloped ones" and the "covered ones", and frightened God' enemies throughout history ...
> And they forgot that the blood of the martyrs on the path of God is the everlasting fuel of the Islamic revolution, and the charges of vigilance and attention, and incitements to power and unity, and reasons for self-sacrifice (*fidā'*) and devotion.
> And you fell, Oh Beheshtī!, blood-stained, your blood mingled with the milk of piety, and your body collapsed in order to prostrate before God, having made the /ritual/ ablution with your own blood, the blood of martyrdom, in an eternal prostration (*sudjūd*). You expired praising God. You expired dressing yourself in the dress of martyrdom, and your pure ghost ascended the ladder of God's pleasure, which it had awaited to meet with desire and patience, just as it had persevered to live in the wounded heart of the *Umma*, in order to force it to continue on the way

of truth, which your body followed carefully and your blood served and the water of the pure martyrs ... and /your ghost expired/ as a vow from us to you that we shall persevere, defying the dangers of the long road—we shall not pay any attention to them, and we shall not permit the weariness to trample down our souls, and we invest our blood and our ghosts as a *wakf* for Islam and the Islamic revolution, until God calls us by his command. "But God makes his light perfect, even if the infidels dislike it".[37]

Comments:
"Blood of God": The meaning is that Beheshtī was so near to God that God is the one who can claim the right to vengeance in accordance with the *lex talionis*.

Miḥrāb of *djihād*: A pun. The author alludes to the common root of the words ḥarb, "war", and miḥrāb, "niche indicating the direction of prayer". The man of prayer dies as a holy warrior.

Abū Dharr (al-Ghifārī): One of the companions of the Prophet, nowadays often quoted as the representative of "radical socialism" in early Islam, and as a harsh critic of social inequities.

ʿAmmār (b.Yāsir): In tradition known as a fervent supporter of ʿAlī b. Abī Ṭālib.

"Enveloped", "covered": Quranic terms (Sura 73 and Sura 74) with special Shīʿī interpretations.

Sudjūd: The metaphor is striking: Beheshtī's body fell down, just as if he were performing the ritual prayer.

Umma: The community of the Muslims.

Wakf: Foundation for religious purposes.

"But God makes etc": Allusion to Sura 61:8 "They want to extinguish with their mouths the light of God, but God makes his light perfect, even if the infidels dislike it".

The wallowing in the sentimentality of blood recurs in the frequent publication of pictures of the blood-stained bodies of the martyrs.[38] In the editorial of the same issue of *Ṣawt al-Umma* the emotional reaction to the June 28th incident makes the writer lose all sense of order and coherence. The article consists of an outpouring of disconnected sentences expressing mourning and faith in the sublimity of martyrdom. This editorial article could itself be called a literary reflection of the Taʿziya ecstasy.[39]

The Taʿziya, in the sense of the ritual mourning connected with the funeral of those considered martyrs, leads to an excitement, to a frenzy on the part of at least some of the participants, allowing us to speak of ecstasy in the meaning of abnormal states of consciousness. As for the burial of the victims of the June 28th outrage, IRP's Weekly Bulletin says:

---

[37] Ṣawt al-Umma 16, Shaʿbān 1, 1401/July 15, 1981, 10. The article is signed "Abū Mikdād".

[38] Cf e.g. the pictures of the corpse and the face of Muṭahharī in IRPWB 1:28, May 8, 1981, front page, and pages 10 and 16.

[39] Ṣawt al-Umma 16, Shaʿbān 1, 1401/July 15, 1981, 3.

... Reports from the cemetery said that because of the massive throng of mourners and their being highly emotional several people became unconscious or were injured.[40]

The pictures published in the newspapers from this occasion, and from the burial of Radjā'ī and Bāhonar[41] are also interesting in this respect. And, as we have seen, this ta'ziya excitement expresses, or is channelled into, actual political action.

References

Periodicals:
Islamic Republic Party Weekly Bulletin. Teheran. (IRPWB).
Kayhan International. Teheran.
Mahjubah. The Magazine for Muslim Women. Teheran.
Ṣawt al-Umma. Teheran.
ash-Shahīd. Teheran.
Tehran Times.
Time. The Weekly Newsmagazine. New York/Amsterdam.

Literature:
Andrae, T. 1923, 1924, 1925. Der Ursprung des Islams und das Christentum. *Kyrkohistorisk Årsskrift.*
Berger, P. 1969. *The sacred canopy.* New York.
Blachère, R. 1949–1951. *Le Coran. Traduction selon un essai de reclassement des sourates.* Paris.
Ende, W. 1977. *Arabische Nation und islamische Geschichte.* Beirut.
Hjärpe, J. 1980. *Politisk islam.* Stockholm.
Hunt, P. 1981. *Uppdrag i Iran.* Örebro.[42]
Inge, W. R. 1912. Ecstasy. *Encyclopaedia of Religion and Ethics.*
Ḳānūn-i asāsī-yi djūmhūrī-yi islāmī-yi Īrān. 1358 (1979). Teheran.
Monchi-Zadeh, D. 1967. *Ta'ziya, das persische Passionsspiel.* Stockholm.
Muṭahharī, M. see the following.
Mutahery, M. 1979. *The martyr.* Karachi. (Also published in Teheran).
Nyberg, E. 1981. *Iran i kamp med det förflutna.* Stockholm.
Paret, R. 1971. *Der Koran. Kommentar und Konkordanz.* Stuttgart.
Strothmann, R. 1961. Ta'ziya. *Shorter Encyclopaedia of Islam.*
Sundén, H. 1966.[4] *Religionen och rollerna.* Stockholm.
— 1974. *Religionspsykologi.* Stockholm.
Veccia Vaglieri, 1971. al-Ḥusayn b. 'Alī b. Abī Ṭālib. *Encyclopaedia of Islam.*

---

[40] IRPWB 1:37, July 10, 1981, 9.
[41] See Kayhan, Shahrivar 10, 1360/Sept. 1, 1981, 1 and 4, and IRPWB 1:45 Sept. 4 1981, 24 and 27, is also interesting in this respect.

[42] I have not been able to procure a copy of the original English version of the book (Inside Iran).

Berserker und Erzbischof—Bedeutung und Entwicklung des altnordischen Berserkerbegriffes

Von ÅKE V. STRÖM

War die Ekstase, bzw. das ekstatische Benehmen, die ausschlaggebende Eigenschaft, die einen Mann zum Berserker machte? Liegt das Berserkersein also auf dem psychologischen Gebiet, wie etwa der Fall ist mit einem Mystiker? (Ström 1970, 222). Diese Frage ist verschiedentlich beantwortet worden, sei es in bezug auf die Bedeutung des Wortes *berserkr,* sei es betreffs des Inhalts der Sache. Die Frage vom Wesen des Berserkers und somit der Berserkerwut muß bis jetzt als ungelöst bezeichnet werden.

1. Die Bedeutung des Wortes

Über die Bedeutung des Wortes *berserkr* gibt es zwei Meinungen, beide merkwürdigerweise im ersten Band eines führenden nordischen Handbuches vertreten, natürlich jedoch in verschiedenen Artikeln (Lid 1956, 502; Bernström 1956, 663). Eine alte Übersetzung aufnehmend, machte Erik Noreen geltend, daß das Wort sowohl aus formalen als auch, und besonders, aus sachlichen Gründen *berserkr<berr serkr,* 'bloßes Hemd', also „im bloßen Hemd kämpfend" bedeute (Noreen 1932, 254). Diese Auffassung des Wortes kehrt noch bei Hans Kuhn wieder: „á berum serk, þad er brynjulaus" (Kuhn 1949, 107, vgl. Bernström 1956, 663).

Dagegen wurde von Nils Lid die Meinung verfochten, daß *berserkr* mit **bernu>bjǫrn,* 'Bär', zusammenhänge (Lid 1956, 502). Gleichzeitig hat Jan de Vries das Wort in derselben Weise als 'Bärenhaut' gedeutet, d.h. es handle sich um „Menschen in tiergestaltiger Vermummung" (de Vries 1956, 454). Noreens Meinung ist „abzulehnen" (de Vries, 1977, 34; so schon Spegel 1712 s.v., Höfler 1934, 170, Note 10 und Dumézil 1931, 81). Ein Berserker war so oder so in Bärenkleider angezogen.

2. Der Inhalt des Begriffes

Auch betreffs des sachlichen Inhalts gehen die Meinungen auseinander. Eine Richtung findet das Typische in der sog. Berserkerwut, der ekstatischen Tobsucht.

Daran geben die Quellen mehrere Beispiele.[1] Eine isländische Sage erzählt von zwei Berserkern, die beide Haukr hießen:

Þeir grenjuðu sem hundar ok bitu í skjaldarrendr ok óðu eld brennanda þerum fotum.

Sie heulten wie Hunde, bissen in den Schildrand und gingen mit bloßen Füßen durch lohendes Feuer. (*Vatsd.* Kap. 46)

Eine andere Saga schildert die Berserkerwut (*berserksgangr*) zwei schwedischer Berserker so:

Þeir gengu berserksgang, ok váru þá eigi í mannlegu eðli er þeir váru reiðir, ok fóru galnir sem hundar ok óttuðusk hvárki eld né járn.

Sie gerieten in Berserkerwut, und sie hatten dann nicht mehr menschliche Natur, wenn sie zornig waren, sondern benahmen sich toll wie Hunde und mieden weder Feuer noch Eisen. (*Eyrb.* Kap. 25)

Hier wird auch das Ende der Berserkerwut beschrieben:

Berserkirnir ... váru móðir mjǫk, sem háttr er þeira manna, sem ekki eru einhama, at þeir verða máttlausir mjǫk, er af þeim gengr berserksgangrinn.

Die Berserker ... waren sehr müde, wie es der Fall ist mit den Männern, die ,,zweigestaltet'' sind, daß sie sehr machtlos werden, wenn die Berserkerwut von ihnen weicht. (*Eyrb.* Kap. 28)

Auch Saxo Grammaticus schildert die Berserkerwut:

Haldanus ... septem filios habebat tanto veneficiorum usu callentes, ut saepe subitis furoris viribus instincti solerent ore torvum infremere, scuta morsibus attrectare, torridas fauce prunas absumere, exstructa quaevis incendia penetrare.

Halvdan hatte sieben Söhne, die so sehr in Zauberei kundig waren, daß sie oft, wenn sie von plötzlichen Kräften der Wut ergriffen wurden, grausig zu heulen pflegten, in die Schilde bissen, feurige Kohlen verschlangen und irgendwelches angezündete Feuer durchdrangen. (*Gesta Dan.* VII, 2:7, vgl VI, 7:5)

Die vielleicht beste Beschreibung gibt Snorri Sturlason, auffallenderweise in der Geschichte der Uppsalakönige:

[Óðins] menn fóru brynjulausir ok váru galnir sem hundar eða vargar, bitu í skjǫldu sína, váru sterkir sem birnir eða gríðungar: þeir drápu mannfólkit, en hvártki eldr né járn orti á þá; þat er kallaðr berserksgangr.

[Odins]Männer drangen ohne Panzer hervor und waren toll wie Hunde oder Wölfe, bissen in ihren Schild und waren stark wie Bären oder Stiere. Sie schlugen die Mannsleute tot, und weder Feuer noch Eisen schnitten in sie. Das wird Berserkerwut genannt. (*Yngl.* Kap. 6)

---

[1] Sämtliche Textstellen über Berserker und Berserkerwut sind in Lagerholm 1927, 143–145 verzeichnet. Die wichtigsten sind in Grøn 1929, 13–26 referiert.

Der älteste, sicher vorchristliche Beleg steht in dem zeitgenössischen Gedicht von Þórbjǫrn hornklofi über die Schlacht bei Hrafnsfjǫrð im Jahre 872 (Noreen, 1932, 247):

Grenjuðu berserkir	Die Berserker heulten,
gunnr var þeim á sinnum,	der Kampf ging auf das Ende,
emjuðu ulfheðnar	die Wolfsverhüllten schrieen
auk ísǫrn dúðu ...	und schüttelten Speere ...
At berserkja reiðu vilk spyrja,	Über das Wesen der Berserker will ich fragen,
bergir hræsævar:	Leich-See-Schmecker (Bluttrinker):
Hversu er fengit	Wie steht es
þeims í folk vaða	mit den kampffrohen Männern,
vígþjǫrfum verum?	die zum Streit gehen?

3. Die psychopathische Erklärung

Auf die letztgenannte skaldische Frage antwortet Nils Lid folgendes: ,,Man kann ein ziemlich klares Bild von ihnen kriegen ... Die Berserker waren psychisch labile Menschen, die durch Suggestion sich selbst einbildeten, sie waren in Raubtierschemen ... einer Art Psychopathen''. Lid legt also das Konstitutive des Berserkerseins in die Veranlagung (psychisch oder sogar psychopathisch) des Menschen, obwohl er auch nebenbei erwähnt, daß die Berserker der Wikingerzeit ,,an die Gefolgschaft des Königs in kleinen Haufen angeknüpft sein konnten'' (Lid 1956, 501 f.).[2]

Wenn die Berserker psychopathisch waren, wie steht es denn mit dieser Sache unter psychiatrischem Gesichtspunkt? Eine Theorie ist schon von dem schwedischen Geisteswissenschaftler Samuel Ödman († 1829) aufgestellt.[3] Sie wurde vom norwegischen Botaniker F. C. Schübeler hundert Jahre später aufgenommen. Sie meinten, die Berserkerwut wäre die Wirkung eines mit Willen durch Fliegenpilz (Ödman: *Agaricus muscarius*, Schübeler: *Amanita muscaria*) hervorgerufenen Rausches (Ödman, 1784, 245; Schübeler 1885, 224). Durch Vergleich mit dargelegter Wirkung des Fliegenpilzes in Kamtjatka[4] glauben sie bewisen zu können, daß die Berserkerwut als psychopathologische Furoranfälle aufzufassen sei. Diese

---

[2] Lids norwegische Text auf ,,nynorsk'' lautet: ,,Ein kan få eit nokolunde klart bilete av dei ... B. var psykisk labile menneske som med suggerering sjølv førestelte seg at dei var i rovdyrham ... eit slag psykopatar''. – ,,Dei kunne vera knytte til kongens fylgje i små flokkar.''

[3] Vor Ödmann (der sonst seinen Namen mit zwei n schrieb) haben folgende zwei über das Berserkertum geschrieben: Hamnell 1709 und Ramelius 1725. Der Erste, der in unsrem

Jahrhundert die Berserker behandelt hat, ist meines Wissens Hermann Güntert (de Vries 1956, 494, Note, schreibt: G. Güntert) in einem schwer zugänglichen Buch (Güntert 1912).

[4] Ein paar Jahre später schrieb Ödmann ein kleines Buch über Kamtjatka, nämlich ,,Beskrifning om Kamtschatka, dess invånare och physiska märkvärdigheter'', Uppsala 1787.

Theorie ist in mehreren pharmakologischen Handbüchern und Konversationslexica 1900–1910 zu finden (Grøn 1929, 6 mit Noten).

Dagegen macht der norwegische Mediziner Fredrik Grøn geltend, daß 1. die Wirkung des Pilzes in hohem Maße von dem Wachstumsplatz abhängig ist, 2. die Wirkungsdauer des Pilzes zu lang ist, 3. das Krankheitsbild ganz verschieden ist (Grøn 1929, 29–33). Statt dessen behauptet er – wie Lid – daß „die Berserker Psychopathen waren, die in hohem Grade für Suggestion und Selbstsuggestion zugänglich waren ... Sie können ohne Zweifel oft dem paranoischen Typus hinzugerechnet werden oder der Klasse der Hystero-epileptiker angehört haben (Grøn 1929. 58).

4. *Die soziologische Erklärung*

Schon 1927 behandelte Lily Weiser [-Aall] die altgermanischen Männerbünde und ihre Weihungen, und sie sah die Berserker als Mitglieder eines solchen Bundes (Weiser 1927, 43–82). Als Vergleich zog sie die südgermanischen Bünde und Weiheriten der Chatten und Harier (*Tac. Germ.* Kap. 31 und 43) heran (Weiser 1927, 31–43). Damit war der Nachdruck von der Berserkerwut an die soziologische Stellung der Berserker verschoben.[5]

Vorzüglich auf germanischem Boden arbeiteten weiter Otto Höfler, der den Zusammenhang „dieser hochaltertümlichen, offenbar ursprünglich theriomorphen Dämonenkrieger" mit dem König hervorhob (Höfler 1934, 67, 264–269), Georges Dumézil, der die Berserker in die indogermanische Gesellschaft soziologisch eingliederte (Dumézil 1939, 79–91), und Rickard von Kienle, der den Männerbund im allgemeinen als Gefolgschaft des Fürsten dargelegt hat (von Kienle 1939, 137–234, vgl. schon Ödman, 1784, 241).

Diese Linie wurde von einer Reihe Komparatisten aufgenommen und von einer uralten indogermanischen Erscheinung beleuchtet, nämlich den kriegerischen Männerbünden, die auf indischem, iranischem und römischem Gebiet in mimischer Vermummung die Vorfahren darstellten und eine spezielle Organisation und Sitte besaß (Wikander 1938, 64–104; Dumézil 1948, 39–54, 150–152: *gandarva's* und *luperci*) bis Geo Widengren die zusammenfassende Darstellung der indogermanischen Gefolgschaft mit ihrer militärischen und religiösen Organisation gegeben hat (Widengren 1969, über Germanen 45–63, 97–101).

Einen wichtigen Einsatz in diesen Zusammenhängen machte schon 1949 Hans Kuhn in einem bahnbrechenden aber leider übersehenen Aufsatz auf Neuisländisch, wo er dem Wort *berserkr* einen fast neuen Inhalt gibt. In

---

[5] Über diese bahnbrechende Arbeit schrieb Professor Noreen in Lund, es lohne sich nicht, auf sie Bezug zu nehmen!! (Noreen 1932, 247). Es ist gefährlich, seiner Zeit voraus zu sein!

dem großen angelsächsischen Gedicht Beowulf aus dem 8. Jahrhundert wird ein Mann in der Leibwache der Fürsten *cempa* genannt, V. 206, u. a. Beowulf selbst, V. 1312, 1525 (Kuhn 1949, 104). Das Wort heißt isl. *kappi* und wird gleichermaßen verwendet. Durch Analyse einer Reihe von Edda- und Saga-Stellen stellt Kuhn fest, daß dieselben Personen abwechselnd *kappar* und *berserkir* genannt werden können, was also zeigt, ,,hve stutt var milli kappa og berserkja" (Kuhn 1949, 110). *Ásmundar saga kappabana* nennt diejenigen *kappar*, die der Hauptperson tötet, *berserkir* (Kuhn 106 f.). Snorri Sturluson spricht von König Rolfs Leibwache als *berserkir*, während *Hrólfs saga kraka og kappa hans* ihnen den Namen *kappar* gibt (Kuhn 109). Arngrims zwölf Söhne mit einer Königstochter heißen in einigen Sagas *berserkir*, so auch im Eddagedicht *Hyndluljóð* V. 24—dasselbe Gedicht spricht aber in V. 18 von *kappar* u.s.w. (Kuhn 110). So war es kein Unterschied zwischen *miklir kappar* und *miklir berserkir* (Kuhn, 108). In Karlamagnús saga sagt man: *vér berserkir og kappar* (Lagerholm 1927, 145). Vgl.: ,,Berserkr est souvent un simple synonym de Viking" (Dumézil 1939, 90). Die Bärengekleideten Krieger der Vendel- und Torslundaplatten können ohne weiters Berserker in der Bedeutung Königswache sein, obwohl sie ohne die geringste Spur von Wut auftreten (de Vries 1956, 454, 498).[6]

5. Eine neue Kombination der Linien

Meine Thesen sind jetzt die Folgenden:

A. Die Kämpfer der fürstlichen Leibwache wurden *kappar, berserkir* und *ulfheðnir* genannt ohne Rücksicht auf irgendeine Berserkerwut.[7]

B. Die Initiation mit Ordalien (vielleicht auch berauschenden Mitteln) können psychologische Zustände erweckt haben, die in gewissen Fällen später wiederhergerufen werden konnten.

C. Diese Zustände können in christlicher Zeit, z.B. unter den Sagaschreibern, den Begriff *berserkr* gefärbt haben.

Den Beweis führe ich folgendermaßen.

A. Die Quellen erwähnen oft Königsmänner ohne Wut, die Berserker genannt werden, z.B. die ganze Verwandtschaftslinie in *Hyndl.* 24, Harald Schönhaars ehemalige Männer Ulfr Bjálfasonr und Berölu-Kári in *Eigla* Kap. 1, ja, sogar in christlichem Zusammenhang: in seinem Vermächtnis 1389 schreibt ein Kreuzbruder Narfue Mathiosson aus Oslo:

---

[6] Über das weitere archäologische Material (Vendel, Valsgärde, Pliezhausen und Sutton Hoo) siehe Ström 1975, 123 Note 77.

[7] Über das Verhältnis der beiden letzteren Begriffen und über die Art des Pelzes siehe näher Höfler 1934, 26, Note 73.

wæll ek lægherstað j sancti Haluarðz kirkiu neer mæistara Oghmunde bærserk frenða minum.

wähle ich Ruhestätte in S:t Halvards Kirche nahe an Meister Ögmund, dem Berserker, meinem Verwandten. (*Dipl. Norv.* IV, Nr. 564, S.422)

In einem Diplom von 1354 verrichtet ein unbekannter Mann, Thorer berserker, eine Flurbereinigung zwischen König Magnus Eriksson und

Olaffuer medh gudz myskun erchibiskup i Nidherass.

Olav mit Gottes Erbarmen Erzbischof in Nidaros. (*Dipl. Norv.* II, Nr. 326, S. 265–268).

Hoffentlich ist Thore nicht während der Verrichtung in Berserkerwut geraten! Späte Sagas wie Barl. sprechen sogar von einem ,,Berserker Jesu Christi'' und dieser als *berserkr Guðs* (Lagerholm, 1927, 145).

B. Über diesen Punkt darf folgendes gesagt werden. Nicht jedermann hatte Zutritt zu den Gemeinschaften oder Kulten der Männerbünde (Höfler 1936, 35). Es war notwendig, eine umfangsreiche Initiation durchzumachen. Vielleicht hat die Volsungasaga in der Erzählung von Sinfjǫtle (*Vols.* Kap. 7 und 8) den nicht mehr verstandenen Initiationsritus für Berserker bewahrt (Weiser 1927, 70–82; Höfler 1934, 199–202; Eliade 1977, 295). Die Königsmänner=Berserker haben, den Quellen nach zu urteilen, einen eisernen oder sogar goldenen Ring bekommen (Höfler 1934, 198f.; 1952, 191f. mit. Note 410; Ström 1969, 704f.).

Zur Initiation gehörte auch Stärke-, Mut- und kriegerische Proben, z. B. einen Feind oder ein gefährliches Tier, besonders einen Bären, zu überwinden und zu töten (*Tac. Germ.* 31: 1f; *Prokop, De bello Pers.* II: 25, Weiser 1927, 73f., Dumézil 1939, 92f.) und dazu Feuerproben (Weiser 75–77).

Ohne Zweifel haben ekstatische Übungen zur Initiation gehört, und vielleicht können narkotische oder andere halluzinogenen Drogen, z. B. Fliegenpilz, dabei wirksam verwendet worden sein. Soweit wir sehen können, war die Verkleidung in Felle ,,the essential moment of initiation into a man's secret society'' (Eliade 1977, 295).

C. In christlichen Gesetzen war *berserksgangr* verboten, und die Strafe dafür war die kleinere Friedlosigkeit, *fjǫbaugsgarðr, Grágás* I: 7, *Grett.* Kap. 19. (über diesen Begriff Ström 1975, 205). Aber schon früh ist etwas passiert: ,,Die vielen Berichte über die Berserker zeigen klar die Entartung und spätere Verwilderung'' (Weiser 1927, 56). Es scheint klar, daß ,,die spätere romantische Literatur ihre ursprüngliche Bedeutung verwischt hat'' (de Vries 1956, 454). Diese Entartung und Verwischung hat die ekstatische Züge in den Vordergrund treten lassen. Die Einübung in Ekstase bei der Initiation kann teils ekstatische Spuren in der Persöhnlichkeit hinterlassen haben, teils in allzu hohem Grade den Begriff *berserkr* gefärbt haben. Wie das Zungenreden in der Pfingstbewegung kann das ekstatische Benehmen ,,als ein bedeutungsvolles Glied in einem Anschlußvorgang eines Individuums an eine gewisse Bewegung aufgefaßt worden" (Holm 1976, 43).

6. *Odin und Berserkertum*

Odin und seine Kämpfer werden von Snorri als Berserker mit Berserkerwut und dazu gehöriger Anästhesie und Furoranfällen beschrieben (*Yngl.* Kap. 6 f.). Auch war ja Odin teils der Gott der Häuptlinge und der Männerbünde teils der Ekstase (Ström 1975, 115–118). Die alte Ekstasesilbe *wōd* kehrt in seinem Namen wieder (Höfler 1973, 286). Überdies hatte er nahe Verbindung mit dem Bären. Die gotischen Könige waren in Bärenpelz gekleidet (Abels 1966, 30). Selbst konnte Odin *Hrjótr*, 'der Brummer', oder *Jǫlfuðr*, 'der braungelbe Arsch', angesprochen werden (de Vries 1957, 65; 1977, 258, 294 f.), ja, er wird einmal *Bjǫrn* genannt (*Harð.* Kap. 15), einmal *Bruno*. 'der Braune' (*Gesta Dan.* VIII, 4: 8).

Die fürstliche Leibwache, die in Bärenpelz gekleidet einen Männerbund mit ekstatischer Initiation darstellte, hat im Zeichen Odins gekämpft. Die psychopathologische Berserkerwut ist aber nicht das Kennzeichnende, sondern ihre königliche und odinistische Verbindung. Vor kurzem hat Höfler darauf gedeutet, daß die ,,Reservekräfte" der Berserkerwut, wie in der Dionysos-Sage, vom Gott bewirkt und verliehen werden (Höfler 1973, 55). Dadurch gehört die Berserker und die Berserkerwut zur Religionsgeschichte, nicht nur zur Psychologie, Pathologie oder Soziologie.

Noch heute trägt die königliche Wache der Svea Livgarde in Stockholm Bärentatzen, gleichwie die Hauptwache auf Amalienborg in Kopenhagen, Royal Foot Guards in Whitehall, Royal Scots Dragoon Guards Band und Canadian Foot Guards. Für die Hochzeit zwischen dem Prinzen von Wales und Lady Diana Spencer wurden 300 Bärenmützen neubestellt nebst den 3 000, die in Großbritannien gebräuchlich sind (Carter 1978, 3). Nur Journalisten und Zuschauer gerieten in Ekstase, nicht die pelzgekleidete Wache. Und doch sind diese Mützen, nach meiner und anderer Meinung (Möhl 1977, 126), ein Rest der Ausrüstung der Berserker, mit denen ein Erzbischof verkehren konnte.

Literatur

Abels, K. 1966. *Germanische Überlieferung und Zeitgeschichte im Ambraser Wolf Dietrich* (*Wolf Dietrich A*). Diss. Freiburg i. Br.

Bernström, J. 1956. Björn. *Kulturhistoriskt lexikon för nordisk medeltid* 1. Helsingfors ...

Carter, N. T. N. 1978. *The bearskin*. London (Stenzil).

Dumézil, G. 1939. *Mythes et dieu des Germains*. Paris.

— 1948. *Mitra-Varuna*. Abbeville.

Eliade, M. 1977. *From primitives to Zen.* Collins. Fount paperbacks.

Grøn, F. 1929. *Berserksgangens vesen og årsaksforhold.* (Det Kgl. Norske Videns-kabers Selskabs Skrifter 1929, 4.) Trondhjem.

Güntert, H. 1912. *Über altisländische Berserker-Geschichten.* (Beilage zum Jahres-bericht des Heidelberger Gymnasiums 1912.) Heidelberg.

Hamnell, O. 1709. *De Magia Hyperboreorum Veterum.* Diss. Uppsala.

Holm, N. G. 1976. *Tungotal och andedop.* Diss. (Acta Universitatis Upsaliensis. Psychologia religionum 5.) Uppsala.

Höfler, O. 1934. *Kultische Geheimbünde der Germannen* 1. Frankfurt am Main.

— 1936. Der germanische Totenkult und die Sagen vom wilden Heer. *Oberdeutsche Zeitschrift für Volkskunde* 10.

— 1952. *Germanisches Sakralkönigtum* 1. Tübingen.

— 1973. *Verwandlungskulte, Volkssagen und Mythen.* (Österreichische Akademie der Wissenschaften. Phil.-hist. Klasse. Sitzungsberichte, 279, 2. Abhandlung.) Wien.

Kuhn, H. 1949. Kappar og berserkir. *Skírnir* 123.

Lagerholm, Å. 1927. *Drei lygisǫgur.* (Altnordische Sagabibliothek 17.) Halle.

Lid, N. 1956. Berserk. *Kulturhistoriskt lexikon för nordisk medeltid* 1. Malmö.

Möhl, U. 1978. Bjørnekløer og brandgrav. *Kuml* 1977.

Noreen, E. 1932. Ordet »bärsärk». *Arkiv för nordisk filologi* 48.

Ramelius, E. 1725. *Berserkus Furorque Berserkius.* Diss. Uppsala.

Schübeler, F. C. 1886. *Viridarium Norvegicum.* Christiania.

Spegel, H. 1712. *Glossarium Suiogothicum.* Stockholm.

Ström, Å. V. 1959. The King God and his Connection with Sacrifice in Old Norse Religion,. *Studies in the History of Religions.* (Supplements to NUMEN) 4. Leiden.

— 1970. Formes de mystique dans le Nord préchrétien. *Mysticism.* (Scripta Insti-tuti Donneriani Aboensis 5.) Stockholm.

— 1975. Germanische Religion. Å. Ström-H. Biezais, *Germanische und Baltische Religion.* (Die Religionen der Menschheit 19,1.) Stuttgart.

Weiser [-Aall], L. 1927. *Altgermanische Jünglingsweihen und Männerbünde.* (Bau-steine zur Volkskunde und Religionswissenschaft 1.) Bühl (Baden).

Widengren, G. 1969. *Der Feudalismus im alten Iran.* (Wissenschaftliche Abhand-lungen der Arbeitsgemeinschaft für Forschung des Landes Nordrhein-Westfalen 40.) Köln-Opladen.

Wikander, S. 1938. *Der arische Männerbund.* Lund.

de Vries, J. 1956, 1957. *Altgermanische Religionsgeschichte* 1–2. (Grundriß der germanischen Philologie 12.) Berlin.

— 1977. *Altnordisches etymologisches Wörterbuch.* Leiden.

Ödman[n], S. 1784. Försök, at utur Naturens Historia förklara de nordiska gamla Kämpars Berserka-gång. *Kongl. Vetenskaps Academiens nya Handlingar.* Tom. V för år 1784. Stockholm.

III

Ecstatic Prophesy in the Old Testament

By GUNNEL ANDRÉ

When speaking of prophets in our culture, we usually have the Old Testament classical prophets in mind. At the mention of prophetic ecstasy the immediate reaction is often, "That would be Saul and the asses or Elijah and the prophets of Baal". A sharp distinction is often made between the so-called primitive prophets and the classical prophets. Bearing in mind that the Chronicles mention chronicles, prophesies, visions and narratives of various non-classical prophets there is a certain danger that we make a distinction between different prophetic types more sharply than was done in Old Testament times.

In this paper ecstasy is treated purely in its own terms, and the literary problems of the OT, such as the age of the texts, the various types of texts, and also the possibility of gradual changes in prophetic activity or the concept of prophecy are disregarded.

I will proceed from the definition of a prophet by Johannes Lindblom, "a person who, because he is conscious of having been specially chosen and called, feels forced to perform actions and proclaim ideas which, in a mental state of intense inspiration or real ecstasy, have been indicated to him in the form of divine revelation" (Lindblom 1973, 46). This definition makes it expedient to begin with a closer examination of the classical prophets. Lindblom himself starts with a thorough study of the primitive prophets stressing that "primitive" is not intended in a pejorative sense. I can only feel that his definition, if it does not exclude, at least strongly modifies some of the texts that are usually presented as examples of ecstatic prophecy and for this reason I will use a different point of departure.

According to the definition a prophet is conscious of having been called. In Isa 6 we find the call of Isaiah in the form of a vision with auditive elements. Isaiah says that at a certain time he *saw* God sitting on a throne, dressed in a mantle, whose train filled the temple. God was surrounded by bewinged seraphim flying around and proclaiming a threefold "Holy". In his vision Isaiah experiences the shaking of the foundations of the thresholds and the smoke filling the temple. He continues to say that in his vision he bewailed himself and his unclean lips. One of the seraphim touched his lips with burning coal from the altar, thereby removing his sin. Then Isaiah *hears* God ask, "Whom shall I send, and who will go for us?" Isaiah volunteers and receives his commission, "Go, and say to this people [. . .] " The message follows.

A closer look at the text proves that the prophet could not possibly be referring to something that his outward eyes and ears see or hear. God is not a person, whom human eyes can see, nor are the seraphim beings which normal eyes can perceive. Burning coal on his lips would have hurt him and prevented him from speaking.

At the same time it is hardly correct to say that Isaiah did not see anything with his normal vision. If the prophet was in the temple at the festival for the celebration of YHWH's kingship it is easy to identify the stimuli that formed what his inward eye saw, viz. the two winged cherubim on the ark turning into flying seraphim. The cherubim were thought of as the throne of the invisible YHWH, who to the prophet's inner eye appeared as a divine king dressed in a royal mantle. Each wing of the cherubim was five metres in length and when these huge statues became living seraphim for Isaiah's inner eye their voices became a thunder which made the temple shake. The smoke from the incense altar was perceived as smoke filling the temple and the coal of the altar became the instrument of forgiveness. The cherubim, which he saw as seraphim, appeared as the council of YHWH, at which a prophet must have sat to be regarded as a true prophet (e.g. Jer 23: 18, 22).

The call of Jeremiah (Jer 1) is also told in a mixture of vision and audition, and it begins with the very common introduction to a revelation, "The word of YHWH came to me", followed by the word of YHWH in 1 sing.form. YHWH and Jeremiah carry on a dialogue where the prophet protests over his mission with reference to his youth. He also says: "Then YHWH put forth his hand and touched my mouth; and YHWH said to me, "Behold, I have put my words in your mouth.' " A summary of the message follows.

Jeremiah then relates two visions in connection with his call. Both of them are introduced by the well-known "The word of YHWH came to me". In the first vision (vv. 11–12) YHWH asks, "Jeremiah, what do you see?" The prophet answers, "I see a rod of almond." YHWH explains, "You have seen well for I am watching over my word to perform it". Whether the prophet actually had an almond-tree in front of him or not is impossible to say. The important thing is that the Hebrew word for almond-tree is *šāqēḏ* and the participial form of "watch over" is *šoqēḏ*. The almond-tree thus gives Jeremiah an association with the watchfulness of YHWH.

The second vision (vv. 13–19) contains the same question, "What do you see?" The prophet answers, "I see a boiling pot, facing away from the north." YHWH explains, "Out of the north evil shall break forth upon all the inhabitants of the land." Then follows YHWH's more precise exposition which among other things contains the exhortation, "But you, gird up your loins; arise, and say to them everything that I command you." In this case too it is hard to say whether the prophet actually had a pot in front of him or not. He could very well have done so while the pot to his inner eye appeared in the north. The fact that he sees the pot in the north is probably to be explained by a mixture of the tradition of the enemy from the north and political clear-sightedness.

The account of the call of Ezekiel (chs. 1–3) is the most detailed narrative and more complicated than the previous ones. In the double introduction Ezekiel himself refers to time and place and says, "The heavens were opened, and I saw visions of God." In the second introduction someone else says that Ezekiel found himself in that particular place at that particular time, and that "the hand of YHWH was upon him there." The vision which follows is full of details and comparisons. Ezekiel sees a fire-flashing cloud coming out of the north, and it is surrounded by brightness and in the middle of the fire there is something *like* gleaming bronze. From the midst of it came the *likeness* of four living creatures, they looked *like* human beings, but nonetheless they had four faces and four wings each. The description continues in the same fashion. The prophet sees YHWH in the same vague way:

Above the firmament over their heads there was the *likeness* of a throne, *in appearance like* sapphire, and seated above the *likeness* of a throne was a *likeness as it were of* a human form. And upward from what had the *appearance of* his loins I saw *as it were* gleaming bronze, *like the appearance of* fire enclosed round about; and downward from what had the *appearance of* fire, and there was brightness round about him. *Like the appearance of* the bow that is in the cloud on the day of rain so was the *appearance of the likeness* of the glory of YHWH. And when I saw it, I fell upon my face, and I heard the voice of one speaking.

This vision displays several features in common with the vision of Isaiah: the fire, the bewinged creatures who behaves partly in the same manner as the seraphim, the thunder, the being resembling a man on a throne, that is a king. Ezekiel sees the throne above the heads of the bewinged creatures, but he mentions no temple, which raises the question, of whether Ezekiel saw his vision in the temple before the fall of Jerusalem as did Isaiah, and thus had the same external stimuli. If so, the note that Ezekiel was in Babylon is secondary. Did Ezekiel see his vision in Babylon thus receiving other external stimuli than Isaiah or receiving none at all? In any case, what Ezekiel sees, he sees with his inner eye.

The vision continues. The prophet has fallen on his face and he hears God talking to him, "Son of man, stand upon your feet, and I will speak with you." Ezekiel describes his reaction, "When he spoke to me, the spirit entered into me, and set me upon my feet; and I heard him speaking to me." The prophet hears YHWH say, "I send you to the people of Israel [. . .] you shall say to them 'thus says YHWH God'." The summary of the message is replaced by the exhortation to prophesy and the unexpected "Open your mouth, and eat what I give you." Ezekiel then describes how a hand offered him a scroll, how the scroll was spread out before him, and how he received a renewed exhortation to eat it. YHWH said to him, "Son of man [. . .] fill your stomach with it", and Ezekiel obeys, "I ate it; and it was in my mouth as sweet as honey."

After YHWH's continuing pep-talk Ezekiel says that a spirit lifted him up and that he heard a roaring "Blessed be the glory of YHWH, wherever it is!" He also heard a thunder from the creatures. The vision ends "The spirit lifted me up and took me away, and I went in bitterness in the heat of my spirit, the hand of YHWH being strong upon me; and I came to the exiles at Telabib, who dwelt by the river Chebar. And I sat there over-whelmed among them seven days." Are these last two verses a part of the vision or not? If they are, then the geographical information means that with his inner eye he saw his experiences as a prophet in the place where he actually found himself, in Babylon. If they describe a real journey, from where did he set out, Jerusalem or Babylon, and how are then the state-ments about the spirit and the hand of YHWH to be understood?

The Old Testament contains more texts featuring the calling of prophets, but these are sufficient examples of the arousal of consciousness. They have been chosen since they also show examples of ecstasy defined as "an intensive experience which totally engages the individual, a psychical state characterized by the fact that the person is much less open to outward stimuli than in a normal state".[1]

It is common to the texts on prophetic calls that the prophets retain their own personalities, that is to say, there is no *unio mystica*. All of them regard themselves as having been called and sent out to be the mouthpieces of YHWH, that is to say, the visions do not primarily concern themselves or their own benefit. On the contrary, they convey to the prophets that they are to face hardships. "Fear not" occurs in some visions. How they reacted physically to these visions we do not know.

---

[1] General definition for the symposium.

With regard to outward stimuli it is very likely that Isaiah's vision was provoked by his visit to the temple, quite possible that Jeremiah really saw a tree and a pot, but unclear how the vision of Ezekiel came about. It is certainly possible and maybe even probable that Ezekiel knew of the vision of Isaiah and that he clothed his own experiences in traditional expressions (cf. 1 Kings 22).

The commissions of the prophets are presented in summary. Their further work is based on new revelations focussed on the message. The prophet is a speaking instrument for YHWH as Aaron was for Moses, "YHWH said to Moses, 'See, I make you as God to Pharaoh; and Aaron your brother shall be your prophet. You shall speak all that I command you; and Aaron your brother shall tell Pharaoh [...]' " (Ex 7:1f.). The prophets often, but not always, begin their oracles with such formulae as "The word of YHWH came to me", "YHWH says", "so says YHWH" etc. As we now have them these are sometimes redactional, although they occur often enough within the oracles to suggest that the prophets themselves used them. It was important to the true prophets to stress that they spoke the word of YHWH and not their own. This is shown by their criticism of false prophets. These were not sent by YHWH but they prophesied in the name of YHWH, speaking the ideas of their own hearts and not those coming from YHWH, they stole prophecies from one another, they were to be placed on a par with diviners, dreamers, soothsayers and sorcerers, they followed their own spirit etc. It was typical of the false prophets to prophesy happiness and welfare.

A true prophet knew that his message came from YHWH and that he was forced, whether he liked it or not, to speak it. They were convinced that it was YHWH speaking to them and acting on them and the terminology is theological. It is therefore difficult to interpret their words in psychological terms.

The redactional heading of the Book of Isaiah says that the book contains the vision of Isaiah concerning Judah and Jerusalem, but the oracles as we now have them are seldom visions. Apart from Ezekiel and Zechariah, the oracles by other prophets are likewise for the most part not in the form of visions. More precisely the prophets express themselves as if they have heard the message. It is mostly impossible to trace what happened to the prophets often, but not always, begin their oracles with such formulae as present it to the audience. A revelation, which in the moment of experience could have been a vision to the inner eye, could, when it is presented to the audience after a shorter or longer period of time, have been interpreted and rationalized to the result, "YHWH says". This process of transformation is in most cases elusive. We only have the result.

The lack of information is not total. Isa 12: 1–4 runs:

As whirlwinds in the Negeb sweep on, it comes from the desert, from a terrible land. A stern vision is told to me; the plunderer plunders, and the destroyer destroys. Go up, O Elam, lay siege, O Merdia; all the sighing she has caused I bring to an end. Therefore my loins are filled with anguish; pangs have seized me, like the pangs of a woman in travail; I am bowed down so that I cannot hear, I am dismayed so that I cannot hear, I am dismayed so that I cannot see. My mind reels, horrors have appalled me; the twilight I longed for has been turned for me into trembling.

It is noteworthy that the panic and deaf-mute state described by the prophet is a result of the vision, fear of the dreadful fate of the country. The inducement of the vision is not mentioned nor do we know in what state the prophet was when he saw his vision.

Several texts in the Book of Ezekiel indicate that the prophet was mute and paralyzed after a vision, e.g. Ez 3: 22–27:

The hand of YHWH was there upon me; and he said to me, 'Arise, go forth into the plain, and there I will speak with you'. So I arose and went forth into the plain; and lo, the glory of YHWH stood there, like the glory which I had seen by the river Chebar; and I fell on my face. But the spirit entered into me, and set me upon my feet; and he spoke with me and said to me, 'Go, shut yourself within your house. And you, O son of man, behold cords will be placed upon you, and you shall be bound with them, so that you cannot go out among the people; and I will make your tongue cleave to the roof of your mouth, so that you shall be dumb and unable to reprove them; for they are a rebellious house. But when I speak with you, I will open your mouth, and you shall say to them [. . .]''

The prophet is told to stay alone as long as the paralysis lasts, but he will be able to speak clearly when it is time to meet the audience. In another case the paralysis is extremely public and meant to be a symbolic act, Ez 4: 4–8:

Then lie upon your left side, and I will lay the punishment of the house of Israel upon you; for the number of the days that you lie upon it, you shall bear their punishment. For I assign to you a number of days, three hundred and ninety days, equal to the number of years of their punishment; so long shall you bear the punishment of the house of Israel. And when you have completed these, you shall lie down a second time, but on your right side, and bear the punishment of the house of Judah; forty days I assign you, a day for each year. And you shall set your face toward the siege of Jerusalem, with your arm bared; and you shall prophesy against the city. And, behold, I will put cords upon you, so that you cannot turn from one side to the other, till you have completed the days of your siege.

The paralysis itself works as an accusation of guilt and the face of the prophet turned towards Jerusalem and his outstretched arm symbolize a threat.

Daniel mentions feebleness (10: 8–11):

> So, I was left alone and saw this great vision, and no strength was left in me; my radiant appearance was fearfully changed, and I retained no strength. Then I heard the sound of his words; and when I heard the sound of his words, I fell on my face in a deep sleep with my face to the ground. And behold, a hand touched me and set me trembling on my hands and knees. And he said to me, 'O Daniel, man greatly beloved, give heed to the words that I speak to you, and stand upright, for now I have been sent to you'. While he was speaking this word to me, I stood up trembling.

A contrary state of severe pain is represented in Jer.4: 19, "My anguish, my anguish! I writhe in pain! Oh, the walls of my heart! My heart is beating wildly; I cannot keep silent." In another place he says, "My heart is broken within me, all my bones shake; I am like a drunken man, like a man overcome by wine" (23: 9).

These texts may suffice as examples. A more extensive study of the material proves the dominance of paralytic reactions over vigorous movements of the body.

The question of how a prophet arrives at a revelatory state of mind is even more difficult to answer, but there are examples. Habakkuk says (2: 1–3):

> I will take my stand to watch, and station myself on the tower, and look forth to see what he will say to me, and what I will answer concerning my complaint. And YHWH answered me: 'Write the vision; make it plain upon tablets, so he may run who reads it. For still the vision awaits its time; it hastens to the end-it will not lie. If it seems slow, wait for it; it will surely come, it will not delay.

Another example occurs in the Balaam-story in Nu 23: 3 ff. "Balaam said to Balak, 'Stand beside your burnt-offering, and I will go; perhaps YHWH will come to meet me; and whatever he shows me I will tell you'. And he went to a bare height. And God met Balaam [...] and YHWH put a word in Balaam's mouth, and said, 'Return to Balak, and thus you shall speak' ". This is repeated, but at the end of the story the following happens (24: 1 ff.):

> When Balaam saw that it pleased YHWH to bless Israel, he did not go, as at other times, to look for omens, but set his face toward the wilderness. And Balaam lifted up his eyes, and saw Israel encamping tribe by tribe. And the spirit of God came upon him, and he took up his discourse, and said, 'The oracle of Balaam the son of Beor, the oracle of the man whose eye is opened, the oracle of him who hears the words of God, who sees the vision of the Almighty, falling down, but having his eyes uncovered'.

Habakkuk (2: 1 ff.) stationed himself on a wall of the fortification to look for God's answer. Daniel had probably fasted for three weeks before a certain vision (10: 2), while Elijah was ordered by YHWH to go and hide by a

13–Religious Ecstasy

brook and drink its water. He was promised that ravens would bring him
bread and meat (1 Kings 17: 2–6).

These texts indicate that the prophets often were alone when they
experienced their revelations. Consequently, we know nothing of the reaction of their environment.

We learn from other texts that the prophets called out their message. The
Hebrew verb *qārā'* basically means "to call aloud". Trito-Isaiah (58: 1) was
ordered, "Cry aloud, spare not, lift up your voice like a trumpet". If Isaiah
(1: 2) and Micah (6: 1) actually yelled when they called on heaven and earth,
mountains and hills as witnesses is hard to tell. It is probably a cultic
expression to be taken less literally.

In some cases (Ez 21: 2; Am 7: 16; Mi 2: 6, 11) "prophesy" is combined
with *hiṭṭîp,* "let drip", which is said sometimes to refer to froth dripping
through the beard (1 Sam 21: 14). In two of the four cases, Amos and
Micah, a non-prophet tells a prophet to stop this activity, and in one case a
false prophet is involved. This does not necessarily mean that the prophets
behaved as if they were mad. It could just as well refer to their boiling rage
and the sprinkling of spit. It could also be a pejorative expression.

A true prophet speaks clearly and distinctly. The criticism of false
prophets also refers to their mumbling (Jer. 23: 31) or their talking unintelli-
gible nonsense. The example par excellence is found in Isa 28: 7–13, "These
also reel with wine and stagger with strong drink; the priest and the prophet
reel with strong drink, they are confused with wine, they stagger with
strong drink; they err in vision, they stumble in giving judgment [. . .] For it
is precept upon precept, precept upon precept, line upon line, line upon
line, here a little, there a little." The translation does not give justice to the
Hebrew text, which runs, *ṣaw lāṣāw, ṣaw lāṣāw, qaw lāṣāw, qaw lāqāw,*
zᵉeršām, zᵉeršām. Is this an onomatopoetic description of the speech of
drunkards, or does it picture the lack of sense in their prophecies? Does it
refer to incessant prophesying or is it pious glossolalia? (Hölscher 1914, 35).
Lindblom hears the babbling of babies (Lindblom 1973, 201, for more
suggestions see Kaiser 1974 ad. loc.). I suggest that Isaiah ridicules the
priests and the prophets, not the other way around.

There are very few suggestions that the classical prophets behaved
strangely when in a revelatory state of mind. The common term is that they
"sought" or "asked" for oracles. People could come to the prophet and
beg him to "ask" God and the revelation is then termed as God's "answer". In some cases (37: 3; 42: 2, 20) Jeremiah is called on to "pray" for
an answer.

Jeremiah has the following passage (29: 26f.), "YHWH has made you
priest instead of Jehoiada the priest, to have charge in the house of YHWH

over every madman who prophesies, to put him in the stocks and collar. Now why have you not rebuked Jeremiah of Anathoth who is prophesying to you?'' Extracted from its context the passage seems to hint that Jeremiah was mad. But these verses are part of a letter, which a certain Shemaiah sent to a priest in Jerusalem. In its turn the letter is part of an oracle, which Jeremiah was ordered to deliver to Shemaiah and the message is a curse on Shemaiah's apostasy. Thus we can presume that Shemaiah bracketed all the prophets he disliked together under the same designation.

Turning to the historical books we get a different picture of prophetic activity. The texts are few and we seldom hear the prophets' own words. It is striking how often they appear in groups.

The two kings of Judah and Israel meet in Samariah during a time of peace to discuss the possible recapture of Ramoth-gilead (1 Kings 22). ''Inquire first for the word of YHWH'', suggested Jehoshaphat of Judah. Ahab of Israel assembled about 400 prophets and asks, ''Shall I go to battle against Ramoth-gilead or not?'' They answered that YHWH tells him to go. In spite of this message from 400 prophets Jehoshaphat insists on asking one more and Ahab suggests Micaiah ben Imlah, although he dislikes this prophet since he only prophecies misfortune. The man who fetches him brings pressure to bear upon him to answer as the other prophets had. Micaiah insists that he will speak as YHWH tells him to. However, he answers like the others, which makes Ahab furious and summons him to tell the truth. The prophet then describes a vision, ''I saw all Israel scattered upon the mountains, as sheep that have no shepherd; and YHWH said, 'These have no master, let each return to his home in peace' ''. Ahab understands this as an oracle of doom and sighs over the hopeless prophet. Micaiah tells another vision:

I saw YHWH sitting on his throne, and all the host of heaven standing beside him on his right hand and on his left; and YHWH said, 'Who will entice Ahab, that he may go up and fall at Ramoth-gilead?' And one said one thing, and another said another. Then a spirit came forward and stood before YHWH, saying, 'I will entice him'. And YHWH said to him 'By what means?' And he said, 'I will go forth, and will be a lying spirit in the mouth of all his prophets.' And he said, 'You are to entice him, and you shall succeed; go forth and do so'. Now therefore behold, YHWH has put a lying spirit in the mouth of all these your prophets; YHWH has spoken evil concerning you. Then Zedekiah the son of Chenaanah came near and struck Micaiah on the cheek, and said, 'How did the spirit of YHWH go from me to speak to you?' And Micaiah said, 'Behold, you shall see on that day when you go into an inner chamber to hide yourself.

The king obeys the false prophets and the result turns out as Micaiah has said.

The last passage very much resembles the classical prophets. Micaiah has with his inner eye seen and heard YHWH sitting on his throne conferring with his heavenly council and asking for a volunteer. The main difference is that it is not the true prophet who volunteers, but the bad spirit. The initiative and order to make Ahab's prophets false prophets comes from YHWH. Micaiah claims to be a true prophet, because he has seen how about 400 prophets became false prophets. He says that he *saw* or *has seen* this which could mean that he saw the vision before he met the kings-he knew in advance what they would ask him. The fact that the prophets are usually calm, often alone, when they see their visions speaks in favour of this, but it can be assumed that the bullied Micaiah was irritated in front of the kings. He was hardly less irritated when one of the false prophets hit him and asked sarcastically, "How did the spirit of YHWH go from me to speak to you?" that is to say, "If you have seen how we received false revelations, how did it happen when you received yours?" Micaiah does not answer this, but like the classical prophets refers to the fact that a true prophet is known by the accomplishment of his message.

This latter is the point of the legend of Elijah and the Baal-prophets (1 Kings 18). Elijah has to prove that YHWH, of whom he is the mouthpiece, is the true God in contrast to Baal. To demonstrate this two altars, one for each side, are to be erected and the challenge is, "You call on the name of your god, and I will call on the name of YHWH". Then Elijah allowed the prophets of Baal to begin:

Then Elijah said to the prophets of Baal, 'Choose for yourselves one bull and prepare it first, for you are many; and call on the name of your god, but put no fire to it. 'And they took the bull which was given them, and they prepared it, and called on the name of Baal from morning until noon, saying, 'O Baal, answer us! 'But there was no voice, and no one answered. And they limped about the altar which they had made. And at noon Elijah mocked at them, saying, 'Cry aloud, for he is a god; either he is musing, or he has gone aside, or he is on a journey, or perhaps he is asleep and must be awakened'. And they cried aloud, and cut themselves after their custom with swords and lances, until the blood gushed out upon them. And as midday passed, they raved on until the time of the offering of the oblation, but there was no voice; no one answered, no one heeded.

When it is his turn Elijah orders quantities of water to be poured over his altar and after this he prays to YHWH and this is the only thing he does. The Baal prophets on the other hand were vociferous for several hours, which makes Elijah mock at them. Moreover, they limp, *pāsaḥ*, around the altar which probably is a pejorative designation for their dancing. They cut themselves, *hitgoded*, with swords and lances. The verb is otherwise used as a part of the foreign and for the Israelite forbidden mourning-ritual (e.g. Deut 14: 1). Here it is clear that the Baal prophets usually behaved in this way. Finally, they were busy with *hitnabbe'*. The verb occurs in Niphal and as here in Hithpael and is in the majority of cases translated "to prophesy". Here it means "rave" and it is doubtful that it has anything to do with "prophecy". To the meaning of *hitnabbe'* we shall return. From the information that they cried aloud until midday and started *hitnabbe'* in the afternoon it may be concluded that they turned from calling on Baal to something else. It is clear that this marks the climax of a form of group-dynamic ecstasy.

A totally different example comes from 2 Kings 5: a Syrian officer by the name of Naaman has been to see the prophet Elisha and has been cured of his leprosy. Gehazi, the servant of Elisha, is uneasy about the fact that Elisha does not accept the gifts of gratitude from Naaman. So he slips out and secures some presents for himself by trickery. When he returns home Elisha asked him where he has been. Another lie: "I went nowhere." Elisha says, "Did I not go with you in spirit when the man turned from his chariot to meet you? Was it a time to accept money . . .?" How does Elisha know what has happened? The bombastic translations, not only into English, suggest that Elisha has been in a state of ecstasy and has seen a vision. This is not the case. The Hebrew text runs, "My heart has not left me", and in Hebrew anatomy the heart is the seat of mental activity. Elisha, knowing with whom he has to deal, simply says, "Do you really think that I don't understand what you have been doing?"

Saul seems to have been a rather neurotic person. His attacks of fury are said to be caused by an evil spirit from YHWH or by YHWH's spirit. As a young boy he is sent away by his father to find his lost asses, and on the way he receives the advice to see Samuel, the seer. The redactor of the text (1 Sam 9–10) explains, "Formerly in Israel, when a man went to inquire of God, he said, 'Come, let us go to the seer'; for he who is now called a prophet was formerly called a seer' ". Before Saul reaches him, Samuel receives a revelation that he should anoint Saul to be prince. This he does. Later he sends Saul away with a detailed description of what is going to happen before they meet again. Among other things this:

You shall come to Gibeath-elohim, where there is a garrison of the Philistines; and there as you come to the city, you will meet a band of prophets coming down from the high place with harp, tambourine, flute, and lyre, before them, and they *hitnabbe'*. Then the spirit of YHWH will come mightily upon you, and you shall *hitnabbe'* with them, and be turned into another man. Now when these signs meet you, do whatever your hands find to do, for God is with you [. . .] When he turned his back to leave Samuel, God gave him another heart; and all these signs came to pass that day. When they came to Gibeah, behold a band of prophets met him; and the spirit of God came mightily upon him, and he *hitnabbe'* among them. And when all who knew him before *saw* how he *nibba'* with the prophets, the people said to one another, 'What has come over the son of Kish? Is Saul also among the prophets?' And a man of the place answered, 'And who is their father?' Therefore it became a proverb, 'Is Saul also among the prophets?' When he had finished *hitnabbeʾ* he came to the high place.

Here we have a clear example of music in connection with *hitnabbeʾ*. It is also said of Miriam, who is called a prophetess in Ex 15:20 that she took a timbrel in her hand and that all the women followed her with timbrels and dancing. The combination occurs in more institutionalized form in 1 Chr 25:1–3, where the list of temple singers mentions the men who were set apart to *nibbaʾ* on lyres, harps and cymbals under the direction of the king and those who should *nibbaʾ* with the lyre in thanksgiving and in praise.

Saul will *hitnabbeʾ* through the spirit of YHWH and *expressis verbis* be turned into another man. This happens and Saul's transformation causes surprise. The question is of course, precisely what caused the surprise? Do they think that he has become a prophet and been received into the prophetic guild or do they ask, "Why does he behave like a prophet when he is not one?"

In order to answer the question we must look at two other texts. The first one is Nu 11 and tells how the people in the desert complain of the lack of food. They are tired of all the manna and ask Moses for meat and nagg at him about the good food they had eaten in Egypt. Moses presents the problem to God and says that he is no longer able to carry the people alone. God tells him, "Gather for me 70 men of the elders of Israel, whom you know to be the elders of the people and officers over them; and bring them to the tent of meeting and let them take their stand there with you. And I will come down and talk with you there; and I will take some of the spirit which is upon you and put it upon them, and they shall bear the burden of the people with you, that you may not bear it yourself alone." The people are promised food until they literally throw up. Moses asks God how he plans to feed the 600.000. The answer is a flip on the nose, "Is YHWH's hand shortened? Now you shall see whether my word will come true for you or not". Moses obeys and the following happens:

YHWH came down in the cloud, and spoke to him, and took some of the spirit that was upon him and put it upon the seventy elders; and when the spirit rested upon them, they *hitnabbeʾ*. But they did so no more. Now two men remained in the camp, one named Eldad, and the other named Medad, and the spirit rested upon them; they were among those registered, but they had not gone out to the tent, and so they *hitnabbeʾ* in the camp. And a young man ran and told Moses, 'Eldad and Medad *hitnabbeʾ* in the camp'. And Joshua the son of Nun, the minister of Moses, one of his chosen men, said, 'My lord Moses, forbid them'. But Moses said to him, 'Are you jealous for my sake? Would that all YHWH's people were *nᵉbîʾîm*, that YHWH would put his spirit upon them!'

The episode ends with the raining of quails and YHWH's wrath over the greed of the people. Moses is not an ordinary prophet, nor are the 70 elders or the two other men prophets, but they do pursue the activity of *hitnabbe'* and apparently for a short while. It gives Joshua an unpleasant sensation, but Moses wishes that the entire people would do the same thing. The question is, *what* do they do? The idea is that they should help Moses with the responsibility for the people after they have received due shares of the spirit upon Moses. If we combine the passage quoted above that Aaron, his prophet, would talk sense to Pharaoh, and the fact that YHWH's spirit was given to kings and prophets when they were inaugurated in their new positions, the text of Nu 11 becomes clear. The text describes how the elders were legitimated as leaders and officers. It is not necessary or even probable that they behaved particularly vigorously. It is rather a question of intensive inspiration in form of possession trance.

The other text concerns Saul (1 Sam 19: 20–24). He sends men to catch the fleeing David:

When they saw the company of the *n^{e}bî'îm* pursuing *nibba'* and Samuel standing as head over them, the spirit of God came upon the messengers of Saul, and they also *hitnabbe'*. When it was told Saul, he sent other messengers, and they also *hitnabbe'*. And Saul sent messengers again the third time, and they also *hitnabbe'*. Then he himself went to Ramah, [. . .] and the spirit of God came upon him also, and as he went he *hitnabbe'* until he came to Naioth in Ramah. And he too stripped off his clothes, and he too *hitnabbe'* before Samuel, and lay naked all that day and all that night. Hence it is said, 'Is Saul also among the prophets?'

It is common to these three texts that they concern persons who are said to receive the spirit of YHWH. None of them is a prophet. None receives a message and nothing points to any kind of speech. Nothing points to vigorous bodily movements, on the contrary, Saul seems to have been paralyzed. Another common feature is that their changes are transitory and a solitary instance. This solitary incident occurs in connection with the inauguration of these persons into a new position. I maintain that these texts, which are the most often cited examples of ecstatic prophecy in the Old Testament, do not actually describe ecstatic prophecy, that is to say, ecstasy "yes", prophecy "no". The texts describe persons who at their inauguration into new functions are legitimated by a solitary state of possession trance, in this case possession of YHWH's good spirit in contrast to YHWH's or anybody else's evil spirit. This means that the proverb "Is Saul among the *n^{e}bî'îm*" signifies, "Is Saul in the state of possession trance, which proves that he is a leader legitimated by YHWH?"

John Sturdy argues that the proverb must have originally circulated on its own and whatever the actual first occasion of its use, the story of it would be later and aetiological. He maintains that the proverb arose as Davidic propaganda against Saul, as the question can be shown to expect the answer "no", which implies: it is a good thing to be a prophet, and Saul is no prophet. I understand the purpose of the two aetiological stories to be to answer "yes" to the question and so they represent a positive (re-?) valuation of Saulite kingship (Sturdy 1970).

Simon Parker claims that as the verb *nibba̓ , hitnabbe̓* in some cases means "be in a possession trance" the noun *nābî̓* in the same text must signify "a person in possession trance" and thus something other than what is generally meant by "prophet" (Parker 1978). In view of the fact that the description in the last three texts of the activity *nibba̓ , hitnabbe̓* is so vastly different to what we know of prophetic activity I agree with Parker.

To summarise one may conclude that the orgiastic, vigorous ecstasy is alien to the Israelite prophets. On the other hand it is found among false and non-Israelite prophets. The ecstasy of the YHWH-prophets, primitive as well as classical is characterized by a calm, sometimes paralytically calm, seeing and hearing the word of YHWH, which they feel compelled to forward.

I started by quoting Johannes Lindblom and I will finish by doing so again, "Modern scholars have attempted to explain the religious experiences of the prophets by the methods of modern psychology with its emphasis on the subconscious or, rather, unconscious sphere of the human mind. For the understanding of the prophetic visions and auditions, their spontaneous and sudden occurrence, and their vivid and fanciful contents, the idea of the effective power of the unconscious is of great help. The application of the psychological methods of Freud or Jung to the experiences of the prophets has, however, not yet proved to be very fruitful. Literary documents from so remote a time cannot yield much to the psycho-analyst. Moreover, the application of these methods demands special qualifications which cannot reasonably be expected of a Biblical exegete. For fear lest I should appear a dilettante entering a domain unfamiliar to me I leave this task to those who are expert in it" (Lindblom 1973, 219).

References

Hölscher, G. 1914. *Die Profeten*. Leipzig.
Kaiser, O. 1974. *Isaiah 13–39*. London.
Lindblom, J. 1973. *Prophecy in ancient Israel*. London.
Parker, S. 1978. Possession trance and prophecy in pre-exilic Israel. *Vetus Testamentum* 28, 3, 271–285.
Sturdy, J. 1970. The original meaning of "Is Saul among the prophets?" (1 Samuel X 11, 12; XIX 24). *Vetus Testamentum* 20, 206–213.

Concepts of Ecstasy in Euripides' "Bacchanals" and their Interpretation

By LILIAN PORTEFAIX

In dealing with ecstasy in antiquity, scholars usually refer to Euripides' "Bacchanals"[1] as one of the most reliable sources with regard to this phenomenon. This drama can also be supplemented by vase paintings, which to a great extent deal with motives from the circle of Dionysos. Furthermore, the "symposium" theme of Dionysos and his *thiasos* is the most frequent motive on vessels and drinking cups in classical Athens (Gericke 1970).

A well-known amphora in Munich, dating from 500–495 B.C., depicts an ecstatic maenad (fig. 1) and the characteristics given by the painter correspond almost in detail to Euripides' description in spite of a distance in time of about a hundred years. The only missing features are the fawn-skin around her neck (111–112) and the wreath of living snakes around her head (101–103). The frieze of the amphora shows the maenad in question in a moment of ecstatic climax which is accented by the painter in locating the toes of her right foot just a little below the border of the frieze.[2] She is dressed in long garb (833), barefooted (665), her head is decorated with a wreath of ivy (80) and her hands are holding the thyrsus-staff (835). Her head is tossed back (865), the eyes turned upwards and the mouth open (1122). In my opinion, the painter has brilliantly represented the rigid body of the maenad with muscles tense just at the moment when she is about to fall senseless to the ground (138). Another vase painting represents this change in the state of ecstasy (fig. 2) and we know from Plutarch that the maenads needed rest and sleep after the rapture (Plu. Mor. 249 E-F).

---

[1] References to the text of the "Bacchanals" in this article are to Arthur S. Way's edition and translation 1942 (Loeb). The "Bacchanals" was Euripides' last drama and he wrote it in Macedonia in 406/05 (Dieterich 1909, P-W VI, 1270). From Diodorus Siculus (IV, 3, 3) we know, that in many Greek towns Bacchic bands of maidens and matrons joined the ecstatic Dionysiac cult every other year, but we can imagine that Euripides met with a more primitive cult in Macedonia. It is the most controversial of Euripides' works, containing many aspects and problems on several levels. This article only deals with one aspect of the drama.

[2] This detail, detaching the maenad from space and time, does not agree with Euripides' description of the experience of ecstasy.

Fig. 1. Maenad in trance. Amphora. Antikensammlungen, München. Inv. 8732 (2344) (Reichhold 1975, Tafel 13).

The artist can only give us the external aspect of ecstasy but Euripides
goes a step further by describing the inner experience in the following way.
The maenads live in the open air on snow-covered Mount Cithaeron,
reclining on pinesprays and oakleaves (684–685) in a fragrance of incense
(148). Young mothers, who had left their babies at home, give their milk to
fawns and wolfcubs (699–703). With their honey-dripping thyrsus-staves
(711) the maenads create water and wine from the rock and their fingers

Fig. 2. Dancing maenads. Red figured lecyte. Sammlung Sabouroff I 55. (Weege 1926, 75).

draw forth milk from the earth (704–710). They tear bulls to pieces (742–744) and a pine from the soil with their hands (1110). They carry fire upon their hair without burning themselves (757–758) and they walk bare-footed in the snow (662–665). When the women are attacked by Pentheus' men they chase them away with their thyrsus-staves (763–764), but they themselves cannot be hurt by the soldiers' iron-javelins (761). When they go plundering goods and babies (753–754) in the Theban lowlands (749–750), they carry the spoils unfastened on their shoulders (755–756). The maenads hear Dionysos' voice calling without seeing him (576–580) and he reveals himself to them in the shape of fire (597). When Pentheus is maddened by Dionysos he imagines himself as seeing two suns and two towns (918–919) and the god himself in the shape of a bull (920–923). Finally, the maenads are said to prophesy when they have the god in their bodies (300–301).

In actual fact, we observe that the ecstatic experience, as depicted by Euripides contains such psychological phenomena as hallucinations, including optical, acoustic and olfactive delusion, anesthesia, delusion as to one's own strength and possession.

Euripides' description can be explained in different ways according to the view taken of religion and its function. In this respect, we shall provide a sociological and a psychological interpretation. Both of these take for granted that the Greek woman was not able to accept her inferior and repressed position. As she was not able to express her dissatisfaction in politics, she had to express her aggressions in a religious context as the only acceptable sphere of activity for women outside the home. Both these theories are founded on comparisons of modern ecstatic cults and modern family patterns.

I. M. Lewis adopts the sociological view (Lewis 1971, 100–127) of the Dionysiac cult and compares it with modern African ecstatic cults on the borderline between Islam and Christianity. In these cults women become physically ill and possessed by a spirit as a result of stress in the home. They are cured through permanent membership of the cult, where through the experience of trance they become on good terms with the possessing spirit. With the authority of the spirit, the women are able to request some relief from housework and also certain gifts such as jewels and other expensive articles from their husbands. The latter accept the demands of the spirit and in this way a balance is established between the sexes. In these cults, possession is looked upon as a sexual unity between the woman and the spirit. In comparing this with the Dionysiac cult, Lewis is of the opinion that it differs from the latter in that the woman in the Dionysiac cult, instead of becoming physically ill, was possessed by some kind of madness manifesting itself in a compulsion to dance and to leave the home. This madness was cured in the cult through a sexual union with the god by means of ecstatic dancing in the mountains and the tearing and eating of animals. In the Dionysiac cult, however, the woman was only temporarily delivered from her duties towards the family during the trance. In any case, she obtained some relief without any restrictions and her husband participated in the cult by yielding to the god in permitting his wife to give free vent to her hostility in this way.

Ph. Slater looks at the Dionysiac cult in a Freudian psychoanalytical perspective (Slater 1968, 219–307) and compares the American middle-class family in the twentieth century with the family situation in classical and post-classical Greece. Here he finds a family pattern characterized by sexual antagonism and segregation. A dominating wife/mother with complete influence over the home threatens and rejects the husband/father, whose hostility in turn originates from a dominating mother. In Slater's opinion the husband tried to limit the power of his wife through keeping her indoors and being away from home as much as possible. Consequently the power of the woman increased in the home but she was frustrated by her isolation and sexual dissatisfaction. Her feelings towards her husband were projected onto their sons and she entered into conflicting relations with them: at the same time as she demanded virility, she denied their sexuality. In Slater's opinion, this is the main reason for homosexuality in ancient Greece. The woman in turn was able to give free vent to her disappointment in the Dionysiac cult by expressing her aggression towards her sons in tearing and eating animals and in obtaining sexual satisfaction through union with the god in a trance.

In my opinion, Euripides' depiction of the experiences of the maenads during the trance can be explained anthropologically as a regression to an earlier state of culture, as opposed to a civilized state. As we noticed earlier, the women are dressed in fawnskins and barefooted, devoting themselves to hunting and warfare in a primitive manner. They do not use any hunting implements, they tear the animals to pieces with their bare hands and eat the meat raw (140). Iron tools are banished. The women tear a fure tree to the soil by means of wooden instruments (1104) and their thyrsus-staves serve as javelins. When plundering the villages of the plains and kidnapping the peasants' babies, they carry their prey unfastened on their shoulders. In this context it may be of interest to note that hunting and warfare have much in common with ecstasy in their basic patterns: a high degree of concentration, silence and tranquility in combination with a sudden change to rapid movement (1084–1090). There are scholars who are of the opinion that the psychological experiences of hunting and warfare of a primitive kind could be the origin of ecstasy (Gladigow 1978, 25).

I believe that the anthropological view can be combined with a religious perspective, which should be the best approach for understanding a religious drama. Considering Eliade's description of "illud tempus" and his theory of the eternal return to this state in myth and cult (Eliade 1976, 438–462) the maenad's experiences in the trance are to be seen as a regression to this original state of which the basic pattern is to be found in Hesiod's Erga (109–118) but also in Plato's description of the reign of Cronus (Plat. Pol. 271). According to Euripides' version the characteristics of this original state are that all boundaries are dissolved. Nature takes part in the maenadic frenzy (726–727) and the boundaries between man and beast are abolished when the maenads give the young animals milk and the god reveals himself in a theriomorphic shape. The borderlines between the sexes are erased; the women have acquired male strength and they appear in male roles as hunters and warriors while at the same time they express their womanliness and maternity. We may note in passing that there are many examples of sex reversals (Segal 1975) in the "Bacchanals" and even Zeus is said to have a "male womb" (527). Furthermore, the boundaries between mortals are annihilated: there is community of property and even of babies. The limits between man and god are destroyed: the maenad maintains herself without working by milk and honey like the gods, she is invulnerable and she carries the divine fire on her head. In my opinion, she experiences herself in the trance as the complete individual, as the androgyne, through unity with the god. This sexual union is reflected in the vase

Fig. 3. Dionysos. Amphora. Antikensammlungen, München. Inv. 8732 (2344) (Reichhold 1975, Tafel 13).

paintings and in the drama: the painter dresses the god in a long womanly garb (fig. 3), and Euripides gives him the epithet "womanly" (θηλύμορφος) (353).

Finally, it is interesting to compare this pattern of ecstatic experience with T. Stace's criteria of mystic experience (Stace 1961, 110). The maenads feel united with nature and with the god and they experience eternal bliss (72). An important point of divergence from Stace's catalogue is that the maenads are still on the borders of time and space. In spite of their ecstatic state they are completely oriented to real life when they gather at an appointed time (723), put their clothes in order (696–698), arrange themselves in ordered ranks (693), sing songs in turns (1057) and finally raise a cult cry together (725). Euripides characterizes their behavior as "good order" (ἐυκοσμία)[3] (693) and the maenads themselves as "wise" (σώφρων) (686, 940). In any case, this does not correspond with the boundless nature of ecstasy and we must consequently ask what was Euripides' purpose in writing his drama. As we have already seen, scholars have explained it in different ways. In this connection, I should only like to make a few comments on Euripides' reasons for using philosophical terms while depicting an ecstatic cult.

Euripides (485/4-407/6) lived in Athens during a time characterized by the overthrow of traditional religion and morality. Some sophists denied the divine basis of these phenomena considering them to be of human origin and a heated debate began about the antithetical concepts *nomos-physis* (Heinemann 1972, 125–147). Euripides was familiar with the different philosophical views and at the same time he criticized the traditional religion (Dieterich 1909, PW VI, 1278). In the "Bacchanals" we find trains of thought which in my opinion are to be found a couple of generations later in the philosophical system of the early Stoics. Without considering the causes of this we can only note that Euripides was a contemporary of Antisthenes (450/45-365), a pupil of Socrates who, according to most scholars,[4] founded the Cynic school, from which the early stoic Zeno (334-236) emanated (Rist 1969, 54–57). Even in the third century B.C. there were impulses to overcome the antitheses *nomos-physis,* and Euripides' last drama is a step in that direction (Heinemann 1972, 166–169). In the "Bacchanals" for example we find an allegorical explanation of the myth of Zeus' rescue of Dionysos from Hera's wrath (288–297). It is interesting to notice the etymological explanation based on the similarity of words,[5] a method which we recognize in early stoicism (Pohlenz I 1948, 97). Furthermore, Euripides has a different opinion about the origin of religion and morality:

Little it costs, faith's precious heritage. To trust that whatsoe'er from Heaven is sent Hath sovereign sway, whate'er through age on age Hath gathered sanction by our nature's bent (νόμιμον ἀεὶ φύσει τε πεφυκός) (893–897) and

In true womanhood inborn (ἐν τῇ φύσει) dwells temperance touching all things evermore (315–316)

---

[3] Barbara K. Gold gives the philological approach in her article "ΕΥΚΟΣΜΙΑ in Euripides' Bacchae", in The American Journal of Philology, 98, 1977, 3–15.
[4] D. R. Dudley is nevertheless of the opinion that Diogenes is the founder of the Cynic school and that there is no direct connection, Socrates—Antisthenes—Zeno (A History of Cynicism, 1938).
[5] The argument is based on the similarity of μέρος, "fragment", μηρός "thigh", and ὅμηρος "hostage" (Euripides, "Bacchanals", 27).

Religion is *nomos;* however, the divine *nomos* anchored in *physis* and the human being has virtue by nature. Euripides attaches religion to nature in a very tangible way in his drama and so did the early Stoics, who had a materialistic view of life (SVF I, 85, 98). Dionysos reveals himself as fire from heaven (1083–1084) and from earth (725–726) and the maenads carry his fire on their heads. Equally the early Stoics characterized their divine principle as fire (SVF I, 537. II 423) and they thought that the destruction of the world would take place through it (SVF I, 98). All nature participates in the maenadic frenzied dance (726) and we find a Stoic line of thought where the soul of the Stoic sage moves in an accordance with the movements of the cosmos (Rist 1969, 88–89). Euripides furthermore anticipates the Stoic ideal of equality on the basis of an equal share in logos (SVF II, 1027) when he states that both the rich and the poor have a share in the wine (421–423) and that the cult is open to everybody (206–209) without any initiations as in the mystery religions (Gatz 1967, 177). Probably he thought that women are more predisposed to religious experience as he makes only the women really meet the god in the drama. Equally, the sex reversals here have their counterpart in Zeno's ideal state which is also a kind of vision of an original state where only the wise are citizens (Pohlenz I, 1970, 137–139). In Zeno's ideal state sexual relations are free, the children of the wise will be loved by all (SVF III, 728), and men and women should wear the same clothes (SVF I 257). Euripides also moves paradise into the sphere of human life; the maenads' experience it "here and now" and not beyond death in a transcendent perspective of time (Gatz 1967, 169). Finally, the maenads are characterized as wise and their wisdom coincides with that of the Stoic sage. We recognize the Stoic *ataraxia* (SVF III, 109) in the following verses.

For it is the wise mans (ὁ σόφος ἄνδρος) part to rein his wrath in soberness (σώφρων) (640–641)

For in his Bacchic rites the virtous-hearted (σώφρων) shall not be undone (317–318) and

O, not with knowledge (το σόφον) is Wisdom (σοφία) tought (396).

Euripides' and the Stoic human ideal are both characterized by moderation and virtue. Euripides has the maenad obtaining wisdom through mystical experience in ecstasy while the Stoic sage attains unity with *logos* in a similar manner as we shall see.

In my opinion, Euripides tried to rescue religion from the attacks of the critics by inventing a synthesis of the antitheses *nomos-physis*. In any case, he did not wish to rescue the traditional religion, but thought that true religion was a religion of nature; he was however afraid of basing it in nature alone without some restraining bonds. These bonds he expressed in "good order", and this concept characterizes the maenadic frenzy. In this drama he shows didactically the consequences of other ways of thinking and the characters have different attitudes towards religion. Cadmus, the townbuilder (171–172), represents at the same time culture and *nomos* and has an opportunistic view of religion (333–336). In the end, his punishment is to be changed into a snake (1330) and he is further doomed to raze important Hellenic towns to the ground (1333–1336). Agaue, on the other hand, stands for *physis*—she is pure nature, she is changed to a beast of prey and tears her own son into pieces (1125–1127). She never attains the balance between *nomos* and *physis,* and she rejects *physis* in favor of *nomos.* When passing mount Cithaeron in her exile she says:

O that afar I might hide me,
Where accursed Cithaeron shall look not on me,
Nor I with mine eyes shall Cithaeron see,
where memorial is none of the thyrsus-spear.
Be these unto other Bacchanals dear. (1383–1387)

Pentheus "the sufferer" represents the openly irreligious attitude (241–246) and at the same time he is the "unnatural" nature due to his perversity towards women (811–816, 1059–1062). Consequently he has to die an unnatural death, sacrificed to Dionysos and torn to pieces by his own mother who is a priestess (1125–1127). For Euripides the truly religious human being is measured and sober (686) and this, in my opinion, is expressed in the fact that the ecstasy in his drama is not connected with drunkenness and sexual excesses (683–688) as for example in the Bacchanalia in Rome (Liv. 39. 8–19). In Euripides' drama the maenad provokes the ecstasy by tossing her head to and fro (fig. 1, 865–866) to the accompaniment of music from flutes (160) and drums (fig. 2. 156). It is interesting to notice that the Stoic also obtained unity with the cosmos through movement. By means of the morally right action he acquired the "right tension" (εὐτονία) in the principal part of his soul (SVF III, 121, 28). It began to move in accordance with the movements of the cosmos and he attained the status of the sage without his own knowledge (Rist 1969, 88–93)—in my opinion a kind of materialistic mysticism.

Euripides defines ecstasy as when Dionysos "throws" Pentheus "out of his mind" (ἐξίστασθαι φρενῶν) (850), but as a matter of fact the maenad is thrown "inside her mind" by the "good order" (εὐκοσμία) in order to experience a harmonious unity with nature.

Finally, we can state that both Euripides and the philosophers thought that the sage was the ideal human being, but Euripides found this ideal within religion and, moreover, in an ecstatic cult—*within* the limits of

14–Religious Ecstasy

reason. Nevertheless, we must express the opinion that the elements of the equation do not fit together—ecstasy and reason are in fact incompatible quantities.

References

Sources

Diodorus Siculus	Library of History, ed. C. H. Oldfather, London 1935. (Loeb Classical Library, vol. 303).
Euripides	Bacchanals, ed. A. S. Way, London 1912. (Loeb Classical Library, vol. 11).
Hesiod	ed. H. G. Evelyn-White, 1914. (Loeb Classical Library, vol. 57).
Livy	ed. E. T. Sage, 1936. (Loeb Classical Library, vol. 313).
Plato	The Republic, ed. P. Shorey. (Loeb Classical Library, vol. 276).
Plutarch	Moralia, ed. F. C. Babitt, 1931. (Loeb Classical Library, vol. 245).
SVF	Stoicorum Veterum Fragmenta, ed. J. von Arnim. Stuttgart 1964.

References

Dieterich, A. 1909. Euripides. A. Pauly – G. Wissowa, *Realencyclopädie der classischen Altertumswissenschaft 6, 1242–1281* (PW).

Eliade, M. 1976. *Die Religionen und das Heilige*. Darmstadt.

Gatz, B. 1967. *Weltalter, goldene Zeit und sinnverwandte Vorstellungen*. Hildesheim.

Gericke, H. 1970. *Gefässdarstellungen auf griechischen Vasen*. Berlin.

Gladigow, B. 1978. Ekstase und Enthousiasmos. *Rausch-Ekstase-Mystik,* hrsg. von H. Cancik. Düsseldorf.

Gold, B. K. 1977. ΕΥΚΟΣΜΙΑ in the Bacchae. *The American journal of philology* 98, 3–15.

Heinemann, F. 1972. *Nomos und Physis*. Darmstadt.

Lewis, I. M. 1971. *Ecstatic religion*. Harmondsworth.

Pohlenz, M. 1970.[4] *Die Stoa*. Göttingen.

Reichhold, K. 1975. *Attische Vasenbilder der Antikensammlungen in München*. München.

Rist, J. M. 1969. *Stoic philosophy*. Cambridge.

Segal, Ch. 1978. The menace of Dionysos: sex roles and reversals in Euripides Bacchae. *Arethusa 11,* 185–201.

Weege, F. 1926. *Der Tanz in der Antike*. Halle.

Gnosis and Mysticism as illustrated by Eugnostos the Blessed

By JØRGEN PODEMANN SØRENSEN

In the second volume of *Gnosis und spätantiker Geist,* Hans Jonas (1954, 222) expressed penetrating insights into what he called the anticipatory function of gnostic mythological teachings: the idea that cosmological mythology may already account for the mystic ascent of the soul to higher forms of consciousness. The very process of gnostic mythology, the emanatory scheme, is self-contained and autonomous in character. The All or the primeval spirit develops or unwraps itself without intervention from outside, and the energy or principle of movement which gives rise to the whole process "ist geistig-seelischer Natur und entfaltet sich auch beim Übergang in die Mannigfaltigkeit ständig in geistig-seelischen Kategorien, die die innere, die wahre Seite der erscheinenden Wirklichkeit, als eigentliche Zustände des Urgeistes, bedeuten" (Jonas 1954, 156). The leading concepts of *gnosis* and *agnoia* add an intellectual aspect of gnostic mythology; the stages in the emanatory scheme are stages in the life of gnosis, i.e. degrees of knowledge (Jonas 1954, 157). Original gnosis is thus contrasted with present agnoia and divided from it by a number of intermediate stages. This mythological or metaphysical foundation of gnosis clearly exhibits the redemptory function of gnosis in the life of the individual; to obtain gnosis is also to return to an unpolluted original condition.

As an account of the descent of original reality to the present deplorable condition, the gnostic cosmological myth is also—by its self-contained, spiritual and intellectual character—a potential account of the mystic way back to the thrones of pre-existence. According to Jonas, however, this potentiality was not realized before the 3rd century; Origen was still a non-mystic, whose philosophical system was later turned into a mystical canon. Whatever the validity of Jonas' analysis of Origen and of his outline of the development of gnosticism from the first to the third century, it is a major achievement to have shown the mystic potentiality of gnostic mythology and systems of thought. When ecstasy entered gnosticism, a path was already blazed for it in gnostic mythology—or perhaps it is better to say that mysticism, including ecstasy, was the natural outcome of intellectual work with gnostic mythology (Jonas 1954, 219 ff.).[1]

For the demonstration of such insights into the relation between gnostic mythology and ecstatic gnosis, the *Letter of Eugnostos* is a far better piece of evidence than anything that was available to Jonas, when he wrote *Gnosis und spätantiker Geist*.

The *Letter of Eugnostos* or *Eugnostos the Blessed* as the text is usually called, has come down to us in two copies, one in *Nag Hammadi Codex III* and another less well preserved in *Codex V*. The text has aroused considerable interest as a possible sample of so-called pre-christian gnosis (Yamauchi 1978, 104–107 incl. further refs.). The present paper, however, will not deal with historical considerations of this kind, its only subject being the content of the letter.

Writing under the programmatic name *Eugnostos* and the more common *Makarios,* the author addresses his pupils or adepts to teach them about god. He starts by refuting three propositions about the nature of the world which to him represent the basic shortcomings of contemporary philosophy, or perhaps of philosophy as such: (1) the world is governed by itself, (2) by a providence, or (3) is subject to predestination. His refutation is neither philosophical in the proper sense of that word, nor does it deal with the implications of these propositions in detail: That which is from itself leads an empty life, providence is foolish, and that which is subject to destiny or fate is something that does not attain knowledge. According to Eugnostos, real insight is not reached through philosophy; what matters is to be able to refute the propositions of philosophy and by means of another proposition to gain access to and reveal the god of truth. The attainment of this, he says, means to be immortal amidst the mortals.

The following, which forms the substance of the text, should thus be taken as an attempt to provide the material for this effort. Philosophical criticism gives place to theological and cosmological discourse of the kind that is common in gnostic literature. We are taught about the eternal, uncreated, nameless and inconceivable god, his antopoi and his intricate emanations with their male and female aspects, about the imperishable aeons, their heavens and firmaments etc. Copious and circumstantial as it is, this cosmology is not complete. The world of perishableness is mentioned and even brought out as opposed to the imperishable aeons, but not elaborated and based on cosmology. Eugnostos deliberately stops before he "leaves the world of imperishableness". It should also be noticed that any

---

[1] These insights as well as the outline of the development of gnosticism from myth to mysticism have been reformulated in Jonas 1974, 291–304, and are utilized on NagHammadi texts in Turner 1980.

escatological perspective is absent from the text. Limitations of this kind are probably motivated by the pedagogical aims of the letter; the accounts of cosmology given by Eugnostos are caracterized by himself as "beginnings of knowledge" (*arkhēnsown*) i.e. the text itself is seen by its author as leading towards gnosis. Already the introduction speaks about the importance of being able to provide an alternative to replace the propositions of philosophy and thus to reveal the god of truth and reach immortality. At the end it is stated that the teachings have been adapted to the background and needs of the receiver:

"But all this, which I have told you above, I have told in such a way that you will be able to bear it, until that which cannot be taught is revealed in you—and all this shall it tell you in joy and in pure knowledge (*sown*)."[2]

Gnostic texts do not often provide information about their *Sitz im Leben,* but the *Letter of Eugnostos* does not leave any doubt. The text is the material for revealing the god of truth, it is preconceived as leading towards that crucial experience where that which cannot be taught is revealed in the pupil. This experience will also comprise what is said in the text "in joy and pure knowledge", i.e. what in the text appears as intricate theology and copious cosmology is supposed, in the experience, to illuminate the pupil from within. This description of *sown* or gnosis clearly points to an experience of the ecstatic type and the *Letter of Eugnostos* can thus be seen as a technique of ecstasy.

The main line of thought in the text is this: In the eternal, unborn, nameless father of the all, all greatnesses and powers pre-exist, and the sources of the wholenesses, i.e. the aeons, are present in him. He does not personally execute the work of creation, but like a reflection of him in a mirror, an antopos, called *Autopator* and *Autogenetor,* appears, and gives origin to an immortal androgynous man.

The male aspect of immortal man is called *perfect Nous,* the female *pansophos Sophia, the mother.* Immortal man becomes the possessor of an aeon, creates gods, archangels and angels and becomes the origin of the next level of emanation, *Son of Man.*

Through the correspondence of Son of Man with his female aspect, *firstborn Sophia, mother of the All,* the next level of emanation, a great androgynous light, is generated. Its male aspect is *Sōtēr, the creator of everything,* its female *Sophia pangenetira* also called *Pistis.* From this pair are generated 6 pneumatic pairs reflecting earlier levels of emanation. Their male names point back to the *antopos* of the father, immortal man, Son of

---

[2] *NHC III,* 90, 4 ff. I follow Krause's translation in *Gnosis* 1971; 2, 37 ff. Parrott (1977, 225) translates: "until the one who does not need to be taught is revealed among you."

Man, and Sōtēr himself; the female names repeat those of the earlier Sophia's. This kind of redundance is what ensures the continuity of the system. Also 6 aeons, to which we shall return later, come into existence. From the 6 pneumatic pairs or 12 powers 36 pairs or 72 powers are generated through processes more arithmetical than sexual in nature. The 72 in turn generate 5 pneumatic beings each, so that the number 360 is reached.

By now we have reached the point where the reflections of imperishableness in the world known by us can be accounted for; our aeon is the reflection (τύπος) of immortal man, time the reflection of the *first-begetter*, i.e. Son of Man, his son again is reflected in some notion of time, regrettably lost in a lacuna. The 12 months of the year reflect the 12 powers or 6 pairs, the 360 days the 360 powers just mentioned. Imperishableness is thus present in our notions of time, not as tangible reality but as τύποι which may be perceived and interpreted.

For the benefit of the 72 powers 12 aeons come into being, so that each aeon may be occupied by 6 powers. In this way 72 heavens originate, each divided into 5 firmaments, so that the number 360 is once more the result. The 3 first aeons are identified as immortal man, Son of Man, and Sōtēr. The first of them is also called *Unity* and *Quietude*.

The rest of the text is a hasty, not very elaborated discourse on the origin of gods, archangels and angels and a few hints as to the further development of aeons, worlds, realms, heavens and firmaments according to earlier prototypes, and their reflections in chaos, the world of becoming and perishableness. In the imperishable part, from the unbegotten farther to the beginning of the revealed part called chaos, everything is light without shade and joy beyond description.

Already Underhill (1930, 97 ff.) emphasized how a doctrine of emanation may serve as a diagram for the mystic, and it is well known that the way of the mystic, his passage through a number of stages on his way towards the thrones of pre-existence, is often seen as a road backwards along the line designed by creation.

To show the diagrammatic function of the emanatory doctrine set forth by Eugnostos it is above all necessary to ascertain what combines the single links of his chain of emanations. In saying that a certain redundance is what holds his system together we have already hinted at this; in a way which is typical for gnostic literature, names, functions, structures are repeated from level to level in the emanatory process, the earlier ones serving as prototypes of the later ones. The system unfolds and develops through processes devoid of any notion of time or action: mirroring, correspondence, or simple multiplication. Of the father an antopos is formed, the male and female aspects "correspond" and thus carry on the emanatory process, powers, heavens and firmaments unfold in uniform schemes as multipla of 6. Even the aeons, originally notions of time, are generated in this timeless manner. The whole emanatory development is governed by processes which in the world known by us occur only in the human brain.

Everything is solidly connected and continuous within one single moment, and plurality is nothing but the kaleidoscopic image of unity—but still the text insists on the division into all the levels and stages of the system. The text can be seen as mediating this basic opposition, and in so doing it contributes explicitly to the theory of this opposition. An important part of the connecting redundance is a chain of psychological concepts, six in number, which—with minor variations—occurs three times. The eternal unbegotten father of the all consists entirely of νοῦς, ἔννοια, ἐνθύμησις, φρόνησις, λογισμός and δύναμις. These elements of the first knowledge of the unbegotten one are sources of the wholenesses, i.e. of the aeons that emanate from the father. They are said to be equal powers, but as imperishable they have a decisive advantage (διαφορά) as compared with everything perishable.

Immortal man, as a reflection of the father, possesses his own νοῦς, ἔννοια, ἐνθύμησις, etc. At this stage the concepts are called equal as far as imperishableness is concerned, but with regard to power there is a διαφορά, a difference, or perhaps better: a hierarchic order between them as a father is related to a son, a son to a thought (ἔννοια) and a thought to the rest. The chain of concepts is hierarchically structured according to the principle which governs the successive levels in the emanatory process. This is further illustrated by pointing out the superiority of oneness to duality, duality to threefoldness, tens to hundreds, etc.

Διαφορά in the first instance denotes the fundamental difference between imperishable and perishable; in the second it denotes the hierarchy of stages merging into or generating each other. The use of the word illustrates the mediating capacity of the system. In its course of development, the system mediates the basic opposition between disparateness and continuity.

This principle is further illustrated in what follows: at the level of the *Sōtēr* the psychological chain unfolds as aeons, this time in a slightly changed form. As an indication of a somewhat lower level νοῦς has disappeared and the aeons now succeed each other in the following order: ἔννοια, ἐνθύμησις, φρόνησις, λογισμός, θέλησις, λόγος.

Such chains of psychological concepts occur several times in gnostic literature. A chain very similar to the one just mentioned is found in a Chinese manichaean treatise (Chavannes-Pelliot 1911). Puech (1978, 2,

100 ff.) regarded such chains as lists of the parts of νοῦς, and they may be so explained in Eugnostos too. The διαφορά-principle set forth in this text, however, necessitates the consideration of the chain as a hierarchical order. In the Chinese treatise the psychological concepts are seen as correlated with levels in manichaean education; in Eugnostos we shall try to show that, taken backwards from λόγος to ἔννοια and νοῦς, they describe the way or the ladder of the mystic towards the thrones of pre-existence, towards ecstasy. It is well known that νοῦς in a gnostic context denotes the highest, the most comprehensive form of consciousness; λόγος may be conceived as opposed to νοῦς—Sallustius, the Neoplatonist, has it that "Mind (νοῦς) sees all things at once", while speach (λόγος) has to express "some first and others after" (*IV*; transl. Murray 1955, 195). The intermediary concepts may then be seen as bridging the gap between λόγος and νοῦς. Θέλησις, will, would thus denote a striving or strong motivation brought about by λόγος and leading towards λογισμός, the conscious, painstaking work with logical and philosophical entities. Φρόνησις, insight, may be seen as the resulting maturity of mind, the necessary basis for the next level, ἐνθύμησις. Ἐνθύμησις in all probability denotes an extreme concentration or the like; ἐνθυμεῖσθαι means to consider something with regard to its importance, value, or dangerousness, thus implying an effort or at least a commitment. But while ἐνθύμησις may denote the mental process or effort without necessarily including its result, ἔννοια seems clearly to denote an insight gained, a principle realized, an accomplished inner thought or concept. In Plutarch, ἔννοια may denote the human knowledge of the gods (*De placitis philosophorum* I, 6 [Moralia XI]). The chain of psychological concepts seems, then, to describe a way towards still higher forms of consciousness, culminating in νοῦς, the human receiver of gnosis which in Eugnostos' doctrine of emanation is identical with immortal man. The mystic's way towards the thrones of pre-existence is also the road to immortality and to the aeon called *Unity* and *Quietude*.

The text of Eugnostos does not permit any statement about the precise psychological nature of the various stages, let alone the psychology of ecstasy as modern psychology sees it. The importance of the text lies very much in the information as to its *Sitz im Leben* given in its introductory and concluding remarks.   This information puts us in a position to see the text as a technique of ecstasy. The copious and circumstantial cosmology set up by Eugnostos is no philosophical theory of the world, but a kind of mandala, which by its very structure exalts the reader above the logos level. By mediating disparateness and continuity the text establishes a road towards the thrones of pre-existence; by integrating psychology and cosmology it brings a whole cosmic drama into the soul—in joy and pure knowledge. Seen as a technique of ecstasy the very copiousness and prolixity of the cosmology makes sense, and the *Letter of Eugnostos* will thus, with its valuable information about its own *Sitz im Leben,* provide an argument for the explanatory value of ecstasy in dealing with gnostic cosmology and emanatory doctrine.[3]

References:

Chavannes, E. –Pelliot, P. 1911. Un traité manichéen retrouvé en Chine. *Journal Asiatique* 557–563.
— 1971 *Die Gnosis 2.* Zürich.
Jonas, H. 1954. *Gnosis und spätantiker Geist* 2, 1. (Forschungen zur Religion und Literatur des Alten und Neuen Testaments. Neue Folge 45.) Göttingen.
— 1974. *Philosophical essays.* Englewoold Cliffs, N. J.
Murray, G. 1955. *Five stages of Greek religion.* New York.
Parrott, D. M. 1977. Eugnostos the Blessed. *The NagHammadi Library in English,* ed. by J. M. Robinson, Leiden.
Puech, H. Ch. 1978. *En quête de la Gnose* 1–2. Paris.
Staal, F. 1975. *Exploring mysticism.* Harmondsworth.
Turner, J. D. 1980. The gnostic threefold path to enlightenment. *Novum Testamentum* 22, 324–351.
Underhill, E. 1930. *Mysticism.* London.
Yamauchi, E. M. 1978. *Pre-Christian gnosticism.* London.

---

[3] The explanatory value of mysticism in dealing with complicated religio-philosophical texts is repeatedly stressed in Staal 1975, notably pp. 47–48 and 90–95.

Ecstasy and Vision

By ANDERS HULTGÅRD

In this paper we shall present some observations on the role played by ecstasy in the activity of the seer, as he emerges in ancient Jewish and Iranian texts.

Ancient Judaism

In the Jewish religious literature of the Hellenistic-Roman period visions are described on almost every page, and visions were the most important means of divine revelation. Here we are immediately confronted with an essential problem. Do these descriptions reflect genuine visionary experiences or is the vision form to be interpreted as a mere literary convention? The problem has often been discussed (e.g. Lindblom 1963, 122–148; Russell 1964, 158–172; Niditch 1980, 158), but no definite solutions have been presented, the main reason being the material itself: a body of texts produced about two thousand years ago, composed, transmitted and reworked in a milieu of which our knowledge is incomplete. The fact that visions were widespread and popular in the ancient cultures of the Mediterranean area and the Near East strongly suggests their conventional use. A critical analysis of many vision texts underlines their traditional and literary character. However, it would be rash to deny that genuine visionary experiences could occur among the circles which produced the apocalyptic writings. The growth and spread of Jewish vision literature would be inexplicable if there were not real visionary experiences at its core. There is therefore some justification in scrutinizing the texts in order to find evidence reflecting the seer's genuine experiences.

In the Jewish texts of the Hellenistic and early Roman period, we do not find any coherent and detailed description of the circumstances under which the seer receives his vision. What we have are allusions and short, sometimes isolated, remarks but, taken together, these indicate an underlying context in which ecstatic experiences seemed to accompany the visions. A pattern may be discerned for the circumstances leading up to the vision itself:

1. There is first a crisis situation (cf. also Niditch 1980, 159) which strongly affects the seer and which manifests itself in grief, lamentation, anxiety and

brooding. The crisis may concern the nation or the community, mankind in general or particular groups within the society. To illustrate this aspect of the pattern, I give some examples:

	crisis situation	seer's emotional manifestations
Daniel 7–10	The persecution of the Jews under Antiochus IV Epiphanes.	"I mourned for three whole weeks" (10:2).
IV Ezra and *II Baruch*	The catastrophy of A.D. 70: destruction of Jerusalem and the Temple.	"I fasted with tears and lamentations" (*IV Ezra* 5:20–21).
		"I wept over Zion and lamented over the captivity which threatened the people" (*II Bar.* 6:2).
I Enoch 14–15	The judgment on the fallen angels and the sons of men.	not explicitly mentioned.
Testament of Levi 2–8	The increasing lawlessness and impiety of men.	"I was grieving for the race of the sons of men" (2:4).

2. Secondly, before receiving the vision, it is often stated that the seer goes away to a lonely or deserted place, in nature or elsewhere. He secludes himself from his normal environment:

Daniel 10:4	"I found myself on the bank of the great river, that is the Tigris" (cf. also 8:2).
I Enoch 13:7	"I went away and sat down at the waters of Dan, in the land of Dan, which is to the south of the Hermon mountains, on their west side."
Test. Levi 2:3	"And when I was feeding the flocks in Abel-Maul."
IV Ezra 9:24 and 26	"Do not fast this time, but go to a flowery field where no house stands ... So I went out, as the angel told me, to a field called Ardat" (cf. also 14:1 and 14:37).
II Baruch 21:1	"I went out from there and sat down in the valley of Cedron in a cave of the earth. There I sanctified myself ..." (cf. also 35:1 where Baruch sits down on the ruins of the holy place).

3. Thirdly, in some vision texts it is emphasized that the seer receives "understanding" before the vision is granted to him. In other words, he has gained an insight into the causes of the crisis situation:

Test. Levi 2:3	"The spirit of understanding of the Lord came upon me and I saw all men corrupting their way."

IV Ezra 5: 22   "And my soul received the spirit of understanding."

4. Fasting and other forms of ascetic practice, purifications and prayer seem necessary to receive visions:

Daniel 10: 2–3   "I refrained from all choice food, no meat or wine passed my lips, and I did not anoint myself until the three weeks had gone by."

I Enoch 13: 7   "I read the account of their petitions aloud" (perhaps a repetitive, chant-like reading as Niditch 1980, 160 suggests).

Test. Levi 2: 4   "And I prayed to the Lord that I might be saved."

IV Ezra 9: 24–25   "Go to a flowery field where no house stands, and eat only what grows there —no meat or wine—and pray unceasingly to the Most High" (cf. also 12: 1).

      5: 13   "But turn again to prayer, continue to weep and fast for seven days" (cf. also 5: 20, 6: 31 and 35).

II Baruch 21: 5   "Go and purify yourself for seven days and do not eat bread, do not drink water and do not speak to anyone" (so also 21: 1).

      47: 2–   "When I arrived there, I sat down and fasted for seven days ...
      48: 1–   and after the seventh day I prayed thus to the Most High".

The points mentioned above may be seen as inducing a state of heightened consciousness and of ritual purity, which prepares the seer for receiving the vision. They also favour the transition to the final state, during which he sees what is hidden from ordinary men. This state of mind may be called ecstasy, although the Jewish texts are very reticent on such matters. There are however indications suggesting real ecstatic experiences similar to those of the shaman, the prophet and other types of religious authority in which ecstasy plays a prominent part.

The beginning of a vision is frequently announced by the indication that sleep overcomes the seer. It may of course be explained by the fact that many visions are thought to occur in the form of dreams seen in the night during the normal sleep. There remain, however, a number of instances where this explanation is less plausible. The introduction to the visions in the *Testament of Levi* describes the patriarch feeding the flocks when understanding from the Lord comes upon him (2: 3). Having finished his prayer (2: 4), he then experiences that "there fell upon me a sleep and I beheld ..." (2: 5). Here the mention of a sudden sleep appears to be quite unexpected, but if interpreted as an ecstatic trance, the reference becomes well-integrated into its context. Other similar cases are found in *I Enoch* 13: 8 and *II Baruch* 52: 8–53: 1.

In addition to the metaphors "sleep" and "fall asleep" to describe the ecstasy of the seer, we find other formulations indicating the state during which the visions are provided. The *Book of Daniel* 10: 5–10 describes the initial stage of a vision. Confronted with the flaming appearance of the angel, Daniel's strength leaves him (v. 8) and he falls "prone to the ground in a trance" (v. 9 *hayīti nirdām;* the latter word is rendered by *katanenyg-menos* in Theodotion).[1] The present structure of the text intends to convey the idea that the seer's reactions are caused by the awe-inspiring appearance of the angel. They may however be interpreted as hints of ecstatic experiences, obscured or given a different context in the literary redaction(s) of the vision. The mention in *II Baruch* 6: 3 of "a powerful spirit" (in Syriac: *rwḥ̄ dḥyl̄*) which lifts the seer upwards is best explained as an expression of ecstasy (see also *I Enoch* 71: 1). The important passage in *I Enoch* chapter 14 records a heavenly tour of the seer to behold the glorious dwelling-place of Yahwe and to receive divine revelation. In this chapter we find an interesting passage (vv. 8–9) describing what may be a reminiscence of genuine ecstatic experiences:

"Behold, clouds in the vision called me and mists summoned me, and the stars in their courses and lightnings hastened me and excited me, and winds in my vision caused me to fly and lifted me upward."

There are two passages in *IV Ezra* (6: 36 and 9: 27–28) where, immediately after the preparatory pattern, we find the remark that the "heart"[2] of the seer was "agitated" or "excited" (Latin text: *turbabatur,* Syriac text: *mštgš hwꜣ*) followed by a direct contact with the divine: "and I began to speak in the presence of the Most High." These formulations can be interpreted as allusions to the ecstasy of the seer.

Indications of faintness, agony and similar phenomena are not infrequently found in connection with the visions. The authors and redactors of the texts often have them appear as the seer's reactions to what is seen. The content of the vision is so overwhelming that the seer's strength fails him, he trembles and is overcome by agony (e.g. *Daniel* 8: 27 and *I Enoch* 60: 1–4).[3] It is possible that these descriptions of faintness and agony originally had a different context, being expressions of the ecstatic state in which the vision was received. This becomes more evident in other cases, e.g. *Daniel* 10: 8, *IV Ezra* 5: 14 and 12: 3. In the two latter passages, we find indications of the seer's physical state when awakening from the vision

---

[1] A similar reaction is described in 8: 18: "When he (sc. the angel) spoke to me, I fell to the ground in a trance."

[2] The word "heart" in these passages reflects a semitic form of expression and should more rightly be translated by "mind".

[3] In *IV Ezra* 6: 37 we find an additional remark which probably indicates visionary ecstasy: "with spirit aflame and in great agony of mind I said."

itself. So it is said in 5: 14: "I awoke with a start, shuddering, my spirit faltered, and I was near to fainting." Such a description is so true psychologically that it is difficult not to see a reflexion of genuine ecstatic experiences.

Ancient Iranian religion

The vision as a primary means of conveying divine revelation also appears in Zoroastrianism and does so with the founder himself, Zoroaster. Although the main source, the Gathas, presents only allusions to Zoroaster's role as a seer, it seems clear that he may be described as a kind of ecstatic visionary.[4] Explicit evidence of visions and their function of granting divine revelations is found in the Middle Iranian texts.

The *Bahman Yašt,* a compilation of diverse apocalyptic materials, records two versions of a dream-vision (I, 1–11 and III, 1–29; edition of Anklesaria 1957) received by Zoroaster. The interesting point in these texts is the intimate relation between ecstasy and the divine knowledge granted to the seer. We also catch a glimpse of the particular technique used for provoking the visionary ecstasy.

Before having the vision, Zoroaster is given a cup of water by Ahura Mazda. While drinking it, Zoroaster receives the divine quality of visionary knowledge:

"And Zoroaster drank from it and he (sc. Ahura Mazda) intermingled the wisdom of omniscience with Zoroaster. Seven days and nights Zoroaster was in the wisdom of Ahura Mazda." (III, 7–8)

The words "wisdom of omniscience" (Pahlavi: *xrat ī harvisp-ākāhīh*) seem to be a technical term indicating the seer's gift of divine vision. The text immediately continues: "and Zoroaster saw ..." followed by the description of the things seen. I have elsewhere (Hultgård 1982, 101–111) illustrated what the Iranian tradition meant by omniscient wisdom. Let me here add some remarks on the ecstatic character of Zoroaster's visions.

The trance state during which the vision is given is described as a sleep. In I, 5 it is said: "When he arose from the sleep ..." and III, 12–13 records something of the seer's physical and emotional experience when awaking from the ecstasy:

"Zoroaster reflected that he had seen (it) in a pleasant sleep granted by Ahura Mazda: 'I am not restored from the sleep', and he took both hands, rubbed his own body: 'I have slept a long time and I am not restored from the pleasant sleep, granted by Ahura Mazda' ".

---

[4] The character of Zoroaster as an ecstatic visionary has rightly been emphazised by Nyberg 1938, 146–187 and Widengren 1968, 86–93.

The manner in which Zoroaster enters into the visionary state is only hinted at, but another tradition recording visionary experiences gives more information. This tradition which is found in *Dēnkart* VII, 4: 84–86 and *Pahlavi Rivāyāt* XLVII, 27–32 describes the heavenly journey of Vištāspa, model of piety and justice in the Zoroastrian religion. Before undertaking his visionary tour, Vištāspa is visited by a heavenly messenger who urges him to drink a cup of haoma (or wine, according to *Pahl. Riv.*) mixed with hemp or henbane (*mang*). He then falls into a deep sleep and his soul is taken to heaven. There he sees things which persuade him to adopt the Zoroastrian faith. The use of a specific beverage to produce a visionary ecstasy is here clearly alluded to and makes it probable that the water mentioned in Bahman Yašt represents a later correction due to the redactor's negative attitude towards this technique of provoking the ecstasy (cf. also Widengren 1968, 91). Vištāspa is however not a divine revealer like Zoroaster and this may be the reason why the conveyance of "omniscient wisdom" is not applied to the figure of Vištāspa.

The *Book of Artāy Virāz* describing the journey of the pious Virāz to heaven and hell is certainly the most spectacular vision text of ancient Iran composed in the Sasanian period. For our purpose, the introductive part (chapters I–III) is particularly important as it shows us how the ecstatic vision was produced. In addition to the consumption of a specific beverage, prepared from wine and hemp (*mad ut mang*, II, 22 and 29–31; cf. also I, 38), we also find some sort of preparatory pattern. First, a special place is selected, presumably in a fire-temple, and the seer undergoes a ritual purification: "and Virāz washed his head and body, and put on new clothes" (II, 25). He then performs the ceremony of the consecrated bread (*drōn*), remembers the departed souls and eats food (II, 28). Three golden cups filled with wine and *mang* are given to Virāz in a ritual manner. The text goes on: "He consumed the wine and the *mang*, and said grace whilst conscious and fell asleep on the cover" (II, 31). The summary of the seer's journey given in III, 1–4 is worth quoting:

"And the soul of Virāz went from the body to the peak of Daiti,[5] (over) the Činvat bridge and came back the seventh day and night (*haftom rōč šapān*) and went into the body. Virāz rose up as if he arose from a pleasant sleep, thinking of Vohu Manah and joyful."

Some points should be commented on. Although the *Book of Artāy Virāz* represents a later stage in the development of Iranian vision texts, it draws

---

[5] According to *Bundahišn* IX, 9, the peak of the Daiti mountain is in the middle of the world and it is from there that the Činvat bridge begins.

on earlier traditions similar to those found in *Dēnkart* VII and *Bahman Yašt,* which have an Avestan background. The term *xvamn ī xvaš* "pleasant sleep" in *Artāy Virāz* III, 3 to indicate the trance state appears in *Bahman Yašt* III, 12–13 as we have seen above. The period during which the ecstatic vision lasts, comprises seven days and nights (*haft rōč šapān; Bahman Yašt* III, 8 and *Artāy Virāz* III, 2). It is noteworthy that the *mang* mentioned in Artāy Virāz II, 29 is qualified as that of Vištāspa, an allusion to the tradition underlying *Dēnkart* VII, 4: 84–86. The words "thinking of Vohu Manah" (*Vahuman mēnišn*) recall the role played by this divine figure in accompanying the seer to the heavenly world (see *Yasna* 51: 16, *Dēnkart* VII, 3: 51–62 and *Zātspram* XXI).

Concluding remarks

The Iranian material shows clearly the importance of ecstasy in the activity of the seer. The ecstatic seeing also means that the visionary shares with Ahura Mazda a divine quality, the "wisdom of omniscience". This feature is clearly expressed with regard to Zoroaster,[6] but it is not evident in the visions of Vištāspa, whose role as a seer seems to have been a more passive one.[7] The granting of the "wisdom of omniscience" appears as a temporary gift (for the details see Hultgård 1982, 111) and it conveys to the visionary a supernatural seeing. The technique of consuming a beverage to which some kind of narcotic (*mang*) has been added, appears to be a typical feature of the Middle Iranian vision texts. It would however be wrong to conclude that this was the only technique applied by the Iranian seers. Other means of provoking religious ecstasy were certainly in use. There is evidence to suggest that chanting was an important method of inducing ecstasy within the early Zoroastrian community (cf. Nyberg 1928, 160–163 and Widengren 1968, 92–93).

Specific techniques for inducing the ecstatic state are not recorded in the Jewish sources. Some elements in the pattern leading up to the vision may be interpreted as parts of a method for inducing the final ecstasy, *i.e.* fasting and prayer; the latter is sometimes described as quite exhaustive, *e.g. Baruch* 21: 26). We do not find in the Jewish material a clear correspondence to the Iranian notion of "omniscient wisdom". The closest examples would be *Daniel* 10: 1 and *IV Ezra* 14: 37–40. In the former passage it is stated that "understanding" (*bīnāh*) came to the seer "in the course of the vision". In *IV Ezra* 14: 37–40 we have an interesting parallel to the drinking

---

[6] The quality of "omniscient wisdom" is also ascribed to the figure of J̌āmāspa, who is, however, not explicitly described as a visionary, cf. Hultgård 1980, 111.

[7] In this respect, Vištāspa conforms very well to the typology of the seer as elaborated by Wach 1944, 351–353.

of the ecstatic cup and the conveyance of the "omniscient wisdom" as recorded in the Iranian texts. The passage is worth quoting in full: "I took with me the five men as I had been told, and we went away to the field, and there we stayed. On the next day I heard a voice calling me, which said: 'Ezra, open your mouth and drink what I give you.' So I opened my mouth, and was handed a cup full of what seemed like water, except that its colour was the colour of fire. I took it and drank, and as soon as I had done so my mind began to pour forth a flood of understanding, and wisdom grew greater and greater within me, for I retained my memory unimpaired".

The context reveals that the passage cited is intended to show how Ezra was able to dictate to the five men the whole revelation given to him by God, but it will certainly also convey an idea of how divine inspiration was thought to be transmitted to the seer. The procedure described looks like a symbolic act, similar to those described with regard to several Old Testament prophets, and performed to illustrate how the seer is inspired with the holy spirit (note the wording "colour of fire"!). It is however possible that we are dealing with an original technique of inducing the ecstatic vision which has been reinterpreted and changed into a symbolic act by the author or the redactors of the Ezra-apocalypse.

References:

Anklesaria, B. T. 1957. *Zand i Vôhuman Yasn* with text, transliteration, and translation in English. Bombay.

Hultgård, A. 1982. Forms and Origins of Iranian Apocalypticism. *Die Apokalyptik im Mittelmeerraum und im Vorderen Orient,* hrsg. von D. Hellholm. Tübingen.

Lindblom, J. 1963. *Prophecy in ancient Israel*. Oxford.

Niditch, S. 1980. The visionary. *Ideal figures in ancient Judaism,* ed. by G. Nickelsburg and J. J. Collins. Michigan.

Nyberg, H. S. 1938. *Die Religionen des Alten Iran*. Leipzig.

Russell, D. S. 1964. *The method and message of Jewish apocalyptic 200 B.C.–A.D. 100*. London.

Wach, J. 1944. *Sociology of religion*. Chicago.

Widengren, G. 1968. *Les religions de l'Iran*. Paris.

Religious Ecstasy in Classical Sufism

By GÖRAN OGÉN

The purpose of this essay is to shed some light on the phenomenon of religious ecstasy as met with in Islamic mysticism and there particularly during its classical period; by the expression "classical Sufism" I do not intend to imply any evaluation but use the phrase solely as a term of convenience to cover the period of Sufi history from about 850 A.D. until *circa* 1100 A.D. (cf. Meier 1971, 551 and 567 sq.), that is, until the incipient upsurge of the conventual orders.

I have only been able to find one previous independent study of religious ecstasy in Islamic mysticism (Gardet 1950).[1] But since this study is based primarily on secondary material *about* the ecstasy of the Sufis,[2] it does not succeed in conveying to the reader any "inside" information from the Sufi ecstatic's world of experience.

This is, therefore, a particularly stimulating task, although it is not without some hesitation that I commit myself to it, for—as Tor Andræ has pointed out in his sympathetic study of some central features in the spiritual climate of early Islamic mysticism—"the Sufi mystics are particularly reticent in their descriptions of ecstasy and offer only brief hints about the wonderful things they have beheld and experienced in the moments of rapture" (Andræ 1981, 132/1980, 106).

Fortunately some new material has been discovered whilst other material has been made more accessible since Andræ's study was published thirty-five years ago, followed by Gardet's account three years later. In addition, I am particularly favoured in being able to use a unique little treatise—unique both in its contents, concerning the experiential world of the ecstatic, and in its circulation, for it is hitherto only known to have been preserved in one manuscript; but more of this unique *document humain* later.

---

[1] The material amassed by Ernst Arbman on Sufi ecstasy in volume two (Arbman 1968, 480–515) of his opulent three-volume work *Ecstasy or Religious Trance in the Experience of the Ecstatics and from the Psychological Point of View* is too hastily and inclusively adopted from translations and secondary literature by European orientalists to be regarded as an independent study of Sufi ecstasy.

[2] It consists chiefly of a translation of a chapter entitled "*Waǧd*" ("Ecstasy") in the well-known Sufi manual *Kitāb at-taʿarruf* by al-Kalābāḏī (d. 995) (Al-Kalābāḏī ed. 1934, 82–83) and of a translation of a poem by al-Ḥallāǧ (d. 922) (Al-Ḥallāǧ ed. 1931, 54–55). It is largely on this paper by Louis Gardet that the chapter "*Extase*" in Anawati-Gardet (1960) and Gardet's article in *Dictionnaire de Spiritualité* (Gardet 1961) are based.

Firstly, some reflections on the concept of "religious ecstasy" in general. What is meant by "religious ecstasy" as a concept in *Religionswissenschaft*? I myself felt the necessity of establishing a certain clarity about the scope of "religious ecstasy" before plunging into the study of the texts, especially since the Greek word *ékstăsis* is not to be found in the Arabic word hoard, neither by itself nor in any translated equivalent. Had that been the case, such a linguistic correspondence might then in the Sufi texts have functioned as a first signal of the presence of the phenomenon, which is the case with many other Sufi mystic categories which, via Syriac, often derive from Greek.[3]

To judge from the literature of *Religionswissenschaft,* the concept of "religious ecstasy" does not seem to have undergone any more exhaustive analysis of meaning or historical description of contents,[4] a fact which might suggest the existence of a consensus regarding the meaning of this concept. It is also possible, however, that such an analysis of meaning and description of contents will prove necessary when the summary of this symposium is to be made and an inventory of the contents of "religious ecstasy" becomes relevant.

In expectancy of such an inventory, I have contented myself with discovering how this concept is *actually* used in the general handbookliterature of *Religionswissenschaft*. For this purpose I have chosen to consult some representative encyclopedias in the field.[5] All these works, with a span of some sixty years, are largely unanimous in their descriptions of what is characteristic of religious ecstasy. These descriptions may be summed up under the following four points:

1. Ecstasy denotes a state in which the ecstatic is aware of being outside himself (RGG; DCR; DS), or in an abnormal state of consciousness (ERE;

---

[3] As, for instance, *gnōsĭs* which, via the Syriac *ĭdŭʿtā*, reoccurs with the Sufis in the Arabic form *maʿrifa; théorĭa* which, via the Syriac *teŭrĭā*, has sprung roots with the Sufis in its Arabic equivalent *mušāhada;* or *anámnĕsis* which, via the Syriac *dŭkrānā* or *ʿuhdānā*, is easily recognizable as *ḏikr* in the Sufi authors, etc.

[4] Thus Ernst Arbman, in his *opus magnum* on ecstasy referred to in note 1, has not, for example, devoted any analysis of length to the definition of ecstasy or the concept thereof.

[5] Viz. 1) *Encyclopaedia of Religion and Ethics* (ERE) from 1912 with W. R. Inge as author of the article (ERE 1912, V 157–159), 2) *An Encyclopaedia of Religion* (ER) from

1945 with R. W. Frank as author of the article (ER 1945, 243), 3) *Die Religion in Geschichte und Gegenwart* (RGG) from 1958 with A. Schimmel as author of the article (RGG 1958, II 410–412), 4) *A Dictionary of Comparative Religion* (DCR) from 1970 with S. G. F. Brandon as author of the article (DCR 1970, 253). I have also compared with 5) *The Oxford Dictionary of the Christian Church* (ODCC) from 1958 with an unsigned article (ODCC 1958, 437) and with 6) *Dictionnaire de Spiritualité* (DS) from 1961 with H. Gratton and O. Leroy as authors of articles (DS 1961, IV 2171–2186) since these more theologically oriented encyclopedias also include common material from *Religionswissenschaft*.

ER; ODCC)—that is, what recent psychology classifies as *Out-of-Body-Experiences* (Grof 1976, 186 sqq.) and generally as *Altered States of Consciousness* (Ornstein 1977, 81 sq.).

2. Ecstasy produces a changed or inhibited reaction to external stimuli (ERE; ER; RGG; DCR; ODCC; DS), inability to experience pain (ERE), passivity along with an intensive joy (ER), a drop in breathing and circulation to a minimum whereby the ecstatic state may exhibit an external resemblance to sleep (RGG); uncontrollable movements may also occur (RGG).

3. Ecstasy is a more or less extreme state of mono-ideism (ERE; ER; RGG) and may entail the cessation of the normally experienced flow of time as linear (RGG).

4. The ecstatic state raises the subject to a higher noetic sphere of consciousness than the common one and allows the subject insights into divine or religious truth, although they may remain inexpressible by way of normal, discursive language (ERE; ER; RGG; ODCC).

Furthermore, experience of levitation may also occur in connection with the ecstatic state (RGG); also the duration of the ecstasy may vary considerably (ERE; RGG).

The neurophysiological and psychological correlates that may possibly be related to the above mentioned manifestations of religious ecstasy I refer to the religio-psychological department for explication.[6] I merely point out that the concept of "religious ecstasy" covers a host of phenomena for which it seems to function as a generic term and that, in the Sufi texts, it is one or several of these phenomena which should indicate the presence of religious ecstasy.

Not unexpectedly, since ecstasy evidently is related to universal categories of experience, I have also come across reports of these phenomena in the Sufi texts. In the Sufi vocabulary there is even a rather differentiated terminology concerning these ecstatic experiences or states; whether different descriptions of one and the same experience are involved or whether the terms actually describe different experiences is a question that we must set aside for the present. There are, however, Sufis expressing the opinion that these different states of mind are based on one single experience in spite of the difference in terms (Al-Kalābādī ed. 1934, 96).

A generic term for these experiences or states is not to be found in the Sufi terminology however, so the problem of which of these phenomena must be present in order for ecstasy to be evidenced—or which of them

---

[6] In particular, the research findings detailed by Stanislav Grof in the account of his LSD- research should be observed in this context (Grof 1976, 104 sqq. and 154 sqq.)

would be sufficient— does not therefore arise for the Sufis. So instead of speaking of religious ecstasy in general, they either refer to the single specific terms in question or else use the plural of one of the words employed to designate one of the terms we include in "religious ecstasy". They thus speak of "ecstasies", *mawāǧīd* from the singular form *waǧd*[7] —if one should at all attempt a translation of this plural. This plural is a genuine Sufi construction and does not otherwise seem to occur in the Arabic language, except as a later borrowing.

As-Sarrāǧ (d. 988), author of the oldest known Sufi handbook, employs the plural *mawāǧīd* a couple of times (As-Sarrāǧ ed. 1963, 296 and 306) and so does al-Kalābāḏī a couple of years later (Al-Kalābāḏī ed. 1934, 99), but it is not—as far as I can see—until al-Qušayrī about a hundred years later that the plural *mawāǧīd* receives a definition. "*Mawāǧīd,*" he writes, "are the fruits of the litanies (*ṯumrāt al-awrād*)," respectively, he continues, "the results of 'clashes' (*natā'iǧ al-munāzalāt*)" (Al-Qušayrī, ed. 1972–74, 217).

In the first definition of *mawāǧīd* as "the fruits of the litanies" al-Qušayrī is most probably referring to the *ḏikr*-litanies, an assumption that is corroborated by a text from as-Sarrāǧ that reads: "One day the forceful ecstasies [that occur] during the intensive *ḏikr*-litanies (*al-aḏkār al-qawīya*) were mentioned in the presence of Sarī as-Saqaṭī [...] 'Yes,' said Sarī, 'if his (the mystic's) face were hit by the sword he would not sense it' " (As-Sarrāǧ ed. 1963, 306). *Ḏikr* we may briefly define as the act of calling God to remembrance verbally and/or mentally (*bi'l-lisān/bi'l-qalb*) through a prayer-formula or a formula of praise (*ḏikr*, pl. *aḏkār* or *wird*, pl. *awrād*); in Arabic, *ḏikr* can imply either the verb or the noun.

As to the second definition of *mawāǧīd* as "the results of the 'clashes' ", the word "clash" here mirrors the fundamental Sufi view of the encounter between God and man as a highly dynamic one. This fundamental view runs through most definitions of the singular *waǧd* which is usually translated by our "ecstasy". "*Waǧd,*" states al-Qušayrī, "is what your heart meets with and what comes upon you without [your] intention or [your] securing [it]" (Al-Qušayrī ed. 1972–74, 217).

In descriptions of this encounter, the following antithetical pairs of concepts are frequently recurrent: "closeness (*qurb*) / distance (*buʿd*)", "presence (*ḥuḍūr*) / absence (*ġayba*)", "attacking (*huǧūm*) / vanishing (*ḏahāb*)", "ecstasy (*waǧd*) / loss [of ecstasy] (*faqd*)", "perplexity (*dahša*) / joyous rapture (*ṯarab*)", "drunkenness (*sukr*) / sobriety (*ṣaḥw*)", "disappearence (*fanā'*) / staying (*baqā'*)".

---

[7] So, for example, al-Ḥallāǧ in his poem *Mawāǧīdu ḥaqqin* (Al-Ḥallāǧ ed. 1931, 54) as an early instance of this usage.

Most of these words, also familiar from the general literature of *Religionswissenschaft* dealing with mysticism, are registered in the earliest Sufi manuals as technical terms, as for example in the above mentioned work by as-Sarrāǧ (As-Sarrāǧ ed. 1963, 333 sqq.), where they are described or defined in a way showing that they express phenomena within the ecstatic category of experience.

But instead of presenting these definitions and descriptions one by one and illustrating them with suitable anecdotal material—interesting and valuable as this might be—it now seems fitting to return to the little treatise I mentioned at the beginning. The work concerned is a small tractate entitled *Kitāb a ṣ-ṣafāʾ* [8] and attributed to al-Ḥarrāz. Al-Ḥarrāz died in 898 A.8D. and thus lived about a hundred years before as-Sarrāǧ, author of one of the earliest Sufi manuals.

This short piece of writing is particularly interesting from two points of view, besides the history of its transmission—it has survived in only one known manuscript according to its editor (Al-Ḥarrāz ed. 1967, 16): firstly, it is a quite rare original document demonstrating the presence of religious ecstasy in the world of Islamic spirituality; secondly, it is notable how the speaker in this text wrestles with the difficulties of expressing, through a literary medium, the experiences and states of mind that the ecstatic encounter with God has provided. Furthermore, this treatise also presents us with an exquisite sample of how the technical vocabulary of Islamic mysticism grows forth from an immediate personal experience, tentatively formulated in a literary form, out of which certain key-words have crystallized into so-called *istilāhāt* or technical terms; to enter upon problems connected with this process, however, would bring us too far afield.

This direct and unelaborated language, so characteristic of most first-hand reports of intensive personal experiences, also makes it difficult to provide an adequate translation, besides the purely formal deficiences of the text in question. I therefore ask for indulgence in respect to the translations to follow, as well as for possible misconceptions of the intended meaning of the original text,[9] for I shall now let al-Ḥarrāz speak mainly for himself for a while. I shall only complement his words with necessary explanations and commentaries and supplement them with the Arabic words that have later become incorporated into the standard Sufi vocabu-

---

[8] I read *ṣafāʾ* with the editor of the text (Al-Ḥarrāz 1967, 22; cf. also the facsimile of the title on page 25 of op. cit.), whereas Fuad Sezgin reads *ṣifāt* (Sezgin 1968, 646) as does Paul Nwyia (Nwyia 1970, 252).

[9] I am very much indebted to the pioneer translation of this text by the late Paul Nwyia in his work *Exégèse coranique et langage mystique* (Nwyia 1970, 256–267) for my own translations from this primitive text. In some cases, however, I deviate from Nwyia's interpretations (cf., e.g., notes 11 and 15).

lary concerning ecstatic experiences and states; it is of course beyond the scope and purpose of this essay to offer a requisite philological and contextual analysis of the writing in question, the aim of the present essay being primarily that of bringing one aspect of Sufi experience—the ecstatic —within the wider orbit of general religious experience and its psychology.

This treatise—which is formally constructed as a dialogue between al-Ḥarrāz and an anonymous seeker—commences with an account of four different ways of responding to God's calling. The first two concern that of the people of the world, the latter two that of the people of God. Let us immediately proceed to the response of the people of God.

While both categories belonging to the people of God choose God rather than the world—even to the extent that the latter is legitimate—yet the majority of those belonging to God miss the point of their choice because—according to al-Ḥarrāz—they are more occupied with the spiritual stations (*maqāmāt*) leading to God than with God himself. From those remaining unaffected by this spiritual gluttony, "God selects them for himself and shows them the greatness of His kingdom in order thereby to subject them to a veritable [spiritual] training, so that they can attack His majesty" (Al-Ḥarrāz ed. 1967, 22).

The expression "attack His majesty" (*al-huǧūm ʿalā ʿaẓmatihi*) is not arbitrarily chosen by al-Ḥarrāz but results from his reading of Sura 6: 75 about Abraham. "Thus," this verse reads, "we (God) let Abraham behold the kingdom of the heavens and the earth in order that he should belong to the convinced ones." This verse al-Ḥarrāz comments in the following way: "He let Abraham behold this in order that he might be able to attack God's nearness and His majesty" (Al-Ḥarrāz ed. 1967, 22).[10]

"Attack God's nearness"—with these words al-Ḥarrāz clearly declares the Sufi point of departure for the encounter with God as a spiritual combat on the part of the mystic. We thus find here a fairly early attempt at the definition of *mawāǧīd*—ecstasies—subsequently given by al-Qušayrī as "the results of the 'clashes' " (cf. supra p. 154).

It is worth while noting that al-Ḥarrāz' use of the rather strong verb "attack" (*huǧūm*)—with its primary association of a hostile and capricious assault—in order to illustrate the active encounter of the mystic with God already occurs in the earliest Sufi handbooks as a technical term *but* in a weaker and more passive sense (As-Sarrāǧ ed. 1963, 341 and Al-Qušayrī ed.

---

[10] This exegesis by al-Ḥarrāz is also literally rendered in as-Sulamī's (d. 1022) collection of Sufi Koran commentaries, his *Ḥaqāʾ iq at-tafsīr*, (Ms. Br. Lib. Or. 9433, fol. 62 a); this circumstance may thus also serve as indirect proof of the genuineness of the authorship of the tractate in question.

1972–74, 251, where its definition is almost synonymous with that of *waǧd* translated above on page 154). In addition, the object of the "attack"— nearness (*qurb*)—has become part of the standard Sufi terminology (Al-Kalābāḏī ed. 1934, 77).

Admonished by his anonymous interlocutor, al-Ḥarrāz now sets out to describe the first spiritual station characteristic of those possessing the spiritual stations of nearness to God, and he begins with: *waǧd*—ecstasy! The first stage of *waǧd* he describes as "concentration of intention (*hamm*) by way of intensive [self-]observation (*murāqaba*), calmness of the limbs through rest, drawing close to God together with little variation in the notions of contemplation (*ḥaṭarāt al-mušāhada*), and with few movements when experiencing the first flashings of the ascending [sun-]light (*bi'dawq ṭawāliʿ al-muṭālaʿ a*),[11] fleeing into solitude (*ʿuzla*), separation (*infirād*), and loneliness (*waḥda*) [...] and seeking rest with Him after the confusion and the multitude of means [employed] in the search of obtainment, and becoming happy with Him and finding intimacy with His word [from Sura 7: 157] 'He lifted their burden from them' [...]" (Al-Ḥarrāz ed. 1967, 23).

From a psychological point of view, one phrase above all in this description might arouse particular interest, viz. "when experiencing the first flashings of the ascending [sun-] light". The expression "first flashings" (*ṭawāliʿ*) is listed in the technical vocabulary of the Sufis and it will thus be profitable to turn directly to as-Sarrāǧ for illumination of this term. "The first flashings (*aṭ-ṭawāliʿ*)," he explains, "are the lights of the realization of God's unconditional unity (*anwār at-tawḥīd*) which shine on the hearts of the gnostics (*al-ʿārifūn*) through their radiation and which through the power of their brightness calm what there is of light in the hearts, just like the ascending sun. When she has arisen, the brightness of the stars disappears from the onlookers as a result of the power of the sun's light in spite of the stars remaining in their places" (As-Sarrāǧ ed. 1963, 345).

But al-Ḥarrāz' friend is not content with this and asks him to describe a spiritual station even better than this first one, so al-Ḥarrāz proceeds to the description of the next spiritual station as: "Stupefaction (*dahša*) from the ominous impressions (*ṭawāriq*) of awe, and bewilderment from continuous exaltation [of God]; as a sincere yearning and as a contentment due to purity of union (*ittiṣāl*), as a consumption of much food without greed as a

---

[11] The original reads ذوق الطوالع المطالع (Al-Ḥarrāz ed. 1967, 23) but in order to obtain a meaningful rendering I suggest we read بذوق طوالح المطالعة as a cor- rection of an unhappy reversal of order. Nwyia, however, follows the original reading in this case and translates with: "[...] ni trop se laisser mouvoir par les premiers éclairs de la connaissance gustative" (Nwyia 1970, 259).

result of being passionately in love, and as an overwhelming wisdom. Most strong gnostics (ʿ*ārifūn*), when experiencing the realities of nearness, start screaming and become stupefied, for they become wild [when they realize] that He is looking at them in various ways until He lets His veil fall over them and shades them in His bosom and lets them enter behind curtains illuminated with His light [. . .] From here they return with splendid marks of honour, not knowing what they have arrived at, for they are stupefied in this spiritual station. When they awaken from their stupefaction they become perplexed over what they have arrived at with [God's] permission; but what they conceal is greater yet" (Al-Ḥarrāz ed. 1967, 23).

After this informative report, in which most of the criteria of ecstasy offered by *Religionswissenschaft* are easily recognizable, al-Ḥarrāz offers an account, no less interesting from the psychologial point of view, about the ecstatic's situation after returning from his ecstatic state.

"You should know," al-Ḥarrāz confides in his friend, "that most of the weeping of the aspirants, their confusion, their screaming, and their movements are the result of grief following upon the spiritual stations [they have experienced] [. . .] And these in their turn are the result of the ascending lights [of the spiritual sun] (*muṭālaʿāt*) due to nearness [to God], for they have beheld Him whom they have not [previously] beheld and they have heard the speech of God Most High that has not [hitherto] been their nourishment. This overwhelms them, for in spite of themselves these ideas (*ḫaṭarāt*) come upon them. And when that comes upon them of which they but seldom have had experience, this astonishes them, and that becomes manifest in them which you [can] see [yourself]. Those who are strong in gnosis (*maʿrifa*) are not affected by this state of mind however" (Al-Ḥarrāz ed. 1967, 24).

The rather surprising expression in the previous description of the second spiritual station of nearness to God as, *inter alia,* "the consumption of much food without greed as a result of being passionately in love" (cf. above), here receives its explanation in the fact that it is now the immediate listening to the word of God Most High that constitutes the main nourishment of the mystic.

At the request of his friend, al-Ḥarrāz now brings him yet deeper into the secrets of nearness to God and makes it clear to him that there now is no further spiritual station to follow but that an intensification of the station in which the ecstatic already dwells takes place, which results in "the forgetting of the lot allotted him by God and the forgetting of his needs with regard to God; God's nearness has cut the mystic off from [his] calling God to remembrance (*ḏikr Allāh*): he *is* now with God and needs no longer call Him to remembrance, and he no longer finds [his own] understanding (*fahm*) interceding between God and him. The attack upon God (*al-huǧūm 'alā Allāh*) has freed him from [the consciousness of] having found God: the slave [of God] becomes abolished (*saqaṭa*)[12] and God [alone] remains (*baqiya*)" (Al-Ḥarrāz ed. 1967, 24)!

Al-Ḥarrāz now experiences the agony of not finding adequate words for communicating what he has undergone and concludes this passage with: "All that I have mentioned to you is different from what I wanted to mention and I do not recognize it and I do not know what I want and I do not know what I say and I do not know who I am or from where I am. You who listen, do you understand what I say? It is a slave who has lost his name and no longer has a name, he is ignorant and no longer possesses any knowledge—but yet he has knowledge and yet he is not ignorant [...] Oh, how I long for one who recognizes what I say and together with me enters into what I say" (Al-Ḥarrāz ed. 1967, 24)!

For the last time al-Ḥarrāz's friend insists on also having the ecstasy of this intensified spiritual station described. And as invaluable help in our understanding of the ecstatic experience of the Sufis, al-Ḥarrāz agrees to this and announces that "he who has been drawn close [to God] (*muqar-rab*)[13] is in reality as if under supervision: he is sought and suspended, without knowledge, understanding, will, sensation, or movement. He is the happiest of creatures, except that those realities of the ecstatic state that are [still] valid for him in his realization of God's unconditional unity (*ḥaqā'iq al-wuǧūd lahū fī't-tawḥḥīd*) come between him and [the final] happiness. His spiritual station consists of a joyous rapture (*ṭarab*) due to continuous beholding of Him, and if it is said to one of those [in this station] 'What do you want?' he answers 'God'. If it is said to one of them 'What is your knowledge?' he answers 'God'. And if his limbs could talk they would say 'God'. For his members, his joints, and his limbs are filled with the light of God. He knows nothing but God and all his knowledge is from God, yes, he himself is from God, through God, unto God, and with God. His identity and his reckoning have vanished (*dahaba*).[14] If one says to him 'What are you?' he would be unable to answer 'I', because of the preponderance of God's decrees. This is the reality of their ecstasy. And when he reaches the peak of nearness, he cannot even say 'God'" (Al-Ḥarrāz ed. 1967, 24–26). This definitive ineffability occurs, al-Ḥarrāz reveals to us, when also the

---

[12] It is interesting to notice how al-Ḥarrāz, known in the Sufi tradition for having been the first to talk about *fanā'* (and *baqā'*) (Su-lamī ed. 1953, 228), not once in this dialogue uses the term *fanā'* but prefers synonyms thereof such as *saqaṭa* or *dahaba* in order to express the underlying experience which has later become conceptualized through the notion of *fanā'*.

[13] According to Nwyia, *al-muqarrab* alludes to *al-muqarrabūn* in Sura 56: 11 and 88.

[14] Cf. note 12.

gnosis [-consciousness] (*ma'arifa*) has left (*dahaba*) the mystic (Al-Ḥarrāz ed. 1967, 26).

After this description of ecstasy, in which we continue to recognize without difficulty most of the criteria of ecstasy that I reported at the beginning (cf. supra p. 227 f.), al-Ḥarrāz resumes his previous, highly interesting description of the ecstatic's situation after the cessation of his ecstasy.

"You should know," al-Ḥarrāz imparts to his friend, "that a life in perfection does not apply to the gnostics and that they are not completely delighted in this station, for after the presence [with God] they are [spiritually] absent even if they are [corporally] present [...] They are without [spiritual] aspiration (*himma*), without purpose, without means, without claim, without flight [into solitude (?)], without ecstasy (*wağd*) and without loss [of ecstasy] (*faqd*) [...] they see His reign as perfect as well as His remembrance (*dikr*) of them as perfect in all matters He has willed [for them]. Their lot from Him is perfect and what is with Him is perfect before they were [born] and after they were [born]. So is His purpose with them and for them perfect. Their calling Him to remembrance (*dikr*) does not add to their nearness to Him, nor does their negligence (*ġafla*) [in calling Him to remembrance] subtract for them from what was [decreed] for them with Him [...]" (Al-Ḥarrāz ed. 1967, 27).

The reality behind this existential suspension and spiritual impotence is the circumstance that the mystic's act of calling God to remembrance (*dikr*) during the ecstatic realization of God's unconditional unity (*tawḥīd*) has become assimilated with the absolute theomnemy (*dikr*) of God's primordial calling to remembrance of His creation, in which no trace of the mystic's own activity remains but only God's acting through the mystic. Al-Ḥarrāz formulates this total monoideization in the words: "God calls himself to remembrance through his (the mystic's) person (*nafs*) when He so desires, He praises himself through his tongue when He desires, and He glorifies himself through his laudations [...] So what place is there for 'I' or for 'You'" (Al-Ḥarrāz ed. 1967, 27)?[15]

---

[15] That is, the ordinary references of identity have become void of meaning. I deviate here from Nwyia's translation which reads: "[...] Il fit mémoire de Lui-même par Lui-même, quand Il le voulut; [...] Il Se louangea par Sa propre langue, quand Il le voulut; [...] Il Se glorifia de Ses mérites dans l'exercice de Sa propre puissance. Où étions-nous, toi et moi" (Nwyia 1970, 265)? The original reads (Al-Ḥarrāz ed. 1967, 27):

والعلم في ذلك انه

نفسه بلسانه حين اراد ومجد

نفسه بنفسه حين اراد وسبّح

فاين انا وانت ذكر

نفسه بحامده في مجاري قدرته

The condition for the mystic's realization of God's unconditional unity (*tawḥīd*) thus consists in a complete forgetting of 'I' and thence of 'You', which al-Bisṭāmī, who died a quarter of a century before al-Ḥarrāz, has expressed in the following words: "Upon the forgetting of one's person, the Creator's calling the person to remembrance follows (*'inda nisyān an-nafs ḏikr bāri' an-nafs*)" (As-Sahlaǧī ed. 1976, 105).

The Sufis, with their well-developed sense for the conditions of the spiritual life, have captured this psychological dialectic between the calling of God to remembrance (*ḏikr*) and the forgetting of self (*nisyān*) in a very eloquent paradox as in the following quotation from al-Wāsiṭī (d. 932): "Those who remember [their act of calling God to remembrance] during their calling God to remembrance are more negligent than those who are forgetful [of their act of calling God to remembrance] during their calling God to remembrance for [the act of] calling Him to remembrance is other than He" (As-Sulamī ed. 1953, 305).[16]

That ecstasy has been a conducive factor for this forgetting of self is obvious. Al-Aʿrābī (d. 952), whose work on ecstasy as-Sarrāǧ has preserved in a summary, was, for instance, quite aware of this, for he writes: "Ecstasy in this world does not consist of the full disclosure [of God] but [is] the heart's contemplation (*mušāhada*) [...] He (the mystic) contemplates [God during ecstasy] out of joy of certitude and purity of theomnemy (*ḏikr*), for [during ecstasy] he is quite alert [inwardly] (*muntabih*)" (As-Sarrāǧ ed. 1963, 311).

Lest we ourselves fall victims to spiritual gluttony in trying to examine the nature of the theomnemy which—according to al-Ḥarrāz—"makes the heart beat from calling God to remembrance, makes the tongue mute, and the value of which nobody knows but God Most High" (ʿAṭṭār ed. 1961, II 38), we shall content ourselves with what al-Ḥarrāz has let us know about the experiences of the Sufi ecstatic. Besides, we have most certainly got to know more about the workings of ecstasy and the secrets of nearness to God than what was intended for the outsider. In a book about the external aspects of intimacy with God, al-Ḥarrāz has stated unequivocally "that

---

I do not think that *bi'nafsihi, bi'lisānihi,* and *bi'maḥāmidihi* should be interpreted as reflexive, an opinion that is confirmed by the following quotation attributed to al-Bisṭāmī

(As-Sahlaǧī ed. 1976, 105):

النفس

كند نسيان النفس ذكر بارئ

[16] The point of the paradox is, of course,

that an awareness of one's own activity of calling God to remembrance during theomnemy distracts the person from perceiving God's antecedent remembrance of him, whereas he who has an undivided awareness of God's primordial remembrance of him and forgets his own activity of calling God to remembrance, perhaps even the external act of calling, during theomnemy has a greater chance of so doing.

what remains of the spiritual stations of intimacy with God is more and weightier than can be put forward in a book; but something may be obtained in discourse with those who know about it" (Al-Ḥarrāz ed. 1975, 73). And discourse with such a person we have been lucky enough to follow!

With regard to one side of the Sufis' ecstasy, al-Ḥarrāz leaves us behind, namely the question whether their ecstasy was spontaneously generated and hence not intentionally induced or whether the Sufi at this time had recourse to expedients for the express purpose of inducing ecstasy—and in that case, which ones.

However, just as we are not over-indulged with first-hand material about the internal dimensions of ecstasy—"for he who asks how good God tastes asks the impossible, for this cannot be perceived through description but only by him who has gotten to taste [and see]" (al- Aʿrābī, ap. As-Sarrāǧ ed. 1963, 313)—likewise we are not over-indulged with first-hand sources about the external dimensions of ecstasy either. This situation holds true at least for the period before the consolidation of the orders (sg. *ṭarīqa*) and their monopolization of the spiritual life, i.e., before the thirteenth century when the ecstasy-inducive rituals we usually associate with this context, such as the *darwīš*-dance, the *ḏikr*-séance, and the *samāʿ*-listening, receive their definitive structures and breakthrough.

And since there now is no al-Ḥarrāz to succour us, we must instead try to shape a picture for ourselves from those disparate notices that are available concerning the external conditions of ecstasy. That the Sufis did employ existent liturgical resources in order to attain an ecstatic state of mind becomes admirably clear from a previously quoted passage (cf. supra p. 229) from as-Sarrāǧ's *Kitāb al-lumaʿ* , where the commentary is reproduced which Sarī as-Saqaṭī (d. 865) gave when he was told of "those forceful ecstasies [that occur] during the intensive *ḏikr*-litanies *and there-with related phenomena that influence the mystic* [. . .]" (As-Sarrāǧ ed. 1963, 306).

In another passage as-Sarrāǧ confirms this circumstance in his own words: "You should know," he writes, "that absence/presence (*ġaybal/ḥuḍūr*), sobriety/drunkenness (*ṣaḥw/sukr*), ecstasy (*waǧd*), attacking (*hu-ǧūm*) and overwhelmings (*ġalabāt*), disappearence/staying (*fanāʾ/baqāʾ*) belong to those states that have been actualized through theomnemy (*ḏikr*) and exaltation (*taʿẓīm*) of God" (As-Sarrāǧ ed. 1963, 344).

In addition to this, as-Sarrāǧ claims that in the traditions (*aḥbār*) there are many reports about those who "heard a word (*kalima*), a *ḏikr*-litany (*ḏikr*), an edifying speech (*mawʿaẓa*), or a fine wisdom-word (*ḥikma*) that gladdened them and elicited ecstasy (*waǧd*) in their inmost (*sirr*) . . ." (As-Sarrāǧ ed. 1963, 295).

Now we also know that there have existed, from the middle of the eighth century, so-called *ḏikr*-sessions (*maǧālis aḏ-ḏikr* or *ḥalaq aḏ-ḏikr*), in which various *ḏikr*-litanies were recited, chosen Koran-words were proclaimed and edifying speech was listened to (cf. Massignon 1968, 105). Although it is not possible to enter into details here, it is in all probability this liturgical milieu, with or without connection to the ordinary divine service, that constitutes the historical background of the subsequent traditional *ḏikr*-séance and *samāʿ*-listening.

Unfortunately, the material at our disposal does not allow us any possibility of judging to what extent the Sufis have purposely utilized these liturgical resources in order to put themselves in an ecstatic frame of mind, or how these gatherings were organized or structured. It was probably not until the so-called educating shaykh (*šayḫ at-tarbiya*) in the eleventh century that these sessions, as far as the Sufis are concerned, received their definitive organization and guidance.

We do know, however, that there were individual Sufis who tried to imitate the ecstatic state and who behaved as if they were in ecstasy (*tawāǧada*)—a feigned ecstasy may also be conducive to real ecstasy. But this is more specifically a Sufi problem proper, concerning genuine and false ecstasy according to their own criteria of judging ecstasy and, in the last instance, a problem which only they themselves are qualified to settle.

In any case, Louis Massignon's statement remains irrefutable: "A fact to be borne in mind," he writes, "is that psalmody based on the Koranic vocabulary remains the main procedure for putting oneself in ecstasy." (Massignon 1968, 106) If we add 'and listening to psalmody', we then obtain a fairly satisfactory picture of the external conditions for the Sufis' ecstasy until the eleventh century, when various innovations begin to appear (Massignon 1968, 106). And as far as the *darwīš*-dance is concerned, it is not until the thirteenth century with Rūmī (d. 1273) that it becomes transformed from an expression of ecstasy—and as such, quite a controversial one (Molé 1963, 147)—into an expedient for ecstasy (Meier 1954, 127). Stimulants such as hashish, coffein, and opium also seem to have been first introduced during the thirteenth century (Massignon 1968, 107).

To illustrate the external conditions of ecstasy I would like to relate, by way of conclusion, firstly the case of at-Tustarī, a contemporary of al-Ḥarrāz, a case which illustrates both the liturgical context of ecstasy and some of its concrete manifestations; and secondly the case of al-Ǧunayd, also a contemporary of al-Ḥarrāz, a case which illustrates spontaneously generated ecstasy.

First, at-Tustarī (d. 896): "It is reported that when Sahl at-Tustarī listened to a *samāʿ* (a kind of musical performance), ecstasy (*waǧd*) manifested itself in him. For twenty-five days he remained in this ecstasy and ate no food. And in spite of it being winter, he sweated to the extent that his shirt became wet. When he was in this state, learned men put questions to him, and he answered 'Do not ask me since a word from me at this point of time is not meaningful to you'' ('Aṭṭār ed. 1961, I 230)!

And finally al-Ǧunayd (d. 910): "'Ǧunayd put a question to Šiblī and said 'What about your theomnemy (*ḏikr*)? You do not heed the true theomnemy, do you?' Šiblī replied 'It is inessential how many times I call Him to remembrance, if He just calls me to remembrance one single time!' At these words, Ǧunayd fell into ecstasy (literally: came out of himself—*az ḫod bešod*)'' ('Aṭṭār ed. 1961, II 148).

References

Anawati, G.-C.–Gardet, L. 1960. *Mystique musulmane*. Paris.

Andræ, T. 1980.[2] *Islamische Mystik*. Stuttgart.

— 1981.[2] *I myrtenträdgården*. Lund.

Arbman, E. 1968. *Ecstasy or religious trance in the experience of the ecstatics and from the psychological point of view 2: Essence and forms of ecstasy*. Stockholm.

'Aṭṭār, Farīd ud-Dın, ed. 1961. *Taḏkirat ul-awliyā'*, *I–II*, edited by M. M. Qazvīnī. Tehran 1339 š.

DCR 1970. *A Dictionary of comparative religion*, ed. by S. G. F. Brandon. New York.

DS 1961. *Dictionnaire de spiritualité*, ed. by M. Viller et al. 4. Paris.

ER 1945. *An Encyclopaedia of religion*, ed. by V. Ferm. New York.

ERE 1912. *Encyclopaedia of religion and ethics*, ed. by J. Hastings 5. Edinburgh.

Gardet, L. 1950. Quelques textes ṣūfis concernant l'''extase''. *Revue thomiste* 50.

— 1961. Extase dans la mystique musulmane. *Dictionnaire de spiritualité* 4, 2068–2072. Paris.

Grof, S. 1976. *Realms of the human unconscious*. New York.

Al-Ḥallāǧ, Ḥusayn ibn Manṣūr. ed. 1931. Le dīwān d'al-Hallāj, essai de reconstitution, édition et traduction, par L. Massignon. *Journal asiatique* 218.

Al-Ḥarrāz, Abū Sa'īd. ed. 1967. *Kitāb aṣ-ṣafā'*, ed. by Q. as-Sāmarrā'ī in his *Rasā'-il al-Ḥarrāz*. Baghdad. (This edition also printed in *Al-Maǧma' al'irāqī. Maǧalla* 15. Baghdad 1967.)

— ed. 1975. *Kitāb aṣ-ṣidq,* ed. by 'Abd al-Ḥalīm Maḥmūd. Cairo.

Al-Kalābāḏī, Abū Bakr Muḥammad ibn Isḥāq. ed. 1934. *Kitāb at- ta'arruf li'maḏhab ahl at-taṣawwuf,* ed. by A. J. Arberry. Cairo.

Massignon, L. 1968.[2] *Essai sur les origines du lexique technique de la mystique musulmane*. Paris.

Meier, F. 1954. Der Derwischtanz. *Asiatische Studien* 8.

— 1971. Ḫurāsān und das Ende der klassischen Ṣūfik. *La Persia nel medioevo*. Rome.

Molé, M. 1963. La danse extatique en Islam. *Sources orientales* 6.

Nwyia, P. 1970. *Exégèse coranique et langage mystique*. Beyrouth.

ODCC 1958. *The Oxford dictionary of the christian church*, ed. by F. L. Cross. London.

Ornstein, R. E. 1977. *The psychology of consciousness*. New York.

Al-Qušayrī, Abu'l-Qāsim. ed. 1972–74. *Ar-Risālat al-qušayrīya*, ed. by ʿAbd al-Ḥalīm Maḥmūd and Muḥammad ibn Šarīf. Cairo.

RGG 1958. *Die Religion in Geschichte und Gegenwart*, ed. by K. Galling 2. Tübingen.

As-Sahlaǧī, Muḥammad ibn ʿAlī. ed. 1976.[2] *An-nūr min kalimāt Abī Ṭayfūr*, ed. by ʿAbd ar-Raḥmān Badawī in his *Šaṭaḥāt aṣ-ṣūfīya* 1. Kuwayt.

As-Sarrāǧ, Abū Naṣr. ed. 1963.[2] *Kitāb al-lumaʿ fi't-taṣawwuf*, ed. by R. A. Nicholson. London.

Sezgin, F. 1968. *Geschichte des arabischen Schrifttums* 1. Leyden.

As-Sulamī, Abū ʿAbd ar-Raḥmān. Ms. Br. Lib. Or. 9433. *Ḥaqāʾiq at-tafsīr*. (British Library Oriental Manuscripts no. 9433.) London.

— ed. 1953. *Ṭabaqāt aṣ-ṣūfīya*, ed. by Nūr ad-Dīn Šurayba. Cairo.

IV

Ecstasy and Mysticism

By HANS HOF

The task I set myself in this paper is that of finding and understanding the structures in human consciousness which characterise the experience of certain kinds of ecstasy. The context in which I try to perform this task is an outline of fundamental changes in consciousness brought about by those methods of meditation which, under optimal conditions, give rise to mystical experience. I define the terms "ecstasy" and "mysticism" within the scope of this outline.

My presentation will be divided into three sections. In the first section I discuss a method of finding and interpreting structures of consciousness relevant for understanding the phenomena of ecstasy and mysticism. In the second section I present the results of an investigation based on the given method: an outline of the realms of human consciousness where different ecstatic and mystical phenomena can be placed. In the third section I offer some considerations regarding the phenomenological method that I recommend for examining the structures of consciousness of ecstasy and mysticism.

1. *Concerning an experimental method in study of ecstasy and mysticism*

Phenomena such as ecstasy and mysticism display both psychological and physical features. We find their defining features within the psychological sphere: what makes ecstasy ecstasy or mysticism mysticism is their psychologically describable features and not the physical ones. The physical features which are a part of these phenomena are usually regarded as secondary in relation to the psychological ones. This relation entails a methodological problem. How does one go about an experimental investigation of phenomena whose main features are to be found in subjective experience? How can one find intersubjective criteria?

A useful approach in obtaining an answer to these questions is shown by the experiences afforded us through the so called "meditation" of the last two decades. I have in mind those forms of meditation that I call "body-centered meditation". By these, I mean those techniques of meditation that aim at activating the nervous system and the brain without any help from ideas that have been induced into the consciousness. In Za-Zen meditation of which I have many years of experience, the physiological states of the body and thereby the states of consciousness change mainly through the adoption of an anatomically well conceived posture and a special technique of breathing.

In explaining the optimal interplay between consciousness and body which is put into action by body-centered meditation, I shall make use of a couple of theories put forward by the neurologist John Eccles and the philosopher Karl Popper in a joint work *The Self and its Brain,* 1978. According to their basic theory, the mental activity of the psychophysical organism is brought about by an interaction between different parts of the nervous-physiological apparatus. In another fundamental theory they claim that the mental activity brought about by interaction in the organism is to be understood as an autonomous entity called Mind or Self and which is not reducible to anything physical.

In discerning and interpreting in a meaningful way the content of the different states and realms of human consciousness which are brought about by body-centered meditation, I have been helped, most of all, by the Czech-american psychiatrist Stanislav Grof's investigations of changes in consciousness. Grof's investigations are carried out with the help of a therapy in which he combined LSD induction and conversational analysis. His experiment is based on a large number of subjects and shows unambiguously that the human psyche or consciousness displays different experiences, and that these experiences among themselves display a definite order. This order is expressed, most of all, by the fact that the maturing of an individual personality in the form of changes related to "self-experience" usually follows a certain order between the realms of consciousness. Grof's survey of the realms or levels of human consciousness is in accordance with the basic experiences of body-centered meditation. These experiences are described in a rich and extensive literature.

Another way of interpreting meaningfully the different realms of human consciousness and their mutual relations is presented in studies in which the interpretations of changes in consciousness by different traditions are compared with experience from different forms of body-centered psychotherapy and personality pedagogies. I have learnt a lot from Ken Wilber's book *The Spectrum of Consciousness, 1977,* which, though it sometimes gives a little too much rein to fantasy, gives an abundance of suggestions from which to choose critically and develop further work.

Among the approaches for understanding and explaining the states of consciousness induced by meditation is the study of the so called "bio feed back". With the help of EEG examinations, for instance, one can establish a correlation between subjective experienced states and objective measurable states in the brain's electrical activity. With this, we have at our disposal a small possibility for an intersubjective control of claims based on subjective experiences such as mysticism and ecstasy with regard to the question of the facticity of such experiences and the explanation of their origin.

2. The structures of consciousness in ecstatic and mystical experience

I shall try to clarify the structures of consciousness that are characteristic of ecstatic and mystical experiences by drawing a map of the changes in a person's self-experience that can be effected by a body-centered technique of meditation. One can differentiate between three types of self-experience actualised by body-centered meditation: externally conditioned self-experience, organism-centered self-experience and the experience of a transcending self. I shall consider each of these individually and examine its individual relation to ecstatic and mystical experience.

2.1. *Externally conditioned self-experiences*

This basic type of self-experience displays two subtypes: self-experience that is related to a person's experience of himself as the subject of his perceptions and the self-picture that is conditioned by the first years of upbringing in the life of a child. I shall call the former *the subject of perception* and the latter *the psycho-dynamically conditioned self-image*.

2.1.1. *The subject of perception.* A person's experience of himself as the subject of perception is fundamental for his self-experience. This statement is confirmed by the changes in a person's perceptual ability that are brought about by meditation. First of all, there is the visual perception which changes in two respects. I shall call one of these changes an increased immediacy in the relationship between perception and the object of perception. This involves a dispersion of, or liberation from learned patterns of interpretation and a higher degree of mental presence in experiencing the object of perception. The second change is a kind of empathy for an insight into the object which is experienced. I call it a transparent experience. In

this the perceived object is changed; it becomes transparent; the demarcations between the object and other objects and its physical stability dissolve and give way to a more uniformly structured content of experience. In the literature, the term "disobjectivising" is sometimes used to describe this phenomenon. Both these changes involve a qualitative change in self-experience. Transparent experience is given first place on our map of self-experience for the location of ecstatic and mystical phenomena.

The type of mysticism that can be placed here is, in my view, identical with extrovertive mysticism in W. T. Stace's classical work *Mysticism and Philosophy*, 1961. He differentiates between this and introvertive mysticism which consists basically of an *unio-mystica*-experience, an experience of the complete oneness of the consciousness with the wholeness of everything that exists. In extrovertive mysticism consciousness of the world remains and in this is experienced a *holon,* a oneness of existence which fills and surrounds the universe. This can be a kind of transparent experience, i.e., a state of consciousness in which the object of consciousness—the wholeness of the physical world—becomes transparent. Such widely differing phenomena and ideas as the ones that Carlos Castaneda writes about in his books on Indian mysticism, drug-induced experiences and the Buddhistic understanding of wholeness as the interdependence of everything can be understood as interpretations of transparent experience.

What has this to do with ecstasy? What takes place in transparent experience is an expansion of consciousness, an expansion which in turn is followed by an experience of pleasure. I believe that we have introduced a class of ecstatic experience. It is distinguished by three features:

(1) the expansion of consciousness; in our example the expansion of consciousness takes place through an experience in which the object of perception becomes transparent.

(2) the expansion of consciousness is followed by an increased degree of intensity in consciousness as consciousness.

(3) the expansion and increase of intensity are followed by an experience of pleasure which absorbs or eliminates other experiences. The experience of pleasure is momentary, i.e., it is fleeting. The fact that the experience of pleasure is momentary is characteristic of the class of ecstatic experience in question here. It is precisely the relationship to time which, as will be shown, differentiates between the types of ecstasy we shall meet on our map of different types of self-experience.

2.1.2. *Psycho-dynamically conditioned self-experience.* The first and basic form of externally conditioned self-experience has been dealt with above as an experience of oneself as the subject of perception. I have called this a person's "first" self-experience because of the fact that self-experience which is vitalised or dynamised through meditation starts with a change in the subject of perception. I call it "basic" because the experience of the self as a subject of the activity of consciousness is central in every type of self-experience.

The next type of self-experience usually activated through the vitalising of self-experience through meditation, I have called a psycho-dynamically conditioned self-image. Similar to the subject of perception, it is externally conditioned. Self-experience here consists of an experienced image of ourselves. It is a result of the psycho-dynamic relationships which are grounded emotionally and during the first years of life between ourselves and our immediate social environment. What characterises this type of self-experience are, primarily, the following two features:

(1) It is a relationship-experience; the image of the self is a product of the relationship-experience.
(2) The self-experience's creating relationships are social relationships.

What takes place in body-centered meditation in relation to the psycho-dynamically conditioned self-image is the bringing to consciousness of the relationship-experience's negative effects that have conditioned the self-image. This bringing to consciousness often expresses itself neurotically and sometimes requires therapeutic help. I mention this for two reasons.

(1) It is necessary for a person to come to terms with difficulties in the experience of his psycho-dynamically conditioned self-image in order to reach the next type of self-experience that is actualised through meditation and which I call the autonomous self. The experience of this is in turn a necessary condition for a genuine transcendent experience or introvertive mystical experience and the ecstasy that can be found in it.
(2) The freeing of a person from difficulties in the experience of his psycho-dynamically conditioned self-image can trigger off an ecstasy of type (1), where expansion of consciousness is followed by increased intensity of consciousness and a momentary experience of pleasure.

2.2. *Organism conditioned self-experience: the autonomous self*

This type of self-experience differs from the two I have described above in that it does not consist of a person's experience of relationship to his environment. It is mainly made up of a person's experience that his psycho-physical organism functions as a whole and in an optimal way according to its own resources. Body-centered meditation can be a part of the explanation of the origin of such self-experience: an improved interaction in the physical part of the organism is brought about through meditation and this in its turn can bring about an improved interplay between itself and consciousness.

An experience such as the autonomous self displays two forms. In one form, a person's experience of his body is central for self-experience. Here we have a subject-object relation between consciousness and body: the body is experienced as an objectively given place for consciousness and its activities. In the other form of autonomous self-experience the subject-object relation is replaced by the experience that man functions purely as the subject of action: man experiences himself as functioning as an integrated psycho-physical organism. This self-experience is not concentrated in the spatially experienced body, but rather in the mental experience of oneself as a dynamic unity.

The transition to a dynamic form of autonomous self-experience has often been compared to a kind of "death-rebirth process". From my point of view, the best description of this process is given by Grof in his works on LSD-therapy: *Realms of the Human Consciousness,* 1975; *The Human Encounter with Death,* 1977, (Joan Halifax is co-author of this book) and *Principles of LSD Psychotherapy,* 1980. What Grof calls rebirth of the autonomous self is the overcoming of a depressive state effected by therapy. The depressive state is described in terms of "oppression" and the overcoming in terms of "consciousness' expansion". This is followed by an ecstatic experience: incresed intensity of consciousness and a positive emotional attitude.

This ecstasy is regarded as having two distinct features in addition to the features that we found in transparent experience:

(1) We found in transparent experience an expansion of consciousness and an increase in its intensity. Here we find another relation to time. The experience of pleasure is constant rather than fleeting; it "goes with time" to use an often quoted expression. The strength of intensity and the positive emotional attitude remain as a constant underlying state of consciousness. This experience, to use a theological expression, gives a *character indelebilis*.

(2) Another distinguishing feature in this experience of the rebirth of the self is a transcending in consciousness towards so called "transpersonal experience". This expression was introduced by the trend in existential humanistic psychology calling itself "transpersonal psychology". By transpersonal experience one is to understand experiences of a superpersonal cosmic unity, i.e., not only the experience of an ultimate dimension of wholeness and oneness in one's own organism but also that of the cosmos as a continuous wholeness.

This cosmic unity can be experienced in different ways. I shall not discuss them here. I shall group them together and call them "transcendence-experience". Common to the different forms of transcendence-experience, is the experience of the personality or self founded on something which broadens or opens itself beyond all concepts of reality, a totally de-objectivised dimension of existence. With this I have come to a third form of self-experience.

2.3. *The transcending self*

2.3.1. *Introvertive mystical experience.* I shall use W. T. Stace's term "introvertive mystical experience" to describe the type of transcendence-experience that I have discussed briefly above. Self-experience which follows introvertive mystical experience is what I call transcending self-experience. Similar to the psycho-dynamically conditioned self-image, transcending self-experience is the experience of a relation but in this case the relation is to the content in the introvertive mystical experience.

Transcending self-experience is connected with ecstatic experience. It is distinguished by ecstasy's three distinct forms: expansion of consciousness, increased intensity and the experience of pleasure.

In the transition to a mature autonomous self-experience—I call it rebirth—an ecstasy whose intensity and positive emotions remained as a constant and underlying state of consciousness took place. This is also the case in introvertive mystical experience. In rare cases something paradoxal can take place with regard to ecstasy's remaining strengthened positive emotions: these are experienced not only as features of the mystical consciousness but also as features of the absolute unity—"a reality beyond reality"—which is the object of mystical experience. I believe that the often quoted terms "bliss" and "light" in reports about introvertive mystical experience can function as metaphysical descriptions of the phenomenon that is discussed here.

2.3.2. *Ecstasy in an absolute sense.* Mircea Eliade puts great emphasis on the distinction between *enstasis* and *ekstasis* in his work *Le Yoga. Immortalité et Liberté,* 1954. This distinction played an important role in the attempts of the scholars Louis Gardet, Louis Massignon and Jacques Cuttat to find a more adequate comparison betwen Christian and non-Christian mysticism. The distinction between *enstasis* and *ekstasis* has often been compared with Plotinus's distinction στάσις ἐν ἑαυτῷ and στάσις ἐν ἄλλῳ; literally "a standing in oneself" and "a standing beyond oneself in another". For Plotinus ecstasy means στάσις ἐν ἄλλῳ.

The two terms "*enstasis*" and "*ekstasis*" are understood as indicating two types of mystical experience. In the case of *enstasis,* the mystic does not go beyond the monistic conceived reality. According to Gardet (*Mystische Erfahrungen in nichtchristlichen Ländern,* 1956) for instance, the profane mystic, i.e., the mystic who does not know the Christian revelation, will, in Sufism, Hinduism and Buddhism, only reach the foundation of his soul which is conceived as one with the absolute. The being that is experienced is an "être pour soi". According to Gardet the experience of the great Christian mystics is different: their consciousness is led to God's being which is an *ens a se,* absolutely distinct from man and his consciousness. Only through the Christian experience of grace is it possible, according to Louis Gardet, to experience the Plotinian στάσις ἐν ἄλλῳ.

The French jesuit Joseph Marechal, who inspired Karl Rahner and others towards a Kantian Thomism, asks the puzzling question: can Plotinus within the framework of his monistic ontology really call his own mystical experience στάσις ἐν ἄλλῳ.

One might ask what exactly does Gardet's and Marechal's question mean? What is the difference between στάσις ἐν ἑαυτῷ and στάσις ἐν ἄλλῳ? I regard this subtle question as a Gordian knot that is difficult to untie. However, I believe that there is an interesting way of letting the sword cut through the knot.

Alfonso Verdú has pointed out in his study on *enstasis* and *ekstasis* (*Abstraktion und Intuition als Wege zur Wahrheit in Yoga und Zen,* 1965) a special form of mystical experience. Verdú finds it in Zen-buddhism and the Buddhist philosopher Nagarjuna. I believe that it is to be found in Master Eckhart. Verdú calls it genuine ecstasy. I would like to call it an ultimate phase of introvertive mystical experience.

This completely different state that the human consciousness steps into is an absolute void of nothingness experienced in consciousness. When the human consciousness is centered in this different state—a στάσις ἐν ἄλλῳ—it acquires the ability to hold the two together in a synthesis: the object of introvertive mysticism and the normal reality, the transcendent and the immanent. Characteristic of this kind of transcendence-experience is that it leads beyond the entities with which one labours in the discussion between monistic and dualistic interpretations of mystical experiences. Sometimes this transcendence-experience has been called "transcendence of transcendence" and it is hereby described as the transcending by consciousness of every intentional object, even beyond "void" understood as an intentional object. The experience of absolute void or nothingness is one side of the transcendence-experience. The other side is the effect of nothingness-experience: it permits a synthesis in consciousness between the two opposing aspects of reality: immanent and transcendent, relative and absolute, differentiated and indifferentiated, empiricism's realistic and introvertive mysticism's idealistic view of reality.

When regarded as a psychological phenomenon, this absolute ecstasy is unique. The experience of the expansion of consciousness together with increased intensity and a constant state of pleasure will, of course, remain as a state of consciousness. But a distinct change in relation to the ecstasy of introvertive mysticism is this: the experience of a transcendent reality is no longer the over-riding one; instead, the empirical reality is experienced as being the only reality, even if it is, after the experience, regarded as being multidimensional. The three common features of ecstasy—the expansion, of consciousness, intensity and pleasure—complement the features that characterise normal consciousness of the empirical world. To use a metaphorical expression: the three features of ecstasy give a kind of vertical perspective to the normal horizontal understanding of reality.

3. *On the phenomenology of mysticism and ecstasy*

In this paper I have provided answers to the question: what ought one to understand by the phenomena of mysticism and ecstasy and how ought the relationship between them be understood? I regard the approach I have used to find these answers as phenomenological.

But what is phenomenology? Or rather, what is a phenomenological method? As far as I can see, there is no uniformly used paradigm indicating what a phenomenological method should look like? This is also true of the academic discipline called phenomenology of religion.

In this concluding section of my paper, I shall reflect a little on the question: what should a phenomenological method look like, when used to investigate such phenomena as mystical and ecstatic experiences, and how should it be motivated scientifically?

My point of departure is a short summary of Ernst Tugendhat's critique of Edmund Husserl's phenomenological philosophy. (E. Tugendhat: *Vorlesungen zur Einführung in die sprachanlytische Philosophie*, 1976, p. 92–106.) I shall firstly present Tugendhat's account of three central themes in Husserl's phenomenology:

(1) A fundamental theme in Husserl's philosophy of science is that in order to understand a phenomenon we have to look at a person's consciousness of the phenomenon. Husserl uses the term consciousness in two senses. The first is *intentionality*. By this, Husserl means that consciousness is always a consciousness or awareness of something. Consciousness is consciousness about something through its activities or intentional acts, such as feeling, thinking and perceiving. The second meaning that Husserl gives to the term ''consciousness'' is *experience*. Husserl gives considerable emphasis to each of these two meanings.

(2) Let us discuss, first of all, consciousness as experience. On it, Husserl constructs the following basic Cartesian tenet: I am certain of that which I experience: I know that I experience this or that. Husserl intends to base the certainty of knowledge on consciousness of a self.

(3) Husserl, however, bases not only the certainty of knowledge but also its essential content on consciousness. In this case, consciousness does not mean experience but intentional act, directed towards an object.

In order to understand a phenomenon we must comprehend it as the object of an intentional act of consciousness. By reductively excluding everything else and intuitively comprehending the content of the act we gain knowledge of the essence of the phenomenon, i.e., its essential features.

Tugendhat makes the following two objections to these fundamental themes in Husserl's phenomenology:

(1) There is no inner perception of the content of consciousness on which I can base a certainty of knowledge. If there is content in a person's consciousness, can he express it in statements that have meaning and which can be understood by others than himself? Conclusion: we do not need to proceed via consciousness; we may instead confine ourselves to language with regard both to knowledge about experiences and the certainty of this knowledge.

(2) A second objection: the content of intentional acts cannot be understood in any other way than via informative statements. We understand the features of a phenomenon's essence via informative statements and thus we have no need to proceed via intentional acts of consciousness in order to reach them. The assertion that there is a statement in which a person A asserts the content in an intentional act and thereby asserts a statement P about the features of a phenomenon can be translated into "A knows that P" which in its turn is equal to the statement "It is true that P".

Concerning phenomena and their features, we need not go via consciousness and its experiences or intentional acts; we can and should instead be satisfied with language and an investigation of linguistic statements about phenomena, and of their truth or falsity according to acceptable criteria.

Before I take sides regarding a Husserlian type of phenomenology and Tugendhat's critique of it, I shall mention another kind of critique of phenomenology other than the philosophical one used by Tugendhat. As is well known, Husserl's phenomenology was carried over into Heidegger's existence-philosophy and into different types of existentialism; one type being existential psychology. It has been said that one of the merits of existentialism is its discovery of the role of consciousness in man's experience of what it is to be man. A criticism that has grown increasingly vigorous during the past 20 years with reference to existentialism's view of man is that it loses sight of the human organism. And yet, within the scope of a basic existentialist humanist view of the nature of man, the relationship between consciousness and body has come into focus variously in psychotherapy, psychology and understanding of man in general. I believe that research in this area has something essential to contribute to a phenomenological approach to phenomena that are related to man's consciousness.

In taking sides on the questions of Husserlian phenomenology that I have mentioned, I shall formulate three theses:

Thesis 1. An empirical method of investigation is to be regarded as phenomenological if, and only if, the investigation takes into consideration the relationship between the phenomenon investigated and human consciousness.

Thesis 2. An investigation whose object is the content of or the product of human consciousness should be formulated as a phenomenological investigation.

Thesis 3. The result of a consciousness-directed phenomenological investigation ought to be adequately tested with the help of linguistic analytical philosophy and body-directed psychology.

By consciousness-directed phenomenology I mean a phenomenology which fulfills the demand stated in thesis 1. By a linguistic analytical philosophy I mean a philosophy which studies the philosophical problems concerning knowledge and ontology via linguistic assertions. By a bodydirected psychology I mean a psychology which studies man's psychological processes in relation to their bodily conditions.

The way in which an interaction between phenomenology, philosophy and psychology according to thesis 3 can and should function can be exemplified with the help of the following example. The example I choose is the phenomenon that I have called *ecstasy in an absolute sense.*

(1) *Concerning the necessity of a phenomenological approach in an investigation of consciousness-related phenomena*

Absolute ecstasy means, as we saw, the experience of a state of consciousness which, it is claimed, is able to cause experience of a synthesis of a transcendent and a non-transcendent dimension of reality. It is easy to realise that a necessary condition for an understanding of statements claiming experience of a synthesis between transcendence and immanence is the psychological understanding of the state of consciousness in which the claimed experience of the synthesis was made. It is only in the context of a psychological understanding of the state of consciousness which is called absolute nothingness that the mystics' claims of a synthesis or an integrated unity of empirical reality and what transcends it becomes meaningful.

(2) *Concerning the desirability of correlating the psychological study of a consciousness-related phenomenon with a study of the phenomenon's bodily conditions*

Of course, the indication of a correlation between an alleged state of consciousness of absolute nothingness, a state in which it is supposedly possible to experience a synthesis of immanence and transcendence with empirically established states of the body, has relevance for the understanding of the phenomenon of absolute ecstasy. By establishing such a correlation, one can place the experience of nothingness in a psychological context which is intersubjectively controllable and, thereby, grant the experience an objective status.

(3) *Concerning the linguistic-analytical task*

By indicating the nothingness-experience's facticity one has of course not said anything about the objective knowledge value of the assertion of an experienced synthesis between transcendence and immanence. The meaning of this assertion, its reference and epistemological status can only be defined through a philosophical analysis of the assertion itself. But even if the investigation in itself is linguistic-analytical it presumably needs support from research into of the genesis of the understanding being expressed in the assertion. The linguistic-analytical investigation will ''hang in the air'' if it is made without consideration of what a consciousness-directed phenomenological and a body-directed psychological investigation have to offer.

I regard my reasoning as an argument for my three theses. With them I opt for a revised version of Husaserl's phenomenological method, and against Tugendhat's critique of Husserl, I wish to claim that consciousness-related phenomena—such as mysticism and ecstasy—cannot be understood except by understanding the states and intentional acts of consciousness in which these phenomena are given.

Ecstasy—a Way to Religious Knowledge —Some Remarks on Paul Tillich as Theologian and Philosopher

By TAGE KURTÉN

Most of the articles in this volume look at *ecstasy* from the point of view of psychology, history or sociology. With my contribution I wish mainly to stimulate some philosophical reflection on ecstasy. This I shall do by presenting some points in the philosophical and theological thinking of Paul Tillich.[1]

In the context of this volume it is possible to argue for a description of Tillich's thought along at least two different lines:

1. He can be looked upon as a religious thinker. In this case he is of interest for religiology[2] mainly as historical material. Then he can be seen as a Christian who in modern time has tried theoretically to reflect upon his own religious faith and the place of ecstasy in that faith.

2. He can also be regarded as a philosopher of religion, who tries to reflect universally and critically upon the phenomena of religion and ecstasy. In that case his main contribution to religiology is to help religiology to reflect upon the question of what possible meaning the concept of "religious ecstasy" can have in a modern scientific context.

This paper will attempt to cast some light on both sides of Tillich's thinking.

---

[1] Tillich was born in 1886 in Prussia. His father was a Lutheran priest. He studied theology and philosophy. In 1911 he became doctor of philosophy, in 1912 licentiate of theology, in both cases on a thesis dealing with Friedrich von Schelling. After World War I he was professor both of theology and of philosophy in Germany. When the Nazis seized power in 1933, he had to emigrate to the USA. There he worked mainly at the Union Theological Seminary until his death in 1965 (Tillich 1952, 16, 18 f.; Pauck 1976, 205 f., 213).

[2] I use the term "religiology" as an "um-brellaterm" for all the disciplines of the scientific study of religion (excluding scientific theology), the main disciplines of which are the history, sociology, psychology and phenomenology of religion. Consequently, "religiology" corresponds to the German word "Religionswissenschaft". I feel it necessary to precise my terminology at this point, because there does not seem to be any generally accepted "umbrellaterm" in English (Pummer 1972, 102 ff.). My use of "religiology" here has a slightly different connotation from that used by Hideo Kishimoto (Kishimoto 1967, 84 f.).

In the most central and extensive work of Tillich, his "Systematic Theology" (ST), we can find a qualification of the term "ecstasy" in connection with his discussion of human reason and the place of reason in a religious (Christian) context. I quote:

> "'Ecstasy' ('standing outside one's self') points to a state of mind which is extraordinary in the sense that the mind transcends its ordinary situation. Ecstasy is not a negation of reason, it is the state of mind in which reason is beyond itself, that is, beyond its subject-object structure. In being beyond itself reason does not deny itself. 'Ecstatic reason' remains reason; it does not receive anything irrational or antirational—which it could not do without selfdestruction—but it transcends the basic condition of finite rationality, the subject-object structure" (Tillich 1951, 111 f.).

How shall we look at this quotation? Can we give it any unambiguous meaning? If so, can the statements in the quotation have some scientifically acceptable meaning? In trying to answer these questions, I must first present some profound features in the structure of the whole of Tillich's thinking.[3]

When looking at Tillich's ideas, it is very important to remember that he strives to be both a philosopher of religion and a Christian theologian, and that these two roles are different, according to Tillich. The philosopher of religion works on a different level from the theologian (Tillich 1951, 9 f.). In any analysis of his thinking it is therefore necessary to discriminate between Tillich's philosophical and his theological statements. Let us first examine some aspects of Tillich's philosopohical thought.

With the help of the following figure it is possible to portray some of the most profound elements in Tillich's philosophy of religion.

In a way Tillich follows Kant in maintaining that the human subject structures "being" (reality)[4] with the help of categories of reason. The most important and profound category is what Tillich calls "the basic

---

[3] There is a high degree of continuity and consistency in Tillich's production from the early 20's until 1965. This makes it important to look at Tillich's early works on the philosophy of science and religion in order to understand his later major work "Systematic Theology" (ST). This fact was pointed out very early in research into Tillich's production (Rhein 1957, 16). Quite recently Joachim Track and Anders Jeffner, for example, have pointed to the same fact (Track 1975, 429 notes 36 and 37; Jeffner 1979, 251).

[4] I here assume that, when Tillich in this part of ST speaks of "being", he means the same thing we usually do when we talk about "reality".

Tillich does not himself use the Kantian term "das Ding-an-sich". His discussion of criticism in his early works nevertheless makes it illuminating to put this term in the figure, in my view (Tillich 1959 a, 309; 1959 b, 236).

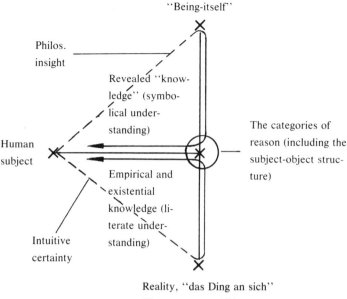

ontological structure'' namely the subject-object structure (Tillich also talks of the self-world structure). Tillich does not find it necessary in ST to make a decision about the degree of truth of the different types of theories of the relation between the mind (subjective reason) and reality (objective reason). The important thing is that there is an interaction between the mind and reality[5] (Tillich 1951, 164 ff., 75 ff. Cf. Tillich 1959 b, 235 f.).

Reality, which according to this can be the object of knowledge, consists of inorganic and organic nature, man and history.[6]

Tillich also follows Kant when he denies the possibility of scientific metaphysics (Tillich 1959 b, 251 f.). In spite of this, Tillich makes a big thing

---

[5] Tillich is not satisfied with the Kantian way of pursuing philosophy. In his writings from the 20's Tillich stresses that the subject has an intuitive certainty of the object, not only that it exists (just as Kant was certain that there must be a ''Ding-an-sich''), but also that it has the qualities which our knowledge says it has. According to Tillich, we can grasp the ''essence'' of things (Tillich 1959 a, 309, 313; 1959 b, 235 ff.).

[6] For Tillich's view on the structure of reality, see Tillich 1963 b, 15–28. Helmut Elsässer has made a most illustrating figure of this side

of Tillich's thinking (Elsässer 1976, 19). See also Tillich's presentation of ''Real''—and ''Geisteswissenschaften'' in Tillich 1959 b.

The knowledge of this reality can in Tillich's view be of a more technical, controlling type or a more existential kind. Here the words of language can also be taken more or less literally. The words immediately grasp reality, according to Tillich (Tillich 1951, 98 f). This side of his epistemology, though it is most interesting, is of minor importance for the problem which occupies us here.

of the so-called ontological argument for the existence of God. Tillich does not mean that the argument could prove the existence of God. The value of it is not in its trying to prove anything. What the argument points out is that the *question* of God is universally valid and philosophically necessary. The philosophical analysis that we meet in the argument gives a description of the way in which potential infinity is present in actual finiteness. What we meet here, present in finitude, is according to Tillich an element which nonetheless transcends this finitude.

"All elaborations /of the argument/ have shown the presence of something unconditional within the self and the world" (Tillich 1951, 206).

This unconditional element Tillich calls *"being-itself"*. However, he stresses that he does not assert by this the existence of a highest being, called being-itself. What comes forth here is "an analytical dimension in the structure of reality". Being-itself is the necessary condition for the self-world, or subject-object structure of reality. In being a necessary condition for the subject-object structure it cannot itself be an object within that same structure (Tillich 1951, 204–208).

What Tillich asserts here is that we have a philosophically valid, and therefore for the whole of mankind common, way to an unconditional element in "reality" as we understand it. This is a very central point in Tillich's thought, which he has elaborated in many works, for example in his "Religionsphilosophie" and also in his most famous "The courage to be".[7] In my figure I try to illustrate this thought with the line that indicates philosophical insight in "being-itself". The term "insight" which I have chosen to use is perhaps too strong. It may invoke the idea of a content, of which it is possible to have some philosophical knowledge. But this is just the opposite of what Tillich seems to be after. Through philosophy we arrive at an awareness of an unconditional premise for the human predicament. In this respect Tillich has, in my opinion, often been misinterpreted.

---

[7] As everyone knows, Tillich can also talk of religion as "our ultimate concern". The problems with this concept I will not discuss here. Here we are interested in the concept "being-itself".

In "Religionsphilosophie" from 1925 he starts from the concept of meaning, and points out that our consciousness of context of meaning presupposes some ground, an *unconditional meaning* which is the guarantee of every particular case of meaning (Tillich 1959a, 318f.).

In "The courage to be" Tillich talks about "God above God" as that which is present in a state of utmost despair, as the last straw to catch at—namely *the fact that* you are in despair. Here we see the paradox that every active negativism must say yes to itself in order to be able to negate itself. (Tillich 1962, 165ff., 178f. I must apologize for using the Swedish translation, but the English original was not available when I wrote this.)

Examples abound both in the Scandinavian and in Anglo-Saxon literature.[8]

This same point, which constitutes the premise for the whole of human culture, is also the premise for religion and its elaboration of the concept of God. Two quotations may serve to sum up the two main points which Tillich finds "hidden" in the classical ontological argument for God:

"Nothing is more important for philosophy and theology than the truth it /the ontological argument/ contains, the acknowledgement of the unconditional element in the structure of reason and reality."

"Unless such an /unconditional/ element were present, the question of God never could have been asked, nor could an answer, even the answer of revelation, have been received" (Tillich 1951, 208 and 206).

Philosophy cannot give any content to "being-itself". But that is just what *religions* try to do, according to Tillich. In the various religious traditions we find concrete expressions of this ultimate reality. But according to Tillich we cannot take the religious expressions of the ultimate ("being-itself") literally. Our language only works adequately within the subject-object structure. When we wish to say something about "being-itself" we must always use language metaphorically, or as Tillich says it *symbolically.*[9] Religious language speaks entirely in symbols about God according to Tillich (Tillich 1951,, 238 ff.; 1963 a, 8 ff.).

---

[8] A Swedish psychologist of religion, Hans Åkerberg, has expressed the opinion that in Tillich's talk about "God above God" we meet the faith of *the most mature religious sentiment* (Åkerberg 1977, XLI f.). This is perhaps true from a psychological point of view, but it does not do justice to Tillich's own way of thinking, in my view. For Tillich, the point "God above God" or "the unconditional" is the *starting-point* of religion. A religion cannot live with only this "pure point", it must have some symbolical expressions besides that.

The American philosopher of religion, Malcolm Diamond, claims in his very penetrating presentation of Tillich's thoughts, that Tillich in ST says that we become aware of being-itself through ecstatic reason (Diamond 1974, 328 f.). This would mean that awareness of the unconditional presupposition belonged to the theological realm (see below, note 10). In fact the treatment of this presupposition in ST belongs to the *philosophical* part of the book. That is, the insight is of a kind which does not demand any "ecstatic reason" according to Tillich.

Some Swedish discussions of Tillich's the-

ory make a similar mistake. They take the concept "being-itself" as if it had some content, as if it were a Christian concept of God (For example Aulén 1965, 157 ff.; Nygren 1972, 320 ff.). As we have seen, it is not Tillich's intention to say anything like this.

Nevertheless, this mistake by the interpreters is understandable. Tillich's terminology is often very vague. In ST I Tillich does say that the statement "God is being-itself" is a nonsymbolic assertion, the only nonsymbolic statement about God. In ST II he, however, corrects this statement (Tillich 1951, 237, 239; 1963 a, 9).

[9] We have here the background to Tillich's famous theory of religious symbols. Because religious symbolism was the focus of the preceding volume in Scripta Instituti Donneriani Aboensis, and Tillich's theory of symbols there was presented by Haralds Biezais, I do not intend to go any further into this question here (Biezais 1979, IX f., XIV f.). A good presentation of the whole of Tillich's theory of symbols can be found in Diamond 1974, 339–354. An interesting interpretation is given i Jeffner 1972, 57 ff.

What religious language talks about always remains a *mystery,* says Tillich. Although "being-itself" is not open to ordinary ways of acquiring knowledge, the awareness of the unconditional element constitutes a need for some sort of knowledge of that element. How can this symbolical knowledge be obtained, according to Tillich? This always happens through *revelation,* says Tillich. It is in this connection we meet Tillich's treatment of "ecstasy".

It is important to stress that Tillich in his presentation of what he means by "revelation" points out that he here moves on a normative (and I would add a theological-religious)[10] level (Tillich 1951, 106ff.). From here on we see Tillich as a religious thinker, not as a philosopher of religion.

For Tillich's treatment of revelation and knowledge of revelation there are three central concepts: *mystery, ecstasy* and *miracle.*

A revelation is something out of the ordinary which "removes the veil" from something hidden, something mysterious. What is hidden is not a mystery if it ceases to be mysterious after the "revelation". Is it not then contradictory to speak of the revelation of a mystery? Not completely, answers Tillich. In the revelation there are cognitive elements, we know more of the mystery after a revelation, than before it: The reality of the mystery has become "a matter of experience" and our relation to the mystery has become a matter of experience (Tillich 1951, 108f.). "The mystery" functions here as a symbol for what was previously called "being-itself".

Every revelation has a subjective and an objective side, and they are both necessary for the revelation. Someone must be seized by the manifestation of the mystery and something must occur through which the mystery of revelation seizes someone, says Tillich. The subjective side is called ecstasy, the objective miracle (Tillich 1951, 111).

A miracle is not an event that happens in contradiction to the laws of nature. It "does not destroy the structure of being in which it becomes manifest". It is an event which is astonishing, shaking, unusual in some way but which manifests itself in a natural phenomenon, in a man or in a historical event. It points to the mystery of being in some way. It is a miracle only if it is received by someone as a sign-event in an ecstatic experience, according to Tillich (Tillich 1951, 115ff., 118ff.).

---

[10] Tillich's treatment of the concept "revelation" in ST is placed in the section which deals with *the theological answer,* not in the one which elaborates *the philosophical question.* (For Tillich's method of questions and answers, "the method of correlation", see Tillich 1951, 59ff.) I take this as an argument for looking at "revelation" as something placed within what Tillich calls "the theological circle", which presupposes that a theologian is religiously involved in his object.

The main characteristics of Tillich's view of religious ecstasy are contained in the quotation at the beginning of this paper. What we have now, is some instruments (thought-structures) which make it easier to understand how Tillich looks at ecstasy. That a miracle can point outside itself to "being-itself", the mystery, is, as we have seen, connected with the necessary condition that a human subject seizes this "self-transcending" of the event. As this transcends the normal categories of the subject's reason, the ecstatic experience means that reason is transcended, too. But Tillich underlines very strongly that this must not happen in a way that destroys reason. That means for one thing that the revelatory knowledge gained from the experience does not add anything to our knowledge of nature or of history. Neither does it give any knowledge about hidden things (metaphysics) or the like. But it has an objective side nonetheless. Much of what is called ecstasy, according to Tillich, lacks this objective side. In such a case it is not real ecstasy, only overexcitement. Overexcitement can be described purely in psychological terms, but that is impossible in the case of real ecstasy, says Tillich (Tillich 1951, 110, 112ff.).

"Ecstasy transcends the psychological level, although it has a psychological side. It reveals something valid about the relation between the mystery of our being and ourselves. Ecstasy is the form in which that which concerns ur unconditionally manifests itself within the whole of our psychological conditions. It appears through them. But it cannot be derived from them" (Tillich 1951, 113).

In Tillich's view rationality is so important an element of real ecstasy that it can be taken as a criterion which discriminates between ecstasy and demonic possession. Demonic possession always destroys the rational structure of the mind in some way, while genuine revelation never does that (Tillich 1951, 113f.).

Summing up, then, it may be said that the cognitive quality of an ecstatic experience mediates some kind of knowledge, according to Tillich. It cannot mediate knowledge of finite objects or relations, the knowledge it gives must be about something else.

"It opens a new dimension of knowledge, the dimension of understanding in relation to our ultimate concern and to the mystery of being" (Tillich 1951, 115).

This is of course an example of religious symbolical knowledge which we have seen as a part of his philosophical ("meta-theological") theory. Religious knowledge, which is symbolical and which is expressed in symbolical language, does not conflict with our ordinary forms of knowledge, it does not "destroy reason".

I hope that I have given enough insight into Tillich's way of thinking to make the quotation from which I started comprehensible. We can now see it as meaningful in the context of Tillich's "thought-world". It is also an example of how a modern Christian thinker can look at "ecstasy" (which does not, of course, mean that every modern theologian looks at these matters in the same way). It is also quite obvious from what we have seen that Tillich's way of treating the phenomenon "ecstasy" does not belong to religiology, if by that term is meant something that could be called an *empirical* scientific study of religion, which is, I think, the generally held view. Tillich would here be of the same opinion. Theology does not belong to the field of empirical, scientific study according to him.

Another question is whether his philosophy of religion is satisfactory, from a scientific point of view.

I think we can look at his philosophy of religion in a broader context. An important problem in the philosophy of religion since the Enlightenment has been how religious language and "religious knowledge" relate to scientific language and scientific knowledge, to put it simply. This development got its most acute expression in the discussion which started from the logical-positivists' criterion of meaning (the possibility of empirical verification). According to this religious language became meaningless. Tillich's philosophy of religion can be seen as an attempt to give meaning to religious language in a culture which is very much coloured by a scientific way of looking at things and of using language.[11]

Seen from this point of view, Tillich's attempt is at least not without relevance for religiology. In a culture where the meaning of religious language is called in question, it cannot be a matter of indifference to religiology whether the religious language is regarded as having meaning or not. If we accept a philosophical theory of meaning which makes religious language meaningless, then religiology will function without conflict only as a historical discipline (because in historical time religious language can be said to have had some sort of meaning), or as a reductionistic behavioral science (religion is *nothing but* a psychological and sociological phenomenon). This way of looking at the matter is of course possible. What a philosopher of religion like Tillich is trying to point out, however, is that this is not the only way of looking at things. He tries to show that it is possible to regard religious language as meaningful even if you have a more or less scientific way of looking at the empirical world.

---

[11] The most important articles in the discussion of religion and the verification-criterion of meaning are to be found in "New Essays in Philosophical Theology" from 1955. Many of the same articles are included in a book from 1975, "The Logic of God". A good analysis of the debate is given in Jeffner 1972.

If we in religiology wish to look at religious ecstasy as something meaningful even today, then we need philosophers of religion, like Paul Tillich.[12]

Anybody interested in a more detailed analysis of Tillich's thought can consult my doctoral dissertation. "Vetenskaplig teologi och dess samhällsrelation" (Scientific Theology and its Relation to Society.) In this thesis I discuss the question of theology as a scientific activity and its relation to church and society. I present three models, on the basis of the works of Paul Tillich, the Swede Anders Nygren and the German Wolfhart Pannenberg, the latter of whom also are both theologians and philosophers of religion.

References

Aulén, G., 1965. *Dramat och symbolerna*. Stockholm.

Biezais, H., 1979. Die Hauptprobleme der religiösen Symbolik. *Religious symbols and their functions,* ed. by H. Biezais. (Scripta Instituti Donneriani Aboensis. 10.) Uppsala.

Diamond, M., 1974. *Contemporary philosophy and religious thought*. New York etc.

Elsässer, H., 1976. Paul Tillich und die Psychoanalyse. *Die Bedeutung Paul Tillichs für die kirchliche Praxis,* hrsg. von W. Schmidt. Stuttgart.

Jeffner, A., 1972. *The study of religious language*. London.

— 1979. The relationship between English and German ways of doing philosophy of religion. *Religious studies* 15.

Kishimoto, H. 1955. *New essays in philosophical theology,* ed. by A. Flew. London.

— 1967. Religiology. *Numen* 14.

— 1975. *The Logic of God,* ed. by M. Diamond and T. Litzenburg, Jr. Indianapolis.

Kurtén, T., 1982. *Vetenskaplig teologi och dess samhällsrelation.* (Publications of the Research Institute of the Åbo Akademi Foundation. 71.) Åbo.

Nygren, A., 1972. *Meaning and method*. London.

Pauck, W. & M., 1976. *Paul Tillich I*. Stuttgart.

Pummer, R., 1972. Religionswissenschaft or Religiology? *Numen* 19.

Rhein, C., 1957. *Paul Tillich*. Stuttgart.

Tillich, P., 1951. *Systematic theology* I. Chicago.

— 1952. Autobiographical reflections. *The theology of Paul Tillich,* ed. by C. Kegley and R. Bretall. New York.

— 1959a. Religionsphilosophie. *Gesammelte Werke* 1. Stuttgart.

— 1959b. Das System der Wissenschaften nach Gegenständen und Methoden. *Gesammelte Werke* 1. Stuttgart.

---

[12] By this I do not mean that Tillich's philosophy of religion is the only acceptable philosophy. I am not even sure if it is philosophically acceptable at all. All I want to stress is the importance of philosophical reflection upon the meaning of religious language.—In this connection I also want to underline that the question of *meaning* is not the same as the question of *truth*. In my article I have not discussed the truth of the religious claims.

— 1962. *Modet att vara till.* Stockholm.
— 1963 a. *Systematic theology* 2. Chicago.
— 1963 b. *Systematic theology* 3. Chicago.
Track, J., 1975. *Der theologische Ansatz Paul Tillichs.* Göttingen.
Åkerberg, H., 1977. Modet att vara till och religionspsykologin. P. Tillich, *Modet att vara till.* Lund.

Psychology, Philosophy, Theology, Epistemology—Some Reflections

By ULF DROBIN

In the following paper I shall stress some points of view that are both trivial and controversial: the implication of the researcher's own world-view for his research; the relationship between theory and *empiri*.

In point of fact, general questions concerning the formation of knowledge, its epistemological propositions and social functions, so much discussed in the humanities and social sciences, have had little impact upon the history of religion, where the theoretical debate seems to remain more specific, more bound to the discipline (or to different disciplines), and where names like Thomas Kuhn, Jürgen Habermas, Michel Foucault etc. are seldom adduced (see for instance Science of Religion, ed. Honko 1979). In the polarization between "positivists" vindicating the notion that theories are abstracted from "reality" and "relativists" maintaining that "reality" is selected and formed according to theories, most historians of religion belong in practice to the first camp, and many belong so exclusively that they do not even acknowledge the problem itself.

The historian of religion is not concerned with metaphysics, but with faith in its human and cultural manifestations. The researcher' own atheistic or religious commitment has no bearing on the result of the investigation, *nota bene* provided that he adheres to strictly empirical principles. Is this *credo* not only a necessary ideal, but also a true description of research? Is an uncomplicated belief in its possible realisation a strength or a hindrance in the pursuit of a relative objectivity that might be attainable outside the predictions of natural sciences? Does the historian of religion have no metaphysical involvement in the material under investigation? Is it without interest whether he is a materialist or a devout religious person, whether he is a believer or non-believer in the physical reality of the gods and spirits he describes, and in the actual efficacy of the sacrifices and other rituals in which he partakes?

Let us take some examples. In his well-known books on the psychology of religion Prof. Hjalmar Sundén tells us that the "experiences" of spirits, gods or God are formed and provoked by frames of reference acquired earlier and suddenly actualized in certain moments of "rôle identification". From the standpoint of common sense, this means that gods and spirits are not real, that they do not have the same ontological status as let us say "experienced"/"perceived" chairs and tables, that they do not exist outside the experiencing subject, but in his inner vision. "In other words just fantasy, imagination, illusion," some university students exclaim negatively when they meet this part of their curriculum, thinking that the originator of the theory is an atheist, who wants to explain away religion. From personal acquaintance I know that Prof. Sundén regards himself as a genuine Lutheran, and I assume that the explanation is not to be found in a schizophrenic contradiction between faith and science, but in liberal Protestant theology.

In the Kantian perspective (Schleiermacher, Söderblom, Otto, Heiler, Tillich etc.) all human reality is subjective, an "inner vision"; time and space, unity and plurality, cause and effect are *Anschauungen* and "categories" within the experiencing subject, through the principles of which the subject organizes his world; the ultimate reality, the Being itself, God, is not of the world of phenomena (Erscheinungen) and cannot thus be understood in the forms of the human world; *cognitions/perceptions* (Erscheinungen/Gegenstände/Phenomena) have no intelligible extra-mental object (noumenon/Ding an sich), since neither unity-plurality, nor extension, nor duration would be applicable; accordingly, God does not reveal himself through *perception,* but through *emotion,* by the "feeling of absolute dependence", through "the state of being ultimately concerned". On the pure philosophical level it would be a pseudo-question to ask if certain phenomena are real or not.

Independent of Sundén's actual philosophical conviction, it is obvious that contradictory assumptions about reality contrasting the naïve realism of positivism with idealism, may by their consequences easily blend together in studies on religion. It might also be added that Sundén follows a normal, traditional strategy of academic writing, whereby—as far as I know—he never states the philosophical premise of his psychology of religion.

If one regards Sundén's 'rôle psychology' as an exposition of both Protestant theology and general psychology, it is tempting to contrast it with a counterpart within the Roman Catholic literature on the psychology of religion, Jean Lhermitte's *Vrais et faux possédés* (1956). The author was a neurologist, a member of the French Académie Nationale de Médecine and associated with the Carmelite Order and the book is provided with the *nihil obstat* and *imprimatur* stamps. The title is significant; *vrais* and *faux* are to be understood literally, as the differentiation between true possession caused by real demons, and false possession caused by mental illness, in which imagined demons are part of the pathological picture. Psychiatric and neurological knowledge is used to distinguish between transcendental and psychopathological etiology, as true possession is thought of as a case for the exorcist of the church and false possession as a case for the psychiatrist of the mental hospital. To the unbeliever it is an extraordinary diagnostic procedure which, epistemologically, might be compared with some Protestant attempts to differentiate between sick and sound religion.

The teaching of the Roman Catholic Church has had its philosophical foundation in St. Thomas Aquinas since the encyclical of Pope Leo XIII in 1879. In principle this still holds true, but in practice this is more evident of the period before 1965. As the philosophical concepts of the discipline of history of religion became established through formative debates and polemics in the first half of this century, I here deliberately identify Roman Catholic philosophy and theology with its official state previous to Vatican II.

In their basic assumptions about reality liberal Protestantism and Catholicism are contrary to each other. In the Aristotelian-Thomistic system "ontology" precedes "gnoseology" and is the teaching of "that which exists", the being as being (*ens secundum quod ens*). The forms are not, as in Kantian philosophy, immanent in the subject, but in the objects of the "outside" world; they are the fundamental constituents of all existing "things" (*entia, substantia*); in the act of knowing the human subject "abstracts" the "form" of the being and receives an "analogous" and intelligible "image" of the extra-mental object, obtains, in short a conceptual knowledge of its "essence".

The transitoriness of the material world—and the possibility of acquiring lasting knowledge in a world of becoming—is as in Aristotle understood by the two corresponding pairs of concepts, expressing the static and the dynamic aspect of reality: *form* and *matter, potency* and *act*. All change (of forms, "transformation") is the transition from potency to act. Matter is the potentiality of form (to change) and form is the actuality of matter.

With an additional closely corresponding pair of concepts Aquinas altered Aristotle's mechanistic system (prima causa, the unmoved mover) into a theocentric system: the concepts of *essence* and *existence*. Essence is **what** a being is, existence that it **is**. Existence is not one quality among others, but, Aquinas says, a miracle. Everything that comes into existence does so by immediate act of God. God **is** *esse* (i.e. actus purus; essence and existence are not twofold in God), all other beings **have** *esse*. He bestows existence at every transition from potentiality to actuality, creates his creation at each moment of time, is both transcendent and immanent, beginner and upholder of everything existent.

The spiritual world of angels, demons (fallen angels) and departed souls, the "pure intelligences", the "spiritual substances", differ from other beings, in that they are not *composita,* as they have form but not matter.

The Thomistic world is rational and 'real' and the human being can through the intellect meet the grace of revelation.

*

Descartes' *cogito, ergo sum* and Berkeley's *esse est percipi,* or the scolastic *scio, aliquid esse*? What comes first, emotion or cognition? The awareness of the very stream of thinking, or the object of the thinking process? Is it possible to think, without thinking something? Are the objects of the "outer" world first "conceptualized" and the ego subsequently "realized" as a unity in its structural relationship to the objects, or the opposite? Do emotions produce objects, or do objects provoke emotions? Is the human world real or not?

What comes first, *The Divinity* or *The Holy*? The religious feeling, or the object of the feeling? The substance or the accident in scholastic language? The inner or the outer world? Kant or Thomas?

These questions can never be answered. But philosophies and theologies provide the answer. The Protestant-Kantian, subjective, idealistic and emotionalistic in one way, and the Roman Catholic-Thomistic, 'realistic' ('objective') and intellectualistic in the other.

Thus Nathan Söderblom, in his famous ERE-article:

Holiness is the great word in religion; it is even more essential than the notion of God. Real religion may exist without a definite conception of divinity, but there is no real religion without a distinction between holy and profane. The attaching of undue importance to the conception of divinity has often led to the exclusion from the realm of religion of (1) phenomena at the primitive stage, as being magic, although they are characteristically religious; and of (2) Buddhism and other higher forms of salvation and piety which do not involve a belief in God. The only sure test is holiness. From the first, holiness constitutes the most essential feature of the divine in a religious sense. The idea of God without the conception of the holy is not religion (F. Schleiermacher, *Reden über die Religion,* Berlin 1799). Not the mere existence of the divinity, but its *mana,* its power, its holiness, is what religion involves. This is nowhere more obvious than in India, where the men of religion, through their art of acquiring holy power, became dangerous rivals of the gods, who, in order to maintain something of their religious authority, were obliged to adopt ascetic holiness themselves (*śat. Brāhm.* ii. 2. 4, ix. 1. 6, 1 ff.). The definition of piety (subjective religion) runs thus: 'Religious is the man to whom something is holy.' The holy inspires awe (religio).

The original idea of holiness seems to have been somewhat indeterminate, and applied to individual things and beings [. . .] (Söderblom 1913, 731).

Söderblom, with his sensitivity to his time, his flexibility of mind and his conspicuous learning, is of course to be seen as one of the founders of the "modern" attitude towards religions within liberal Protestantism. With the same right he may be viewed as the logical outcome of the Schleiermachian theology, as a representative of the new philosophy of mission (the 'fulfilment doctrine'; Sharpe 1975, 163), as the given answer to the inherent atheism of the evolutionary anthropology of religion, as the antipode of the 'realistic' apologetical endeavours within the Roman Catholic history of religion (Anthropos), as well as the defence of the church in an age of "science" and secularism, a defence rather by harmonizing inclusivity than antagonistic exclusivity, possible through the pure subjective position.

What Söderblom offers is not an empirical insight but a religious value to the history of religion.

The same is even more obvious in Rudolf Otto's *Das Heilige, Über das Irrationale in der Idee des Göttlichen und sein Verhältnis zum Rationalen,* published in 1917.[1] The book is written like a poetical grammar of the Irrational with strongly literary, one might even say liturgical qualities. It has been widely read (44th edition 1979) and has more than most other books served as a manual of faith for intellectual Protestants. Its well-known main categories are in themselves very emotionally charged and suggestive: *das Rationale als Prädikat an einem Irrationalen, das 'Kreaturgefühl' als Reflex des numinosen Objekt-gefühls im Selbstgefühl, das Numinose, das 'Ganz andere', das mysterium tremendum et fascinans, horrendum, energicum, mirum, augustum* etc.

Religion, according to Otto, had its beginning in *awe* (Scheu), in the numinous *Urschauer,* the *stupor,* the feeling of *'Gänsehaut'* and *'völlig auf den Mund geschlagen sein'.* This original feeling has no connection whatsoever with morality. It is a quality *sui generis,* irreducible to anything else and can only be described by analogy. Through the incitements and stimuli of the "outer objects" the awe-experience externalizes itself into the outside world, where "something" is permeated with the numinous feeling of being "wholly other", and in the next stage is rationalized into concepts of souls, ghosts, spirits, gods. The 'creature-feeling', again, is an emotion, which like a shadow follows the awe-experience, projects into the numinous object and reflects to the subject, now as a consciousness of the numen and *eine Abwertung des Subjekts hinsichtlich seiner selbst.*

---

[1] Otto had already 1909 developed his basic views in *Kantisch-Fries'sche Religionsphilosophie und ihre Anwendung auf die Theolo-* *gie.* For the connection between Söderblom and Otto see Edsman 1966, 24–25.

This kind of psychology and history of religion was unacceptable to Catholics of traditional or official persuasion. The philosopher and psychologist Joseph Geyser, a well-known expert on Aristotle and the medieval philosophy, published in 1921 a booklet *Intellekt oder Gemüt?*, where he analyzed Otto's theory of knowledge from an Aristotelian point of view and very lucidly demonstrated that Otto's emotionalist psychology is far from the common sense position of general psychology. For instance:

Ein Gefühl kann gewiss auf ein ,,Objekt ausser uns" gerichtet sein. Dass aber dieses Objekt ,,ausser uns" existiere, das können wir vorstellen und denken, jedoch nicht ,,fühlen" (Geyser 1977, 312).

Indirectly, Geyser's critique elucidates the dilemma of all idealism: the difficulty of being consistent. Otto applies the Kantian categories to the reality (contents) of religion, but not to the reality of "ordinary life". They refer to the religious conceptions and concepts which grew out of emotion, not to the "things" of the natural world. It is religion that is an "inner world", of which it is possible to gain knowledge only by experience and without perceiving in the ordinary meaning of the word.

Geyser cannot agree. To him religious reality exists outside the human being and the way to religious knowledge is in principle the same as all other acts of knowing:

Kein Gefühl entsteht in uns ohne eine Ursache. In dieser Ursache hat es darum auch sein intentionales Objekt. Aber diese Ursache selbst kommt uns oft nur dumpf zum Bewusstsein und tritt daher hinter der Deutlichkeit der erlebten Gefühlsreaktion völlig zurück. Zugleich sucht sich unser Ich aber doch in der Regel ein ihm einigermassen deutliches Objekt für seinen Gefühlszustand. In Erfüllung dieses Triebes findet es dann dieses Objekt nicht selten in bestimmten schon von ihm besessenen Wahrnehmungen, Vorstellungen oder Zuständen. Manchmal aber phantasiert und erdenkt es sich auch ein Objekt hinzu. Durch dasselbe wird dann wieder rückwärts das Gefühl gesteigert oder sonstwie modifiziert. Dieses phantasierende Vorstellen ist jener Vorgang den Otto als die nachträgliche Rationalisierung eines vorausgegangenen irrationalen Erlebnisses bezeichnet. So etwas kommt in unserem Bewusstsein vor. Doch berechtigt das nicht dazu, in das ,,irrationale", d. h. emotionale Erlebnis selbst und als solches ein Bewusstsein hineinzulegen, das seiner Natur nach gar nicht Gefühl sein kann, sondern Vorstellen und Wissen ist. Das ist das nach meiner Ansicht prinzipiell Fehlerhafte an der Darlegung Ottos vom Erfassen des mysterium durch das menschliche Bewusstsein (ibid., 317–318).

Pater Wilhelm Schmidt—the founder of the Roman Catholic school of the history of religion, the so-called Anthropos School or the Vienna School —indeed reacted strongly against Otto's *Das Heilige*, wrote a book directed against Otto which turned all of Otto's theses upside down: *Menschheitswege zum Gotterkennen. Rationale, Irrationale, Superrationale: Eine religionsgeschichtliche und religionspsychologische Untersuchung* (1923).

Non-evolution, the central place of the Supreme Being (das Höchste Wesen, God), the objective validity and moral quality of early man's religion are emphasized and long quotations are abstracted from the first volume of Schmidt's later monumental *Der Ursprung der Gottesidee* and from his, by then, famous handbook on dogmatics and apologetics *Die Uroffenbarung als Anfang der Offenbarung Gottes* (1911). Holiness is—from the beginning—the attribute of the Supreme Being.[2]

In the point of intersection between Otto's and Schmidt's psychology and history of religion the fundamental difference between Protestant and Catholic teaching emerges perhaps more clearly than in any other context.

*

Such questions as whether the human world is subjective or objective, whether the subject "creates" an internal world or in an "analogous" way "registers" or "records" an external reality are, of course, as far beyond all *empiri* as is the physical existence or non-existence of spiritual beings (or God). But these religious, non-religious, philosophical and epistemological propositions, which are void and meaningless from the point of view of *empiri*, necessarily condition our orientation in the world, as well as the methodology and *empiri* of research.

The phenomenological school of the history of religion[3] developed from, and was made possible by, liberal Protestant theology. In the Kantian perspective, the actual contents of alien religion could be denied and interpreted into the subjective idealist scheme of the interpreter's own religion. Religion, but not religions, *Wesen,* but not *Erscheinungsformen,* essence, but not externals, evidenced of God. Religion was something *sui generis* not to be reduced to anything else. Reductionism became the most pejorative word in the discipline. The very interpretation could be taken as a proof of God's existence (as in Söderblom's case, Andrae 1931, 328).

To illustrate the ideo-historical background of the discipline in theology, mission and adaptation to the scienticism of the secularized environment is no criticism but an explanation of the social formation of the ideas and necessary for a deeper understanding of the phenomenological paradigm. Now, it can be maintained that it was precisely the subjective perspective, which, by allowing or even requiring unbiased study of other religions,

---

[2] See also Schmidt 1930. Bornemann 1974 and Pajak 1978 elucidate Schmidt's shifting position towards revelation. For the implication of Thomism in the history of religion see Drobin 1979, 186–218.

[3] "The phenomenological school" here includes authors such as G. van der Leeuw, F. Heiler, C. J. Bleeker, etc., and excludes authors such as P. D. Chantepie de la Saussaye, R. Pettazzoni, G. Widengren and Å. Hultkrantz, who use the term phenomenology without the Kantian (-Husserlian) implication. See further, Pettersson and Åkerberg 1981 and Waardenburg 1972. Compare also the discussion in Temenos, vol. 9, 1973, between P. Kvaerne and W. C. Smith.

made a science of religion possible. This would be true as far as it is possible to speak about *one* scientific perspective. Phenomenology (or comparative religion within the phenomenological tradition) has its merits in description, in *Verstehen,* in the emphatic understanding of the individual religious actor, and has contributed greatly to the knowledge of man's manifold spiritual worlds. Problems arise when it comes to explanation; and it should be borne in mind that the borderline between explanation and description is fluid, that explanatory ideas always "colour" description. Here the religio-centric attitude of the paradigm (but not necessarily of the conscious mind of the individual researcher) conflicts with research traditions within psychology and sociology, which are secular at the very roots of their development.

Let us consider social anthropology, a discipline which also studies religion. It might be said that here is a very natural "division of labour", that for social anthropology the goal is the understanding of society by comprehending the unconscious social network manifested in beliefs and rituals, while for history of religion the goal is the understanding of religion by conceiving its socio-cultural setting. This sounds simple but might under the surface hide epistemological propositions less harmoniously related to each other.

The philosophical premises of social anthropology go back to Marx, Durkheim and the *année sociologique* school. The central idea, taken from Marx, but by Durkheim used with another intent and in another context is the notion that the consciousness of the indivudual is a social product (Firth 1972; Zeitlin 1968, 234–280). This means that the categories of thinking, perceptions and values in the individual are determined by the individual's social existence, his relations to others; that the social tradition is reproduced and repeated in the individual as is language in the individual speaker. The society is not the sum of its individuals, is not an abstraction confronting the individual, but the opposite. The individual is an "abstraction", a variable of the determining constant—the society. Via British functionalism, French structuralism and up to modern cognitive studies this basic thought is constitutive.

There is a close connection and an obvious opposition between Protestant phenomenology and Durkheimian sociology. Both adhere to Kant. To the phenomenologist the categories of time, space, class, number, cause etc. are immanent in the subject (the individual mind), by which it structures its world, *and* beyond which it experiences—uniquely, independently and self-subsistently—the ultimate and undivided Reality. To the anthropological sociologist, however, the categories of duration, extension, causation, classification etc. are immanent in the society, through the principles by which the society as an organic whole bears and moulds its members into the social unity. The society, not the individual, is unique, independent and self-subsistent. Religion is a power of the utmost importance through which the society expresses itself:

> For a long time it has been known that the first systems of representations with which men have pictured to themselves the world and themselves were of religious origin. There is no religion that is not a cosmology at the same time that it is a speculation upon divine things. If philosophy and the sciences were born of religion, it is because religion began by taking the place of the sciences and philosophy. But it has been less frequently noticed that religion has not confined itself to enriching the human intellect, formed beforehand, with a certain number of ideas; it has contributed to forming the intellect itself. Men owe to it not only a good part of the substance of their knowledge, but also the form in which this knowledge has been elaborated.
>
> At the roots of all our judgements there are a certain number of essential ideas which dominate all our intellectual life; they are what philosophers since Aristotle have called the categories of the understanding: ideas of time, space, class, number, cause, substance, personality, etc. They correspond to the most universal properties of things. They are like the solid frame which encloses all thought; this does not seem to be able to liberate itself from them without destroying itself, for it seems that we cannot think of objects that are not in time and space, which have no number, etc. Other ideas are contingent and unsteady; we can conceive of their being unknown to a man, a society or an epoch; but these others appear to be nearly inseparable from the normal working of the intellect. They are like the framework of the intelligence. Now when primitive religious beliefs are systematically analysed, the principal categories are naturally found. They are born in religion and of religion; they are a product of religious thought. This is a statement that we are going to have occasion to make many times in the course of this work.
>
> This remark has some interest of itself already, but here is what gives it its real importance.
>
> The general conclusion of the book which the reader has before him is that religion is something eminently social. Religious representations are collective representations which express collective realities; the rites are a manner of acting which take rise in the midst of the assembled groups and which are destined to excite, maintain or recreate certain mental states in these groups. So if categories are of religious origin, they ought to participate in this nature common to all religious facts; they too should be social affairs and the product of collective thought (Durkheim 1976, 9–10).

Different societies categorize reality differently. Socially determined variance is the constant of human reality. Society is, as is repeatedly stressed by Durkheim, something irreducible, something *sui generis* (ibid. 16, 418). Whereas in the one system we have religion (or God), in the other system we have Society.

Methodological conflicts between historians of religion and social anthropologists are *legio*. The historian of religion declares that the social anthropologist, who analyses religion in terms of social organisation, has neither the right understanding of religion as a phenomenon *sui generis,* nor the right understanding of the individual in religious life; that the approach of the social anthropologist is *reductionistic* and thus never can reach the very core of religion. The social anthropologist, again, states that the historian of religion illegitimately isolates religion from the wider concept of culture, and accordingly fails to see the meaning of religion in the network of social organisation and identification; that the historian of religion does not have a *holistic* approach, which to the social anthropologist is the essential prerequisite for a deeper understanding.

In other words, each party accuses the other of reductionism, and the words reductionism and holism have an ideological charge. In both cases epistemology and theory are mostly mistaken for *empiri.* Each perspective is, of course, governed by world view and intention and is completely legitimate (compare Sacrifice, eds. Bourdillon and Fortes 1980 and Drobin 1981).

In social anthropology there is a built-in conflict between political world views, which obviously also includes historians of religion: the respective views of Durkheim and Marx. To Durkheim society itself is the constant and is a homogenous, harmonious and homeostatic organism; to Marx the "mode of production", the shifting socio-economic conditions between groups, or classes, is the constant; the one model stresses harmony and non-change, the other disharmony and change. Now whether indigenous culture, and by analogy religion, is a great value *per se,* or an obstacle to development and justice, is finally a political jugement on a scale from conservatism to socialism, which might support an interest in segregation as well as in assimilation (compare Gluckman 1975 and Myrdal 1968).

With these short reflections I should like to emphazise that the history of religion necessarily has a social function, be it religious or non-religious. Some questions that are experienced as problems of *empiri* might on closer consideration be expressions of conscious world views, of loyalties, or of such unconscious views as are merely part of the terminological and verbalistic tradition of the discipline (this one or others); the paradigm of handbooks by which each discipline introduces itself to the student. It is, of course, not to be expected, nor even to be hoped, that history of religion should refer to a body of people with the same outlook on the world and the cosmos. It will remain as fragmented as society is elsewhere. Too strong a belief in objectivity, actual or pretended, might produce subjectivity of either a naïve or a hypocritical kind.

Statements about human and social reality are mostly true or false from a certain point of view. Objectivity in a deeper sense must be multi-dimensional and complex. Both the object beheld and the beholder must be taken into consideration. Ideally, there should be (a) knowledge of the material (which cannot but be unsatisfactory, as "material" always is a "cut", a "bracketing", in a wider reality); (b) knowledge of the system of thought, the intention, that structured the presentation of the material; (c) comparison with other, different and similar, presentations of material of the same type; (d) some knowledge of one's own intention.

This ideal, which can never be fully realized, might be compared with optics. One photographic angle never provides a "true" picture. One must go around the object to obtain additional perspectives.

Philosophies and theologies are explicit logical systems. They can be studied in the same manner as mathematical propositions and their consequences. Religions are implicit world views. They can be studied only through implicit world views.

References

Andrae, T. 1931. *Nathan Söderblom*. Uppsala.

Bornemann, F. 1974. P. W. Schmidt und die Bücherzensur (1909–1912). *Verbum. Romae, Apud Collegium Verbi Divini* 2, 15.

Drobin, U. 1979. *Afrikanska religioner i västerländska belysningar*. (Skrifter utgivna av Religionshistoriska institutionen vid Stockholms universitet.) Stockholm.

— 1981. Review of Sacrifice, ed. by M. F. C. Bourdillon—M. Fortes. *Ethnos* 46, 1–2.

Durkheim, E. 1976. *The elementary forms of the religious life*. London.

Edsman, C.-M. 1966. Ur Nathan Söderbloms arbetsverkstad. *Religion och Bibel* 25. Uppsala.

Firth, R. 1972. *The sceptical anthropologist?* (Inaugural Radcliffe-Brown lecture in social anthropology. From the proceedings of the British Academy 58.) London.

Geyser, J. 1977. Intellekt oder Gemüt? *Die Diskussion um das ,,Heilige"*, hrsg. von C. Colpe. Darmstadt.

Gluckman, M. 1975. Anthropology and apartheid: the works of South African anthropologists. *Studies in African Social Anthropology*, ed. by M. Fortes—S. Pattersson. London etc.

Kværne, P. 1973. "Comparative religion: whither and why?" *Temenos* 9.

Lhermitte, J. 1956. *Vrais et faux possédés*. (Bibliothèque Ecclesia 19.) Paris.

Myrdal, G. 1968. *Objektivitetsproblemet i samhällsforskningen*. Stockholm.

Otto, R. 1909. *Kantisch-Fries'sche Religionsphilosophie und ihre Anwendung auf die Theologie*. Tübingen.

— 1929. *Das Heilige*. Gotha.

Pajak, S. 1978. *Urreligion und Uroffenbarung bei P. W. Schmidt*. (Studia Instituti Missiologici Societatis Verbi Divini.) St. Augustin.

Pettersson, O.—Åkerberg, H. 1981. *Interpreting religious phenomena*. (Acta Universitatis Lundensis.) Lund.

274

Sacrifice, 1980. Ed. by M. F. C. Bourdillon–M. Fortes. London.

Schmidt, W. 1910. *L'Origine de l'idée de Dieux*. Paris.

— 1911. Die Uroffenbarung als Anfang der Offenbarung Gottes. *Religion, Christentum, Kirche*, hrsg. von G. Esser–F. Mausbach. Kempten–München.

— 1912. *Der Ursprung der Gottesidee* 1. Münster in Westfalen.

— 1923. *Menschheitswege zum Gotterkennen*. München.

— 1930. *Handbuch der vergleichenden Religionsgeschichte*. Münster in Westfalen.

Science of religion: studies in methodology, 1979. Ed. by L. Honko. The Hague etc.

Sharpe, E. J. 1975. *Comparative religion*. London.

Smith, W. C. 1973. "The finger that points to the moon." *Temenos* 9.

Sundén, H. 1966. *Die Religion und die Rollen*. Berlin.

Söderblom, N. 1913. "Holiness." *Encyclopædia of religion and ethics* 6. New York.

Waardenburg, J. 1972. Grundsätzliches zur Religionsphänomenologie. *Neue Zeitschrift für systematische Theologie und Religionsphilosophie* 14.

Zeitlin, I. M. 1968. *Ideology and the development of sociological theory*. Englewood Cliffs, New Jersey.

The Unio Mystica of Teresa of Avila—Two Classical Presentations in the Light of Psychology

By HANS ÅKERBERG

Task and method

It is generally maintained within the Carmelite tradition that Teresa (1515–1582)[1] showed an extraordinary facility in describing the stages of mysticism with experimential vigour and deep intensity, compared for example to John of the Cross, whose mystical presentation is of a more dogmatic and systematic nature. In this sense she would appear to be unsurpassed within the entire Roman Catholic mystic tradition.

It would thus appear logical to attempt a case study[2] of her religious and mystical development, beginning with her writings, all of which are clearly more or less autobiographical. It is nevertheless my opinion that such an idiographic study would be methodologically most risky. This is partly because the material, despite its often obvious autobiographical nature, is not of a type that may be explicitly described as personal documents of a more intimate character, and partly because the material is so historically remote that it may be too difficult in certain contexts to ascertain in depth its reliability in points of detail or even its general source value. In addition, it is always uncertain when the subject is a woman, exactly how much of the published material represents authentic and uncensored notes and how much has undergone revision on the advice of her confessors.

This study is not, therefore, devoted to a given period in her personal, mystical development. Such a task, for the reasons mentioned above, would be far too hypothetical and also exceed the scope of this paper. The task on which I have focused, rather, is of a direct immanent, comparative character. I intend to compare two classical presentations by Teresa of the

---

[1] Teresa was canonized on March 12, 1622 and elevated to *doctor ecclesiae* by Pope Paul VI on September 27, 1970.

[2] For the meaning of *case study*, see our work 1981 b. Parts of this work are found published under the title "Tre interpretationskomponenter" in *Svensk Teologisk Kvartalskrift* 1981, 108–122. A considerably larger portion from the same book is to be published in German in volume 15 of *Archiv für Religionspsychologie* (under the title "Drei Interpretationskomponenten") and soon in English, too, in another international publication.

significance of *unio mystica,* firstly her description of this in the *Libro de la vida* (1565; hereafter referred to as *Life*), and secondly her presentation of the same mystic element in the book *Castillo interior o Las moradas* (1577; hereafter referred to as *Interior Castle*).[3] This paper does not then primarily encompass a study of Teresa's development between 1562 and 1577, but rather a purely comparative study of the two distinct presentations of *unio mystica* given in the previously mentioned books.

But even such a limited task has its risks. It is, for example, often very difficult to know for sure whether similar expressions in two such works, separated by a period of time, may also be assumed to have analogous meanings. Teresa can very well use identical or similar words and expressions at two different times to describe two completely or partly different experiences. Verbal similarity is, in other words, no guarantee that the experiences themselves are analogous. To overcome this problem as far as possible one must therefore view every statement against its general and detailed contextual background. There are thus certain general frames of reference to be taken into consideration. In this sense, Teresa's forms of expression are certainly not without influence from earlier traditional material. This is important for understanding both of her presentations, but of special significance in the context of the *Life*. Between the account in the *Life* and that of the *Interior Castle* there appears yet another influence of paramount importance for Teresa, namely the meeting with John of the Cross in 1567.[4] The latter influence was so powerful, as will be clearly shown later, that it simply changed Teresa's view on important and decisive points concerning the mystic goal and the mystic path.

We thus come to another methodological question concerning the choice of theory with which, setting aside problems of source criticism and of tradition and context, we will attempt to interpret and understand[5] the differences between Teresa's two presentations of *unio mystica* already cited. We firstly need a theory which has something to say about the major goals of mysticism and which may also be used for a careful analysis of the

---

[3] I here use various volumes of E. Allison Peers's edition of the *Complete Works of St. Teresa* (which is a translation from the critical edition of P. Silverio de Santa Teresa CD: Santa Teresa de Jesús Obras, 9 vol., Burgos 1915–24). For *Life,* I use the edition from 1972, vol. I, and for *Interior Castle* I use an edition from 1963, vol. II.

[4] John of the Cross (1542–1591) was declared beatified by Pope Clemens X in 1675 and canonized by Pope Benedict XIII in 1726. Pope Pius XI, in 1926, elevated him

into the level of *doctor ecclesiae* (doctor mysticus). In the presentation below I utilize E. Allison Peers's edition *The Complete Works of Saint John of the Cross,* 1974 (a translation from the critical edition of P. Silverio de Santa Teresa, Burgos 1929–31).

[5] Concerning the implication of the terms 'interpretation' and 'understanding' see Åkerberg 1981 b, 67–72. (This section is also part of the material found in note 2 in German in volume 15 of *Archiv für Religionspsychologie.*)

steps on the path of mysticism. For this type of analysis I prefer Nathan Söderblom's theory distinguishing between "mysticism of the infinite" and "mysticism of personal life", which I have presented and analyzed in other works (see Åkerberg 1975; 1981a, 164ff; 1981c). Furthermore, we also need a theory with whose help it is possible to link the concepts of "religious maturity" and "mysticism", a combination which has not, to my knowledge, been the object of a separate study.[6] For this task I choose G. W. Allport's theory of "the mature religious sentiment" and its developing characteristics (Allport 1968, 59–83) in combination with W. James's criteria of saintliness (1928, 272ff.).

A few introductory comments should be made concerning Nathan Söderblom's distinction within mysticism. In a coming paper (Åkerberg 1981c) I have attempted to systematize what often appears to be rather disparate research on mysticism, and to present the premises and potential of Söderblom's distinction in relation to such a systematization. Thus, taking into consideration both older and more recent mystic research, I have divided the material into five major categories, interrelated in such a way that categories 2–5 are all subordinate to category 1. These five categories are: (1) *The major mystical goals,* (2) *The mystical path,* (3) *The mystical experience,* (4) *The mystical language,* and (5) *The religious mystic.* Categories 2–5 may be regarded as subordinate to category 1 because they are all dependent upon a basic categorization of the major goals of mysticism, which is the starting point for a more detailed study of almost any special problem within mysticism. Category 1, in my view, is therefore fundamental for most of the research concerning aspects of mysticism. It is to this main category (and even partially for questions within category 2) that Söderblom's distinction of mysticism belongs.

One half of the distinction—"mysticism of the infinite"—can characterize the mystical elevation, where the unifying experience with the suprahuman eliminates every perception of concrete and abstract elements from the sensate world. The experience lies beyond what the normal waking consciousness is able to register and what man after the experience is able objectively to express. It is something of a fleeting "existence beyond", which reforms a man's entire life, providing him with a "truth" and a goal to reach for and lifting him beyond this world's suffering and other earthly premises and conditions. In its most pure and cultivated form one finds this basic type of mysticism among such thinkers as Plotinus and Shankara, but

---

[6] The relationship between "religious maturity" and "mysticism" has been dealt with, however, in some earlier works. Cf. Åker-berg 1975a, 23; 1975b, 218ff; 1977, XLff.; 1980a, 44; 1981a, 165f. (See even Nilsson 1980 and Hoffmann 1982.)

it is also found here and there within sporadic nature mysticism, to name another example.

In contrast to this type of mysticism, Söderblom sets what he calls "mysticism of personal life". The experience of a deep, direct contact with suprahuman "reality" can also be realized through other states than the world-forsaking, ecstatic heights. The human experience of "divine self-communication" (this is Söderblom's way of describing the concept of revelation) also knows another way. Experience does not here have its foremost support in ecstatic raptures of the "existence beyond", even if such experimental states may also be found occasionally or in the initial phase of a personality mystic's development. On the contrary, they have their religious experimential foundation[7] in a 'faith' (a "conversion" to "religious maturity" intensifying the degree of belief),[8] which often grows strongest when the factors of suffering are greatest.[9] While "mysticism of the infinite", a way for "the upper ten thousand", implies an experience of oneness with the suprahuman beyond this life's suffering and this world's material structure, the "mysticism of personal life" encompasses a meeting with God in the midst of life's problems and struggles, in the midst of the world in which one lives and labours. In this meeting, which can be experienced at a deep level of faith within the framework of the normal waking consciousness, the dialogue between an "I" and a "Thou" never ceases.

Against the background of Söderblom's distinction, it is quite clear that what the psychology of religion has consistently regarded as "mysticism" is what he calls "mysticism of the infinite". As a special basic type of mysticism, "mysticism of personal life" has received practically no attention at all,[10] though it is most clearly represented by entire mystic traditions and by individual mystics who, traditionally, are always placed within the sphere of mysticism. Here we have, for example, the Jewish philosopher Martin Buber, and here we also find within Christian mysticism such a *doctor ecclesiae* as John of the Cross. For him—a point I shall develop further below—as for other "personality mystics", the last step "of the mystic ladder of Divine love", the complete union with God (which "causes the soul to become wholly assimilated to God", *Dark Night*, 441),

---

[7] Regarding the various possibilities contained in the concept "experience", see Åkerberg 1981 a, 144 ff. (the "experience group") and ibid., 151 ff.

[8] See here Allport's (1968) and Clark's (1968) usage of the term 'faith'. See also my *pro gradu* dissertation 1975 b, 34 passim.

[9] See here Clark 1968, 227 ff. (*"How does*

belief become faith?") and 232 ff. (*"How is faith kept creative?"*). Cf. my dissertation 1975 b, 61 f.

[10] I have pointed out this earlier in Åkerberg 1975 b and 1981 a. This is also maintained with emphasis in the forthcoming work 1981 c.

is not possible to attain here in life, but can only become a "reality" when the soul at the moment of death "goes forth from the flesh" (ibid., loc cit.).

Since Söderblom's distinction, as should be apparent from the above presentation, is concerned with a psychology of personality, it can also be characterized by reference to the anthropological aspect in this context. "Mysticism of the infinite" in its purest form presumes what in theology is usually described as a Pelagian view, that is, a view of man proceeding from the postulate that man is *by nature* a good and autonomous being, provided with a completely free will. In the opposite way the "mysticism of personal life" has, where it occurs in its purer forms, presupposes of a clearly antipelagian anthropology, that is, that man is viewed as *homo peccator,* without the ability to do good or establish a contact with God *on his own.* Between these two poles there exists a continuum of varying forms of semi-pelagianism, that is, views that to varying extents ascribe to man the ability to do good and to exercise a free will. One could, more popularly, say that in later anthropologically blended forms the thought is implied that God and man can meet so to speak "half way".

An additional implication in Söderblom's distinction is provided by his concepts of "practice" and "spontaneity". This pair of concepts functions within the sphere of the distinction like a calibrating instrument, which should ideally allow fine adjustments to be made with greater certainty regarding the position of various mixed forms of mysticism which might be found along the continuum between the two opposing poles. The word "practice" implies varying forms of methodic, religious training, and "spontaneity" implies characteristics of self-surrender.

The decisive question for the present study is now, where within the distinction area Teresa's view of *unio mystica* should be placed. We know that she confesses to an anthropological view which includes a certain tendency to characteristics of semipelagianism, although with a clearer tendency towards "mysticism of personal life" than "mysticism of the infinite". But is this so of all of her published presentations? How does a comparison between the descriptions of the *unio mystica*-state in *Life* and in *Interior Castle* emerge on this point? Is it possible to verify, which is my thesis, that Teresa's view on this main question has undergone a clear change, from a description in the former work to an account in the second, and that this change indicates a distinct tendency of her mystical view to move closer to a clearer form of "mysticism of personal life" in her work *Interior Castle*? The task of this study is thus, taking into consideration the question of source criticism and the question of tradition and context, to carry out a comparative analysis of the presentations of *unio mystica* in the two previously mentioned classic works, in order to ascertain whether the latter presentation, which has primarily served as the guide for her followers, does not provide more pregnant characteristics of "mysticism of personal life"—in direct line with the mystical teaching derived from John of the Cross—than those indicated by the first, shorter description of the same state in *Life*. Since it is my thesis, as I have previously mentioned, that there does exist such a difference in the two presentations, I shall also in this analysis compare the relevant passages in *Interior Castle* with the mystical teaching of John of the Cross. As Söderblom indeed maintains with his distinction of mysticism, namely that it should not be carried to excess as there are always certain shades of "infinity-" as well as "personality character" (both "practice" and "spontaneity") in every mystic, so the comparative analysis in the present study should not encourage extremely extrapolated results. A certain degree of care is called for, for the methodological reasons previously mentioned. This, however, in no way hinders us from forming the reasonably reliable conclusions necessary to prove the validity of the thesis I have presented.

When it comes to the collective research on Teresa together with other accounts of her life and mystical teaching, we find that this collective literature has mainly proceeded from attempts to relate her teaching to her religious development, despite the extremely difficult problems of source criticism I have mentioned above. The source problems, however, entail that all of these studies and thereby their attempts at analysis are more or less speculative judgments. Strong emphasis has thus been given to her auditions, visions and other phenomena connected with prayer experiences within the framework of her meditative and contemplative life.[11] A number of researchers, especially from an earlier period, have in the reductionistic spirit initiated by Ludvig von Helmholtz and often called "medical materialism",[12] diagnosed her as a pronounced hysteric.[13] Even if such a medical diagnosis does not in itself imply devaluation or doubt regarding the nature and importance of her experiences,[14] it has nonetheless contributed over a long period of time to an oversimplified presentation of her mysticism in varying circles. From an empirical standpoint, however, such

---

[11] See here among others, Heiler 1918; Poulain 1921; Leuba 1925; Andrae 1926; Zaehner 1957; Sundén 1966 and 1971. Among the works which deal with her life more generally can be mentioned Auclair 1950 and Leroy 1962. More popularized works and articles written in Swedish include i.a.: Theeuwes 1963; Stinissen 1972; Arborelius 1980; Steinmann 1981.

[12] Concerning the characteristics of "medical materialism" and an attempt to deal with this view, see James 1928. (Cf. here also Åkerberg 1980a.)

[13] Among scholars who have largely dealt with Teresa's mystical experiences from such a reductionistic perspective are i.a.: Hahn 1883; Delacroix 1908; Leuba 1925.

[14] See here especially James 1928, 4ff; Underhill 1930, 58 and 267; Pratt 1930, 369f.

research contributions are of quite limited interest. Where they do not contain direct metaphysical statements, they instead consist, for the most part, of highly speculative judgments. For this reason we here set them completely aside. Of considerably greater interest, however, are the studies and descriptions dealing with ecstasy and the relationship between the descriptions of mysticism in *Life* and *Interior Castle*.[15] Even if we here too find clear examples of reductionistic explanations, we also find certain points which should be considered in this presentation. This is especially true of those points including hypotheses about the influence of John of the Cross on Teresa and her further development of *unio mystica* in *Interior Castle*. Nevertheless, none of these studies deal more explicitly with the question which is the task and main thesis of the present study.[16] It is therefore my hope that this paper will provide a new contribution and a new perspective to the collective research on Teresa.

Focusing Ecstasy

When it was maintained above that *Life* was edited in 1565, this should not be seen as the date for the book's actual composition. This classic autobiography was preceded by a long birth process.

In the year 1554, Teresa underwent the religious stage of development which the Carmelite tradition usually calls her "definitive conversion".[17] In the same year or perhaps the following year she made her first attempt to write her life history, but the entire work seems to have been impeded by her feelings of inability to correctly describe the state in which she had moved through "the conversion". This first attempt was apparently followed by two additional attempts, which were intended to be submitted to

---

[15] The works primarily referred to will be mentioned in conjunction with the study of *Interior Castle*.

[16] Concerning more modern works which deal with or touch upon questions within the framework of my study—without ever considering the relationship between characteristics of "mysticism of the infinite" and "mysticism of personal life" in the mystical teaching of Teresa—see note 47 below.

[17] See here for example, Arborelius 1980, 18. Teresa describes this dramatic experience in *Life*, chap. IX. Hypothetically—taking into consideration the somewhat unreliable nature of the source material (see my presentation above)—this experience and its results could very well be interpreted with the aid of H. Sundén's role theory (see Sundén, 1966

and 1969). Teresa writes of this experience, which occurred while reading St. Augustine's *Confessiones:* "When I started to read the *Confessions* I seemed *to see myself in them* (my italics) and I began to commend myself often to that glorious Saint. When I got as far as his conversion and read how he heard that voice in the garden, *it seemed exactly as if the Lord were speaking in that way to me, or so my heart felt*". (my italics) It here seems to be a question of a role adoption, implying an identification process leading to a dual role situation, that is, Teresa experiences the words in *Confessiones* which accompanied Augustine's conversion as words also directed at her from God. Thus, the dramatic experience follows.

the tests of a couple of Jesuits. However, even these drafts have been lost. In her pronounced need of theological guidance, Teresa later wrote a fourth version, which she allowed a few highly-esteemed priests to analyze and of which certain parts are found fragmentarily in *Relaciones* 1–3.[18] This version should be seen as the first more complete attempt at an actual edition of her life history. It was followed only a few years later by the final, definitive edition of *Life,* which is the object of this study and which is the only version remaining in its entirety today.

From this short summary of the compositional process of *Life* we can state two things. Because of the many versions, attributable among other things, to Teresa's circumspection—the Inquisition had established its headquarters in Toledo in 1485[19]—and because of the analyses at the hands of different priests *Life,* despite the apparent spontaneity in places, cannot by itself, that is, without authentic and correctly time-related letter material, be viewed as a genuine, personal document of a purer type.[20] It does not therefore enable us to make any deeper analyses of the development of Teresa's religious personality, a view implying a certain amount of criticism toward some earlier research. However,—and this is the other point—*Life* is very suitable for the type of analysis which I intend to present in this study. The various preliminary versions have led to a final product, whose aim neither she herself—though she calls the book "her soul"—nor her priestly revisors and advisors viewed as pure autobiography, but rather and perhaps chiefly as a guide to and about the stagelike development of prayer normally used within monastic life. The book's structure is, thus, edited to be an instructive work, and even if it contains many personal expressions special to Teresa, it is at the same time a presentation which has been revised in order to be an acceptable dogmatic document for the Church. It is from this latter perspective that, within the framework of this paper, the book will be the object of psychological analysis and comparison.

Of the 40 chapters that make up *Life,* it is especially chapters 11–21 which are of specific interest for the present study. Teresa describes there the path of prayer in four stages, and my analysis will focus upon the last two steps in this development, chapters 16–21, where the path to a state of *unio mystica* is described and characterized.

---

[18] These *Relaciones* are found in Peers's edition under the title *Spiritual Relations,* vol. I, 301 ff.

[19] Concerning the Inquisition as a possible source of threat to Teresa, see Auclair 1950, 110 and Sundén 1971, 25.

[20] Concerning questions of source criticism and material grouping, see my methodolog-ical work 1981 b, 14 ff., 33 ff. and 58 ff. (In note 2 above concerning the German translation of parts of this work, there are important questions on the problem of source criticism under the subtitles "Quellenkritik und Materialgruppierung" and "Sicherstellungsniveaus".)

Before we reach this description of the path of prayer, it is of importance to attempt to chart summarily the main influences on Teresa before and during the period when the book was written. What do we know generally about this and what is found on this question in the first 10 chapters of *Life* in which Teresa describes her life history up to the "definite conversion"?

The entire problem of the current of influences seems complex and difficult to chart if one desires a more detailed account. However, certain clear characteristics can be seen in the long period of absorbed tradition related here (including the first fifty years of Teresa's life), which are of importance for the present continued presentation.

She received the first marked influence from her family home. Both her mother, who died in 1528 when Teresa was only thirteen, and her father, of whose death struggle (1543) she gives a detailed description marked by the deepest piety ("He looked like an angel", *Life*, VII, 44), had a strong intensity of faith. Here Teresa saw faith at work and it was here that she was taught about biblical figures and the importance of prayer. At the age of 17 she entered the convent school of the Augustinian nuns in Avila, where she remained for about one and one half years and where she apparently received her first instruction on the life and works of Augustine among other things, instruction which would later have a dramatic continuation during her lifetime. Already in 1536 she was adopted as a novice at the Carmelite Convent of the Incarnation in Avila. During a trip in 1538, she received a book from her uncle which was of very great importance for her, the Franciscan Francisco de Osuna's *Tercer Abecedario* (Third Spiritual Alphabet). This book "treats of the Prayer of Recollection" (*Life*, IV, 23), and after reading this work she began to go "the way of prayer with this book for my guide" (*Life*, loc. cit.). Already at this point, she arrives, at certain times and for very short instants, at the stage she would later term the "experience of Union". Teresa, who while reading Osuna's work had serious health problems—fragile health followed her throughout life— shows a remarkable sensibility and openness in relation to the account she was reading. Perception and action preparedness are apparently constantly at a peak for her, especially readiness for a special type of role adaption with its elements of identification processes and possible dual role situations which follow (Hjalmar Sundén's terms in connection with his role theory; see note 17). At the same time this is indicative of her apparent need for guidance and tradition adoption. The continuation of her life also reveals a series of similar active reading processes. Here can merely be named the influences of Pope Gregory's *Moralia in Job* (*Life*, V, 30), Augustine's *Confessiones* (ibid., IX, 56; see note 17), Franciscan Bernardino de Laredo's *Ascent of Mount Sion*[21] and certain other spiritual writings.[22] Summarily, Teresa writes about the relationship between the influences and one's own experiences: "The blessings possessed by one who practices prayer—I mean mental prayer—have been written of by many saints and good men. Glory be to God for this! If it were not so, I should not have assurance enough (though I am not very humble) to dare to speak of it." (*Life*, VIII, 49 f.) With the above mentioned influences it is plausible also to include confessors' influences (here mainly Father Garcia de Toledo), and the influence of continually utilized sermons (ibid., VIII, 53), even if Teresa herself can also maintain that: "... I have no learning, nor have I led a good life, nor do I get my information from a learned man or from any other person whatsoever" (Ibid., X, 61).

Against the background of the influences exemplified above, all of which have been selectively adopted into a collected tradition pattern,[23] Teresa now presents an experience-packed description of the path of prayer in the remainder of *Life* (chapters 11–21). It appears that her selection has mainly been guided by her own disposition for extravagant prayer states. Thus, it does not seem unreasonable to assume that out of the various influences, whether or not they can be seen as the fruits of reading or are the results of personal contacts, she has adopted and personally interpreted precisely those passages that could be viewed as support for a clearly semi-pelagian view of man founded, experimential world with extraordinary and—to use Söderblom's terms—partly infinity-tending states and phenomena. At the same time a very clear consciousness of sin becomes prominent, as part of a personally experienced relation to God and probably also reinforced by her contacts with her confessors and in the light of the threat of the inquisition. Summarily stated, it thus appears that her basic view of God and relationship to God have certain characteristics of infinity character,

---

[21] See Arborelius 1980, 14.

[22] Here we should mention the Spanish Dominican and revivalist preacher Vincent Ferrer's spiritual work *Tractatus de vita spirituali*, which Teresa can have read in a Spanish translation from 1515 (see *Life*, XX, 128). However, it seems less probable to me that Teresa was also strongly influenced by John Tauler (as Underhill wishes to maintain, 1930, 464), since he represents a completely different type of mysticism in line with *Theologia Germanica*, a mystic tradition which is predicated on a more antipelagian anthropology than the mysticism represented by Teresa (see here Åkerberg 1981 a, 162). In what

way and to what possible extent Ignatius Loyola influenced Teresa (see here Underhill 1930, 468 and Sundén 1971, 25) is more difficult to ascertain.

[23] On the premises for the selective adoption of tradition, see my methodological work 1981 b, 46 f, where I deal with this problem starting from three questions: Why does the individual adopt of the given tradition pattern? Why does the individual adopt what he adopts? What function does the adopted tradition pattern then have in the individual's own situation? (This material, too, is found in the German translation, note 2 above, in volume 15 of *Archiv für Religionspsychologie*.)

which yet with a consciousness of sin as corrective, never allows her to completely leave the area of "mysticism of personal life". That this is so, is clearly seen through a more thorough study of her teachings on the path of prayer in *Life,* but the tendency, as previously stated, has already been visible earlier in the book's introductory autobiographical part (chp. 1–10). As a summarizing example of this suggested tendency and as a transition to her description of the four steps on the path of prayer, we may cite the following passage from chapter 10:

When picturing Christ in the way I have mentioned, and sometimes even when reading, I used unexpectedly to experience a consciousness of the presence of God, of such a kind that I could not possibly doubt that he was within me or that I was wholly engulfed in Him. This was in no sense a vision: I believe it is called mystical theology. The soul is suspended in such a way that it seems to be completely outside itself (*Life,* X, 58).

From this standpoint, which, partly from another perspective, has also been discussed in certain earlier research,[24] Teresa now begins, with the aid of a parable, to describe the four steps of prayer. The soul is here likened to a garden which can be watered in four different ways, and these ways are comparable to the four steps on the path of prayer:

Let us now consider how this garden can be watered, so that we may know what we have to do, what labour it will cost us, if the gain will outweigh the labour and for how long this labour must be borne. It seems to me that the garden can be watered in four ways: by taking the water from a well, which costs us great labour; or by a water-wheel and buckets, when the water is drawn by a windlass (I have sometimes drawn it in this way: it is less laborious than the other and gives more water); or by a stream or a brook, which waters the ground much better, for it saturates it more thoroughly and there is less need to water it often, so that the gardener's labour is much less; or by heavy rain, when the Lord waters it with no labour of ours, a way incomparably better than any of those which have been described (*Life,* XI, 65).

With the aid of this parable Teresa now describes "these four methods of watering by which the garden is to be kept fertile" (ibid., loc. cit.). Thus, when she begins with the first step and turns to "the beginner", one must, as when reading the works of John of the Cross for example, understand "the beginner", not as one recently initiated into belief or even an individual between secondary and primary religiosity,[25] but rather as a person who, seen in the context of today's more "common" religious situation, has already made considerable progress on the path of faith and prayer. Nonetheless, such a person within the framework of Teresa's prayer perspective is a "beginner".

---

[24] See, among others, Pratt 1930, 349 and Zaehner 1957, 104 f.

[25] Here I use these categorizations in accordance with Clark 1968, 23 f.

What Teresa wishes to emphasize above all in this description of the first step is that it is extremely laborious to undergo. The beginners become "servants of love", "for it will fatigue them to keep their senses recollected, which is a great labour because they have been accustomed to a life of distraction" (ibid., XI, 66). Teresa accentuates here the great difficulties always present in a cultivated mysticism and which include the emphasis in the introductory phase on attempts to eliminate the sensory impressions of the world. In her own case, this step has apparently taken many years.[26] What is particularly emphasized here is the importance of the exercise, about whose conditions she writes on the one hand, in the manner of infinity mystic, that it is a question of "how much we can attain by our own power" (ibid., XII, 70), but about whose premises she also writes frequently and decisively, as a personality mystic, saying: "Once more I repeat my advice that it is very important that we should not try to lift up our spirits unless they are lifted up by the Lord" (ibid., XII, 73). To be hindered in one's continued striving to go further on the path of prayer, or to believe too much in one's own power, is according to Teresa a direct example of "the devil's doing" (ibid., XIII, 77 et passim).

From this first step she now goes on to describe the second degree of prayer, which she also calls "the Prayer of Quiet", while at the same time in conjunction with the conclusion of the first step she also urges—something valid for all her teaching on mysticism—that "there is no state of prayer, however sublime, in which it is not necessary often to go back to the beginning" (ibid., XIII, 80). By the term "Prayer of Quiet" Teresa wishes to emphasize the quite pronounced difference between this step of prayer and the former. While the first was a question of endurance of exercise and intensive prayer work, which required all of man's power resources and continual attempts at complete concentration, the second step is on the contrary a direct relief for him.[27] Earlier she was a laboriously working "servant", but she now becomes a resting, receptive worshipper. "Everything that now takes place brings the greatest consolation, and so little labour is involved that, even if prayer continues for a long time, it never becomes wearisome" (ibid., XIV, 84). This entire stage is character-

---

[26] Teresa herself writes: "These trials bring their own reward. I endured them for many years;" (*Life*, XI, 67).

[27] "Having now spoken of the labour and manual effort with which this garden is watered when one draws water from the well, let us now speak of the second way of drawing it which is ordained by the Lord of the garden. By using a device of windlass and buckets the gardener draws more water with less labour and is able to take some rest instead of being continually at work. It is this method, applied to the prayer called the Prayer of Quiet, that I now wish to describe" (*Life*, XIV, 83).

ized by a deep, joy-filled harmony, which, perhaps not least because it is at the same time remote from man's normal needs for dependency relationships to "worldly things", provides a clear indication that it is beginning to assume a supernatural character. The individual that experiences this stage is therefore often afraid of losing it, and all too many—as Teresa repeatedly points out (ibid., XV, 90 et passim)—believe that at this stage of prayer they have already arrived at the goal for "recollection" and, maybe, contemplation. Concerning the relationship to God during this state, Teresa presents this quite clearly within the categories of "mysticism of personal life". It is not man himself that "waters the garden", but rather all occurs through the action of a personal God, while at the same time man retains the faculties of his soul and yet rests.

The following degree of prayer appears radically different in exactly this sense; Teresa also describes it as "a sleep of the faculties" (ibid., XVI, 96). Here man releases the majority of the faculties of the soul, and is on his way to leaving normal waking consciousness. The soul has begun—to use Teresa's terms—an "exile" (ibid., XVI, 98) which expresses the view that this step in prayer is a transitionary stage. While the first step on the path of prayer, which Teresa describes here, is a laborious and exercise-filled step which can take a long time, often many years of struggle, the remaining three steps are all of rather short duration. Man is the passive receptive partner in all of the last steps, and in the third step, which has a clear pre-ecstatic character, the "pleasure and sweetness and delight" is "incomparably greater than in the previous state" (ibid., XVI, 96). The only faculties of the soul which have not left the normal waking state are the "memory" and "the imagination". These "make such turmoil within it /the soul/ that they leave it helpless" (ibid., XVII, 103). On this only partly conscious level a form of emancipation process is taking place, in which man, because of the "sleep" of the other faculties of the soul, cannot take active part and which has as its goal the complete union, or as Teresa carefully expresses it, implies "nothing less than an all but complete death to everything in the world and a fruition of God" (ibid., XVI, 96).

From this third step, Teresa now *attempts* to go on to describe the fourth and last degree of prayer. It is, as she carefully emphasizes, only an attempt since, as opposed to the earlier prayer steps where some of the faculties of the soul were still in conscious function, the fourth step implies a complete release of all the faculties of the soul from the normal waking state of consciousness. Teresa, in other words, attempts here to speak of the unspeakable. She attempts to describe what man experiences during "the union", the state where he completely abandons normal waking consciousness. In Teresa's description we find, for example, all of W. James's four classic criteria.[28] I have already hinted at a first characteristic in the "ineffability" which is clearly present at the beginning of chapter XVIII. In the chapter that follows she provides a clear example of the "noetic quality" of the state ("Then its /the soul's/ past life comes up before it and all the truth of God's great mercy is revealed. The understanding has no need to go out hunting; for its food is already prepared." *Life,* XIX, 112). In addition, the characteristic which James refers to as "transiency" is found in a number of places (see ibid., XVIII, 109 et passim), and as far as "passivity" is concerned, even this characteristic is apparent in long passages (for example, ibid., XVIII, 108 f.). Thus, Teresa's attempt at describing the "union" implies all the criteria for an experience beyond the normal waking state of consciousness.

If we now go further and study the actual essence of this *unio mystica,* we find that Teresa consistently divides it into two integrating elements or degrees, the "union" on the one hand and the "ecstasy" on the other. Both are parts of the same prayer step, but the "ecstasy" is something of the climax of this junction. Thus she can write: "It is quite clear what union is—two different things becoming one" (ibid., XVIII, 106), while she also accentuates: "This elevation of the spirit, or union, is wont to come with heavenly love; but as I understand it, the union itself is a different thing from the elevation which takes place in this same union." (Ibid., XVIII, 107). She strives very hard to underline this distinction between the "union" and the varying expressions for the "ecstasy" even in the following:

I should like, with the help of God, to be able to describe the difference between union and rapture, or elevation, or what they call flight of the spirit, or transport—it is all one. I mean that these different names all refer to the same thing, which is also called ecstasy. It is much more beneficial than union: the effects it produces are far more important and it has a great many more operations for union gives the impression of being just the same at the beginning, in the middle and at the end, and it all happens interiorly. But the ends of these raptures are of higher degree, and the effects they produce are both interior and exterior (ibid., XX, 119).[29]

With the aid of the parable of the garden which is watered in different ways, Teresa lets us understand that the state of *unio mystica* is, of itself, achieved when the Lord of the garden provides heavy rains, that is, when the power of the suprahuman sphere is united with the "human flower" in the garden. However, when this suprahuman sphere of power once again

---

[28] James 1928, 380 ff. Regarding Underhill's criteria for mysticism and W. T. Stace's characterization of the mystic experience, see my critical presentation in Åkerberg 1981 a, 154 ff and 158 ff.

[29] Cf. Pratt 1930, 420 ff. (see there the point in note 56) and Leuba 1925, 165 f. (see there especially also note 2).

raises itself from the earth like a cloud, it may happen that it draws the soul of man up with it "and begins to reveal to it things concerning the Kingdom that He has prepared for it." (Ibid., loc. cit.) It is this later "elevation" which Teresa calls the "ecstasy" and which is not a prayer step separate from the "union" as she presents it but simply a higher degree within this fourth step on the path of prayer.

The "things concerning the Kingdom" which people experience in this "ecstasy" are "delight", and they result for her in a number of phenomena which she summarily describes as "true revelations, great favours and visions" (ibid., XXI, 135) and among which in turn she especially stresses levitation in this account (ibid., XX, passim).

From the state of the fourth step of prayer man gradually returns to normal waking consciousness. This occurs only gradually as the varying faculties of the soul once again resume their "normal" functions in a given order, and this occurs through a powerful experience of pain: "And now comes the distress of having to return to this life" (ibid., XX, 127). It appears here to be a question of a powerful experience of abandonment and of what we might try to describe as a general feeling of being astray after the extremely marked experience of oneness, which just seconds earlier had placed the individual in a diametrically opposed state. However, she also sees this pain as a "favour", the task of which is to cleanse and chasten the soul and to prepare it, inspired by the *unio mystica* state, to function "correctly" in the tasks of earthly life.

This summary of Teresa's presentation of the path of prayer up to *unio mystica* is quite sufficient for our purpose within the framework of the present study. The goal of prayer is apparently to come to a "union" with the possibly heightened degree of "ecstasy" in a state which lies completely beyond normal waking consciousness. For whoever has experienced "ecstasy", prayer is in reality focused toward this goal, and the path there goes via the long and difficult first step and then through the shorter and increasingly passive steps of "Prayer of Quiet" and "sleep of the faculties". This entire prayer development and especially its last step clearly display the character of "mysticism of the infinite". The faculties of the soul, which together represent the "ego", are increasingly dissolved from their normal functions, resulting in a final, though short, state of a form of "union" where a dialogue between "I" and "Thou" is not possible to maintain. And this is exactly one of the characteristics of "mysticism of the infinite". However, that this state is not nevertheless a question of some form of "mysticism of the infinite" is apparent through Teresa's continually repeated view of the relationship to God and the anthropological conditions. While "mysticism of the infinite" proceeds consistently from man's completely free will and free opportunities—the Pelagian view—Teresa constantly maintains the personality mystical view with regard to divine sovereignty and man's total dependence upon "His Majesty, the Lord". Thus, if one views Söderblom's mystic distinction as a polar system with the two opposed pure poles, "mysticism of the infinite" and "mysticism of personal life", and with all the composite forms on a continuum between these two extremes, one can, in view of Teresa's presentation of *unio mystica* in *Life,* place it summarily within the area of "mysticism of personal life" but at the same time far from the pure pole of this last form of mysticism.

Beyond Ecstasy

I have now presented and, with the aid of Söderblom's distinction within mysticism, also analyzed one of the two classic presentations by Teresa where she stepwise divides the path of prayer forward towards *unio mystica.* In *Life,* which was edited in the version we have today in 1565, she divides the path of prayer, as we have seen, into four steps. The last step can be termed a very mild form of "mysticism of personal life", taking into consideration the relationship to God and the character of the anthropological question, since the experiential state also contains certain phenomena and characteristics of "mysticism of the infinite". On a continuum with "mysticism of the infinite" and "mysticism of personal life" in their pure forms as contrary poles, Teresa's description of the *unio mystica* in *Life* is definitely found on the "mysticism of personal life" side of the continuum, but somewhere between that side's outer pole and middle point with a fairly clear tendency in the latter direction.

In *Interior Castle,* Teresa's second classical presentation of the step-like development of prayer, the *unio mystica* state is presented, as we shall see, in a quite different way on some decisive points when compared with the presentation in *Life.*

Between these two presentations—*Interior Castle* was written by Teresa in 1577—some events have occurred which are important to note when attempting an analysis of this latter book. She has during this period, between 1565 and 1577, received some new and important influences, which have necessarily affected her entire Christian view. She has probably also during this time personally undergone a continued deepening religious development, and these factors among other things have combined to leave their mark in a series of writings[30] which appeared during these years and

---

[30] Here may be mentioned *Way of Perfection* (1566), *Exclamations of the Soul to God* (about 1569), *Conceptions of the Love of God* (probably written between 1571 and 1573) and *Foundations* (1576).

in which it is possible to discern certain tendencies toward a further development of the path of prayer described in *Life*.

As far as Teresa's adoption of tradition is concerned, something which continues even after the writing of *Life,* this is apparently of two types. The one type is a retention of the influences that have affected her earlier (Noyen 1974, 18), even if they now—and this is an important point—have, through continued reading, become deepened within her. In the other type, she has taken up completely new impulses from other places. Through her many journeys from 1567 onwards for the purpose of establishing new convents, she comes into contact with new priests and with other important Church figures. But she probably also gathers some new fruits from her reading during this period. Thus, research has speculated among other things about the possibility of influence from the Flemish Franciscan monk Ruysbroeck regarding Teresa's division of the *Interior Castle* into seven mansions.[31] Regardless of the likelihood of this possible influence, it is, however, my decided opinion that a completely different influence has dominated her development up to the writing of *Interior Castle*. I am referring here to her contact with John of the Cross. That this contact actually meant a lot for her development and her later writings has of course certainly been emphasized previously by a number of scholars.[32] However, the way in which it has influenced Teresa, by affecting her mystic insight and directing it towards what I have here termed a further more pronounced "mysticism of personal life" has not, as far as I know, been the object of a more explicit hypothetical study before. To prove such a movement in her mystic teachings towards an increasingly obvious "mysticism of personal life", from the presentation in *Life* to the presentation in *Interior Castle,* is the main thesis of this study. To carry out at the same time some comparisons with the mystic views characteristic of John of the Cross and to assume that the latter's mystic teaching is the primary psychological factor behind Teresa's changes of direction, is *per se* an interesting hypothesis which also finds a good deal of support within the framework for this paper.

. Teresa met John of the Cross for the first time as early as 1567 during a trip to Medina del Campo. From that point on they maintained contact during the ensuing years. Immediately before the summer of 1572 John of the Cross came to Avila to function as confessor for the nuns at the Convent of the Incarnation at which Teresa was prioress. Even though he

---

[31] Cf. here Sundén's point in the work from 1971, 35 and 39 and his references in note 8, p. 35.

[32] See, among others, Baruzi 1931, 156 ff.; Sanson 1953; Sundén 1971, 34 f.

had not at this time written any of his known works, it is, however, clear for a number of other reasons that he influenced Teresa on decisive points in her basic mystic view (and thereby also, even if this question lies outside the present study, in her mystic development, since she wrote against the background of her own experiences). A number of things support such an assumption. It was Teresa who, in her continual search for knowledgeable priests and guides, took the initiative for the first meeting with the renowned John of the Cross who was also well-known for his biblical knowledge. It was also Teresa who—judging from notes, descriptions and letters (even though we know that John of the Cross consciously did away with Teresa's letters seeking counsel)—continued to maintain the initiative and became increasingly dependent upon the young priest. After his arrival at the convent of the Incarnation in Avila in 1572, he also became Teresa's major discussion partner and teacher (cf. Theeuwes 1972, 33 ff.), and she emphasizes in a number of letters his exceptional knowledge and piety and calls him unquestionably a saint. It was also after the contacts and discussions with John of the Cross that Teresa's description of the life of prayer and its mystic direction seriously began to display tendencies towards change. Thus it seems apparent, for example, that the varying phenomena which, according to Teresa, follow ecstasy (visions, auditions, levitations) occur less frequently for her after the teaching she has received from John of the Cross. Even if, as has already been mentioned above, he did not leave any writings or fragments from the time before 1578, it must be viewed as entirely reasonable to assume that the basic theological and mystic view which he began to propound in 1578, is *in summa* the same as he had communicated in his teaching during his time at the convent in Avila and which, Teresa, among others, was influenced by. That he had not written anything earlier, can very possibly be explained by his characteristic piety of humble introversion, and that from the year 1578 he began to work on his writings has, in turn, an equally simple and reasonable explanation. It was in the August of that year that he succeeded in obtaining release from his imprisonment in the Calced Carmelite priory at Toledo, where he had been taken in the December of the previous year as a result of the Calced Carmelites' opposition to the radical monastic reform, which the Discalced Carmelites attempted to carry out and of which John of the Cross was one of the energetic supporters. The imprisonment in Toledo with all its privations and the contempt shown by the leaders of the Calced Carmelites demonstrated for John of the Cross the great seriousness of the struggles over reform efforts, and it was probably the need for a more active intervention in these efforts that stimulated his decision to begin to write down the mystical teaching which he earlier had only given verbally.

From what has been said above, it is, therefore, from the viewpoint of source criticism, fully reasonable to make certain careful comparisons between Teresa's main work from 1577, *Interior Castle,* and the teaching of John of the Cross, as presented, for example, in such works as *The Ascent of Mount Carmel* and *Dark Night of the Soul.*[33] Even if these works were first started in 1578, they would most probably conform on decisive points with the uniform and consistent teaching which John of the Cross had earlier provided and for which he was known in Teresa's circles.

What then is the sum of John of the Cross's teaching? Obviously, I do not here have the space to provide even a partially complete answer to this question. This would require a complete larger work in itself. However, it is fully possible in consideration of aim and main thesis of the present study, to focus on such points in the teaching of John of the Cross that demonstrate the universal goal of this form of mysticism, and which make comparisons with Teresa's mystical presentations possible on a reasonable and meaningful level.[34]

What should be primarily emphasized with John of the Cross and his mystical teaching is his realistic foundation and his strong repudiation of all paramystic phenomena (everything that Teresa in the fourth step of prayer in *Life* terms ecstasy and classes as the special characteristics of ecstasy: visions, auditions and other phenomena). Such occurrences are indeed occasionally to be found on the mystical path of prayer, but they are not, according to John of the Cross, worth striving for and are in no way—which is most important to underline—a sign of *unio mystica.* On the contrary, they can occasionally simply be a sign of "melancholy or some other imperfection with respect to sense or to spirit" (*Ascent,* Vol. I, 14), (and it is striking that a mystic of the 16th century points out as obvious what later mystic research during the 20th century should present as an occasionally reasonable though often strongly overprescribed hypothesis). In *Ascent* and *Dark Night,* which to a large extent deal with the same problems and which may have been worked on concurrently, John of the Cross describes in stages the "night" which man must go through on the way towards the goal of prayer. While the former work speaks of what man himself must undergo, such as certain forms of ascetism, the second work deals with how God intervenes and continues the purification up to its completion in the *indissoluble* union. In both cases it is a question of a path through various hardships and sufferings of "the night", a chastening, a stripping away of

---

[33] In the following I utilize Peers's abbreviations of these titles: *Ascent* and *Dark Night.*
[34] Concerning the problem of comparison of religio-psychological data, Åkerberg 1981 a, 144 ff. ("the experience group" with a differentiation of the term 'experience'), 151–168 ("Comparative Studies on Mysticism") and 168 ff. ("A Tentative Solution Model").

all that man by his nature feels dependent on in the material world. In *Dark Night* he then differentiates between "the Night of Sense" and "the Dark Night of the Spirit". In the first state man experiences symptoms of a form of aridity, which reveals itself in feelings of joy impeded and stagnation, and likewise in an inability to continue discursive meditation. However, whoever succeeds in surmounting this step can leave attempts at meditation for a subsequent, restful contemplation, which is the first more pronounced characteristic of the mystic path. This prayer step, which in certain respects seems to have similarities to the state which Teresa in *Life* calls "Prayer of Quiet", can according to John of the Cross last for several years. However, for the individual who has achieved this step in the mystical development of prayer and who—as is often the case in processes of religious growth—believes that he has already attained the goal, "the horrible" "Dark Night of the Spirit" can come as an unexpected and harrowing experience. When it begins with all its force, man must suddenly take upon himself and bear all the anxiety which follows the transformation of the faculties of the soul and their direction towards a completely new reference system and its conditions. This change, which leads to a complete and conscious restructuring of the entire perceptual field, brings various forms of suffering in combined periods of light and darkness, but can in turn also result in God lighting and more distinctly maintaining a passive "flame of love" in the individual. The "night" is then past and the state of *unio mystica* can commence. This latter development up to the mystical goal is especially dealt with by John of the Cross in *Spiritual Canticle* (also begun 1578–79) and in *Living Flame of Love* (written in two weeks in about 1585).

If one attempts, from the viewpoint of Söderblom's distinction of mysticism to classify the nature of the mysticism John of the Cross has expounded in his teaching, one finds that, with regard to both the image of God and the relationship to God, it clearly lies within the area of "mysticism of personal life". Those hints of a semipelagian anthropology which possibly sometimes can appear in his writings—perhaps especially in *Ascent* (if one reads this work separately and tendentiously), is opposed very clearly and thoroughly in the other writings through the insistence that God's "grace" is the only refuge and hope in man's "obsessions" and other sufferings. The mysticism represented by John of the Cross has no hint whatsoever of an impersonal relationship to God. The infinitymystical, ecstatic elevations beyond existence, which, for example, are the goals for Polotinus's mysticism and of which we also find some clear characteristics in Teresa's fourth prayer step in *Life* (even if there they are presented in combination with a non-infinity mystical view of man), are completely excluded from the path to *unio mystica* presented by John of the Cross. The path there, like the final goal itself, does not imply any ecstatic transcendence beyond the normal waking state of consciousness or a dissolution of one's own "ego", but rather continues the entire time, though in varying senses because of the marked restructurings of the perceptual field, to consist of an "I"—"Thou" relationship of man towards God. The *unio mystica* state here is not, as in "mysticism of the infinite" of a transient nature, but a unification, distinct from "mysticism of personal life", a state which is lasting, in the life of worship as well as in the life of normal daily activities. The individual can say here in the words of Paul from Gal. 2:20: "I am crucified with Christ: nevertheless I live; yet not I, but Christ liveth in me".[35] In *Dark Night* (Vol. I, 441) John of the Cross adds further that the complete union with God, which "causes *the soul to become wholly assimilated to God*" (italics mine) and which is the final goal of "mysticism of the infinite", cannot occur until the moment of death when the soul leaves the body.

Against the background of this compressed presentation and characterization of the mysticism which John of the Cross expounds in his teaching, we will now look at the second of Teresa's two classic descriptions of the path of prayer previously mentioned in this paper. I am referring to the book which is generally regarded to be her most important writing, namely *Interior Castle,* which she wrote very quickly (in a few months) in 1577.

As the title already implies, Teresa uses in this account a different basic parable for the meeting between God and man than that used in *Life*. Here she likens the soul to a castle, which has many rooms ("just as in Heaven there are many mansions", *Interior Castle,* I, 1, 201) but whose interior can also be seen as seven concentric circles, which mainly represent the seven steps which lead up to the goal: the meeting with God in the inner circle, the centre of the soul.

The door through which one enters the castle is prayer. This implies radically that those who do not pray cannot enter into the castle either, that is, they cannot develop in their life of faith. Teresa terms such people (with reference to Joh. 5:5) as "paralysed souls" (ibid., I, 1, 204). With a certain amount of contrast to the presentation in *Life,* where the first step of prayer already assumes a marked decision by the individual to begin to wander along the path of prayer, Teresa thus begins the description in *Interior Castle* from the "relative religious zero point" (my expression), where man

---

[35] This Scriptural passage is quoted and explained by John of the Cross in *Spiritual Canticle* (which he began in 1578–79), vol. II. 65, 135, 238, 294 and in *Living Flame of Love* (about 1585), vol. III, 51 and 143. (Concerning its currentness within the Carmelite Order today, see, among others, Stinissen 1973, 731).

is a pure beginner at prayer with perhaps only a few opportunities for prayer a month (see ibid., loc. cit.). In the first three Mansions (totalling five chapters) she describes the development of prayer up to the actual mystical prayer, which begins with the fourth Mansions. The third Mansions here seem to be mainly commensurate with what she has earlier described in *Life* as the characteristics of the first step of prayer.[36]

When we arrive at the fourth Mansions, prayer has gone over into actual mysticism. Here it is not man who works with his prayer struggle, but rather he here passively and momentarily receives what God during short periods of time can give him of inner strength. Teresa calls this "consolations from God" and compares the state in its main characteristics[37] with what she described in *Life* as "Prayer of Quiet" (ibid., IV, 2, 236). Quite generally she characterizes this fourth Mansions as "a dilation or enlargement of the soul" (ibid., IV, 3, 244), in which one of the faculties of the soul—the will (ibid., IV, 2, 238)—is released by being drawn into the castle's centre. This experience can, despite the joyous harmony of the state in general, give rise to certain problems for the individual. Because of pride or because of a striving to come even further in the soul's unification with God, a few can succumb to exercises of piety that are a direct danger to health. Teresa gives here a sharp warning against various forms of unhealthy mystic endeavour, which would be worthy of special attention within mystic research.[38]

After the step of the "Prayer of Quiet", which often occurs suddenly but may continue for several days or longer (since the faculties of the soul still,

---

[36] Cf. here Stinissen 1972, 237. (J. H. Leuba makes a somewhat hasty and careless comparison here between Teresa's description of the path of prayer in *Life* and *Interior Castle* respectively: "In the *Autobiography*, the Ascent to God is divided into four stages or 'states' [...] But in *Interior Castle*, these four stages are divided into six, and a new one is added" (Leuba 1925, 163).

[37] Teresa herself notes that in some places comparisons between the presentations in *Life* and *Interior Castle* may be hazardous if pressed. See for example, *Interior Castle*, IV, 2, 238.

[38] Teresa writes (ibid., IV, 3, 245 f.): "There is one peril of which I want to warn you, though I have spoken of it elsewhere; I have seen persons given to prayer fall into it, and especially women, for, as we are weaker than men, we run more risk of what I am going to

describe. It is this: some women, because of prayers, vigils and severe penances, and also for other reasons, have poor health. When they experience any spiritual consolation, therefore, their physical nature is too much for them; and as soon as they feel any interior joy there comes over them a physical weakness and languor, and they fall into a sleep, which they call 'spiritual', and which is a little more marked than the condition that has been described. Thinking the one state to be the same as the other, they abandon themselves to this absorption; and the more they relax, the more complete becomes this absorption, because their physical nature continues to grow weaker. So they get it into their heads that it is *arrobamiento*, or rapature. But I call it *abobamiento*, foolishness; for they are doing nothing but wasting their time at it and ruining their health."

with the exception of the will, function "normally"), the very short and likewise momentary degree of the fifth Mansions can commence. Teresa uses the same term for this step as she used in *Life* for the fourth step of prayer, namely "Prayer of Union". However, one now finds a clear difference between the descriptions of this fourth step of prayer in *Life* on the one hand, and the fifth Mansions in *Interior Castle* on the other. Even if, in the fourth degree in *Life,* Teresa differentiated in turn between the elements of "union" and "ecstasy" and associated the climax with the latter element, it is not difficult to see that both of these elements, which in *Interior Castle* are now nearly commensurate with the fifth and sixth Mansions, have a milder and much less dramatic emphasis than was the case in *Life.* In that work, ecstasy was focused on as the final goal of the path of prayer. In *Interior Castle,* one is aware from the beginning of the description in the fifth and sixth Mansions according to which the goal is found *beyond* ecstasy. Indeed, the state of the fifth Mansions implies that all the "inner" faculties of the soul are released from their normal ways of functioning, which is also a condition for the experience of "union" to have a noetic quality ("By means of the senses and faculties she could not understand in a thousand years what she understands in this way in the briefest space of time." Ibid., V, 4, 265), but this release from the normal waking way of functioning is not presented as a final goal for the path of prayer but now—as opposed to the description in *Life*—is rather a step towards a more distant and deeply embedded goal. The dramatic presentation of the fourth step of prayer in *Life* is now markedly de-emphasized and the entire description is now expressed in terms of bridal mysticism, inspired mainly by the Song of Songs (see for example, ibid., V, 1, 252 and V, 4, 264 f.). It is reasonable even at this point to assume the influence of John of the Cross (whose writings contain over one hundred and fifty references to this biblical book). The careful presentation of the "union" in the fifth Mansions, which indirectly implies that there exists a deeper and distinct union further on, can be seen as another result of John of the Cross's influence.

Thus, if the fifth Mansions is clearly a milder and more cautious account of the conditions of union than what Teresa has earlier described within the framework of the fourth step of prayer in *Life,* then such characterization must be valid to an even greater degree with reference to her description of the state in the sixth Mansions. This also deals partly with "ecstasy", which was the object of a purer description in the second element of the fourth step of prayer in *Life,* but here in *Interior Castle* this continued inner process towards "Prayer of Union" has received a more careful and differentiated emphasis. The sixth Mansions, which forms the book's long-

est section (with eleven chapters), points directly (see for example, ibid.,
VI, Chp. 1, 2 and 7) towards the seventh Mansions, and the entire presentation is marked by the symbolism characteristic of bridal mysticism. Teresa
also calls the state "the Betrothal" and thereby points indirectly towards
yet another step, namely "the Spiritual Marriage" in the seventh Mansions.
This symbolism appears in various places in the tradition. It is found in
Bernhard of Clairvaux, but Teresa could also find it in her closest environment—namely in John of the Cross (cf. Lapauw 1981, 153). Viewed in its
entirety, the state in the sixth Mansions cannot be said to be dominated by
ecstasy and rapture (terms which according to Teresa are largely identical
in context) but rather by all the difficulties and pain-filled purging processes
which are the conditions for a "Spiritual Marriage". Instead of being
similar to the presentation of "the ecstasy" in the fourth step of prayer in
Life, the description of the state in the sixth Mansions is much more
strikingly reminiscent of the experimential elements which John of the
Cross presents in *Dark Night*. The quickly changing sequenses of experience have something of the character of *mysterium tremendum et fascino-
sum* (R. Otto's terminology in *Das Heilige*). Teresa writes on the one hand
that the sixth Mansions result in "pain", "tears" and "sighs" as a consequence of the many obsessions that accompany "the Betrothal", not the
least of which is the constant doubt and conflict over the problem of
whether or not it is God or the Devil that elicits the various phenomena.[39]
However, on the other hand, she makes it clear that this purging process is
only possible for man to bear because he is repeatedly released from his
struggles by a series of raptures. "And now you are going to see what His

---

[39] Analogous to the points made by John of
the Cross concerning possible physical or
mental instability or disturbance in connection with certain forms of phenomena, Teresa
also writes of persons who have had visions
and auditions the following balanced words:
"The real solution is to see that such people
have less time for prayer, and also that, as far
as is possible, they attach no importance to
these fancies. For the devil is apt to take
advantage of the infirmity of these souls, to
the injury of others, if not to their own as
well. Both with infirm and with healthy souls
there is invariably cause for misgivings about
these things until it becomes clear what kind
of spirit is responsible. I believe, too, that it
is always better for them to dispense with
such things at first, for, if they are of God,
dispensing with them will help us all the more
to advance, since, when put to the proof in
this way, they will tend to increase. Yet the
soul should not be allowed to become depressed or disquieted, for it really can not
help itself." (*Interior Castle,* VI, 3,
280.)—These and other statements by Teresa
and John of the Cross may be worth careful
consideration from those concerned with the
psychology of religion who—often without
any or sufficient knowledge of theology or
the history of religion—are interested in possible correlations between, for example, visual and auditive phenomena on the one hand
and physical or mental instability on the other. Within most cultivated mysticism such
phenomena are more or less considered paramystic, and they are very seldom allowed to
occupy a central place in various teaching
traditions of mysticism.

Majesty does to confirm this betrothal, for this, as I understand it, is what happens when He bestows raptures, which carry the soul out of its senses;'' (*Interior Castle*, VI, 4, 286 f.). Here we find a clear reminiscence of Teresa's earlier presentation of "ecstasy" in *Life* and thereby also a minor difference between her own view and the teaching presented by John of the Cross,[40] but the phenomena accompanying "ecstasy", when not only the inner but also the outer faculties were released from their normal functions, are de-emphasized in their entirety and seem to be affected by some powerful influence. Visions are now dominated by the intellectual type, and the levitation phenomenon is distinctly less prominent. Throughout the entire account the fundamental anthropological idea is to be found— as in most of *Life* as well—demonstrating the nature of the relationship to God: "May it please His Majesty often to bestow this prayer upon us since it brings us such security and such benefit. For, as it is an entirely supernatural thing, we cannot acquire it" (ibid., VI, 6, 302). The view of man expressed points very clearly towards "mysticism of personal life", although, as we have seen, this book too, in the descriptions of the fifth and sixth Mansions still has certain vestiges of infinity mysticism. Nevertheless, viewed within the framework of the entire book with its guideline to the seventh Mansions, this section stands in closer relation to the "mysticism of personal life".

Elements of suffering and rapture are thus not the final goal on the path of prayer. "The Betrothal" in the sixth Mansions is simply yet another step towards the central state of the life of faith, a step beyond ecstasy towards "the Spiritual Marriage". That we now find ourselves on the firm ground of "mysticism of personal life", is already implied although that union is not of a transitory nature but has rather a more lasting character. Already in the sixth Mansions Teresa gives some indications anticipating "the Spiritual Marriage", "where in a wonderful way the soul never ceases to walk with Christ our Lord but is ever in the company of both His Divine and His human nature" (ibid., VI, 7, 306). The permanency of this union in the seventh Mansions is supported in several places in the context of descriptions of this later state. Teresa summarises this as: "the soul remains all the time in that centre with its God" (ibid., VII, 2, 335; see i. a. even ibid., VII, 1, 332 and VII, 2, 338). This is not, however, to be interpreted to mean that man in the seventh Mansions lives in some sort of lasting ecstatic state. On

---

[40] Another point where Teresa deviates somewhat from John of the Cross, concerns the use of discursive meditation. While John of the Cross maintains that this meditation can be put aside in favour of contemplation, when the individual has difficulty in meditating with a focused thought content, Teresa maintains that there is a need for discursive meditation even for later steps of development on the path of prayer.

the contrary, Teresa herself is very careful to differentiate clearly the experience of union that occurs in the fifth mansions from that occurring in the seventh:

And His Majesty is pleased that it should not be as on other occasions, when He has granted it raptures, in which I certainly think it is united with Him, as it is in the above-mentioned Prayer of Union, although the soul does not feel called to enter into its own centre, as here in this Mansion, but is affected only in its higher part (ibid., VII, 1, 331).

"The Spiritual Marriage" is furthermore completely different to "the Prayer of Union" inasmuch as it is a state retained during all of life's various conditions and the different tasks of the day (the faculties of the soul are not released; ibid., VII, 3, 342), and inasmuch as these conditions of life in the sense of temporary obsessions, can serve as reminders that a *complete union* with God is never possible in this life ("this great favour cannot be fulfilled perfectly in us during our lifetime"; ibid., VII, 2, 333).

Here the influence of John of the Cross is clearly seen coming to the fore. The similarity between his mystical teaching—criticising undue emphasis in the life of prayer on powerful raptures and emphasizing the mild "flame of love" which in this life can never attain complete union with God (see above p. 295)—and Teresa's presentation of the seventh Mansions in *Interior Castle,* are striking on point after point. Her indirect allusion to Gal. 2:20, which is a central verse of Scripture for both John of the Cross and all "mysticism of personal life", is yet another example of this personality mysticism in the seventh Mansions, while it also suggests further support for the hypothesis that John of the Cross is the most important psychological influence (see ibid., VII, 3, 338 and VII, 3, 340). It is also possible that, when Teresa herself points out that her momentary transition to the seventh Mansions came to pass in connection with a special occurrence during a Mass celebrated by John of the Cross,[41] this can be of interest regarding the importance of the influence of John of the Cross on Teresa.

---

[41] Teresa writes: "When I was at the Incarnation, during the second year I was Prioress there, on the octave-day of Saint Martin, I was making my communion, and the Father, Fray John of the Cross, who was giving me the Most Holy Sacrament, divided the Host between another sister and myself. I thought he was doing this, not for lack of Hosts, but because he wanted to mortify me, for I had told him that I was very pleased when the Hosts were large ones, though I knew I should be receiving the Lord, whole and entire, if I took only the smallest particle. 'Have no fear, daughter', His Majesty said to me, 'that anyone will be able to part thee from Me.' [...] Then He revealed Himself to me, in an imaginary vision, most interiorly, as on other occasions, and He gave me His right hand, saying to me: 'Behold this nail. It is a sign that from to-day onward thou shalt be My bride'" (*Spiritual Relations*, XXXV, Peers's edition, vol. I, 351 f.).

The entire description of the seventh Mansions has bewildered a number of scholars.[42] There has been a desire to place Teresa among the infinity mystics, a procedure which has certain possibilities if one chooses to treat certain passages in *Life* tendentiously and at the same time ignore her anthropological view, but the presentation in the seventh Mansions of *Interior Castle* is impossible to include in such a pattern. For here, a completely different form of mysticism is involved—"mysticism of personal life". However, this is not an example of the type in its more extreme forms. Teresa does not, for instance, speak explicitly of any *terrores conscientiae* (see Åkerberg 1981a, 165f.). But it is, nonetheless, a clear form of "mysticism of personal life" with marked tendencies to coinside with the mysticism present in John of the Cross's writings.[43] It also demonstrates, as does *all* "mysticism of personal life"—and even many forms of more deeply rooted "mysticism of the infinite"—all the characteristics of mature religious sentiment.

If one considers W. James's classical characteristics of mature religion ("Saintliness", James 1928, 272ff.), one finds that his concept of the "fundamental inner condition" of the state together with its "characteristic practical consequenses" coincide extremely well with Teresa's description of the seventh Mansions (and in many respects even with earlier steps of prayer). As far as "the inner conditions" are concerned, these are a direct consequence of wandering on the path of prayer, and regarding external "practical consequences", it is two characteristics in particular that she emphasizes: what James describes as "strength of soul" and "charity". The former of these two is characterized by an overcoming of the dominat-

---

[42] Among the references to researchers mentioned in the text and notes, special emphasis may be given to J. H. Leuba. In his strongly reductionistic work *The Psychology of Religious Mysticism*, Leuba makes the assertion (in reference to Teresa's presentation of the seventh Mansions in *Interior Castle*): "We shall see that there are sufficient reasons for rejecting this last degree as being the product of a confusion and for regarding the four stages of the *Life* as the more satisfactory division" (1925, 163). In the following discussion Leuba attempts, in a somewhat construed manner, to defend his special mystic view, in which no room is found for Teresa's seventh degree of prayer or for "mysticism of personal life" in general. Leuba expands the discussion directly into completely unprovable speculations, and his account on

this point can in no way be regarded as scientifically valid.

[43] In this connection I only wish to mention *en passant* the interesting question of whether and to what extent there can possibly exist a connection between the distinctions "mysticism of the infinite"—"mysticism of personal life" on the one hand and the psychological typology "Healthy-mindedness"—"Suffering" (Clark 1968, 154–187) on the other. It seems apparent in most cases that tradition factors have a guiding function for the direction of an individual's mysticism. Whether mental dispositions, too, can from a psychological point of view influence the mystical nature and/or degree is, however, also an important but as yet unconsidered question.

ing power of fear ("Come heaven, come hell, it makes no difference now!",
James 1928, 273), and Teresa also writes about the goal "to lose the fear
which previously she sometimes had of the other favours that were granted
to her" (*Interior Castle*, VII, 1, 333). It is in other words, almost a question
of some form of "assurance of salvation" in Luther's sense. In the same
way, Luther may provide an object of comparison for the characteristic
which James calls "charity" and which, according to Teresa, is the foremost characteristic of a correctly developed mystic life of prayer. Luther,
as we may recall, presents a model for the deep love of one's neighbour in
each one striving to "be every man's servant". Teresa uses similar expressions in a couple of places: "Therefore, sisters, if you wish to lay good
foundations, each of you must try to be the least of all" (ibid., VII, 4, 347),
and further: "Do you imagine it is a small advantage that you should have
so much humility and mortification, and should be the servants of all ..."
(ibid., VII, 4, 349).

In a similar way, G. W. Allport's six criteria of religious maturity
coincide extremely well with Teresa's presentation of the seventh Mansions. The most important of these criteria, namely the functional autonomy of mature religious sentiment (Allport 1968, 72) is to be found very
clearly in Teresa's description: "... this impulse, or whatever it is called,
proceeds from the interior of the soul" [...] "... this interior movement
proceeds from the centre of the soul and awakens the faculties" (*Interior
Castle*, VII, 3, 340f.; see even ibid., VII, 4, 347). With the same evidence,
it is also possible to show that Allport's other five criteria have their full
counterparts in Teresa's text.[44]

What should be of special interest for mystic research here, over and
above the evidence of the clear relationship between the criteria of religious
maturity and Teresa's mystical teaching in *Interior Castle,* is that within the
field of mature religion it is possible to differentiate this qualitatively
conditioned state. Allport has, indeed, suggested that this mature religious
state also presupposes a subsequent development so that faith does not
stagnate and decline (he says that mature religious sentiment is after all
heuristic by nature; Allport 1968, 81 ff.), but research attempt has not been
made to differentiate this stage of religious development. I should therefore
like to present here, as a first attempt, a broad model of differentiation for
the mature religious stage. If—as in my dissertation on Nathan Söderblom's

---

[44] The mature religious sentiment as *well differentiated* (see *Interior Castle,* VII, pas-sim), as *consistent in its moral consequences* (see ibid., VII, 3, 339 and 4, 346), as *compre-hensive as a philosophy of life* (see ibid., VII, 3, 338f.), as *integral* (see ibid., VII, 3, 339) and as *heuristic* (see ibid., VII, 4, 347 et passim). The underlined characteristics are presented by Allport 1968, 59–83.

religious development (1975 b)—I assume that "conversion" is the point at which an individual moves to a mature religious stage, then we can continue with a differentiation of this stage into two main steps, *before* and *after* the evidence of mystical characteristics.[45] Even if the border between these two main steps may in many cases (momentary transitions excepted) appear rather flexible, it should, however, be possible to maintain such a division and it should be of value, *at least* for the type of piety which develops via a maturation process into "mysticism of personal life". The mystical teaching of John of the Cross can provide an account of such a path of development. In the present study I have tried to show that Teresa, too, describes a very similar process in the *Interior Castle*.

Brief Reflections

In this short study a comparison has been made between two classical descriptions of the path of prayer given to us by Teresa in the works *Life* and *Interior Castle*. With Söderblom's distinction between "mysticism of the infinite" and "mysticism of personal life" as a psychological instrument, I have tried to show, in direct contrast to much other mystic research (although there are clear exceptions),[46] that Teresa's mystic presentation lies in its entirety within the domain of "mysticism of personal life". In *Life* she does demonstrate, it is true, tendencies remote from the extreme of "mysticism of personal life" and she also sanctions there certain conditioned phenomena of "mysticism of the infinite", but a very clear movement occurs in *Interior Castle* towards a purer "mysticism of personal life", although neither Teresa nor John of the Cross can ever be said to represent the extreme of "mysticism of personal life". She maintains an anthropological view throughout, however, characteristic of a personality mystic's relationship to God and displaying that view of man together with that image of God. This relation to God is also marked in *Interior Castle* by a pronounced "I"—"Thou" relationship vis-à-vis God. In the seventh Mansions, where man on the last step of prayer arrives at the centre of the castle and thus of the soul, it is not a question of a state beyond normal waking consciousness with—as in "mysticism of the infinite"—"the ego's" dissolution into the cosmos or into the suprahuman sphere, but

---

[45] Concerning a general definition of "mysticism", see Söderblom 1975, 83. Such an attempt to define this phenomenon does, however, need a more stable and differentiated classification of the criteria. When does "mature religion" deepen into "mysticism"? Here is an important topic of research.

[46] Hints of a questioning of the character of "mysticism of the infinite" within Teresa's mysticism can be found in, for example, Underhill 1930, 170 and Zaehner 1957, 104 f.

rather an experience within the framework of the functional consciousness, which, incidentally, is also sharply emphasized by the Carmelites themselves.[47] Exercise dominates here to be sure, as in all other cultivated mysticism, during the first steps of prayer, but in the seventh Mansions the spontaneity of a faith in God becomes increasingly clear. Thus, we find ourselves in all aspects firmly within the "mysticism of personal life". The examples of raptures, still found in de-emphasized form in *Interior Castle*, are essentially to be viewed as reminiscences of her earlier experiences and teaching. They are found more carefully expressed, but they no longer retain any central place in the presentation.[48]

My main task, in accordance with my thesis, has been to show this movement in Teresa's mystical teaching towards an increasingly pronounced "mysticism of personal life" in *Interior Castle*. But one hypothesis I have simultaneously tried to find support for is the role of John of the Cross as the decisive influence upon Teresa's development. Whether Teresa obtained the idea of dividing the path of prayer into seven steps from Ruysbroeck or not—a question which may be difficult to prove conclusively,—it is not, however, primarily his mysticism which is represented in *Interior Castle*. This account is highly reminiscent, as I have tried to suggest above, of the mystical teaching which John of the Cross began to write down after his imprisonment but which he had expounded for many years to Teresa, among others, in contact before and during his period as confessor at the Convent of the Incarnation in Avila.

Söderblom's distinction is a well-designed instrument, permitting a cor-

---

[47] In a completely new work by Camillus Lapauw OCD, *Teresa von Avila, Wege nach Innen,* the author writes as follows with regard to Teresa's mysticism, on the basis of an indepth analysis of *Interior Castle:* "Die teresianische Mystik ist zunächst eine personale Gottesmystik. Ziel der Innerlichkeit und der Einkehr ist keine Versenkung in eine Leere, kein Einswerden mit einem kosmischen Allgrund und keine Erleuchtung im buddhistischen Sinn. Die von Teresa vorgelegte und gelehrte Mystik beruht auf einer persönlichen Begegnung, einer Hingabe an ein Du, einer Lebensgemeinschaft" (1981, 218). See here, too, the references to relatively new literature on Teresa, provided by Lapauw on page 222. (For the loan of Lapauw's work, which is as yet unobtainable in Sweden, and for help with other bibliographical information, I wish to thank Anders Arborelius OCD and Wilfrid Stinissen OCD.)

[48] Here one can perhaps attempt a very careful comparison between Teresa and Sundar Singh. While the latter, after a conversion of dramatic character in 1904 found his piety changed in a new direction, from "mysticism of the infinite" towards "mysticism of personal life" after this marked change of mystic type still retained a disposition towards certain ecstatic states (see Söderblom 1975, 168–209), Teresa also apparently had difficulty in leaving the raptures during her later, more pronounced period of "mysticism of personal life". (See here Åkerberg 1981 c.) In both cases, however, the ecstatic states increasingly assume a more de-emphasized character, and for neither of them do these raptures play a central role in their later forms of mysticism.

rect understanding of the type of mysticism represented by both John of the Cross as well as Teresa. The mystical teachings of both try to show a way to *unio mystica* which is possible in this life and which is not based upon a Pelagian anthropology. All the primary characteristics of this teaching thus lie clearly within "mysticism of personal life".

References

Allport, G. W. 1968. *The individual and his religion*. New York.
Andrae, T. 1926. *Mystikens psykologi*. Uppsala.
Arborelius, A. 1980. Företal till Teresa av Avila. *Boken om mitt liv*. Helsingborg.
Auclair, M. 1950. *La vie de Sainte Thérèse d'Avila*. Paris.
Augustine (354–430) *Confessiones*.
Baruzi, J. 1931. *Saint Jean de la Croix et le problème de l'expérience mystique*. Paris.
Clark, W. H. 1968. *The psychology of religion*. New York.
Delacroix, H. 1908. Études d'histoire et de psychologie du mysticisme. *Les grands mystiques chrétiens*. Paris.
Etchegoyen, G. 1923. *L'amour divin*. (Bibliothèque de l'école des hautes études hispaniques.) Paris.
Ferrer, V. (1350–1419) 1515. *Tractatus de vita spirituali*.
Gregory I (540–604) *Moralia in Job*.
Hahn, G. 1883. Les phénomènes hystériques et les révélations de Sainte Thérèse. *Revue des questions scientifiques* 13/14.
Heiler, F. 1918. *Das Gebet*. München.
Hoffmann, D. 1982. *Der Weg zur Reife*. Stockholm.
James, W. 1928. *The varieties of religious experience*. London–New York–Toronto.
John of the Cross (1542–1591), 1974. *The complete works of St. John of the Cross* 1–3, ed. by E. A. Peers. Glasgow.
de Laredo, B. 1535. *Subida del Monte Sión*.
Lapauw, C. 1981. *Teresa von Avila, Wege nach Innen*. Innsbruck.
Leroy, O. 1962. *Sainte Thérèse d'Avila*. (Les Études carmélitaines 45.) Paris.
Leuba, J. H. 1925. *The psychology of religious mysticism*. London.
Nilsson, L. 1980. Expansiv tro. *William James då och nu*, ed. by O. Pettersson–H. Åkerberg. Lund.
Noyen, C. 1974. Företal till Teresa av Avila. *Den inre borgen*. Helsingborg.
de Osuna, F. *Tercer Abecedario*.
Otto, R. 1917. *Das Heilige*. Breslau.
Poulain, A. 1921. *Des graces d'Oraison*. Paris.
Pratt, J. B. 1930. *The religious consciousness*. New York.
Sanson, H. 1953. *L'ésprit humain selon Saint Jean de la Croix*. Paris.
Silverio de Santa Teresa. 1915–24. *Santa Teresa de Jesús Obras*. 9 vol. Burgos.
— 1929–31. *Obras de San Juan de la Cruz*. Burgos.
Stace, W. T. 1960. *Mysticism and philosophy*. Philadelphia–New York.
Steinmann, A.-E. 1981. *Karmelitorden*. Helsingborg.
Stinissen, W. 1972. Teresa av Avila. *Meditation och mystik*, utg. av H. Hof–W. Stinissen. Karlskrona.
— 1973. En kristen livsstil. *Svensk Kyrkotidning* 67.

Sundén, H. 1966. *Die Religion und die Rollen*. Berlin.
— 1969. Die Rollenpsychologie und die Weisen des Religionserlebens. C. Hörgl–K. Krenn–F. Rauh, *Wesen und Weisen der Religion*. München.
— 1971. *Teresa från Avila och religionspsykologien*. (Acta Universitatis Upsaliensis. Studia Historico-Ecclesiastica Upsaliensia 20.) Uppsala.
Söderblom, N. 1975. *Till mystikens belysning*. Lund.
Teresa of Avila (1515–1582), 1963–72. *Complete works of St. Teresa* 1–3, ed. by E. A. Peers. London.
Theeuwes, J. 1963. *Teresa av Avila*. Hälsingborg.
— 1972. *Johannes av Korset*. Stockholm.
Underhill, E. 1930. *Mysticism*. London.
Zaehner, R. C. 1957. *Mysticism, sacred and profane*. London.
Åkerberg, H. 1975 a. Inledning till Söderblom, N. *Till mystikens belysning*. Lund.
— 1975 b. *Omvändelse och kamp*. Diss. Lund.
— 1977. "Modet att vara till" och religionspsykologin. P. Tillich, *Modet att vara till*. Lund.
— 1981 a. On the comparability of religio-psychological data. O. Petrtersson–H. Åkerberg, *Interpreting religious phenomena*. (Acta Universitatis Lundensis. Sectio I Theologica Juricica Humaniora 36.) Stockholm.
— 1981 b. *Tolkning och förståelse*. Lund.
— 1981 c. Oändlighetsmystik och personlighetsmystik. *Religion och Bibel* 40.
— 1982. Drei Interpretationskomponenten. *Archiv für Religionspsychologie* 15.